A HISTORY OF
AMERICAN ARCHAEOLOGY

A History of American Archaeology

THIRD EDITION

Gordon R. Willey
HARVARD UNIVERSITY

Jeremy A. Sabloff
THE UNIVERSITY OF PITTSBURGH

W. H. FREEMAN AND COMPANY

NEW YORK

Illustrations:

(p. ii) Catherwood's drawing of a stela at Copan. (From Catherwood, 1844)

(p. xiv) Scenes from the Mexican Codex Féjerváry. (From Kingsborough, 1831–1848)

Library of Congress Cataloging-in-Publication Data

Willey, Gordon Randolph, 1913–
    A history of American archaeology / Gordon R. Willey, Jeremy A.
Sabloff. — 3rd ed.
      p. cm.
    Includes bibliographical references and index.
    ISBN 0-7167-2370-0. — ISBN 0-7167-2371-9 (pbk.)
    1. America — Antiquities. 2. Indians — Antiquities. I. Sabloff,
Jeremy A. II. Title.
E61.W67   1993
970 — dc20   92-35643
                                                                   CIP

PRINTED IN THE UNITED STATES OF AMERICA

1 2 3 4 5 6 7 8 9 0 RRD 9 9 8 7 6 5 4 3

To Philip Phillips,
to whom archaeology has always
been anthropology

Contents

Preface to the Third Edition

It is more than twenty years since we began researching and writing *A History of American Archaeology,* which was first published in 1974. In the midst of the early years of the New Archaeology, we felt that it was critically important to place the intellectual developments of the 1960s in historical perspective. Given the pace of growth of American archaeology and the continued demand for copies of this work, as well as a number of helpful comments, we soon felt it necessary to revise and expand the first edition of this book. The second edition appeared in 1980 and, to our surprise and delight, has continued to be of wide interest to both professional scholars and students.

As the intellectual scene of the 1980s and 1990s continues to advance and to grow increasingly complex (and occasionally strident), there is a feeling in some quarters that the discipline may have lost its way. We do not believe this to be the case and, in fact, believe that the field is poised to take new leaps forward in understanding America's past. Nevertheless, it is true that students have few written works to help them gain a general perspective on current debates in American archaeology. Nor can they find guides that will help them build a framework for evaluating the various agendas competing for the future direction of American archaeology. Our hope is that this third edition will provide a useful historical matrix for the modern intellectual themes and disputes.

Finally, it is worth emphasizing that we have always viewed this book as an introduction. Clearly, a variety of histories of American archaeology are needed. Our book does not pretend to be comprehensive; it does not even attempt to broach, for example, many fascinating questions of social history. We can only hope that many new histories of American archaeology will be forthcoming in the not-too-distant future.

In addition to our previous acknowledgements, we would like to give special thanks to Merrilee Salmon and Robert W. Preucel for their helpful comments and encouragement on our revisions of Chapter Six.

We also wish to express our gratitude to all those colleagues and students, too numerous to name individually, who directed us to new references, sent us reprints, and provided us with additional illustrations. Finally, the enthusiasm and support of Jerry Lyons, Diane Maass, and their colleagues at W. H. Freeman is greatly appreciated.

GORDON R. WILLEY
JEREMY A. SABLOFF
December 1992

Preface to the Second Edition

The innovations that began in American archaeology in the early 1960s have continued unabated to the present and have prompted this second edition of *A History of American Archaeology*. For this second edition, we have made some minor changes in the first five chapters, mostly brief textual, footnote, or bibliographical additions. The original Chapter Six has been slightly rearranged, with some additions and deletions. Chapters Seven and Eight are new. Chapter Seven treats, in a highly selective way, what has been going on in New World archaeological research in the late 1960s and 1970s, particularly the innovations of the past two decades. Chapter Eight is concerned with formulations in method and theory in the context of the New Archaeology of the 1970s. The orientation and nature of these two new chapters are described more fully at the close of Chapter One.

That we devote three chapters to the past two decades may seem to some to be an excessive preoccupation with the current and fashionable. Others may feel that the events of these past two decades should compose the real body of the book, with all that led up to them a mere introduction recounting the follies and foibles of a premodern era. To either critic, we would say that we have taken a middle course. To the first, we will admit that what we have set down here in Chapters Six, Seven, and Eight will be reduced with the historical perspectives of the future; but our recording of the 1960s and 1970s will provide a record of the outlooks, controversies, and biases of our own time as viewed by two of its participants. To the second critic, we can only answer that the past shapes the present. No individual, no institution, no intellectual tradition can ever fully escape from its generic forbears, and archaeology is no exception.

In this second edition, the footnotes are placed at the ends of chapters, and many new titles have been added to the already extensive bibliography. As we said in the first edition, the book is designed so that the reader may pursue matters of special interest in much greater detail through the references. All the original illustrations have been retained and several new ones added to the new chapters.

In preparing the second edition, we have had aid and advice from L. R. Binford, L. S. Cordell, and R. S. MacNeish. Whitney Powell (artist) and Hillel Berger (photographer), both of the Peabody Museum staff at Harvard, helped us with the illustrations in Chapters Seven and Eight. Maria von Mering Huggins prepared the new index, and Richard J. Lamb of W. H. Freeman and Company was of constant assistance in helping us ready the manuscript for publication.

GORDON R. WILLEY
JEREMY A. SABLOFF
October 1979

Preface to the First Edition

AMERICAN ARCHAEOLOGY—as all archaeology—is now in a phase of critical self-appraisal. Recent innovations in method and theory have aroused interest and argument in a way that has never occurred before within the discipline. This is the occasion, we believe, for a review of the full course of its development. In this way, we can appreciate new developments in relation to those that have gone before; and from this historical perspective we may also see more clearly the significance of the new directions in which the field is moving. Being a pioneer effort, this book was not conceived of as definitive in any sense. Rather, it is hoped that it may be the first of a genre which will stimulate further critical reflections and writings on the intellectual history of the subject.

It is inevitable in a work of this sort that the authors draw not only upon formal writings but upon the informal conversations and interchanges with professional colleagues dating back over a period of a good many years. Our debts to many of these people will be made clear throughout the text and footnotes; to the others, we offer our general, but nonetheless grateful, thanks. For his special efforts in calling our attention to numerous, but not well-known, references that bear upon the early history of North American archaeology, we wish to express our special appreciation to Stephen Williams. It should also be noted that some of the ideas of the book were first launched and discussed in a Harvard seminar on the history of American archaeology which was offered by one of us (Sabloff) in the fall of 1969, and we acknowledge the aid and interest of the students of this seminar group.

A word should be said about the extensive system of notes and the bibliography. This is not undue pedantry. Although we have attempted to write a text that can be read without necessary reference to the notes, the latter are a very integral part of the book, especially for the student. It is obviously impossible to describe in detail the various examples of archaeological operations or ideas of interpretation with which we are dealing. Recourse to the source material undoubtedly will be desirable for many readers. We have gone to some pains to make this possible with our notes and references.

We take this opportunity to thank Katherine W. Willey and Paula L. W. Sabloff for their critical readings of the manuscript and Maria von Mering Huggins for the final typing. The bibliography was put in final form by Isabelle Center. Maps and charts are the work of Symme Burstein of the Peabody Museum staff.

Finally, it is our pleasure to thank Glyn Daniel, archaeologist, editor, and instigator of various series of archaeological publlications, for his invitation to us to prepare such a book. His encouragement, together with the patience and help of the editorial staff of Thames and Hudson, have, in very large measure, made the book possible.

GORDON R. WILLEY
JEREMY A. SABLOFF

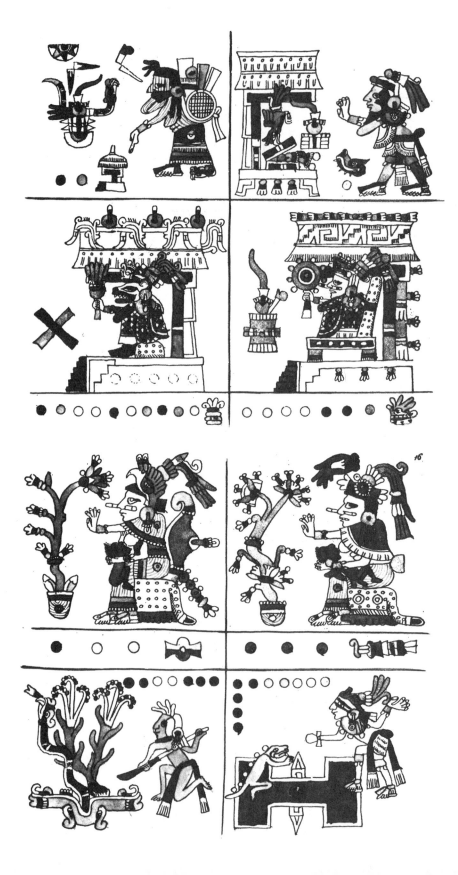

The present state of archaeology cannot be divorced from its past state.

GLYN DANIEL

Introduction

Archaeology: 1. Ancient history generally; systematic description or study of antiquities. 2. spec. The scientific study of the remains and monuments of the prehistoric period.
THE OXFORD UNIVERSAL DICTIONARY, 1955

THE NATURE OF ARCHAEOLOGY

F̲ew dictionary definitions are ever wholly satisfactory in capturing the substance and meaning of complex subjects. This is certainly true for the discipline of archaeology. The one we have cited is adequate, although only in a general way. It is true that most devotees of the subject, amateur or professional, would agree that archaeology is concerned primarily with the prehistoric past, that, in the consideration of this past, the emphasis is on material or artifactual remains, and that the data are approached systematically, as regards description, classification, and comparison. But our principal objection to such a definition is that it does not specify the basic goals of the discipline, at least as we conceive them. Accordingly, we offer a modified definition to begin this historical account of the development of archaeology in the Americas. Archaeology[1] is the study of the human cultural and social past whose goals are *to narrate* the sequent story of that past and *to explain and understand* the events that composed it. The discipline attempts to achieve these goals by surveying, excavating, and analyzing the remains and monuments of past cultures and the contexts in which they are found

Given such a definition, archaeology has an obvious alliance with history, for both history and archaeology deal with the human past. Both are concerned with the narration of that past and with its explanation. Their differences are primarily those of method rather than philosophical outlook. History orders and presents the past with the aid of textual references that were coexistent with that past; archaeology relies, as the dictionary definition informs us, on material remains and monuments, and, further, it relies on the distinctly archaeological methods and techniques of their recovery and preservation. There are, of course, instances where the two disciplines converge to contribute to an elucidation of the human past, as in those cultures where contemporary written records are few in number, selective in subject matter, or imperfectly translated, and where it is necessary to supplement them with the archaeological recovery and interpretation of artifacts and monuments.

Archaeology is also allied with anthropology. Anthropology is fundamentally a generalizing and comparative discipline. It begins with the particulars of human societies and cultures, but its most distinctive characteristic is its comparative point of view. The purpose of this comparison is, ultimately, to explain and understand the ways in which cultural and social forms come into being, function, and change, or, more briefly, an understanding of process. At this point, there is, by tradition, some philosophical distinction between archaeology as history and archaeology as anthropology. That is, many historians have dealt with the past in particularistic or idiographic terms, whereas in archaeology there has been a somewhat greater trend toward comparative generalization. (However, Spengler and Toynbee, historians by training and method, were interested in explaining the past in general comparative or nomothetic terms.) Conversely, archaeologists often have been and are concerned with the specific event rather than the generalization that may be drawn from a comparison of events.

It is, thus, our definition and conception of archaeology — whether in its American version or elsewhere — that its objectives are narration, explanation, and understanding, that it is both allied to history and to anthropology, and that its procedures are particularizing (idiographic) and generalizing (nomothetic) (see Trigger, 1970, 1989; Spaulding, 1968; Clarke, 1968, pp. 12–14; see also Chapter Six). For, although all these dualities are conceptually separable, they are not mutually exclusive. On the contrary, they are inevitably related. This interrelationship is to be recognized in the simple fact that, to explain past events, it is necessary to describe and to plot them in space and in time and that, conversely, such events cannot be described satisfactorily until they are to some extent understood.

Although interest in the past is very old and virtually universal, archaeology as a discipline is a western European development (see Daniel, 1950, 1964, 1967, 1968; Clark, 1939; Bibby, 1956; Lynch and Lynch, 1968; Clarke, 1968, pp. 4–11; Trigger, 1989). It has its traceable roots in the humanistic antiquarianism of the Italian Renaissance. This antiquarianism was founded on the discoveries of the monuments of Classical

ARCHAEOLOGY
IN WORLD
HISTORICAL
PERSPECTIVE

antiquity. The Renaissance findings, for the first time, gave western Europeans a comparative point of view about other cultures. This was the seed idea for both archaeology and anthropology. It was now known that another way of life, another civilization that rivaled and, in many ways, surpassed that of fourteenth and fifteenth century Italy, had once existed in the distant past. The conception of cultural difference in time (the essence of archaeology) was extended to the acceptance of contemporaneous cultural differences in geographic space (a primary tenet of anthropology) (Rowe, 1965).

After the Renaissance, archaeology as humanistic antiquarianism took two courses. In northern Europe, especially England, France, and Scandinavia, such antiquaries as William Camden (1551–1623), John Aubrey (1626–97), William Stukeley (1687–1765), and Rasmus Nyerup (1759–1829) studied the local mounds and monuments of their countries and set down accounts of their observations. The other course was followed by scholars like Giovanni Belzoni (1778–1823), who journeyed to the Classical world and the Near East and brought the treasures of these lands back to rich patrons in northern Europe. Belzoni was, perhaps, more romantic grave-robber than scholar; but, toward the end of the eighteenth century and the beginning of the nineteenth, more serious students followed such dilettanti. For example, a valuable by-product of Napoleon's Egyptian campaign was the introduction of French scholars to Egyptian antiquities, an event that led eventually to the work of people like Denon and Champollion and the truly archaeological achievement of the deciphering of the Egyptian hieroglyphs.

It was, however, the first of these two courses of humanistic antiquarianism that led more directly to what can be rightly called the first systematic archaeology. This occurred in Denmark, where, in 1819, J. C. Thomsen (1788–1863) followed up the work of Nyerup by organizing the national museum of that country along the lines of the Three-Age system. This system was predicated on the belief that the ancient inhabitants of Europe (and probably other parts of the world as well) had passed, successively, through ages characterized by the use of stone, bronze, and iron implements and weapons. The idea itself was not new. Greek and Roman historians and philosophers of Classical times had suggested it, and various European antiquarians of the late seventeenth and eighteenth centuries referred to it. By the early nineteenth century, it was in historical accounts and school books available in Denmark. Thomsen, however, was the first to apply the stone-bronze-iron classification to substantial collections of actual specimens, to insist that the classification corresponded to a sequence of chronologically defined periods, and to go on from the identification of stone, bronze, and iron materials to stylistic seriations of weapons and tools that could be correlated with the three ages (Trigger, 1968b; 1989, pp. 78–81).

Thomsen's work was continued by his younger colleague, J. J. A. Worsaae (1821–85), who enunciated some of the first important principles of archaeology, including the notion that objects accompanying the same burial are generally things that were in use at the same time and that were usually placed in burial association at the same time (Rowe, 1962a). This is the basis of grave lot segregation and of the chronological seriation of such lots.

At about this time, another line of investigation was beginning that was to merge with the Danish advances in the development of archaeology. For many years, flint artifacts had been observed in geological strata, but their significance was not appreciated until Lyell revolutionized geology with his fluvial or depositional theories of that science in his *Principles of Geology* (1830–33). Then, in 1836–37, the French scholar Boucher de Perthes announced discoveries of human-made artifacts in deep geological strata, claiming for them great antiquity. The idea that humans and their artifacts could be of such great age aroused a storm of opposition, both religious and scientific; however, the idea proved to be the beginning of Paleolithic archaeology. By 1860, with the support of Sir John Evans and others, the scientific world had accepted Boucher de Perthes' discoveries. The dimension of time, which had begun to transform antiquarianism into archaeology with the Danish Three-Age system, was now seen in all its implications for history and prehistory. Moreover, the presence of archaeological materials in different geological strata, and in strata that were found superimposed one over the other, introduced the vital concept of stratigraphy to the emerging archaeological discipline.

Still another intellectual force appeared in the mid nineteenth century to aid in the growth of archaeology as well as anthropology. The year of 1859 was the year of Darwin's *The Origin of Species*. The book, together with Huxley's impassioned stand in its favor, had a revolutionary impact on all science and learned thought. From biological evolution, the idea of progress was extended to the history of human societies and cultures; and two of the founders of anthropology, E. B. Tylor (1832–1917) and L. H. Morgan (1818–81), saw in this principle of cultural evolution, and in the findings of archaeology with its Three-Age system and its demonstrated great antiquity of humans, the data from which to construct a model of the human social and cultural past. This model—the sequence of Savagery, Barbarism, and Civilization—had, in turn, a profound effect on archaeology as well as on all philosophies of history and society.[2]

Finally, and less specifically, there were other influences converging to aid in the development of archaeology in the early and middle nineteenth century. There was the general rise and appreciation of science, a trend that had begun in eighteenth-century rationalism and had gathered momentum from that time forward. Closely interrelated with this was the rising industrialism of western Europe and America and the expansion of the power of these regions to what had been unexplored and exotic parts of the world. Industry had an obvious, direct alliance with fields like geology and the physical sciences; together with the exploration and exploitation of far corners of the world, it also had a more subtle, but very real, conditioning effect in bringing about an intellectual climate in which anthropology and archaeology could flourish.

The latter part of the nineteenth century and the first part of the twentieth, up to the time of World War I, saw great progress in archaeology. Schliemann, Petrie, Sir Arthur Evans, and others conducted long-term operations in the Classical World and the Near East; Stephens, Catherwood, and others explored the Maya ruins of the New World; in England, General Pitt-Rivers set new standards of professional excavation; and, in the United States, Putnam began the training of a generation of professional archaeologists. After World War I, archaeologists became more aware of the importance of chronology, not simply as the great developmental span of humankind's passage through the Three-Age system or the levels of Savagery to Civilization but as the means of ordering culture units or culture complexes in regional archaeological sequences. Problems were conceived of as more strictly historical, in the sense of spatial-temporal relations between cultures and in the tracing out of diffusion. Generally, this was carried out within the limits of a regional framework, for this was a time of intensive regional specialization, but there were some outstanding broader historical syntheses, of which V. Gordon Childe's *The Dawn of European Civilization* (1925) and *The Most Ancient East* (1934) are of primary importance.

From preoccupation with strict historical schematics came a gradual shift toward an interest in the more detailed reconstructions of prehistoric lifeways within individual sites and culture units and in the workings or functionings of cultures. This began with a consideration of cultural-natural environmental relationships but spread from there to other aspects of culture, especially those of social structure. These trends began even before World War I but have grown in importance, in both Europe and America, since then (Trigger, 1968b). They have led to attempts to understand culture process, to explain the past, and, in these attempts, archaeologists have called more and more upon other sciences — mathematics, physics and chemistry, geology, biology, and botany — and have designed research projects of an interdisciplinary nature.

At the same time, attempts to understand human behavior, particularly symbolic behavior, have continued the alliance of archaeology with a variety of humanistic disciplines.

In American usage, the term *archaeology* is applied both to the discipline itself and to the subject matter. That is, *archaeology* and *prehistory* are employed interchangeably. In Europe, *archaeology* is more apt to be reserved for the discipline, whereas *prehistory* refers to the substance. This is not a matter of great moment, but it is mentioned here to avoid confusion or misunderstanding in later contexts.

There is still another distinction about this same pair of words that the reader should keep in mind. In the New World, the whole range of the prehistoric past may be referred to as either *prehistory* or *archaeology*, without reference to chronology or to level of cultural development. This contrasts, again, with European usage, where earlier or simpler cultures are assigned to prehistory, and terms such as *Classical archaeology* or *Egyptology* designate the study of later or more advanced cultures (Clark, 1939, Chapter 1).

With these few preliminary observations, we can now go on to say that American archaeology, as the name implies, refers to the practice of archaeology in the New World. The subject matter of this practice is, for the most part, the prehistoric or Pre-Columbian past of this New World. More specifically, this means that the peoples under consideration are the ancestors of the American Indian and the Eskimo-Aleut. The geographical range includes both major continents and the islands of the Arctic, Greenland, and the Antilles. The chronological span is from the first inhabitation of these lands, certainly as far back as 10,000 B.C. and quite likely earlier, to the coming of the Europeans in A.D. 1492.[3] Although American archaeology is largely concerned with the Pre-Columbian inhabitants of the New World, it may also pertain to the historical European period. Thus, the establishment of a European trading post among the Native Americans of interior Georgia in the eighteenth century may be an event that is now known only, or principally, from what has been found in the ground by archaeologists. Nor does American archaeology have to be restricted to an involvement with Native Americans. Historic-site archaeology may pertain wholly to European-derived Americans—for example, to Colonial Williamsburg or to an American Civil War battle site.

In brief, and by widest definition, if archaeology is the telling, explaining, or understanding of the past through archaeological methods and techniques, the American version of archaeology simply limits the field geographically.

AMERICAN
ARCHAEOLOGY:
A DEFINITION

Map of the Americas showing the three major divisions: North, Middle, and South.

As we have already implied, the practice of archaeology in the Americas did not develop in isolation from that of Europe (Hallowell, 1960; Willey, 1968a). There was first a long period of antiquarian interest, much as there was in the Old World. It began with the European conquests and continued into the nineteenth century. As in Europe, this American antiquarian interest was also channeled along two courses. Count Waldeck and Lord Kingsborough, with their studies of the Aztecs and the Maya, can be seen as the counterparts to the dilettanti who traveled to the ancient world of Greece and Rome; others, such as Thomas Jefferson or Caleb Atwater, digging in the mounds of the Eastern United States, remind us more of the English or Danish antiquaries. The mid-nineteenth-century synthesis of the Danish Three-Age system, the realization of the geological antiquity of humans, and Darwinian evolutionism made themselves felt in the Americas very soon after they were developed in Europe. Subsequent American developments, again, show parallels to the European ones. The archaeology of the high civilizations of Mexico and Central America tended to focus on the humanistic concerns of art, iconography, and documentary materials; that of the simpler cultures of North America was more in the natural science tradition, with interests directed toward artifact typology, geological stratigraphy, and even digging techniques. But this divergence was by no means complete, even in the nineteenth century; and, in America, as in Europe, these lines have been converging in the twentieth century.

THE PRESENT BOOK

It is the purpose of this book to provide a history of the development of the discipline of archaeology as it has been, and is being, practiced in the Americas. Thus, our emphasis will be on the *doing* of archaeology. We will be concerned with the way problems of cultural history have been conceived by the archaeologist and how these conceptions have changed through time. In pursuing this theme, we will examine research strategies and methods employed in carrying them out—how data have been obtained and analyzed, and conclusions drawn therefrom. In other words, what is projected is an intellectual history of the subject. This should be more than a listing of new methods and discoveries as these have appeared from time to time. We will attempt to give the reader an appreciation of the intellectual climate of the various times under consideration and of the influence of other disciplines and philosophies on American archaeology. What we will be arguing is that American archaeology is as good as its concepts and that the history of its development is related very directly to the addition of new and better concepts as these apply to the dimensions of form, space, and time and to the circumstances of context, function, and process. In so doing, we will be discussing and emphasizing those works that are most closely linked with the introduction and uses of new and important concepts. Sometimes these have been presented by their authors as explicit methodological and theoretical innovations while in other instances they have been implicit in substantive data or interpretations. Even with these criteria, we cannot be encyclopedic but, on the contrary, consciously selective.

This history is in no way intended as a summary of substantive results. Although archaeological strategies and methods cannot be entirely separated from archaeological data, we will be involved only in a limited way with substantive findings.[4]

At the time of the first edition of this book, there had been no modern full-scale histories that embraced all of American or New World archaeology.[5] However, we were then influenced in the organization and treatment of our work by various shorter works and unpublished lecture courses, which foreshadowed what we are trying to do here. The earliest of these was a lecture course given by the late W. D. Strong at Columbia University in 1940, Method and Result in American Archaeology.[6] Strong was a student of Kroeber's, and he took from Kroeber an anthropological outlook with a definite historical bias; nevertheless, Strong conceived of archaeology as a science, which was, in his words, "part history, part anthropology." He was interested in the specifics of history and in the way these might be viewed in more general schemes of cultural evolution. In one of his lectures, he made the statement that "only a trained anthropologist could be a good archaeologist." Of published works that deal wholly or in part with the history and development of method and theory in American archaeology, we should mention Walter W. Taylor's *A Study of Archaeology,* which appeared in 1948. Primarily a critique of current theoretical orientations and practices in American archaeology, it also offered a historical perspective on the development of the discipline. Other articles or books that treat, to a greater or lesser degree, the development of American archaeology, surveying either all or parts of the New World, include a paper by N. C. Nelson (1933), a summary statement by W. D. Strong (1952), a review by J. B. Griffin (1959), a primarily ethnological-anthropological history by A. I. Hallowell (1960), comments by Frederick Johnson (1961), E. N. Wilmsen's (1965) considerations of late Pleistocene studies, Robert Silverberg's (1968) popular book about the "Moundbuilders," studies of particular regions or periods by J. E. Fitting (1973, ed.), P. J. Lyon (1969), F. B. Kirbus (1976), and Brian Fagan (1977), and general syntheses of the subject by D. W. Schwartz (1967, 1968), G. R. Willey (1968), and Shirley Gorenstein (1976). For more recent years, this is by no means a complete listing, as the topic of the history of the discipline has increasingly attracted the attention of archaeologists. A great many articles of historical perspective on the field, particularly in the 1980s, have been published. Some of these are cited in the pages which will follow.[7] However, one very important new source deserves special mention: B. G. Trigger's *A History of Archaeological Thought* (1989), which includes much information of relevance to American archaeology.

The Strong lectures and many of these writings share a common outlook, in that all tend to view American archaeology as passing through more or less similar periods of development. The organization of the present book follows such a period scheme. This is clearly laid out in our chapter headings. However, as Schwartz has argued in his paper, we are dealing with intellectual attitudes and, although the history of these attitudes can be usefully conceptualized into periods or eras, they must also be appreciated as trends through time, for there is a considerable overlapping from one period to the next.

Our first period and trend is designated as the *Speculative Period* (Chapter Two). This follows the terminology of Schwartz's article, and we believe it to be appropriately descriptive of the basic attitude toward the antiquities and peoples of the New World during this period. The opening date for the period can be set at the "discovery" of America in 1492. After this event, European soldiers, explorers, priests, settlers, and savants indulged in speculative writings and discussions over the meaning of the New World and its inhabitants. We bring the period to a close at a date that we set, somewhat arbitrarily, at about 1840. By this time, the world was moving into the beginnings of a scientific era, and, in the Americas, the decade of the 1840s marked the appearance of the first major archaeological writings in which systematic description outweighed speculation. There had been precursors to this kind of factual, descriptive archaeology in the years before, but from this time on, it came increasingly to the fore.

We have applied the name *Classificatory-Descriptive* to this trend of factual archaeology and to the new period (Chapter Three). The title signifies the emphasis on systematic description of archaeological remains and monuments and on the classification of these data in accordance with formal typologies. The American archaeological publications that herald the period are the important monographs by Stephens and Catherwood, *Incidents of Travel in Central America: Chiapas and Yucatan* (1841) and *Incidents of Travel in Yucatan* (1843), and the notable book by Squier and Davis, *Ancient Monuments of the Mississippi Valley* (1848). The period, defined as extending from 1840 to 1914, saw a continued increase in classificatory-descriptive work at the expense of the sheerly speculative, although the latter did not disappear entirely. The period was also marked by the first professionalization of the American archaeological discipline, with the establishment of museums and university departments in the latter third of the nineteenth century. It was also the age of Darwin, Huxley, and Spencer in England and the time of the spread of the theory of evolution from there to other parts of the world. Such influences were felt as early as the 1860s and 1870s on the American side of the Atlantic. Evolutionism was, in effect, the first process to be evoked or used by American archaeologists, in however naive a manner.

The threshold of World War I may be taken to mark the inception of our third period in American archaeological development, the *Classificatory-Historical* Period. The year 1914, following general usage, is designated as a mean date for the first carefully and consciously controlled — and culture-historically productive — archaeological stratigraphy in the New World, a credit that traditionally is shared by Gamio, for his Valley of Mexico excavations (1913)[8] and by Nelson with his somewhat more refined work in the Galisteo Basin of New Mexico (1914, 1916). The name for the period was selected to emphasize the historical or chronological interests that dominated it. The classificatory objectives of the preceding period were combined with archaeological chronology building, and the results were regional or areal chronologies, or space-time charts, of culture units or complexes. This, of course, was related to refinements in culture-unit definitions, in stratigraphic and seriational procedures, and to the introduction of absolute dating techniques. It was to be a period in which American archaeology's ties to ethnology and social anthropology were continued and made even closer than before. This came about administratively, through departmental organization in universities, and ideologically, in the transfer of concepts from ethnology-social anthropology to archaeology. The direct-historical approach, or the working from the ethnographic present to the archaeological past, and the uses of ethnographic analogy in archaeological interpretation, both of which flowered in this period, are examples of this interdisciplinary stimulation. Less felicitously, the strong antievolutionary bias of American social anthropology of the period was also passed on to archaeology. As we have defined the period, it spans the years between 1914 and 1960, and, as such, it embraces almost the entire history of what still must be called *modern archaeology* in the Americas. Because of this, we have devoted two chapters to the Classificatory-Historical Period. The first (Chapter Four) is concerned with the earlier years, from 1914 until 1940. Most of the archaeology done in these decades was historically oriented only in the rather limited sense of being the geographical-chronological plotting out of monuments and remains. There were certain exceptions, however; some archaeologists attempted to go beyond this and to reconstruct and narrate a story of the past which had more semblance to life. Between 1940 and 1960, there was a very definite shift of interest in this direction. Attempts were made to recover cultural contexts as well as to erect space-time frameworks of artifact types and to place artifact types and complexes into prehistoric patterns of behavior and to explicate function. All of this involved more intensive studies of the remains themselves, especially in conjunction with their natural environmental settings and with the inferences as to ecology that could be drawn from these conjunctions. It also involved an increased interchange of ideas between archaeologists and social anthropologists. These developments are treated in a second chapter devoted to the Classificatory-Historical Period (Chapter Five).

In our previous editions, we had referred to the most recent period as the *Explanatory Period,* but we feel this is too limiting and too confining a title for all that has happened in American archaeology since 1960. Many elements of what we now call the *Modern Period* can be seen earlier, especially in the latter half of the preceding period, but it was not until after 1960 that methodological and theoretical considerations became of prime importance as American archaeologists attempted to grapple with problems of process in culture change and the nature of social behavior in the past. These innovative attempts were often referred to as the *New Archaeology* or *Processual Archaeology.*

In our discussion of these innovations, we will try to sort out the new from the old. We will begin by examining the strong continuation of an earlier culture-historical approach, relating this to processualism and the reemergence of cultural evolution. Systems theory and the ecosystem concept will be reviewed, as well as deductive reasoning and the positivist philosophy of science, both major tenets of the New Archaeology. The nature and uses of ethnographic and historic analogies will be considered, showing their uses in both culture-historical and functional-processual contexts. We will follow this by giving some attention to the *Post-New Archaeology, Postprocessual Archaeology,* or contextual and critical archaeology of the late 1970s and 1980s.

Throughout the book, we will make every effort to illustrate theoretical and methodological arguments with examples drawn from recent American archaeological research.

Our treatment of the Modern Period will be a single chapter, the final Chapter Six. In our first edition of this book (1974), we dealt with the decade of the 1960s and largely with the Processual or New Archaeology. In the second edition (1980), we again reviewed the 1960s and moved on into the 1970s, devoting three chapters to these decades. We admitted then that such a detailed coverage of these last two decades was disproportionately large for any work claiming to be a full history of the American archaeological field. For this third edition, we have treated the last three decades—from 1960 to 1990—in a single chapter again. Even this, perhaps, is disproportionate, given the length of the book, and we are well aware that only time and the distance of retrospection can give archaeologists a more insightful appraisal of this Modern Period. But, to quote ourselves from the previous edition, "we are interested in the directions in which the field is moving. What we say here is necessarily ephemeral, but perhaps it will serve as one contemporary record for the historian of the future."

NOTES

1. Archaeology is most usually spelled with *ae* (as separate letters or as a ligature), and this spelling will be followed here; however, some American archaeologists and institutions substitute *e*.

2. This idea of human social and cultural evolution is much older than the mid-nineteenth century (Harris, 1968, pp. 29–31).

3. This is not meant to exclude Europeans or other inhabitants of the Old World who happened to arrive in the New World prior to 1492. Thus, the Viking presence, now documented in Newfoundland *ca.* A.D. 1000, is certainly within the compass of American archaeology, as would be any Asiatics (such as Jomon voyagers from Japan *ca.* 3000 B.C.) who may or may not have reached the coasts of South or Middle America.

4. For such syntheses of substantive archaeology of the Americas, see Willey (1966–71), Jennings (1968, 1989), or Fiedel (1987). Given the extensive nature of the present book, its vast subject matter, and its limited length, we have relied almost entirely upon the published record rather than upon more informal unpublished sources.

5. Some works in the nineteenth century, such as

Haven's *Archaeology of the United States* (1856) or Winsor's *Narrative and Critical History of North America,* Vol. I: *Aboriginal America* (1889), trace through the development of theoretical thinking about American antiquities and inhabitants to their respective times.

6. Willey was a student in the course and subsequently taught it at Columbia in 1942–43. See also Strong (1952). Mention should also be made here of a Harvard course, History of American Archaeology, offered in 1960–65 by Stephen Williams (Belmont and Williams, 1965), which influenced us and our book.

7. As this edition went to press, a useful new edited collection of essays on the history of American archaeology was published: *Rediscovering Our Past: Essays on the History of American Archaeology,* edited by Jonathan E. Reyman (1992).

8. Gamio's (1913) pioneering work was carried out in 1911, at the urging of A. M. Tozzer and Franz Boas. Nelson's fieldwork (1914, 1916) was carried out from 1912 to 1915. Even earlier, Holmes (1885) had made more general references to cultural stratigraphy in the Valley of Mexico.

CHAPTER TWO

The Speculative Period (1492–1840)

We must not lose sight of the fact that modes of thought
at any given time were firmly rooted in the ethos of that
time and were severely circumscribed by the extent of
knowledge then current.

EDWIN N. WILMSEN

A DEFINITION OF
THE PERIOD

The Speculative Period is really a prelude to our story. The collection of virtually all the archaeological data uncovered during this period, with a few notable exceptions, was incidental to other pursuits. American archaeology was not established as a vocation or a discipline until well after 1840 and did not even become a popular avocation until the beginning of the nineteenth century. However, there were mounds and artifacts and a wide variety of antiquities, as well as the Native American population, which could not be ignored, and speculation about all of these was rife. We can only sample the fascinating multitude of written comments and discourses on American antiquities and the Native Americans from 1492 to 1840.[1] Hopefully, though, we will succeed in conveying some of the flavor of this first period in the history of American archaeology.

The entire three and a half centuries of the period were pervaded by a general intellectual atmosphere of armchair speculation about the origin of the Native Americans. Emerging from this, however, were three trends of thinking, which contain within themselves the seeds of the archaeological discipline in the Americas.

The first of these trends pertained principally to the sixteenth and seventeenth centuries. Its focus was Latin America, and it consisted mainly of chronicles by men who accompanied the Spanish Conquistadors and works describing the nature of Native American cultures by priests and other administrators. The latter studies would be called "administrative spin-off" in modern parlance.

The second trend began in the eighteenth century and was particularly strong in the early nineteenth century. It consisted of accounts by explorers and travelers, mainly in North America but occasionally in Latin America, who described ruins and mounds in their reports and speculated at great length on the origins of their finds. The object of their travels often was to produce a book of literary merit. The approach, especially in the nineteenth century, was natural scientific in tone, and almost everything that was observed was recorded. It should be stressed that we are concerned here only with those early chroniclers and explorers who had some historical or antiquarian interests. There were a number of writers who provided ethnographic descriptions of Native American groups from the sixteenth through the nineteenth centuries. These ethnographic documents have been and continue to be of great use to the archaeologist for general and specific ethnographic analogies and for showing continuities of various customs (Hole and Heizer, 1969, pp. 181–183). However, we are particularly interested in those writers who not only described the Native Americans but who showed an interest in the past history of Native American customs and artifacts and speculated on their origins. Many persons, for example, described the life of the Aztecs and the Maya at the time of the Conquest, and these primary sources of data have been widely used by archaeologists. But, a few of the writers, such as Bernardino de Sahagun and Diego de Landa, also revealed archaeological interests and asked what we would consider archaeological questions in their works. These latter writers were forerunners of the later eighteenth- and nineteenth-century explorers and archaeologists who also asked such questions as "Whence?" and "What happened?" in their descriptions of customs of Native Americans and archaeological ruins they encountered.

The third trend was almost ephemeral and actually marked the first stirrings of the later descriptive-historical trends, which began about 1840. It consisted of the few efforts that had archaeology as their primary concern. The people who went out and excavated or undertook archaeological surveys in the eighteenth and nineteenth centuries, such as Jefferson or Atwater, were at best archaeologists by avocation. Nevertheless, they originated a trend that blossomed later in the nineteenth century, as a general interest in archaeology was sparked by discoveries throughout the Americas and in Europe.

It is obvious that these trends do not form a tight typology, nor are they intended to. There is a definite overlap among them, not only in time but occasionally in content, too. For example, the sixteenth-century archaeological expeditions of Diego Garcia de Palacio to the Maya site of Copan, Honduras, and the nineteenth-century one of Antonio del Rio to Palenque, Mexico, were ordered by governmental directive. In addition, the chroniclers and early forerunners of the discipline of archaeology indulged in speculations as to Native American origins which were no less imaginative than those of the explorers and writers of belles-lettres. In fact, it is rampant speculation, whether of an enthusiastic or restrained or of a logical or illogical variety, that links all the trends and characterizes the entire period.

The dominance of a speculative mode of thought during the period is certainly due to a number of factors. The most important ones probably were a paucity of reliable archaeological data, the lack of European models of archaeological reasoning that the American worker could emulate (Hallowell, 1960, p. 74), the significance of a literary approach in much of the archaeologically relevant writing, coupled with the virtual nonexistence of a tradition of scientific explanation and the deeply rooted acceptance of theological explanations of natural and cultural phenomena. All these factors, plus, on the one hand, a continuing sense of wonder and amazement at the exotic nature of the New World as more and more of it was explored, and, on the other, the immediate need to create a heroic history for the new land (especially in North America) (Silverberg, 1968), made speculation the dominant element in all discussions of the architectural ruins and material culture of the ancient inhabitants of the New World.

It should be clear that, when we speak of speculation, we are talking about nonscientific conjecture.[2] Such conjecture was rampant in this time period, because the observers of archaeological phenomena had little or no hard data for comparisons with their observations or in many cases had no information whatsoever on which to base their speculations. It obviously is quite difficult to produce credible reconstructions without a good foundation of reliable data. However, even in the few cases where primary excavated or surveyed information was available, the workers of the period did not use these data carefully to build or test hypotheses. Rather, the raw data and speculation tended to be compartmentalized. A case in point, which we shall soon return to, is the work of Caleb Atwater, who, after meticulously describing his studies of the mounds of Ohio, proceeded to link the mounds to peoples from "Hindostan" (Atwater, 1820). One reason for this kind of thinking was the lack of any tradition of scientific reasoning. An archaeological tradition worthy of that name had to await the intellectual migration from Europe of books such as Charles Lyell's *Principles of Geology* in the 1830s. It also was not until the early nineteenth century that would-be archaeologists in the Americas had any good European models for their archaeological methods and theories. Until the work of Thomsen, Worsaae, and, later, Boucher de Perthes, there simply were no archaeological studies that could be used by American archaeologists to point their own work in the proper direction.

Without any intellectual tradition in the Speculative Period from which a scientific archaeology might have developed, theological explanations remained the accepted means of reconstructing events of the past. The sword certainly cut both ways, since the strength of theological thought militated against purely scientific modes of thinking. The discovery and recognition of Late Pleistocene populations in the New World, for example, had to await the Darwinian Revolution (see Wilmsen, 1965, p. 176), just as it did in the Old World.

To our mind, the phrase *discovery of the Americas,* as found in many history books, is most often used in a completely European-ethnocentric manner. The idea that Columbus "discovered" America would probably have been seen as an unbelievable joke by the many millions of Native Americans who had lived in the New World since their distant ancestors had first arrived in the Americas at least 12,000 years prior to Columbus' expedition (Deloria, 1969; Josephy, 1970). Even in relation to European voyages, it has been clear for many years that the Norsemen visited North America a number of centuries before Columbus. Nevertheless, it was Columbus' voyage and later voyages in the sixteenth century that had such great intellectual impact on European thought. In this sense, one might say that these exploratory voyages were discoveries relating to the European mind. As has been pointed out by Rowse (1959): "The Discovery of the New World, it has been said, is much the greatest event in the history of the Old.

The new explorations had tremendous significance for European philosophical thought in addition to their importance for the politics and economics of the time. They generated much excitement and stirred the imagination of the intellectuals of the sixteenth century. Crone (1969, p. 176) has put it well: "The Age of Discovery . . . was not so much a break with the past and a new departure, but rather a quickening of pace, a stimulus to nascent ideas. The New World provided, as it were, a gigantic laboratory in which the speculations of Renaissance man could be tested, modified, and developed."

The explorations of the very late fifteenth and the sixteenth century presented the European philosophers and intellectuals with a number of pressing questions, which demanded immediate answers. One of these questions, and the one of paramount importance for an under-

THE AMERICAS:
DISCOVERY AND
ORIGINS OF THE
NATIVE AMERICANS

standing of the beginnings of American archaeology, was "Who are the Indians[3] of the New World?" The first question which arose with respect to the Native Americans concerned their identity or origin. It seems a natural enough question and the only one which at the time could be considered speculatively, that is, without waiting for the tedious accumulation of additional facts (Nelson, 1933, pp. 88–89). The answers to this question were not long in coming and were as varied as they were plentiful. Many, if not most, of the proposed answers appear totally outlandish to the modern archaeologist, but at the time they were taken quite seriously. As Spinden has so cogently remarked (1933, p. 220): "It seems that the manifestly impossible has a vastly greater appeal to the imagination than the merely improbable."

The question of who the Native Americans were and where they came from was of great importance, because, to Europeans, who had been taught that everyone was descended from Adam and Eve and that, at the time of the universal flood, only Noah and his family survived (Hallowell, 1960, p. 4), the inhabitants of the New World either had to be related to some descendants of Noah or else were not human. Some of the early Spanish explorers and settlers believed that the latter was the case and that the Indians were beasts. But, after several key rulings culminating in the historic Papal Bull of Pope Paul III in 1537, and through the efforts of men such as Antonio de Montesinos and Bartolomé de las Casas, it was established that the Native Americans were indeed human, that they should be treated as such, and that every effort should be made to propagate the faith among them (Hanke, 1949, 1951).

From the moment that knowledge of the discoveries made by the early explorations spread throughout Europe, there were innumerable writers who were willing to speculate on the origins of the Native Americans. One of the favorite opinions of those men who were theologically inclined was that they were descendants of the Ten Lost Tribes of Israel.[4] Diego Duran, for one, favored this hypothesis (Huddleston, 1967, pp. 38–41). James Adair, an influential eighteenth-century American writer, also believed in it (Adair, 1775), as did such an eminent nineteenth-century antiquarian as Lord Kingsborough (1831–1848).

Another popular explanation was that the Native Americans came from the lost world of Atlantis. This hypothesis, which was inspired by Plato's discussion of Atlantis, was suggested as early as 1530 by the poet Fracastoro and in 1535 by Gonzalo Fernandez de Oviedo y Valdes (Wauchope, 1962, pp. 30–31). This explanation, along with its companion, the land of Mu hypothesis, has fallen from its early popularity, but is still revived on occasion by diehard supporters in the twentieth century.

ATLANTIS INSULA

Late seventeenth-century map of the Americas. This is an extract from Sanson's map, with the New World conceived of as the "Island of Atlantis." (From Winsor, 1889)

Several Dutch scholars also entered the debate quite vigorously in the mid-seventeenth century. De Groot supported the idea that the origin of the Native Americans lay across the Atlantic in Scandinavia, the land of the Norsemen. De Laet and Horn, on the other hand, believed that Scythians from Central Asia and others were responsible for the people of the New World (DeGroot, 1963; de Laet, 1643, 1644; and Horn, 1652, as cited in Spinden, 1933).

Cortez talking with the Aztecs.
(From Sahagún, 1950–3)

Many other writers also looked to Asian countries, such as China, Korea, or India, for the source of the peoples of the New World. Some suggested long boat trips as the means of these migrations. Indeed, the suggestion that the origin of the American Indian lay in Asia was first made in a form which almost has a modern ring. As far back as 1590, Fray José de Acosta, in his *Historia Natural y Moral de las Indias,* suggested that the Americas were peopled from Asia by means of a slow overland migration. Although Acosta did not rule out the possibility of ship-wrecks landing people in the New World, he felt that "small groups of savage hunters" who took an overland route with "short stretches of navigation" accounted for most of the original population of the Americas. He guessed that this migration may have occurred as early as one to 2,000 years before the Conquest (Beals, 1957; Wilmsen, 1965, p. 173; Huddleston, 1967, Chapter II). Acosta's proposal is especially remarkable in light of the relatively meager geographical knowledge of the time. The existence of a land bridge or a narrow strait between the Old and New Worlds was nothing more than a possibility to the writers of the day.

By the mid-seventeenth century, at least as early as 1637 (Wauchope, 1962, p. 85), the presently accepted hypothesis that the first migrant to the New World arrived from Asia via the Bering Strait was being seriously considered. In 1648, Thomas Gage stated that the New World was originally populated by people coming out of Asia through the Bering Strait area. He was also one of the first writers to note the racial resemblances between the Native Americans and the peoples of Mongolia in northeast Asia and used this evidence to support his argument (J. E. S. Thompson, 1958, p. 92). By the time that Cook completed the mapping of the Bering Strait area, Pfefferkorn could say in a book published in 1794, that "it is almost certain that the first inhabitants of America really came by way of the strait" (Treulein, 1949, p. 161, as quoted in Ives, 1956, p. 420; see also Wilmsen, 1965, p. 173).

By the end of the eighteenth century, it could be stated with some certainty that the origins of the Native American lay in Asia and that they did indeed migrate to the New World via the Bering Strait. But this did not put an end to the rampant speculations that had typified the previous three centuries since the discovery of the New World and that continued unabated well into the nineteenth century. Nor did the growing acceptance of the origin of the Native American in Asia mean that the archaeologically inclined writers had any notion of when the first migrations actually took place or what was the way of life of the first inhabitants of the Americas, although they did not hold back their varied speculations.[5] It was not until 1845 that a distinguished scholar, Albert Gallatin, could firmly state (p. 177): "From whatever place the people of America came, the first important question is the time of their arrival." As Wilmsen has pointed out, the writers of what we have called the Speculative Period had no concepts of time, space, or culture to handle the idea of what some archaeologists now call "Early Man" (Wilmsen, 1965, p. 173). The beginnings of these concepts had to await the birth of the discipline of archaeology in the Classificatory-Descriptive Period.[6]

Brief mention should be made here of certain writers whom we might consider as the earliest forerunners of archaeology in the Americas or, better yet, the forerunners of the forerunners. At the time of the Spanish Conquest and shortly thereafter, a number of writers, both Spanish and Native American, wrote down descriptive statements about the nature of the native cultures immediately preceding and during the Conquest as well as narrative descriptions of the Conquest itself. These ethnographic descriptions have provided the archaeologist with a wealth of information about the civilizations of Mesoamerica[7] and the Peruvian area[8] just before they were virtually obliterated by the Conquistadors. Some of the writers also showed a keen interest in the past history of these native civilizations. This kind of interest and curiosity, to our mind, marks the first stirrings of interests, which more than three centuries later led to the establishment of American archaeology as a viable academic discipline.

THE EARLY CHRONICLERS AND HISTORICAL INTERESTS

We should further point out that the Native American peoples themselves were not without historical interests. For example, some native documents or codices, carvings, and paintings in Mesoamerica, which include of chronicles, genealogies, or historical statements, have been preserved in the original or in post-Conquest copies.[9] As Leon-Portilla has stated (1969, p. 119): "The Pre-Columbian man truly realized the significance of what we call history."

The body of *Historias* and the other documents, which includes discussions of the pre-Conquest histories of the peoples of Mesoamerica and the Peruvian area and varies in length from occasional comments to huge multivolume books, is relatively large. The reliability and utility of these works are also variable. Yet, some of these books, such as those of the Franciscan Fray Bernadino de Sahagún[10] and the Dominican Fray Diego Duran[11] on the Aztecs, and Garcilaso de la Vega's *Royal Commentaries of the Incas,*[12] to name just three, definitely display intellectual leanings that we would have to stamp as historical. Since the pre-Conquest past is now the province of the archaeologist, these works are obviously of interest to us. We do not have the space to consider them all, but they should be singled out as the prehistoric baseline of the history of the archaeological discipline.

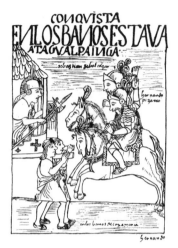

Pizarro and the Inca. A drawing from the chronicler Guaman Poma de Ayala (1613).

Among the early Spanish and Native American chroniclers, Bishop Diego de Landa and Fray Bartolemé de las Casas deserve special mention. Landa, of all the writers of the sixteenth and early seventeenth centuries, shows perhaps the strongest interest in archaeological ruins as well as in reconstructing the history and way of life of a Native American culture—in this case, the ancient Maya. In his *Relación de las Cosas de Yucatán*,[13] he describes ruins such as Chichen Itza and even gives a plan of the main temple there. He offers a political history of the Maya, discusses the nature of their society, daily life, and technology, and describes many of the material artifacts and religious practices. In addition, he gives a good working description of the ancient Maya hieroglyphic and calendrical systems. One has only to look at the many varied entries under *archaeology* in Tozzer's syllabus of the *Relación* (Landa, 1941, pp. 276–282) to appreciate the kind of archaeological data supplied by Bishop Landa. The Bishop must have been an interesting character, since he was both a persecutor and destroyer of Maya documents and a preserver of the details of the Maya way of life in his own writings. Nevertheless, as Tozzer has said as regards the content and importance of the *Relación:* "The source material presented by Landa includes practically every phase of the social anthropology of the ancient Mayas, together with the history of the Spanish discovery, the conquest and the ecclesiastical and native history, together with the first accurate knowledge of the hieroglyphic writing" (Landa, 1941, p. vii).

Fray Bartolemé de las Casas was also a bishop, for a short time, of Chiapas in Mexico-Guatemala. He is best known as a champion of the rights of the Indians of the New World, and much of his life was spent trying to convince his fellow clergy and the Spanish Crown to treat the Native Americans in a fair and humane manner and to appreciate the value of their civilizations. Two of Las Casas' great works were the lengthy *Apologetica historia de las Indias* (Casas, 1909) and the *Historia de las Indias* (Casas, 1927). In one of his many penetrating books on Las Casas, Lewis Hanke devotes a full chapter to proving that Las Casas was an anthropologist (Hanke, 1951, Chapter III). Hanke not only proves his case in general, but he also provides evidence that indicates there is good reason to consider Las Casas as a forerunner of nineteenth- and twentieth-century American archaeologists. First, "He looked at all peoples, the ancient Greeks and sixteenth-century Spaniards as well as the newly discovered New World natives, as human beings in different stages of development from rude beginnings to a higher stage of culture" (Hanke, 1951, p. 62). That is, Las Casas, even as early as the sixteenth century, had at least a rudimentary concept of an evolutionary scale of cultural development.

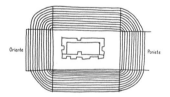

A sixteenth-century drawing of the Castillo at Chichen Itza, Yucatan, Mexico. This is certainly one of the first archaeological plans of an American ruin ever published. (From Landa, Tozzer, ed., 1941)

In addition, Las Casas was one of the first, if not the first, to provide a discussion relating environment and culture in the New World. In a tone we would now consider strongly deterministic, Las Casas spends the first thirty-two chapters of the *Apologetica* describing "minutely the favorable physical conditions in the New World which make it inevitable that the Indians are men of wise understanding. He shows himself a forerunner of Jean Bodin, usually considered the first European environmentalist" (Hanke, 1951, pp. 70–71).

Third, as Huddleston (1967, pp. 23–24) has pointed out, Las Casas indicates in his *Historia* that the history of the native inhabitants of the New World might have been quite ancient. Regrettably, Las Casas did not elaborate his brief comments on human antiquity in the Americas, and, unfortunately, the interests and leads of clerics like Landa and Las Casas were not really followed up for many years, even centuries.

F̲or a century and a half to two centuries after the Conquest and the writings of the early chroniclers, there was much new European exploration and settlement throughout the New World and a rapid growth of European colonies in the Americas.

This period, however, produced only sporadic writings, such as those by Du Pratz (1758), that were of any relevance to the history of American archaeology and ethnography. New editions, collections, and critical evaluations of the early writers were made throughout the seventeenth to nineteenth centuries (including *The History of Mexico* by Clavijero, first published in 1780–81[14] and *The History of America* by Robertson in 1777), and unpublished documents were discovered and finally published. All in all, though, these works were no different in historical spirit from the ones we have already noted.

Beginning in the latter part of the eighteenth century, a new trend emerged, centering much more on North America than on Latin America. Archaeology still had not appeared as an avocation, let alone a profession, but there was much new exploration, resulting in new data on ruins, mounds, and artifacts. In turn, speculations about these remains began to have a real data base and became progressively more informed.

Much of the new data on the archaeological ruins was a by-product of observations made by explorers who were not specifically interested in collecting archaeological information. Rather, they attempted to record data about everything they saw in their travels. Their approach can best be labeled as *natural scientific* and is typified by the work of such writers as William Bartram (1791). Interpretations of the mounds varied from sober discussion to bizarre speculation.

THE EXPLORERS
AND THE
ARMCHAIR
SPECULATORS

A complementary trend, which definitely overlapped the natural scientific-exploratory one, can be termed *literary*. The ultimate aim of many of the explorers was to return home and write a work of literary merit that recounted all the writer's observations. One did not have to travel to write such a book. There were many "armchair explorers" who produced books on the history of the Americas. Many of these nonambulatory writers had friends, such as missionaries or army men, who would correspond with them and describe the nature of the "West"–which, until the beginning of the nineteenth century, still lay east of the Allegheny Mountains. These reports not only mentioned mounds but also provided much new data on the living Native Americans.

From the pens of some of the travelers and the armchair scholars came the myth of the Moundbuilders in North America. Robert Silverberg (1968, p. 57) has traced the beginnings of the myth as far back as 1785, although its real heyday was in the nineteenth century. In brief, the myth held that the multitude of mounds or ruins, which were constantly being discovered in Ohio and other frontier areas as the colonists pushed to the west, could not have been built by the relatively few Native Americans who were then residing in these areas. Instead, they must have been erected by a more civilized and populous race that had disappeared a long time ago.

The reasons for the rise of the myth, which was not laid to rest until the end of the nineteenth century, when Cyrus Thomas (1894) reported on the Bureau of Ethnology's Moundbuilder studies, were many. One of the most important was the need for the creation of a heroic past, which might resemble that enjoyed by Europe. As Silverberg (1968, p. 57) has said, "The dream of a lost prehistoric race in the American heartland was profoundly satisfying; and if the vanished ones had been giants, or white men, or Israelites, or Danes, or Toltecs, or great white Jewish Toltec Vikings, so much the better."

A second significant reason was the widely held North American belief that the Native Americans were savages who were incapable of building the mounds. The Spaniards saw the wonders of Tenochtitlan, capital of the Aztecs, the public works of the Incas, or the other great achievements of Middle and South America, and they were interested in using the Native Americans as labor. The English in North America, especially after the French and Indian War, saw the Native Americans as warlike degenerate savages who were occupying land the new settlers wanted for their own use.[15] It was inconceivable to much of the literate public of Eastern North America that the culture of the Native Americans or their ancestors was civilized enough to have built the mounds. Nevertheless, there were some to whom this notion was not beyond the pale. By the beginning of the nineteenth century, two basic positions had

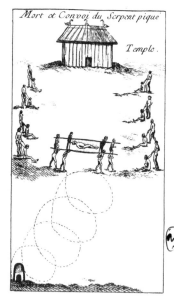

Funeral ceremony of the Natchez, at the end of the seventeenth century. There is a temple on a mound in the background. The dead man is being carried on a litter, and his several retainers are being strangled preparatory to being buried with him. (From Le Page Du Pratz, 1758)

An important early European view of the southeastern Native Americans is provided in the illustrations of Jacques Le Moyne (1591), who accompanied the French settlers to northeastern Florida in the 1560s. This drawing shows a burial ceremony with the grave or small burial mound outlined in arrows and topped by a conch-shell drinking vessel. The mourners surround the mound, and in the background is a palisaded village. Pictures such as this were either unknown to or ignored by early writers on the Moundbuilder controversy.

emerged regarding the origins of the mounds: either the Moundbuilders and the Native Americans (or their direct ancestors) were one and the same people, or the Moundbuilders, whose hypothesized origins were as varied as those first proposed for the peopling of the New World,[16] were an ancient race who had died off or moved away, to be replaced by the later Native Americans.

No links could be seen between the contemporary natives and the mounds by most observers of the time. Although observations made

by De Soto's exploratory party in the southeastern United States, reported in the works of Garcilaso de la Vega[17] and the "Gentleman of
Elvas,"[18] definitely showed Native Americans building and using
mounds in that area, these data were forgotten. Instead, various speculative origins for the mounds were proposed, and the debate over these
hypotheses became heated. In fact, so little was known about the
mounds at the beginning of the controversy that two such eminent men
as Benjamin Franklin and Noah Webster could seriously state in 1787
that the mounds might have been built by De Soto himself.[19]

Toward the end of the eighteenth century, new and better data on
the mounds began to pour in, and the problem of the identity of the
Moundbuilders became more clearly defined and emerged as a public
concern. Observations on the mounds were made by such travelers as
Kalm (1772), who also found artifacts in New Jersey that had a Quaternary or Recent geological date (see also Nelson, 1933, p. 90; Zeisberger,
1910; Carver, 1779; Barton, 1787, 1797, 1799; Bartram, 1791; Madison,
1803; Harris, 1805; Stoddard, 1812, and Brackenridge, 1813, on Louisiana;
Haywood, 1823, on Tennessee; and Rafinesque, 1824, who located hundreds of sites in Kentucky).

Benjamin Smith Barton traveled in Ohio and published a book in
1787, which said that the mounds he had observed in the course of his
travels had been built by Danes, who then migrated to Mexico and
became the Toltecs. In a later book in 1797 and in an article in 1799, he
did not pursue this earlier opinion but concentrated more attention on
the living Native Americans and suggested the ancestors of the Native
Americans might have built some of the mounds: "I do not suppose
that these more polished nations of America have passed away. Some
of them, it is probable, are extinguished. But of others, I suppose that
it is chiefly the strength and the glory that are no more. Their descendants are still scattered over extensive portions of this continent . . ."
(Barton, 1799, p. 188). Barton believed that the Native Americans came
from Asia—which, by the end of the eighteenth century, was the
generally accepted opinion. Moreover, he commented that the date of
this arrival might have been earlier than the theologically accepted date
of 4004 B.C. given by Archbishop Ussher for the Creation (Barton, 1797;
Wilmsen, 1965, p. 174). This opinion of Barton's was one of the first
attempts to give a real time-depth to the Pre-Columbian history of the
New World.

The natural historian William Bartram was the son of the famous
botanist John Bartram of Philadelphia. He traveled extensively throughout the southeastern United States with his father and then by himself
in the 1770s and published an important book on his travels in 1791. This
work included descriptions of many mounds, and Bartram reached what

Silverberg has called the "conservative" conclusion that, although the ancient mounds had not been built by the contemporary Native Americans, they had been built by other unspecified Native Americans. Bartram also was in correspondence with Barton and provided him with much data on the mounds of the Southeast, including descriptions of Creek Indian mound-building and use. Unfortunately, these observations of Bartram's did not reach the general public until 1909, after a series of mishaps that prevented earlier distribution of these data (Silverberg, 1968, pp. 33–42).

The Right Reverend James Madison and the Reverend Thaddeus Harris were on opposite sides of the argument concerning Native Americans as Moundbuilders, with Madison defending the proposition and Harris opposing it. John Haywood, in his book on the state of Tennessee, maintained that the Cherokee had built at least some of the mounds. The publication by the missionary John Heckewelder of a work on the Lenni Lenape several years earlier (1819) had made public their legends of a group of tall people with a high culture had lived near the Mississippi River when the Lenape tried to move through the area. Those supporting the Native Americans as moundbuilders said that this group were Cherokees who later moved south; the "lost race" or "mysterious Moundbuilder school" held that the legends provided conclusive evidence for their side (Silverberg, 1968, Chapter 2). H. H. Brackenridge published an article in 1813 on the mound question and a book in 1814 on Louisiana. In his article, he made the important distinction between burial and temple mounds and stated his view that the former were earlier. This definitely was a precocious statement and foreshadowed later chronological and conceptual developments by a number of decades (Belmont and Williams, 1965). However, Brackenridge held the popular view that such peoples as the Toltecs had built the mounds of North America before migrating south to Mexico. Amos Stoddard, who wrote another book on Louisiana, included a chapter on antiquities in which he supported the hypothesis that Welshmen were the great Moundbuilders.

Army men, such as General Parsons, General Putnam, and Captain Heart, who were stationed in Ohio, also contributed useful information in the late eighteenth century through letters and maps.[20] Putnam's map of the earthworks at Marietta, Ohio, has been called by Shetrone (1930, pp. 9–13) "the genesis of the science of archaeology in the Americas." We would not be so generous. The map was simply a part of the burgeoning data on the mounds that had begun to accumulate in the late eighteenth century.

The Reverend Cutler also explored the Marietta mounds, which were at the site of a colonial town, and attempted to date them by

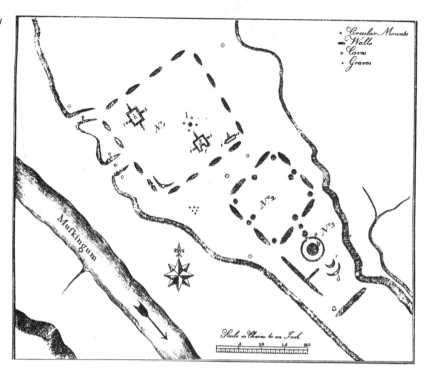

counting the number of rings on the trees that had grown on top of them
(Silverberg, 1968, p. 30). In this effort, we can see one of the earliest
attempts at absolute dating in the New World. Tree-ring dating, of
course, has become immeasurably refined in recent decades and now
serves as a useful dating tool in some areas, especially the southwestern
United States.

Some well-known public figures also became involved in the debate
on who had built the mounds. Governor De Witt Clinton (1820) wrote
about the mounds of western New York state and held that they were
built by Scandinavian Vikings. Albert Gallatin (1836), Secretary of the
Treasury and well-known linguist and ethnologist, linked the Moundbuilders and southward-migrating Mexicans, although he perspicaciously stated that agriculture may have diffused in the opposite direction, northward from Mexico to North America. Finally, General
William Henry Harrison (1839), who later became President of the
United States, described some of the antiquities of the Ohio Valley. He
supported the anti-Native American or "lost race" side of the Moundbuilder debate. Another President with archaeological interests, Thomas
Jefferson, did not become involved in the debate, although he made

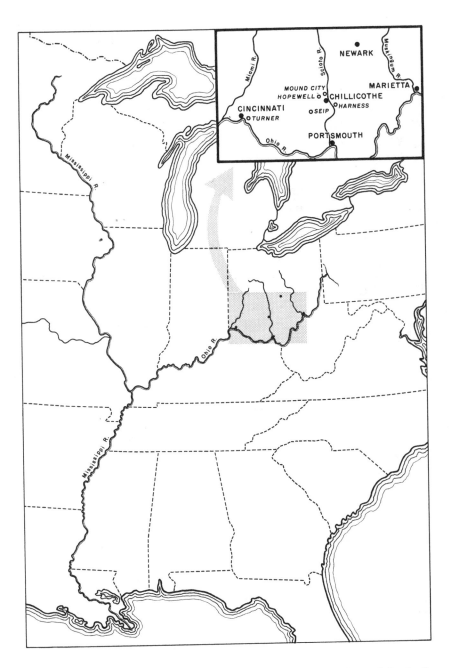

*Map of the Ohio and Mississippi
River Valleys.*

important contributions to the development of archaeology. We shall
return to him shortly.

As the Moundbuilder debate escalated in participants, hypotheses,
and partisanship, the general public was caught up in the arguments and

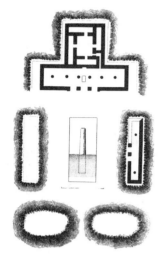

Plan of the ruins of Mitla, Oaxaca, Mexico. (From Humboldt, 1814)

added their numbers to the whole intellectual furore. The evidence for this interest was made clear in 1833, when Josiah Priest's *American Antiquities and Discoveries in the West* sold 22,000 copies in thirty months, a great number for that day, and soon became "established . . . among laymen as a kind of archaeological classic" (Silverberg, 1968, p. 83). Unfortunately, this book made no archaeological contribution, as it championed the most bizarre hypotheses and data. Nevertheless, it did reflect the general feeling of the day which was on the side of the "lost race" of Moundbuilders school of thought.

The "lost race" idea, however, received a blow in 1839, when the famous physical anthropologist S. G. Morton published his *Crania Americana*. Morton had taken measurements of eight skulls from mounds as well as skulls of recently deceased Native Americans. He concluded that there was just one race represented in his sample, although he further stated that the race consisted of two families, the Toltecan and the Barbarous, which he differentiated purely on cultural and not on physical grounds (Silverberg, 1969, pp. 106–109). Thus, although the people who supported a separation of early civilized Moundbuilders from later savage Native Americans could not claim any more that the Moundbuilders were a different race, the rest of their arguments remained intact for the moment.

Several others made solid contributions to the small but growing body of archaeological data that existed by the end of the Speculative Period. Winthrop Sargent collected artifacts, which we can now identify as Hopewellian, and a report on them was published in 1799, *Transactions of the American Philosophical Society* (Sargent, 1799). N. F. Hyer first described the now famous ruins of Aztalan in Wisconsin in 1837 (Hyer, 1837), and one year later R. C. Taylor wrote about the mounds of Wisconsin, with special attention to the fascinating effigy forms (Taylor, 1838). Finally, in 1839 in Missouri, the fossil-hunter Albert Koch uncovered the skeleton of a mastodon, an extinct elephant, in association with some stone artifacts. Koch, who was somewhat of an entrepreneur and showman, displayed the mastodon in a traveling show before selling it. The skeleton then went to the British Museum, while the artifacts ended up in Germany (Montagu, 1942), the association between the artifacts and skeleton not being considered important enough to keep the finds together. The time was not yet ripe for the acceptance of great age for the stone artifacts, and Koch's contemporaries were not willing to accept the significance of the finds or their association. Koch was ridiculed and his discovery forgotten for many years.

All the attention we have just paid to developments in the United States should not be taken to indicate that there were no archaeological activities in Latin America in the seventeenth to early nineteenth centuries, although most of the activity was in North America. For example, the Mexican-born creole scholar, Don Carlos Siguenza y Gonqora, undertook actual archaeological excavations at Teotihuacan as well as collecting both specimens and early historic manuscripts (Bernal, 1980, pp. 49–54). Other important individuals included Alexander von Humboldt, who travelled throughout the Americas. In his writings, which can be considered as perhaps the epitome of the natural-science approach discussed earlier, he described a number of ruins, especially in Peru and Mexico (Humboldt, 1811). He also made other contributions

Drawing of an Oaxacan (Monte Alban style) funerary urn. Although correct in some features, it is inaccurate in others. (From Kingsborough, 1831–48)

Drawing of a Maya priest figure and accompanying hieroglyphic text. The rendering has many inaccuracies and is greatly inferior to the later work of Catherwood. (From Del Rio and Cabrera, 1822)

to American studies, most notably in cartography. As H. E. D. Pollock has said: "[Humboldt] stands . . . as a landmark in his diligent accumulation of data, in his unbiased presentation of material, and in his attitude toward the remains of antiquity as fragments of history" (Pollock, 1940, p. 183).

In relation to the prehistoric architecture of Middle America, Walckenaër, de Larenaudière, and Jomard (1836) called for the cessation of speculation and the beginning of adequate recording and mapping of archaeological remains (Pollock, 1940, p. 184). Their plea, which was definitely nonspeculative in tone, was at least partially answered within a few years by Stephens and Catherwood. Other travellers, such as Waldeck (1838), Dupaix (1834), and Galindo (Ian Graham, 1963) made minor contributions. In South America, Lund began working in the Lagoa Santa Caves of Brazil in the mid-1830s, but his work was not completed and published until the following period Lund (1842, as discussed in Nelson, 1933, p. 90).

Earlier, we commented on the many collections of Conquest and pre-Conquest documents that were made in the Speculative Period. Perhaps the most important of these collections, commentaries, and histories was Lord Kingsborough's lavish, nine-volume *Antiquities of Mexico,* published between 1831 and 1848. Kingsborough gathered together a number of documents and added his own comments on various antiquities in an effort to prove that the native inhabitants of Middle America were the descendants of the Ten Lost Tribes of Israel.[21] Kingsborough's volumes revealed a great enthusiasm for the antiquities of Mexico, an enthusiasm that reflected the growing nineteenth-century interest in the past of the New World and that helped bring about the birth of archaeology in the Americas. Although *Antiquities of Mexico* is, in most respects, a work of the Speculative Period, its author devoted his whole life to the study of antiquities. This kind of full-time activity, albeit by someone who did not need to practice archaeology for a living, marked the beginning of a trend that was more typical of the following periods.

Thus, by 1840, public and scholarly interest in the antiquities of the New World was very high; yet, most of the published accounts of mounds and other archaeological phenomena remained speculative and were often by-products of other endeavors. Debate on the Moundbuilder question was heated but generally uninformed. There were no full-time archaeologists, nor were there many people among those who followed archaeology as an avocation who were willing to carry out archaeological fieldwork to verify or diagnose their theories and speculations. There were, however, a few important exceptions to this, and these exceptional scholars clearly stand out today as the forerunners of the established discipline of archaeology that was to come into being after 1840.

U p to this point, we have been concerned with the ephemeral beginnings of American archaeology. Various slender threads of archaeological reportage have been traced. Some of these threads are obviously tied to later trends; others are only peripherally related. On the whole, though, in a period that lacked all the hallmarks of an established archaeological discipline, including clear goals, professional archaeologists, archaeological courses in colleges, archaeological texts describing accepted methods, concepts, and theories, and detailed cultural historical reconstructions, there was little sign of the kind of work and publication that marked the following Descriptive-Historical Period. Speculation on a narrow data base was the rule. Three exceptions stand above their contemporaries; they are, indeed, the true forerunners of American archaeology. The two most important of these forerunners largely eschewed speculation. One of them further realized that archaeology must be attacked by posing problems, undertaking excavations, presenting data, and answering problems in a rigorous manner. In his hands antiquarian interests began to become archaeological ones.

In 1784, Thomas Jefferson, later to become the third President of the United States, decided to discover the nature of the barrows or burial mounds found on his property in Virginia. "That they were repositories of the dead, has been obvious to all; but on what particular occasion constructed, was a matter of doubt" (Jefferson, 1944, p. 222). To solve this problem, Jefferson took the extraordinary step of carrying out a relatively well-controlled excavation.[22] Jefferson carefully trenched the mound and recognized strata that had no correspondence with each other. He discovered a large quantity of skeletal material and found that the bones had been placed in the mound and then covered and that this process had been repeated many times. The mound had gradually reached its final height of twelve feet through the accumulation of skeletons (Jefferson, 1944, pp. 222–224). As Lehmann-Hartleben (1943, p. 263) states, Jefferson's excavation "anticipates the fundamental approach and the methods of modern archaeology by about a full century," and actually more. Sir Mortimer Wheeler, perhaps the most eminent authority on the nature of archaeological excavation, has labeled Jefferson's work "the first scientific excavation in the history of archaeology." He further notes that "it was unique not only in its age but for long afterwards" (Wheeler, 1956, p. 6).

THE FORERUNNERS
OF AN
ESTABLISHED
DISCIPLINE OF
ARCHAEOLOGY

Thomas Jefferson, 1743–1826. (From the American Philosophical Society)

The real significance of Jefferson's digging was threefold. First, the very fact that he excavated at all was important, since few individuals throughout the Speculative Period undertook such a step. Second, Jefferson's excavations were sufficiently careful to enable him to observe the nature of the strata in his trench. Third, and probably most important, "the excavation [was] . . . made, not to find objects, but to resolve an archaeological problem" (Lehmann-Hartleben, 1943, p. 163).

As regards the general Moundbuilder problem, Jefferson would not commit himself. He took the cautious, but for his time, laudable, position that more data were needed to answer the question. Jefferson also became President of the American Philosophical Society, which was located in Philadelphia, the intellectual capital of the United States during much of the Speculative Period. The members of the Society took an active interest in the Moundbuilder debate, published many archaeologically relevant papers, and collected archaeological objects. In 1799, as President of the Society, Jefferson sent a circular letter to a number of correspondents to obtain data on archaeological remains. The circular began by stating (Sargent: American Philosophical Society, 1799, p. xxxvii): "The American Philosophical Society have always considered the antiquity, changes, and present state of their own country as primary objects of their research." Among the other things, the circular called on its recipients "to obtain accurate plans, drawings and descriptions of whatever is interesting, (where the originals cannot be had) and especially of ancient Fortifications, Tumuli, and other Indian works of art: ascertaining the materials composing them, their contents, the purposes for which they were probably designed, etc."

The discussion of the kinds of information solicited in the circular also included the following:

> With respect to the [above], the committee are desirous that cuts in various directions may be made into many of the Tumuli, to ascertain their contents; while the diameter of the largest tree growing thereon, the number of its annulars and the species of the tree, may tend to give some idea of their antiquity. If the works should be found to be of Masonry; the length, breadth, and height of the walls ought to be carefully measured, the form and nature of the stone described, and the specimens of both the cement and stones sent to the committee.

In many respects, the directions and general tenor of this paragraph can be seen as the theme of one of the major trends of the succeeding Classificatory-Descriptive Period. Thus, we can see that at least a good part of the orientation of the discipline of archaeology was present as far back as the end of the eighteenth century, but such works as the circular called for were not carried out until the post-1840 era.

Although Jefferson has often been referred to as the "father of American archaeology," he had no immediate intellectual offspring. Unfortunately, Jefferson's influence as an archaeologist apparently was not important for either his contemporaries or even the next generation.[23] As we hope will become clear, we do not believe that one can point to a single individual as the progenitor of American archaeology but must view the rise of the discipline in terms of the culmination of both specific antiquarian and general intellectual trends in the New and the Old Worlds.

The American Philosophical Society was not alone in its effort to encourage the collection and publication of archaeological data. In 1812, the publisher Isaiah Thomas founded the American Antiquarian Society in Massachusetts. Its purpose was (Shipton, 1945, p. 164–165): "the collection and presentation of the antiquities of our country, and of curious and valuable productions in art and nature [which] have a tendency to enlarge the sphere of human knowledge, aid in the progress of science, to perpetuate the history of moral and political events, and to improve and instruct posterity." The Society was the first of this kind in the Americas, and its early members included such famous men as Thomas Hart Benton, Lewis Cass, Henry Clay, DeWitt Clinton, C. C. Pinckney, and Daniel Webster (Shipton, 1945, p. 165). It was the American counterpart of European antiquarian societies (Wissler, 1942, p. 195; Silverberg, 1968, p. 59), and its creation was a reflection of a growing public interest in the history of North America and an increase in popular scientific curiosity (Shipton, 1967, p. 35). The founding of the Society was an important event in the history of American archaeology, since it gave the growing but diffuse interest in archaeological concerns a focal point. The Society in and of itself did not change the contemporary antiquarian interests into true archaeological ones, but it did publish one of the most significant studies of the Speculative Period and was associated with several important works during the early Classificatory-Descriptive Period.

In the first volume of the American Antiquarian Society's *Transaction*, dated 1820, there appeared a work by Caleb Atwater entitled "Description of the Antiquities Discovered in the State of Ohio and other Western States." Atwater lived in Circleville, Ohio and was the postmaster there (Hallowell, 1960, p. 79). He explored many of the mounds of his home town and the surrounding region of Ohio and provided the best descriptions and plans of these mounds that had yet been made. Mitra, in his *A History of American Anthropology* (1933, p. 99), has said that "the first true archaeologist was . . . Caleb Atwater." Atwater was ahead of his time in certain respects but very much a part of it in others. From the point of view of his influence upon his contemporaries and those who were immediately to follow him, he was the most important figure of the Speculative Period.

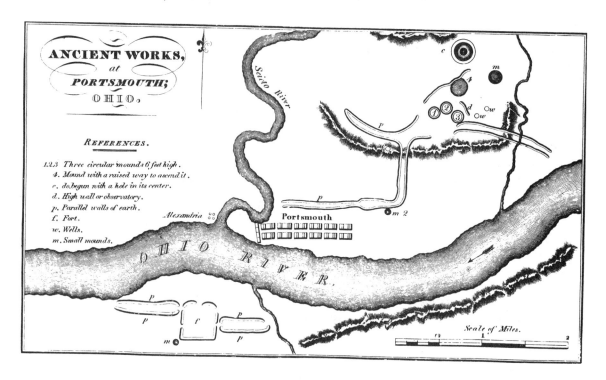

Map of ancient earthworks at Portsmouth, Ohio. (From Atwater, 1820)

Atwater's book really has two parts, the descriptive and the speculative. Unfortunately, the latter did not really follow from the former. The purely speculative section, though, is clearly separated from the descriptive one. In his descriptions, Atwater used a relatively simple three-part classification for the observed remains: (a) modern European; (b) modern Native American; (c) Moundbuilder. In his speculative section, Atwater proposed that the mounds had been built by Hindus who migrated from India and who later moved to Mexico. As regards the latter point, Atwater was apparently influenced by Humboldt's writings. He also speculated that the Native Americans, with their simpler culture, had arrived in the Americas before the more advanced Moundbuilders and afterward moved into areas vacated by the latter (Atwater, 1820). Compared to other writers of his day, Atwater was relatively restrained in his speculative hypotheses (Silverberg, 1968, p. 74).

As we now know, Atwater's ideas were incorrect; but there was one other individual in this period who deserves mention here and who was not wrong. Dr. James H. McCulloh, Jr. an armchair antiquarian,[24] wrote two books: *Researches in America,* in 1817 (second edition), and *Researches Philosophical and Antiquarian Concerning the Aboriginal History of America,* in 1829. His principal contribution was his denial that there was an early separate Moundbuilder culture. In the second Appendix of his 1829 work, actually the most important section of this book, he carefully sifted all the previous written evidence and concluded that the Moundbuilders and the Indians were one and the same race and that the Native Americans were capable of building the mounds. McCulloh (1829) also reviewed data on the high civilizations of Latin America and the cultures of the natives of North America.

Samuel F. Haven, who agreed with McCulloh's views, said of his work in 1856: "No more perfect monument of industry and patient research connected with this subject has been published."[25] Cyrus Thomas concurred, calling McCulloh's conclusions "remarkable" for the time.[26] However, McCulloh's views were unpopular and some people found the book difficult to read. Clark Wissler (1942, p. 201) has stated: "Had McCulloh possessed a great mind like Gallatin he would have produced the first great classic critique upon the culture origins of the aboriginal civilizations of Mexico and the Andean region instead of producing a poorly organized and ineffectual book. Nevertheless he deserves a place in the history of anthropological thought during the period 1800–1860." We would tend to agree with Haven and Thomas and feel that Wissler's criticism demands more than could have been expected of any American antiquarian of McCulloh's time.

As of 1840, American archaeology as a scholarly discipline simply did not exist. There were virtually no full-time practitioners of archaeology and no professionals. There was no field methodology, and the conceptual inventory was minimal. The data base was very slim, and chronological knowledge, either absolute or relative, was rudimentary at best. It was generally accepted that the New World was peopled from Asia via the Bering Strait, but beyond that there was little agreement or knowledge. There were some survey data on the mounds of the Ohio Valley and the southeastern United States. Some of the major ruins in Mexico, Guatemala, and Peru were recognized and some details of them known. Most of the area of North America was archaeological *terra incognita*, as were vast territories of South and Central America.

Nevertheless, there were bright spots, and certain signposts for future developments were already in existence. The outline for what had to be done in terms of the initial steps of gathering data in North America had been presented by the American Philosophical Society in its 1799 circular, and a model of how to investigate archaeological problems was present in the excavations of Thomas Jefferson. The framework of an archaeological survey could also be seen in Atwater's Ohio mound studies.

AN APPRAISAL
AND SIGNS FOR
THE FUTURE

Moreover, by the fall of 1839, John L. Stephens and Frederick Catherwood had already begun their travels in Middle America. Grave Creek Mound in Ohio had been dug, and Henry R. Schoolcraft was soon to study it and publish his results. In 1826, James Smithson, an Englishman, left a half million dollar bequest to the young republic of the United States to found an institution "for the increase and diffusion of knowledge among men" (Washburn, 1967, p. 106). As a result, the Smithsonian Institution, which was to have such a profound influence on the history of American archaeology, was founded in 1846.

By 1840 in the Old World, Lyell had already produced his *Principles of Geology,* and Darwin had made his momentous voyage on the *Beagle.* In addition, the Danes had begun to make important archaeological advances. The lack of European models to which scholars in the New World could turn was soon to be rectified.

Finally, travel was becoming easier in the Americas, and the United States began to spread westward. With this burgeoning expansion, a new spirit could be seen. As William H. Goetzmann (1966, p. 232) has said:

> The professional explorer and scientist began to take to the field in the 1840s, and with his appearance came a new and significant refinement, not only in the scientific approach to the West, but in all aspects of the search for knowledge. The basis of geographic discovery shifted from the simple notation of landmarks and natural wonders, of settlement sites and overland trails, to the scientific assessment of basic resources, and serious study of primitive cultures different from our own. . . .

All these events and nascent trends led, in the second half of the nineteenth century, to the birth of the discipline of American archaeology. But the incipient discipline in 1840 still had a long, long way to go to become a science.

NOTES

1. For supplementary reading, see Belmont and Williams (1965); Hallowell (1960); Haven (1856); Silverberg (1968); Wauchope (1962); Willey (1968); Wilmsen (1965); Winsor (1889); Huddleston (1967); and S. Williams (1964).
2. *Speculate:* to form conjectures regarding anything without experiment. *Funk and Wagnall's New College Standard Dictionary* (1956).

3. A misnomer deriving from Columbus' belief that he had landed in India.
4. Huddleston (1967) argues that it did not become popular until the latter part of the sixteenth century and that many writers to whom this theory is attributed, such as Las Casas, did not believe in it.
5. The Moundbuilder versus the Native American

debate only began in earnest in the nineteenth century.

6. For further discussion of the many wild speculations as to the origins of the Native Americans see Robert Wauchope (1962) and Williams (1991).

7. Mesoamerica includes central and southern Mexico and northern Central America (see Willey, 1966, p. 85, for a more exact definition).

8. The Peruvian coast and highlands and the adjacent highlands of Bolivia (Willey, 1971).

9. The Mixtec codices would be just one example (see Spores, 1967).

10. Sahagún (1950–63), the Anderson-Dibble edition (in English and Aztec).

11. Fray Diego Duran (1964), the Hayden-Horcasitas edition (in English).

12. Garcilaso de la Vega (1966), the Livermore edition (in English).

13. Landa (1941), the Tozzer edition (in English).

14. Clavijero (1817), the Cullen edition (in English).

15. There were also Spaniards who thought of the Native American as savages; nevertheless, there appears to have been general attitudinal differences between the Spanish and the English as well as the French (Spencer and others, 1965, pp. 496–7).

16. Obviously, the question was basically the same, since it was not supposed that there were any predecessors to the Moundbuilders in North America.

17. Garcilaso de la Vega (1951), the Varner edition (in English).

18. Elvas, Gentleman of (1907), in English.

19. Webster, the famous lexicographer, later retracted this opinion (Shetrone 1930, p. 14).

20. Parsons (1793) and (in a letter written in 1786) Heart (1792).

21. Wauchope (1962, pp. 50–53); see also Ian Graham (1977) for background and colleagues of Kingsborough and Bernal (1977) for detail on this era of Mesoamericanists.

22. As early as the sixteenth century, explorations with ancient ruins as their object were undertaken; but Garcia de Palacio's trip (1840) to Copan and Del Rio's (1822) to Palenque had little import for, or impact on, the growth of American archaeology.

23. As Wheeler (1956, p. 43) has said referring to Jefferson's excavations: "Unfortunately, this seed of a new scientific skill fell upon infertile soil."

24. Although McCulloh saw military service in Ohio (Silverberg 1968, p. 58), he was basically armchair-bound (McCulloh, 1829).

25. Haven (1856, p. 48), quoted in Mitra (1933, p. 104).

26. Thomas (1894, p. 600), quoted in Silverberg (1968, p. 58) and Hallowell (1960, p. 81). We will return to this question of Moundbuilder vs. Native American again in Chapter Three. It is not altogether a simple issue; from early on, as in the case of McCulloh, there were scholars who were convinced of a long continuity of the Native American past which would embrace the builders of the Tumuli of the eastern United States as well as their more recent descendants. At this early juncture, such persons were usually in the minority and in opposition to the more popular opinion which saw the Moundbuilders as a "lost race" (see Dunnell, 1991 for another view).

CHAPTER THREE

The Classificatory-Descriptive Period (1840–1914)

The field investigator [of the Western United States] was spurred on to one of the most rapid and complete inventories ever made on any portion of the globe, and the best scientific minds were so busy recording the mass of data that they had little time to formulate hypotheses about the meaning and utility of it all.

WILLIAM H. GOETZMANN

A DEFINITION OF
THE PERIOD

The Classificatory-Descriptive Period is distinguished from the preceding Speculative Period by a distinct change in attitude and outlook on the part of many of the major archaeological workers and writers.[1] However, the intellectual trend that characterized the Speculative Period did not suddenly come to an end in 1840—the Speculative mode of thought remained a very important element of the Classificatory-Descriptive Period. But the principal focus of the new period was on the description of archaeological materials, especially architecture and monuments, and rudimentary classification of these materials. Throughout the period, archaeologists struggled to make archaeology into a systematic scientific discipline. They did not succeed, but they laid the foundations for many of the achievements of the twentieth century.

Intellectual developments and the emergence of new ideas in Europe had significant effects on the rise of American archaeology in the middle and late nineteenth century. Among the developments were the discovery of great human antiquity in the Old World, the publication of Darwin's *Origin of Species,* and the rise of the science of geology. Simultaneously, the beginning of professional archaeology in Europe, together with the upsurge of science and scientific thought at the expense of theological dogma, were in turn reflected on the American continents.

Throughout the Classificatory-Descriptive Period, there was a steady increase in the discovery and description of antiquities as the United States expanded westward and as Euro-Americans penetrated into other parts of the North and South American continents.[2] In the United States, this work was sponsored by the government, universities, museums, and scientific societies. Archaeology became both an established vocation and a recognized avocation. Toward the end of the period, it began to be taught in universities, so that a generation of professionally trained archaeologists became active in the early years of the twentieth century. The alliance of American archaeology and general anthropology began in this period, both academically and in the field. The importance of this union for the conceptual development of American archaeology, and particularly that of the United States, was longlasting, as we shall see later.

In North America, the earlier research interests in the mounds and earthworks of the Eastern United States was maintained, and there was continuing interest in the controversial question as to who had built the mounds. Were they a "lost race" of Moundbuilders or simply the ancestors of the Native Americans? Another focus of attention was the problem of the earliest inhabitants of the New World. Discoveries of Pleistocene inhabitants of the Old World spurred American archaeologists to hunt for comparably early remains on their side of the Atlantic. Unfortunately, the period was characterized by a lack of a rigorous chronological perspective and the development of methods that would lead to such a perspective. On the other hand, typological, classificatory, and geographical distribution studies went forward. In Middle America, the trends were somewhat similar, although there were some significant differences. These were occasioned by the extraordinary richness of the Pre-Columbian remains, the presence of native writing systems, and the strong influence of European humanistic scholarship. All of these gave the archaeology of this area a different flavor from that of North America. In South America, there was relatively less archaeological exploration, but what there was remained Classificatory-Descriptive. A singular exception was the development of an area chronology in Peru by the German scholar Max Uhle.

The major concern of archaeologists in Eastern North America during the period was the mounds of the Ohio and Mississippi Valleys and surrounding areas. The Moundbuilder controversy persisted throughout the nineteenth century, particularly in popular publications, and was not really laid to rest until the publication of Cyrus Thomas' monumental report on the mound explorations of the Bureau of (American) Ethnology in 1894.[3]

The first major contribution of the period was *Ancient Monuments of the Mississippi Valley* by E. G. Squier and E. H. Davis, which appeared in

ARCHAEOLOGICAL RESEARCH IN NORTH AMERICA

Ephraim George Squier, 1821–1888.
(From the National Anthropological
Archives, Smithsonian Institution)

1848. This work was the best descriptive study published until then, and its intellectual orientation typified the new trends that emerged during the Classificatory-Descriptive Period (Haven, 1856, p. 122). Squier, an Ohio newspaperman who later became a diplomat and traveled widely in Latin America (Tax, 1975), and Davis, a physician from Chillicothe, Ohio, accurately surveyed a vast number of mounds, excavated in some, and brought together in their book the survey data of other workers. There also was a salvage aspect to their work, in that many of the mounds were being destroyed as the pioneers pushed westward.

The overall tone of *Ancient Monuments of the Mississippi Valley* was descriptive, not speculative. As Squier (1848, p. 134) said:

> At the outset, all preconceived notions were abandoned, and the work of research commenced, as if no speculations had been indulged in, nor any thing before been known, respecting the singular remains of antiquity scattered so profusely around us. It was concluded that, either the field should be entirely abandoned to the poet and the romancer, or, if these monuments were capable of reflecting any certain light upon the grand archaeological questions connected with the primitive history of the American continent, the origin, migration, and early state of the American race, that then they should be carefully and minutely, and above all, systematically investigated.

It is evident that the descriptive tone of the volume was not only due to the authors' inclinations but to those of the renowned scientist and Secretary of the Smithsonian Institution, Joseph Henry, who edited the Squier and Davis manuscript before publication. As Wilcomb Washburn (1967, p. 153), working with Henry's correspondence, has noted: "Henry insisted upon throwing out some of the engravings Squier had prepared which were not 'of an original character,' and he drew a tight line on the manuscript itself so that 'your labours should be given to the world as free as possible from everything of a speculative nature and that your positive addition to the sum of human knowledge should stand in bold relief unmingled with the labours of others.'"

The volume was the first publication of the newly founded Smithsonian Institution and appeared in its Contributions to Knowledge series. Moreover, Squier and Davis had the support of the American Ethnological Society, which corresponded with them in the field and helped arrange the publication of the monograph. The active involvement of a government body as well as a professional anthropological society in archaeological fieldwork and, especially, publication also indicated a marked change in the trends of archaeological development in the New World.[4]

Edwin Hamilton Davis, 1811–1888.
(From the National Anthropological
Archives, Smithsonian Institution)

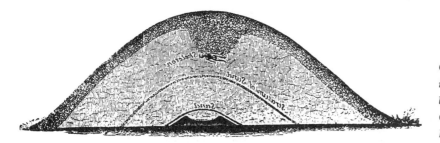

Cross-section drawing of the internal construction, including a burial, of Mound 2 in the Mound City, Ohio group. (From Squier and Davis, 1848)

It should be noted that Squier and Davis used a rudimentary functional classification for the mounds and asked some questions about the probable uses or purposes of such archaeological structures. These questions were formulated as quite explicit hypotheses, and they went further in suggesting lines of investigation that might be pursued to verify or disprove their suppositions. In so doing, they anticipated, in a degree, the modern method of formulating hypotheses and testing expectations.

The Grave Creek Mound in West Virginia. (From Squier and Davis, 1848)

An artist's conception in the mid-nineteenth century of a group of sepulchral mounds. (From Squier and Davis, 1848)

Even with all the praiseworthy aspects of *Ancient Monuments of the Mississippi Valley*, the speculative mode of thought still retained a significant role in that work. Squier and Davis adhered to the "great race of Moundbuilders" theory and felt that the Native Americans or their ancestors were not capable of erecting the mounds. The subsequent migration of the Moundbuilders to Mexico was considered a likely possibility. They rejected the hypothesis of Whittlesey that there were two peoples in Ohio, one in the North and one in the South.[5] Whittlesey was attempting to differentiate between two mound-building cultures in Ohio — actually a chronological rather than a geographical distinction, which was made many decades later; but Squier and Davis felt that the geographical differences were no greater than are to be expected between the structures of a sparse frontier population.

Before taking up a diplomatic post in Nicaragua, Squier also explored the mounds of western New York, and in 1849 the Smithsonian Institution published this work, too (Squier, 1849). Squier made the New York survey, because he wished to learn more about the Moundbuilders and felt that the origins of the Ohio Moundbuilders might be in western New York. He hypothesized that the remains in both areas would be quite similar. Squier found, to his surprise, that there was good evidence that the Iroquois Indians had built many of the mounds in New York.

This discovery apparently did not change his opinions about the identity of the Ohio Moundbuilders, but he was forced to distinguish between the Ohio and western New York areas and abandon his hypothesis.

Another contemporary study of the mounds was made by I. A. Lapham in Wisconsin. Lapham surveyed and explored the many effigy mounds of that state with the support of the American Antiquarian Society; the Smithsonian published his findings in 1855.

We have noted that, although popular and some scientific opinion of the mid-nineteenth century favored the "separate Moundbuilder race" theory, there were some opposing views. These were that the ancestors of the modern Native Americans had built the mounds and that the Native Americans and the Moundbuilders were one and the same group. Foremost among the scholars holding this latter view were Samuel F. Haven and Henry Rowe Schoolcraft.

Two site maps of mounds and earthworks. Left: the Dunlaps Works, Ross County, Ohio. Right: the ancient works in Athens County, Ohio. These maps far surpassed in care and accuracy any maps that had preceded them. (From Squier and Davis, 1848)

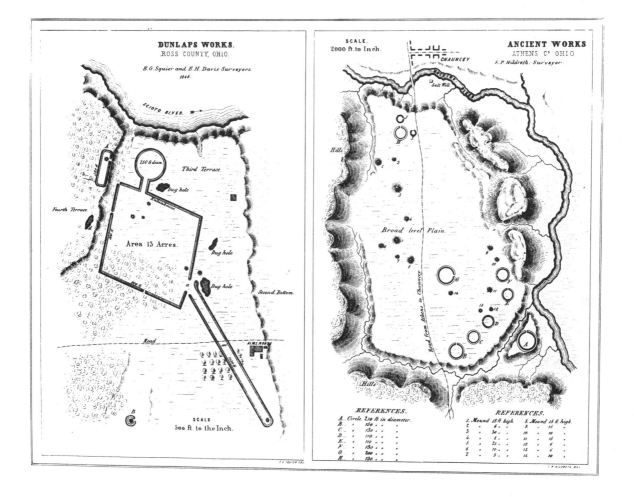

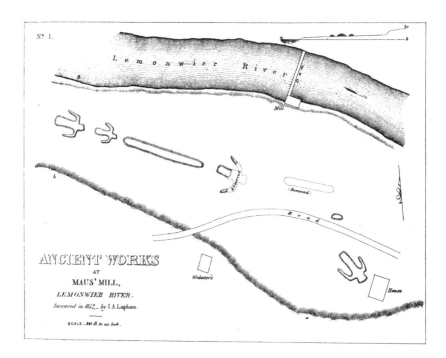

Lapham's map of the ancient works at Maus' Mill, Wisconsin. (From Lapham, 1855)

Samuel F. Haven, 1806–1881. (From Winsor, 1889)

In his important review of the state of North American archaeology in 1856, Haven, the Librarian of the American Antiquarian Society, carefully sifted the available archaeological data and came to the conclusion that the "ancient lost Moundbuilder race" hypothesis was untenable (Haven, 1856). His study, which was commissioned and published by the Smithsonian Institution (Fewkes, 1897, p. 751), was a model of reasoned description and discussion in comparison with the speculative works that had dominated the literature until then. Haven's archaeological outlook typified the new, increasingly professionalized descriptive trend, which was to dominate the period by its close.

Henry R. Schoolcraft also opposed the prevailing Moundbuilder hypotheses in his writings, although he had supported them earlier in his career. After examining the remains from the Grave Creek Mound in West Virginia, Schoolcraft, who was generally sympathetic toward the Native Americans, decided that there were cultural continuities from the Moundbuilders to the contemporary native inhabitants of the Eastern United States (Schoolcraft, 1854, pp. 135–136). He further felt that the mounds need not have been built by peoples with an advanced civilization but could have been constructed by peoples at a barbarian level of culture. Unfortunately, Schoolcraft's views were buried deep in his unindexed (at that time)[6] and rambling six-volume *Historical and Statistical Information Respecting the History, Condition, and Prospects of the Indian Tribes of the United States*, which appeared 1851–57, and probably few people read it at the time (or since, for that matter).

Another important work that was published at this time was Daniel Wilson's two-volume *Prehistoric Man: Researches into the Origin of Civilization in the Old and New World* (1862, plus two later editions). Although Wilson did not agree with Haven's and Schoolcraft's forward-looking views that the ancestors of the Native Americans had built the mounds, he did not indulge in wild speculation about the origins of the Moundbuilders, favoring Mexico as the Moundbuilder homeland (see Silverberg 1968, p. 179). Wilson's general view of archaeology was relatively advanced for the time. As he noted at the beginning of his book (1862, p. vii): "To confine our studies to mere antiquities is like reading by candle-light at noonday; but to reject the aid of archaeology in the progress of science, and especially ethnological science, is to extinguish the lamp of the student when most dependent on its borrowed rays."

The Moundbuilder debate raged through the decades from the 1850s into the late 1890s and was accompanied by continued amateur "pottings" of mounds. Such excavations and studies were sponsored by individuals or local amateur societies.[7] Many popular books of highly varying quality, by authors from both sides of the Atlantic, such as Pidgeon (1858), Lubbock (1865), Baldwin (1872), Foster (1873), Larkin (1880), Bancroft (1882), and Nadaillac (1884), kept the fires lit and helped to add many an additional wrinkle to the hypotheses as to where the Moundbuilders came from, when they thrived, and where they went. The general public remained caught up in the excitement of the debate. But, for many, the interest was more than pure curiosity. The Native Americans of North America were in the process of being exterminated as the United States spread westward, and the more primitive they were thought to be, the easier it apparently was to justify their destruction or displacement. As Silverberg (1968, pp. 159–160) has pointed out: "The controversy over the origin of the mounds was not merely an abstract scholarly debate, but had its roots in the great nineteenth-century campaign of extermination waged against the American Indian."

In opposition to this popular trend, there was another one that, by the end of the period, had built up a strong enough foundation to sweep the popular-amateur approach into the background. This new tide, whose first waves we noted earlier, was the increasing professionalization of archaeology. It was certainly related to the huge growth of science in the United States and the rapid rise and expansion of universities

Cyrus Thomas, 1825–1910. (From the National Anthropological Archives, Smithsonian Institution)

(Freeman, 1965). The heyday of local scientific societies quickly drew to a close at the beginning of the twentieth century, as amateur enthusiasts were replaced by local college and university scholars and researchers. This trend was as true for archaeology as it was for other disciplines (McKusick, 1970, pp. 2–3, 1991).

In addition, a number of archaeological journals and professional societies were born during this period. Such journals as the *American Antiquarian* (founded in 1878 by the Reverend Stephen D. Peet) (Haynes, 1900, p. 32; Peet, 1892–1905) and the *American Anthropologist* (founded in 1888) were particularly important. The American Association for the Advancement of Science (Anthropology Section), the Anthropological Society of Washington (later the American Anthropological Association), and the Archaeological Institute of America (now mainly interested in Old World archaeology) were among the more important societies. The last, in fact, asked Lewis Henry Morgan, one of the most eminent American anthropologists of his day, to prepare a plan in 1879 for archaeological exploration and research in the American field (Hallowell, 1960, p. 54).

Two institutions in particular had immeasurable impact on the dawning age of professional archaeology in the nineteenth century. They were the Smithsonian Institution (founded in 1846) and the Peabody Museum of Harvard University (founded in 1866). The former, especially, laid the foundation for and dominated the Classificatory-Descriptive Period of American archaeology. In the persons of such men as Powell, Thomas, and Holmes, the Smithsonian Institution and two of its arms, the Bureau of Ethnology (founded in 1879 with Powell as its head

A mound in Fort Pickering, South Memphis, Tennessee. (From an original pencil sketch in the manuscript of Cyrus Thomas' mound surveys: the National Anthropological Archives, Smithsonian Institution)

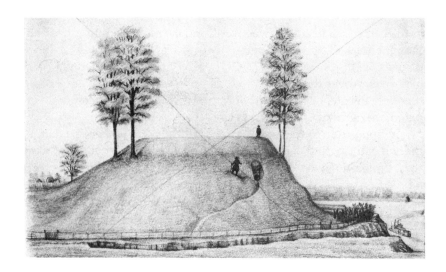

*Major John Wesley Powell
(1834–1902) consulting with a
Native American on the Kaibab
Plateau, near the Grand Canyon of
the Colorado River in northern
Arizona. This picture was taken by
Hilliers on the Powell Expedition of
1871–5. (From the National
Anthropological Archives,
Smithsonian Institution)*

and renamed the Bureau of American Ethnology in 1894) and the National Museum (also founded in 1879), provided some of the most influential scholars of the period. As Hallowell (1960, p. 84) has forcefully stated in relation to the former, "it was under the auspices of the Bureau of American Ethnology, in short, that, through a series of widely gauged programs, the empirical foundations of archaeology in the United States were established on a broad geographical scale."[8]

Cyrus Thomas of the Bureau of Ethnology was responsible for completing the demolition of the "lost Moundbuilder race" hypothesis in 1894. John Wesley Powell (the great explorer, who descended the Grand Canyon rapids of the Colorado River in a boat), the Director of both the Bureau of Ethnology and the United States Geological Survey (Darrah, 1951; Judd, 1967), picked Thomas, an entomologist from Illinois, to head a Division of Mound Exploration in 1882. Powell wanted to concentrate on ethnological and linguistic pursuits, but the U.S. Congress insisted that the Bureau of Ethnology spend $5,000 a year on mound studies (Judd, 1967, pp. 18–19).

Thomas was at first a believer in the "separate Moundbuilder race" hypothesis, but, after he began working in the field, he changed his mind and soon became a champion of the opposing view. This latter view was also strongly held by Powell, as can be seen by reading any of his introductions to the *Annual Reports* of the Bureau of Ethnology in the later 1880s and early 1890s. Other workers in the Bureau, such as Henshaw (1883), also attacked the "lost race" hypothesis in no uncertain terms. Thus, Powell's Bureau of Ethnology became the leading advocate of the idea that the ancestors of the Native Americans built the mounds, a view that is now accepted as fact and that carried the day well before the end of the Classificatory-Descriptive Period. Unfortunately, this triumph may have had some ironic results in helping to retard certain developments in the archaeology of the eastern United States and in North American archaeology in general, as we shall see later; at the same time, it did nothing to change the prevailing popular attitudes against the Native American.

Upon receiving his appointment from Powell, Thomas quickly realized that he would have to undertake an extensive program of survey and excavation to salvage many mounds that were being rapidly ravaged and to maximize his labor force throughout all four seasons of the year (also see Jeter, ed., 1991). The data his able assistants uncovered convinced him that the connections between the mounds and the Native Americans were clear. Furthermore, he felt that different tribal groups had built different mounds (Thomas, 1894, p. 528). Although he attributed too many of the mounds to a post-European time of construction and was not alert to the possibilities of cultural sequence or development, Thomas' basic views were in other respects modern in tone.[9]

Thomas' conclusions were published in the monumental twelfth *Annual Report* of the Bureau of Ethnology in 1894. Utilizing culture-area units, this work presented all the Bureau's data on the mound explorations and effectively brought a long era of speculation to an end, at least among the growing group of professionals in the field. In fact, the Report has recently been said by one archaeologist to mark "the birth of modern American archaeology" (Jennings, 1968, p. 33).

Thomas, who was interested in such subjects as Maya hieroglyphics in addition to the mounds, also wrote a general text in 1898 summarizing North American archaeology. Of all the archaeologists at that time, he was probably most qualified for the task.

Another major contributor to the solution of the Moundbuilder question was Frederic Ward Putnam, Curator of the Peabody Museum

SECTION OF SHELL-HEAP
Six inches of modern soil
(Later stage) Fine thin pottery beautifully ornamented. Neatly made implements of bone, shell, etc. Axes, arrow and spear heads of stone; also stone-beads and objects of stone used in games Three feet
Two feet of soil containing a few fragments of pottery
(Middle stage) Better pottery, rudely ornamented. Primitive implements of bone and shell Four feet
(Earlier stage) Rude, heavy pottery, destitute of ornament Three feet

A stylized stratigraphic diagram from S. T. Walker's shell-mound excavations in Florida. (From Walker, 1883)

Shell-mound at Old Enterprise, Florida. (From Wyman, 1875)

from 1875 to 1909 and Peabody Professor of American Archaeology and Ethnology from 1887 to 1909. Putnam was one of the leading figures of the Classificatory-Descriptive Period, both as an excavator, or excavator sponsor, and as an administrator or founder of museums and departments of anthropology.

Before discussing Putnam's role in the growth of American archaeology, we should take note of the earlier history of the institution with which he was associated for so many years. The Peabody Museum of Harvard University was founded in 1866 through the efforts of O. C. Marsh, a nephew of George Peabody. Marsh had been influenced by Lyell, who had advised him to take up archaeology in the Americas. Marsh participated in excavations in Ohio and was the prime mover behind Peabody's gift to Harvard.[10] The first Curator of the Peabody Museum was Jeffries Wyman, a famous natural scientist of the day. Wyman excavated shell-mounds on the Atlantic Coast and then, more importantly, on the banks of the St. Johns River, Florida (Wyman, 1868a; 1875).

Wyman's shell-mound excavations reflected the influences of similar work in Europe. The immediate catalyst was the publication by the Smithsonian Institution of an English translation of an article by Morlot on the shell-middens of Denmark as well as the Swiss lake dwellings

Archaeologists photographed at the Chillicothe Group, Ohio. Frederic Putnam (1839–1945) is at the right with C. L. Metz next to him. (From the Peabody Museum, Harvard University)

(Morlot, 1861). This publication also stimulated the work of J. J. Jones in the shell-mounds of Nova Scotia.[11] Wyman's work helped prove conclusively that the shell-mounds were artificial and that they predated the time of the Native Americans.[12] Wyman was also able to recognize some

The Peabody Museum of Harvard University in 1893, during Putnam's time. (From the Peabody Museum, Harvard University)

The Middle American exhibits at the Columbian Exposition of 1892 in Chicago, Illinois. (From the Peabody Museum, Harvard University)

stratigraphy in them and showed that the heaps of the St. John's River region were different from those of other regions.

One other significant shell-midden excavation of the time was by S. T. Walker at Cedar Keys, Florida (Walker, 1883; Bullen, 1951). Walker recognized strata in the midden and defined several periods on the basis of changing pottery styles. Walker, however, treated the cultural strata like geological ones and generalized a sequence for a whole region. Unfortunately, the work of Wyman and Walker had little effect on the archaeology of Florida and failed to provide an impetus for the building of cultural chronologies.

It was after Wyman's death in 1874 that Frederic W. Putnam became the Curator of the Peabody Museum. Putnam's original professional interests were in zoology but turned to archaeology and general anthropology after his new appointment. Putnam has been called the "father of American archaeology" (Dexter, 1966b). Although we would not go that far, we would agree that he was a major force in its development. Perhaps it might be best to label Putnam, if one must attach labels to great figures, as the "professionalizer of American archaeology." Besides bringing the Peabody Museum to a position as one of the leading anthropological institutions in the United States, Putnam was in charge of the Anthropology Building and Exhibit at the 1892 Exposition in Chicago; he helped found the Field Museum of Natural History in Chicago, the Department of Anthropology at the University of California (Berkeley), and the Anthropology Department of the American Museum of Natural History (Dexter, 1966a). He also was the Secretary

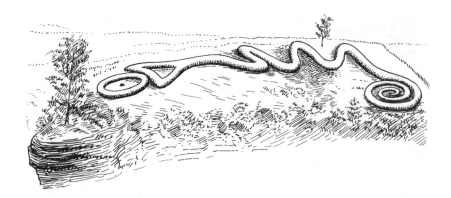

Artist's drawing of the Great Serpent Mound in Ohio. (From Putnam, 1890)

of the American Association for the Advancement of Science for twenty-five years.

Putnam's archaeological interests lay in two areas: the mounds of the Ohio Valley and the study of Late Pleistocene peoples. In relation to the former, he and his associates excavated at Madisonville, the Turner mounds, and at the Great Serpent Mound, among others (Dexter, 1965; Morgan and Rodabaugh, 1947, p. 6). He even obtained the Serpent Mound for the Peabody Museum to save it from destruction; the Museum later turned the mound over to the State of Ohio. Putnam also dug in Tennessee and analyzed and published the prehistoric collections from California obtained by the Wheeler Geographical Expedition. His excavations were models of good technique for the time, and he trained many students in the basics of scientific surveying and mapping, digging, cross-section drawing, and the careful plotting and recording of finds (Putnam, 1886). He also recognized stratigraphy in the mounds of the Ohio Valley, but he did not go on from there to form local or regional cultural sequences.

Putnam's second main interest was in proving the great antiquity of human occupation in the New World. That is, he believed and wished to prove conclusively that people were present in the Americas many thousands of years ago and that they arrived before the end of the Pleistocene Ice Age. To this end, he sponsored various archaeological projects, including the work of C. C. Abbott in the Trenton Gravels of New Jersey. Abbott (1876) discovered tools made of argillite that "looked" early; some appeared in strata which he believed dated to Glacial times. At the time, there was some support for the views of Abbott and Putnam, although it was later shown that the layers were of much more recent date (see Richards, 1939).[13]

The Trenton Gravels finds were just one facet of a major debate that

Drawings of Trenton Gravel "paleoliths." (From Haynes, 1889)

was waged toward the latter part of the Classificatory-Descriptive Period and well into the Classificatory-Historical Period. Many other discoveries were brought forward as proof of an early peopling of the Americas, and this view, which was also supported by such scholars as Henry Haynes (1889), held sway for much of the nineteenth century.

The desire to prove the great antiquity of people in the New World had been stimulated by discoveries in the Old World, where a Pleistocene and Paleolithic date had been demonstrated for Boucher de Perthes' discoveries in France. These discoveries, together with the triumph of Darwinian evolution and its implications, overrode the limiting theological views concerning the age of humans.[14] The publication of such

Putnam in his 1890 mound excavations in the Little Miami Valley, Ohio. (From the Peabody Museum, Harvard University)

popular books as Lubbock's *Prehistoric Times,* which went through many editions, further created interest in the subject in the Americas. It was believed by many that humans had first reached the New World in Glacial times, and a few even believed that the date might be pre-Pleistocene (Whitney, 1872). Unfortunately for the successful demonstration of an early human presence in these continents, Quaternary geology was very imperfectly understood in the Americas in the nineteenth century. It was not known just when the Pleistocene had ended nor to what date such extinct animals as the mastodon had survived. Nor was there a refinement of geological-archaeological excavation techniques that would have been of help in resolving the question of human presence during the Pleistocene.

Even today, in the Americas, the whole situation concerning the Late Pleistocene is disputed on many fronts. This Pleistocene presence is clearly demonstrable, but just how early humans arrived in the New World is still a source of debate. The circumstances are not comparable to the Old World where remains of the genus *Homo* may be dated in hundreds of thousands of years and where the stone artifacts made by these people are found in relatively great numbers in numerous deep Pleistocene deposits. It comes as no surprise, then, that archaeologists in the nineteenth century rushed precipitously into an archaeological situ-

An Ohio mound excavation in 1889, a trenching operation under the direction of C. L. Metz. (From the Peabody Museum, Harvard University)

ation that required methodological care and rigorous standards of proof. Every new find that appeared to have some antiquity on the basis of rude-looking tools or putatively ancient geological associations was proclaimed as a conclusive proof of the antiquity of humans in the New World.

But, as virtually all the supposed finds of the Glacial Age (either artifactual or human) turned out to be unacceptable, the pendulum of opinion began to swing in the other direction. The two scholars most responsible for this change were William Henry Holmes and Aleš Hrdlička.

Holmes was first trained as an artist, but, after traveling in the Western United States with the United States Geological Survey, his interests soon turned to geology and then to archaeology. He worked in the United States National Museum and the Bureau of American Ethnology for much of his career and succeeded Powell as chief of the Bureau in 1902. As we shall see later, he also did a brief stint of fieldwork in Mexico. Holmes was particularly interested in prehistoric ceramics and stone technology, and his classificatory work helped set the stage for typological developments in the following period (see Holmes, 1903). In relation to stone technology, his studies of these "paleoliths," which were claimed by others to be artifacts from Glacial times, showed that these implements were actually rejects of much later native craftsmen (Holmes, 1892; Hough, 1916, p. 195). This work convinced him that people did not reach the New World until after the Pleistocene, and he became a strong defender of this point of view.

Hrdlička also had a major effect on American archaeology, although his role has often been misinterpreted.[15] A physical anthropologist, he was brought to the United States National Museum in 1903. He became Curator of the Division of Physical Anthropology in 1910.[16] Hrdlička was particularly interested in early finds and studied almost all the alleged early sites and associated skeletal material that were discovered in the early part of the twentieth century. He was relentless in his criticisms of the supposed early datings of these finds and often sloppy techniques involved in their excavation. He did not certify as acceptable any of the early discoveries of the time, although he still believed that evidence would be uncovered that would show that people first came to the New World more than 10,000 years ago (Hrdlička, 1925). As time went on, Hrdlička came to be somewhat dogmatic in his rejection of new finds (Schultz, 1945, pp. 312–313), and, as Frank H. H. Roberts has stated, an atmosphere of fear pervaded the Late Pleistocene scene, with many workers afraid to face Hrdlička's scathing attacks. "The question of early man in America became virtually taboo, and no anthropologist, or for that matter geologist or paleontologist, desirous of a successful career

Carved stone tablet from an Ohio mound. These curious and small objects possibly were used as textile or body stamps. They are associated with either Adena or Hopewellian cultures, possibly both. Finds like this helped to maintain a popular faith in the mysterious Mound-builders, as opposed to the Native Americans. Such beliefs persisted long after the scientific excavations of Putnam and Thomas and their contemporaries. (From the Peabody Museum, Harvard University)

William Henry Holmes, 1846–1933. (From the National Anthropological Archives, Smithsonian Institution)

Holmes was the great classifier of eastern North American pottery. Among other things, he identified and segregated the fiber–tempered wares of Florida. Many years later, these wares were demonstrated to be the earliest pottery of America north of Mexico. (From Holmes, 1903)

would tempt the fate of ostracism by intimating that he had discovered indications of a respectable antiquity for the Indian" (Roberts, 1940, p. 52).

Nevertheless, as Clewlow has perceptively pointed out, Hrdlička's work must be evaluated in terms of its historical context (Clewlow, 1970, p. 32). Instead of looking at Hrdlička as a negative force, his criticisms of various archaeologists should be seen as an attempt to bring some degree of rigor and an established mode of validation into archaeological field-work and interpretation. That is, he may have helped to hold back Late Pleistocene studies in a substantive sense, but he advanced the cause of American archaeology as a whole by attempting to make its methodology more scientific. Thus, Hrdlička was helping to lay the foundation that made possible the transition from the Classificatory-Descriptive Period to the Classificatory-Historical Period. Whether the price that had to be paid was equal to this advance is, of course, another question.

The net result of all the early claims and the disproofs by Holmes, Hrdlička, and others was that, by the end of the period, there was little time-depth to American prehistory. The concatenation of circumstances that led to this situation had a major impact on the development of American archaeology. We will further discuss this impact in our review of Classificatory-Descriptive Period concepts and again in the following chapter.

As we have mentioned, archaeology, or at least an interest in antiquities, spread geographically during the Classificatory-Descriptive Period. As explorers and later new populations moved into areas hitherto the preserve of the Native American, such as the southwestern United States, there was an explosion of *descriptive* archaeological knowledge. In other areas, too, such as the southeastern and northeastern United States and even Alaska, the growing group of professional archaeologists carried out valuable new work.

Much of the early archaeological work in the western areas of the United States was done by members of expeditions or took the form of surveys by the federal government (Goetzmann, 1959, 1966). It often consisted simply of descriptions of ruins, especially in the Southwest, although, as the period progressed, there was more and more excavation. In the Southwest, the first descriptions of archaeological remains were by William H. Emory, who "almost singlehandedly . . . began the study of Southwestern archaeology" (Goetzmann, 1966, p. 255; Emory, 1848), J. H. Simpson, the Kerns, and other members of topographic surveys organized by the United States Army. Later investigators included individuals from the Bureau of Ethnology and members of private expeditions, such as James Stevenson (husband of the ethnographer Mathilda Coxe Stevenson and associate of Major Powell), the Mindeleffs, the Wetherills, A. Bandelier, F. H. Cushing, J. W. Fewkes, B. Cummings, G. Nordenskiöld, and E. L. Hewett, who all braved less than ideal working conditions to advance the descriptive state of archaeological knowledge. Frank Hamilton Cushing, the leader of the privately sponsored Hemenway Expedition, helped pioneer the direct-historical approach in the Southwest and combined both ethnography and archaeology in his work (Cushing, 1890); such scholars as Bandelier, Hewett, and Hough showed a precocious interest in Southwestern chronology and made some fairly accurate guesses about sequences there (Bandelier, 1892; Hewett, 1906; Hough, 1903). In other words, Nels C. Nelson and A. V. Kidder, both pioneers of the following Classificatory-Historical Period, did not make their striking archaeological advances in a vacuum.

In the southeastern United States, Clarence B. Moore visited and explored a number of key sites in his private houseboat. Many of the sites were located, naturally, on or near the various rivers of the area.

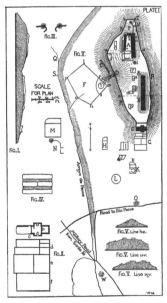

Bandelier's plan of the ruins of Pecos, New Mexico. (From Bandelier, 1881)

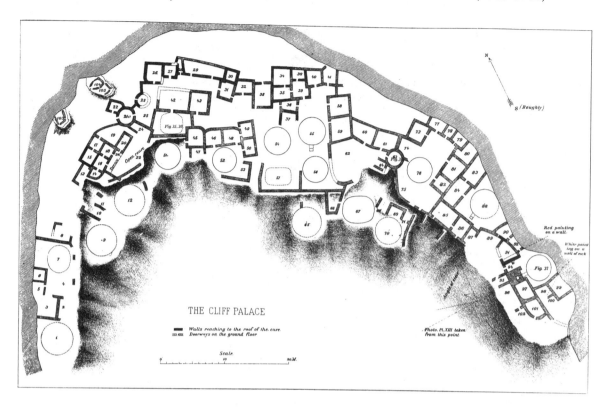

THE CLIFF PALACE

Walls reaching to the roof of the cave.
Doorways on the ground floor

Scale.

Gustav Nordenskiöld's plan of the Cliff Palace, Mesa Verde, Colorado. (From Nordenskiöld, 1893)

Moore published a number of descriptive reports with voluminous illustrations concerning this work (for example, see Moore, 1896, 1902, 1910). Earlier, C. C. Jones had studied the antiquities of Georgia. Gates P. Thurston had worked in Tennessee in the late nineteenth century, and somewhat later, H. I. Smith excavated the Fox Farm site in Kentucky (Smith, 1910).[17] Others working on the eastern seacoast and in the Ohio Valley included Gerard Fowke, who also excavated in the Southeast, Willoughby, who worked in several regions, including Maine and Ohio, and various individuals, such as Volk, Cresson, and Metz, who excavated under the auspices or sponsorship of Putnam.

W. K. Moorehead studied some of the mounds of Ohio, including Fort Ancient and the Hopewell Mound group, and, later, he published his studies on the state of Maine and on the great site of Cahokia in Illinois (Moorehead, 1892, 1922, 1928). He also wrote the two-volume *The Stone Age of North America* and was director, for many years, of the Department of American Archaeology of the Phillips Academy, Massachusetts.

In Quebec, Canada, John W. Dawson, a geologist and the principal of McGill College and University, also undertook some important archaeological work. Of major interest were his attempts to link artifacts excavated in western Montreal with the Iroquois village of Hochelaga, which was visited and described by Cartier in 1535. As Richard S. MacNeish (1981) has noted: "Here not only was the birth of Canada's archaeology, but perhaps the beginnings of the direct-historic approach." Dawson summarized many of his findings in his book *Fossil Men and Their Modern Representatives*, first published in 1880.

Dawson took the unusual step of trying to flesh out the archaeological picture of prehistoric life in the Old World through comparison with archaeological information from America rather than vice versa. In comparing the "hoes" of the Moundbuilders of the Mississippi Valley with flint implements of the Somme Valley in France, Dawson (1880, p. 17) states: "In following out these comparisons, moreover, I do not wish to restrict myself to the mere similarity of implements and other remains, but to present such pictures of the actual life of the American Indian as may enable us to place ourselves in his position, and to view things from his standpoint. By thus sitting at the feet of the red man, we may chance to discover some truths which the learned archaeologists of the old world have not yet attained; and in any case may hope to present some interesting and instructive pictures of primitive man in the old world and the new."

Photograph of Spruce Tree House, Mesa Verde, Colorado, taken at the turn of the century. (From the Peabody Museum, Harvard University)

Pottery found by C. B. Moore in the sand burial mounds of the St. John's River, Florida. (1) Duval's Landing (2,3) Tick Island. (From Moore, 1894)

Pottery from the Maine shell-mounds. These vessels were identified as "Algonquian" by Willoughby. While it is possible that this ethnolinguistic identification was correct, it is now known that pottery such as this dates to the first millennium A.D. and is of general Hopewellian affiliation. (From Willoughby, 1909)

Finally, in our brief survey of some of the scholars who added to our descriptive knowledge of eastern North American prehistory in the Classificatory-Descriptive Period, we should note the works of William C. Mills on the mounds of the Ohio Valley. Mills, curator for the later part of his life of the Museum of the Ohio Archaeological and Historical Society, can be seen as a significant transitional figure between the myth-demolishing Cyrus Thomas in the Classificatory-Descriptive Period and the cultural-typologizing W. C. McKern in the Classificatory-Historical Period.

After excavating various mound groups in Ohio, Mills could separate a Fort Ancient from a Hopewell culture (Mills, 1906, 1907; Schwartz, 1967, pp. 26ff.), but chronology was still a matter of guesswork. In other words, at the beginning of the twentieth century, an attempt was being made to see cultural variety within what had been thought of as *mound culture*. Moreover, these newly defined cultures were not classified solely on the basis of geography (or space), as was the case in Thomas' work (1894), but by cultural similarities. Mills was not the first to do this—Thurston, for one, had defined a Stone Grave culture (or *race*, as he called it) in Tennessee (Thurston, 1890; Schwartz, 1967, p. 26)—but he based his cultural definitions on careful excavation and analysis. He was unable, however, to align these cultures on the basis of stratigraphy to construct a regional sequence. This is not to say that Mills was unaware of time;[18] he simply lacked an archaeological basis to discuss it scientifically.

In the Far West and Alaska, such archaeologists as H. I. Smith, Max Uhle, and N. C. Nelson, as well as the eminent naturalist W. H. Dall, all made significant contributions. Dall and Uhle are especially important because of their attempts to apply stratigraphic methods to build chronologies. Dall was a conchologist and natural scientist who participated in several expeditions to Alaska. During one of these, he had the opportunity to excavate a series of shell-mounds on the Aleutian Islands. He published his results in an article entitled "On Succession in the Shell-Heaps of the Aleutian Islands," which appeared in Volume I of Major Powell's *Contributions to North American Ethnography* in 1877.

Dall trenched several shell-mounds and was able to recognize strata in them. Moreover, he was also able to formulate a three-period chrono-

Copper and imitation deer antler headdress. This find was made in a burial mound of the Hopewell Group. Freshwater pearl beads, copper breastplates, and other ornaments were found in association. (From Moorehead, 1892)

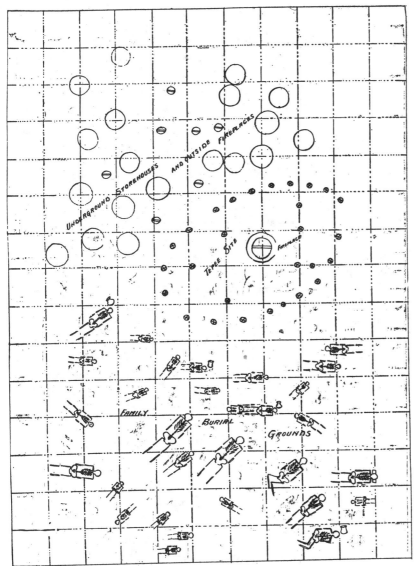

Gridded field plan of burials, house ring (as indicated by postmolds and fireplace), and other fire areas and storage pits. Mills' work in this case involved greater reporting and recording accuracy of excavated features than had heretofore characterized Ohio Valley archaeology. (From Mills, 1906)

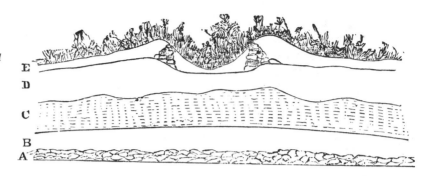

Dall's cross-section of a shell-mound excavation in the Aleutian Islands, Alaska. (A) original hardpan, (B) echinus layer, (C) fishbone layer, (D) mammalian layer, (E) modern deposits and vegetable mold. (From Dall, 1877)

logical scheme for the mounds based on the stratigraphy. As Dall states (1877, p. 47): "[The ditch] gave us a clear idea of the formation and constitution of the shell-heaps; enabled me to distinguish between the different strata and their contents; to make the observations repeatedly; to fully confirm them by experience in many localities; and thus to lay the foundation for the generalizations suggested in this paper." He goes on to conclude (pp. 49–51):

> That a gradual progression from the low Innuit stage to the present Aleut condition, without serious interruption, is plainly indicated by the succession of the materials of, and utensils in, the shell-heaps of the islands. . . .
>
> That the stratification of the shell-heaps shows a tolerably uniform division into three stages, characterized by the food which formed their staple of subsistence and by the weapons for obtaining, and utensils for preparing this food, as found in the separate strata; these stages being—
>
> I. The Littoral Period, represented by the *Echinus* Layer.
> II. The Fishing Period, represented by the Fishbone Layer.
> III. The Hunting Period, represented by the Mammalian Layer.
>
> That these strata correspond approximately to actual stages in the development of the population which formed them; so that their contents may appropriately, within limits, be taken as indicative of the condition of that population at the times when the respective strata were being deposited.

In addition, Dall recognized the probable influence of the environment on the differential development of culture on the islands, although, in typically unfortunate nineteenth-century terminology, he talks of lower and higher stages of culture. Perhaps Dall's geological knowledge and background as a naturalist enabled him to view the archaeological data in a more skillful manner than many of his contemporaries.[19]

It is unfortunate that Dall's excavations were not followed up in new localities and that his article and three-period scheme, along with the methodology used to formulate it, seem to have had no impact at all on other archaeologists of the time. Both the remoteness of the Aleutians and lack of follow-up excavations may have helped to obscure Dall's advances.

Max Uhle, fresh from his excavations in Peru, made a significant breakthrough in his excavations at Emeryville Shell-mound in the San Francisco Bay area of California (Uhle, 1907). Uhle, a German, had been trained in his native land before coming to the United States. He excavated in Peru for both the University of Pennsylvania and the University of California. These important digs will be discussed later in the South American section. At Emeryville, Uhle clearly excavated parts of the mound "stratum by stratum" (p. 8). He discusses the age of the mound and the cultural stages represented by the ten principal strata. He even includes a table that shows the number of implements in the mound, stratum by stratum (p. 39), and he clearly indicates that "it is evident that the character of the objects in the upper strata is entirely different from that of the implements which are found in the lower beds" (p. 39). Uhle also recognized continuity from stratum to stratum. Uhle compares the Emeryville Shell-mound with others on the West Coast, East Coast, and even in Denmark. He argues that it was occupied for more than a thousand years and that cultural change is definitely evident in the changing contents of successive layers. Uhle's work was followed by that of Nels C. Nelson, a student of A. L. Kroeber, at the Ellis Landing Shell-mound and others of the San Francisco Bay region (Nelson, 1909, 1910). Nelson, however, did not advance Uhle's work and in contrast to his later innovative work in the Southwest, tended to be much more cautious in his interpretations than Uhle (Rowe, 1962).

Unfortunately, Uhle's work did not have the impact that it deserved. Certain aspects of his Emeryville report might leave something to be desired, but Uhle still saw the significance of culture change through stratigraphic succession. However, A. L. Kroeber, who was in charge of the Department of Anthropology at the University of California and was the administrator of the Hearst funds that supported the work of Uhle and other archaeologists, did not approve of Uhle's conclusions. It is ironic that Kroeber, who within a decade became a champion of the historical use of archaeological data, was unable to accept Uhle's findings. In his contribution to the *Putnam Anniversary Volume* in 1909, Kroeber blasted Uhle's conclusions, although he did not mention Uhle by name. "The one published account of a systematic though partial exploration of a shell-heap of San Francisco Bay," he states, "upholds the view of a distinct progression and development of civilization having taken place during the growth of the deposit. An independent examina-

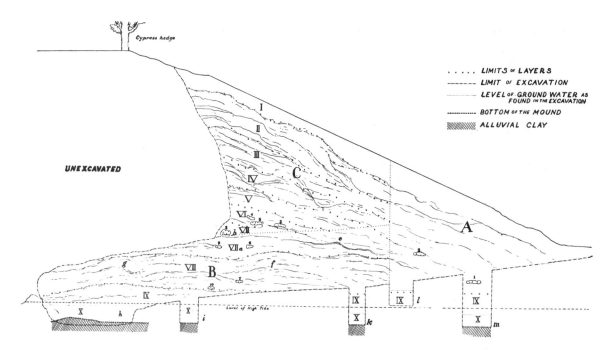

Cypress hedge

. . . . . LIMITS of LAYERS
--------- LIMIT of EXCAVATION
.... LEVEL of GROUND WATER as FOUND in the EXCAVATION
----------- BOTTOM of the MOUND
///////// ALLUVIAL CLAY

UNEXCAVATED

Level of High Tide

Uhle's cross-section drawing of strata in the Emeryville (California) Shell-mound. (From Uhle, 1907)

tion of the material on which this opinion is reared, tends to negate rather than to confirm it" (Kroeber, 1909, p. 15). Kroeber was unable to accept evidence of microchange or small-scale cultural process in the archaeological record. As Rowe has so perspicaciously noted: "Kroeber at this time [1909] visualized cultural change in terms of major shifts in technology and subsistence, any changes of less moment were insignificant. He could not comprehend Uhle's interest in all changes, however minute" (Rowe, 1962, pp. 399–400). Within a decade after Uhle's California excavations, archaeologists in southwestern North America and Mexico did master the description of cultural microchange and laid the foundation for the Classificatory-Historical Period; however, explanation of these changes was not to be seriously attempted in the Americas until after 1960.

ARCHAEOLOGICAL
RESEARCH IN
MIDDLE AMERICA

The development of archaeology in Middle America (or Mesoamerica) paralleled that of North America in general trends, although its tempo and concerns were quite different from those of North America. Middle American archaeology had also been influenced by Europe, but more by individual Europeans than by general intellectual or archaeological developments there, in contrast to North America. The differences between the two areas were obviously related to the relative richness and grandeur of the Middle American remains as well as the presence of a great native literature and indigenous writing systems. These latter attracted the interests of European and North American scholars, who devoted much energy to their study and decipherment. The differences in outlook and consequences of the Spanish Conquest versus the English and French colonization, noted in the previous chapter, are also relevant in terms of the development of differences in the two areas.

The beginning of the Classificatory-Descriptive Period in Middle America was marked by the two explorations in Yucatan and Central America by John L. Stephens, a lawyer (Von Hagen, 1947), with Frederick Catherwood, an architect and artist, and the publication of their *Incidents of Travel in Central America, Chiapas, and Yucatan* in 1841 and *Incidents of Travel in Yucatan* in 1843 (Catherwood, 1844). Stephens had previously traveled extensively in the Old World and had published three accounts of his explorations (Stephens, 1837, 1838, 1839). The work of Stephens and Catherwood literally opened the field of Mayan archaeology in particular and Mesoamerican archaeology in general. As Pollock (1940, p. 185) has said:

> The explorations alone of these men would mark them as important figures in Maya archaeology, but the straightforward uncolored description of Stephens, and the accurate drawings of Catherwood, assisted by the use of daguerreotype and camera lucida, left a work of immense value. Stephens' sound opinion, moreover, as to the indigenous origin of the ruins and their lack of tremendous age was of great importance at a time when there was so much loose thought on the subject.

The two *Incidents of Travel* . . . were widely read and stimulated new explorations and writings. Moreover, like *Ancient Monuments of the Mississippi Valley* by Squier and Davis, the volumes of Stephens and Catherwood became models for new work.

These two explorers were followed by a diverse and colorful group of men, including Charnay, a Frenchman who made the first photographs of Maya ruins (Charnay, 1887); Le Plongeon, who made some early excavations and was one of the most fantastic characters in American archaeology (Wauchope, 1962, pp. 7–21); Alfred P. Maudslay, an Englishman who explored and mapped many sites, including Yaxchilan and Copan, and published the huge *Biologia Centrali Americana*, which includes four volumes of archaeology (Maudslay, 1889–1902; Thomas, 1899); Teobert Maler, who worked for the Peabody Museum and mapped, photographed, and carefully described a number of Maya ruins (Maler, 1901, 1903, 1908); Adolph Bastian and S. Habel, two Germans who wrote about the sculptures of Santa Lucia Cotzumalhuapa in

Drawing of Stela 2, Copan, Honduras. (From Maudslay, 1889–1902)

Drawing of a palace at Yaxchilan. This site was designated as "Lorillard City" by Charnay. (From Charnay, 1887)

the Guatemalan Highlands (Bastian, 1876; Habel, 1878); Karl Sapper, a geographer and ethnographer, who classified ruins into architectural types and related these to ethnographic and linguistic areas (Pollock, 1940, p. 190; Sapper, 1895); Thomas Gann, a doctor, who surveyed and excavated in Honduras and British Honduras (Gann, 1900); and E. H. Thompson, the American Consul in Yucatan, who dredged the great Sacred Cenote at Chichen Itza and explored other ruins (E. H. Thompson, 1897, 1898, 1904).

The Maya area was the center of most of the activity, but work was also done in Central Mexico. Leopoldo Batres worked at the great site of Teotihuacan (Batres, 1906); Zelia Nuttall published studies on a wide variety of Mexican archaeological topics (Nuttall, 1910);[20] W. H. Holmes, whom we discussed earlier, also made an important contribution to Mesoamerican archaeology. In *Archaeological Studies among the Ancient Cities of Mexico,* Holmes classified ceramic vessels and various kinds of ceremonial architecture and attempted careful archaeological comparisons (Holmes, 1895–1897).

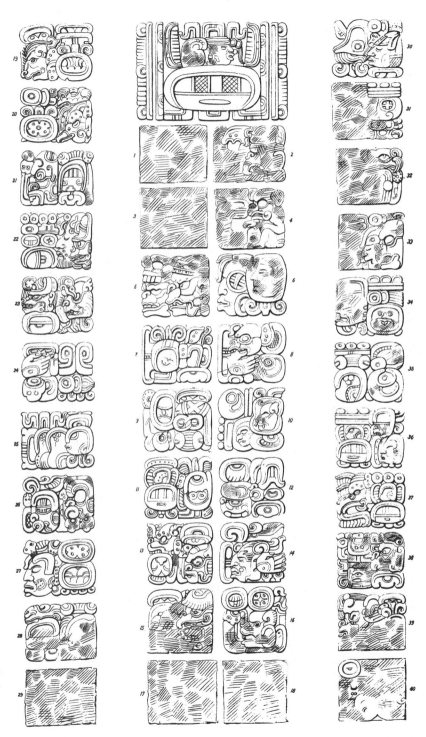

An Initial Series and hieroglyphic text from the back and sides of Stela 2, Copan, Honduras. Drawings such as this were invaluable to the interpreters of Maya glyphs, such as J. T. Goodman. (From Maudslay, 1889–1902)

The combined work of these men and women helped to form the descriptive background of Middle American and especially Maya archaeology and paved the way for the advances of the following Classificatory-Historical Period.

The first important large-scale excavations in Middle America were undertaken at the major Classic Maya center of Copan, Honduras, by

An example of Maler's fabulous photography, this one of Stela 11, Seibal, Peten, Guatemala. (From the Peabody Museum, Harvard University)

E. H. Thompson using a palace room at Labna, Yucatan, Mexico, as an office ca. 1890. (From the Peabody Museum, Harvard University)

W. H. Holmes' drawing of the ruins of Teotihuacan in the Valley of Mexico. The artist's view looks from back of the Pyramid of the Moon down the Street of the Dead. The famed Pyramid of the Sun (B) lies on the left, as does the enclosure (E) designated as the Ciudadela. This sketch is an example of Holmes' masterly draftsmanship. It is amazingly accurate, even though done impressionistically. (From Holmes, 1895–7)

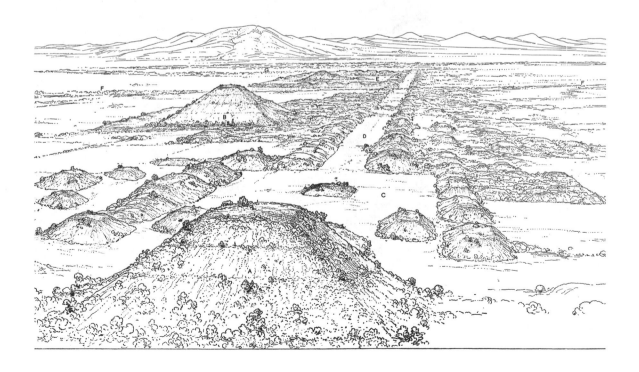

Photograph of a Copan stela taken during the Peabody Museum's excavations of the 1890s. Compare with Catherwood's drawing of Copan Stela 2 (frontispiece). (From the Peabody Museum, Harvard University)

the Peabody Museum of Harvard University. The work was conducted by M. H. Saville, John Owens, who died in the field, and G. B. Gordon; and the results were published as part of a new series of Memoirs of the Peabody Museum (Gordon, 1896, 1902; Saville, 1892). These reports were almost totally descriptive in content and tone. New steps forward were taken with the work of Alfred M. Tozzer[21] and R. E. Merwin in the Maya Lowlands and Edgar L. Hewett and Sylvanus G. Morley at Quirigua. In descriptive treatments, their works were virtually modern in the accuracy of recording and completeness of presentation. They also attempted some chronology, but this was through relating their excavated buildings and tombs to hieroglyphic inscriptions and Maya calendrical dates recorded on associated monuments (Tozzer, 1911, 1913; Hewett, 1912; Morley, 1913; Pollock, 1940, pp. 191–192; Merwin and Vaillant, 1932).

It is in the realm of hieroglyphic inscriptions and native literature that a second important theme emerges in our survey of Mesoamerican archaeology during the Classificatory-Descriptive Period. This

The Maya ruins of Palenque, Chiapas, Mexico. Photograph taken early in the twentieth century. (From the Peabody Museum, Harvard University)

Sculptured head of the "Maize God" from Copan, Honduras. (From the Peabody Museum, Harvard University)

Temple I at the Maya Lowland site of Tikal, Guatemala. Photograph taken at the time of Tozzer's explorations there (ca. 1911). (From the Peabody Museum, Harvard University)

field of study was dominated by Europeans, including the Abbé Brasseur de Bourbourg, Ernest W. Förstemann, Edward Seler, and Léon de Rosny, although such Americans as Cyrus Thomas, D. G. Brinton, Joseph T. Goodman, and Charles P. Bowditch also made important contributions.[22] The interests of most of these scholars were definitely humanistic in nature, and none of them, with the exception of Thomas, was actually a practicing field archaeologist. Their studies, however, did aid Mesoamerican archaeologists in several significant aspects.

The work of Förstemann, who has been called "the father of Maya hieroglyphic research" (J. E. S. Thompson, 1958b, p. 43) on the Dresden Codex (an original Maya book) led him to the decipherment of much of the numerical and calendrical data in it.[23] It thus became possible for archaeologists to date inscribed monuments in the Maya area. The work of Brasseur de Bourbourg on Landa's *Relación de las Cosas de Yucatán* and native Maya documents from Yucatan and the Guatemalan Highlands (Brinton, 1882, 1885), respectively, provided much useful data that archaeologists could use for numerous analogies with Maya civilization of more ancient times and gave a great appreciation of the development and richness of that civilization just prior to the Spanish Conquest.

The wealth of data on the Maya, as well as the other great civilizations of Mesoamerica, was later to prove a boon to archaeologists, as they began to investigate scientifically processual problems, such as the rise of settled village life and civilization and the development of cities and the state. The rich data, however, had a somewhat negative impact as well. For many decades throughout the Classificatory-Descriptive and Classificatory-Historical Periods, the relatively vast quantities of data about the elite aspects of Maya civilization, especially the religious, and the obvious magnificence of elite architecture and art arrested the archaeologists' attention and kept their efforts within an artificially narrow scope. Historical reconstruction of the Mesoamerican past became the historical reconstruction of the elite past. This narrow purview was not to be modified until late in the Classificatory-Historical Period.

Finally, in more general terms, we should note Prescott's monumental account of the conquest of Mexico by the Spanish (Prescott, 1843). In this connection, the doubts of Lewis Henry Morgan and Bandelier as to the culturally advanced nature of the Aztec state should also be pointed out (Morgan, 1876; Bandelier, 1877, 1878, 1879). The question was one of both interpretation and classification. Morgan and Bandelier reasoned from prior evolutionary assumptions and tended to belittle the accomplishments of the Aztecs, believing that there was no true Native Ameri-

Charles P. Bowditch, 1842–1921 from a portrait by Ignace Gaugengigl. Bowditch, an accomplished scholar in Maya astronomy and mathematics, was the principal patron of Harvard's Peabody Museum in its early Maya archaeological program. (From the Peabody Museum, Harvard University)

Pages from the Dresden Codex, which was the document used by Förstemann in much of his decipherment work. (From Kingsborough, 1831–9)

can civilization. Although it is now quite apparent that Morgan and Bandelier were wrong, their raising of these questions about the cultural level and the nature of Aztec sociopolitical organization foreshadowed concerns of a later period, when archaeologists turned to questions of cultural development.

In 1914, at the very end of the period, Thomas A. Joyce, a British archaeologist, was able to draw together all the available archaeological data on Mesoamerican archaeology in a general work entitled *Mexican Archaeology* (Joyce, 1914). He attempted to set up a chronology for the area, based on the dates on carved Maya monuments and the sequences offered by native legends and traditions. One year earlier, however, an even more important study was produced by H. J. Spinden (1913). *A Study of Maya Art* was definitely a precocious work, which still provides many stimulating hypotheses about Maya culture. Most significantly, Spinden attempted to order Maya art chronologically, with the evolutionary development of stylistic traits as the framework for this chronological sequence. By 1914, a new age in Mesoamerican archaeology was definitely dawning.

Conventional archaeology of the Classificatory-Descriptive Period was carried out in a number of places in South America. Much of it approached the tradition of Stephens and Catherwood — that is, travelers' accounts, well illustrated and generally accurate in factual reporting. Peru, that area of the continent with the most spectacular ruins, attracted the most interest, and books on the archaeology (and living native peoples) of Peru began to appear in the 1850s and continued on into the twentieth century. Among some of the best known are those by Tschudi

ARCHAEOLOGICAL RESEARCH IN SOUTH AMERICA

The Inca ruins of Ollantaytambo, Peru. (From Squier, 1877)

The "Gateway of the Sun" at Tiahuanaco, Bolivia. (From Squier, 1877)

Max Uhle, 1856–1944. (From Museum für Völkerkunde und Vorgeschichte, Hamburg)

(1869), Castelnau (1852), Wiener (1880), Middendorf (1893–1895), and Squier (1877) of Mississippi Valley fame. Perhaps the leading Peruvianist of the time, in the sense of high quality of scholarship, was Sir Clements Markham (1856, 1871, 1892, 1910). Excavation accounts, too, were published in the period, including those of Reiss and Stübel (1880–1887) and Bandelier (1910). But the outstanding figure for the Classificatory-Descriptive Period in Peru, and in South America as a whole, was Max Uhle. Uhle was more of an archaeologist, in the present sense of that word, than any of the others. His substantive contributions were great, and, from a methodological standpoint, he should be regarded as an important transitional figure between the Classificatory-Descriptive and the Classificatory-Historical Periods.

Uhle[25] was born and trained in Germany, beginning in philology but switching soon after receiving his academic degree to archaeology and ethnography. While a curator in the Dresden Museum, he met

Alphons Stübel, who, with Wilhelm Reiss, had just excavated the Ancon cemetery on the Peruvian coast. Stübel collaborated with the young Uhle on a study of notes and photographs Stübel had made at Tiahuanaco. Together, they brought out *Die Ruinenstaette von Tiahuanaco* in 1892. That same year, Uhle began field research in South America and continued there intermittently, for over thirty years. His most brilliant work was in Peru and Bolivia in the 1890s and the first decade of the twentieth century. Later, he was to work in Chile and Ecuador.

His museum work in Germany had given Uhle a commanding knowledge of Inca and Tiahuanaco pottery and sculptural styles, and this served him well in his major field excavation in Peru, at the great site of Pachacamac, just south of Lima, on the Peruvian coast. It was here that he set the first important stake in a Peruvian area chronology. Knowing the Inca materials from the site to be just anterior to the Spanish Conquest, and knowing Tiahuanaco and Tiahuanaco-like styles to be fully Pre-Columbian, he reasoned that a third distinct style of pottery, which showed no Tiahuanacoid influence but was sometimes associated with Incaic pieces, had an intermediate chronological position. In other words, Uhle was applying both stylistic and associational seriation on a

Excavating in the cemetery of Ancon, coastal Peru. (From Reiss and Stübel, 1880–7)

Drawings of pottery from the Ancon cemetery. These specimens are represented with good accuracy and can be easily identified as to styles as these are defined today. (From Reiss and Stübel, 1880–7)

The "Gateway of the Sun," Tiahuanaco. This photograph was taken by Stübel in the late nineteenth century. Compare it with Squier's drawing on the following page. (From Stübel and Uhle, 1892)

similiary principle. He was familiar with stratigraphic principles, and some grave and structural superpositions at Pachacamac further verified this sequence; yet, most of Uhle's Peruvian digging was a search for graves and a careful recording of grave-lot associations, so that he never put stratigraphy to the test there in refuse excavations. However, in an interim between the Peruvian expeditions, he did stratigraphic digging in the California shell-mounds. The Pachacamac explorations were published in 1903, in Philadelphia, by the University of Pennsylvania, and the report remains one of the monuments of American archaeology. Uhle went on from the Pachacamac findings to propound a Peruvian area-wide chronological scheme. Other coastal excavations indicated that earlier advanced styles antedated Tiahuanaco stylistic influence. He thus had a four-period sequence:[26] (1) early regional styles; (2) Tiahuanaco-influenced styles; (3) late regional styles; and (4) Inca-influenced styles. The efficacy of the chronology was demonstrated at a number of places along the Peruvian coast, including the Rimac, Ancon, Chancay, and Moche Valleys (Uhle, 1910, 1913a, 1913b; Kroeber, 1926). It utilized the principle of *horizon styles* — in this case Tiahuanaco and Inca — and it has withstood the test of seventy years of subsequent research, being modified only by the discovery of earlier archaeological cultures and horizons.[27]

Diagram of the "Gateway of the Sun," Tiahuanaco. Prepared as a key to the iconographic descriptions of the text. (From Stübel and Uhle, 1892)

In 1912, Uhle left Peru to work in Chile and, later, in Ecuador. Although he contributed significantly to the developing discipline of archaeology in both countries, his overall success was somewhat less. In Chile, Incaic and Tiahuanacoid relationships were pointed out, and Uhle recognized the North Chilean coastal preceramic cultures (Uhle, 1916, 1919, 1922a). He dubbed the latter "Paleolithic," but, as Rowe has explained, he was claiming no great age for them, only "exercising the comparative method of the cultural evolutionists" (Rowe, 1954, p. 15). In Ecuador, there was more of a descriptive archaeological base than there had been in Chile. This went back to the systematic work of Federico Gonzáles Suárez, beginning in 1878 (Gonzáles Suárez, 1878, 1892, 1910), and also included explorations, excavations, and publications by the North Americans G. A. Dorsey (1901) and M. H. Saville (1907–10), both protégés of Putnam, and the French anthropologist Paul Rivet (Verneav and Rivet, 1912–1922). What the situation needed was sound chronological ordering. The task, however, was more difficult than in Peru; for one thing, there were no easily recognizable horizon markers. Incaic influence could be identified in parts of the country, but the attempt to extend the Tiahuanaco horizon so far north met with failure. By this time, too, Uhle's interests in work of confined regional scope seemed to be lagging. His later Ecuadorian writings show an increased tendency to follow out extreme diffusionist theories, with the Middle American Maya, about which he knew nothing at first hand, seen as the point of origin of New World higher cultures (Uhle, 1922b, 1923). Uhle remained in Ecuador until 1933,[28] and after this he continued writing and library and museum research up to the time of his death in 1944; however, it is a fair judgment to say that his truly influential work was over long before this and that, indeed, it had been done in Peru before 1912.

In retrospect, Uhle appears at the very top of any list of the outstanding archaeologists of the Classificatory-Descriptive Period; in fact, he

The central figure from the "Gateway of the Sun," Tiahuanaco. Photography of this excellent quality characterized some of the archaeological work of the latter part of the Classificatory-Descriptive Period. (From Stübel and Uhle, 1892)

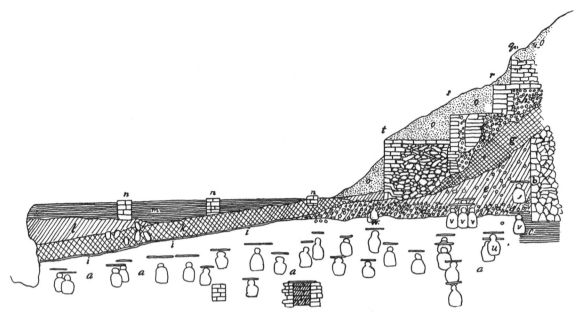

Uhle's cross-section drawing of architectural and grave stratigraphy at Pachacamac. (From Uhle, 1903)

The ruins of Pachacamac, Peru. (From Uhle, 1903)

helped transform American archaeology of that period and bring about a new era. He was ahead of any of his contemporaries in a realization of the importance of chronology. This is summed up perfectly in his statement: "In Americanist studies, the first thing that had to be done was to introduce the idea of time, to get people to admit that the types could change."[29] This shows a sophisticated awareness of cultural microchange of the sort that Flinders Petrie was then propounding, and Uhle had been influenced by Petrie (Rowe, 1954, pp. 54–55). In fact, Uhle's archaeological sophistication must be attributed, in very large part, to his European background, training, and continued contacts. He was not hampered by the parochial view of many of the Americans, both North and South, who tended to conceive of New World archaeology as a kind of undifferentiated time-plane of the Native Americans and their forbears. Uhle was able to apply seriational and limited stratigraphic methods to resolve problems of chronology. He was clearly at his best when operating with the specifics of a relatively limited cultural-geographical area, such as Peru; and, in our opinion, his cultural evolutionary theoretical orientation stood him in good stead here.[30] It convinced him that "the types could change" through time. When he projected these theories farther afield, he was on shaky ground; neither the information nor the proper comparative approach was at hand. An excess of uncritical diffusionism also marred his later work.

Nowhere else in South America was there anyone of Uhle's stature as an archaeologist. Perhaps, if Baron Erland von Nordenskiöld had gone in more for archaeology, rather than restricting his principal efforts to ethnography, he would have made comparable contributions to prehistory. Nordenskiöld's one serious archaeological field attempt, the excavation of dwelling and burial mounds in the Bolivian lowlands, resulted in important stratigraphic observations on one mound and the definitions of an earlier and a later culture. This was published in 1913, at the very close of the Classificatory-Descriptive Period (Erland von Nordenskiöld, 1913). Another case of stratigraphy or superposition was recorded a few years earlier by the Argentine archaeologist J. B. Ambrosetti, who, excavating at Pampa Grande, in the northwestern part of that country, defined a grave sequence (Ambrosetti, 1906). Argentine archaeologists were quite active in the late nineteenth and early twentieth centuries, working from museums and universities. As in the United States, the methods were classificatory and distributional, and archaeological remains were studied in concert with ethnography and ethnohistory. Ambrosetti (1897, 1902, 1906, 1908) was the best of the group, in many ways comparable—in his broad knowledge and careful reporting—to W. H. Holmes in North America. An Argentine colleague, S. Debendetti (1910, 1912), deserves mention, as do the Swedish explorer-archaeologists Eric Boman (1908) and Count von Rosen (1904, 1924). For the Argentine lowlands, L. M. Torres (1907, 1911) made a valuable contribution on Paraná delta archaeology, and F. F. Outes (1897, 1905, 1907) established himself as the leading authority on the archaeology of the Pampas-Patagonia. This was also the time of Ameghino's claims for very early artifacts from the Argentine littoral, claims which Hrdlička and others effectively demolished (Ameghino, 1911, 1918; Hrdlička and others, 1912).

Elsewhere in South America, archaeology of the period was descriptive and occasionally classificatory, and sometimes there were attempts to relate archaeological remains to historical Native American groups. The latter exercise was often quite uncritical, with the proof of prehistoric-to-historic continuities assumed. William Bollaert (1860) wrote on Colombia, and Vicente Restrepo (1895) brought out his well-known monograph on Chibchan ethnohistory and archaeology. Marcano (1889) and Karl von den Steinen (1904) reported on excavations in Venezuela. J. W. Fewkes (1907, 1922) was a principal worker in the West Indies, and Thomas A. Joyce (1916) devoted a part of a book to the archaeology of that area. This same book of Joyce's also included Central America, where Squier (1852, 1853), Holmes (1888), MacCurdy

Plan and cross-section drawing of burial enclosure in Costa Rica. (From Hartman, 1901)

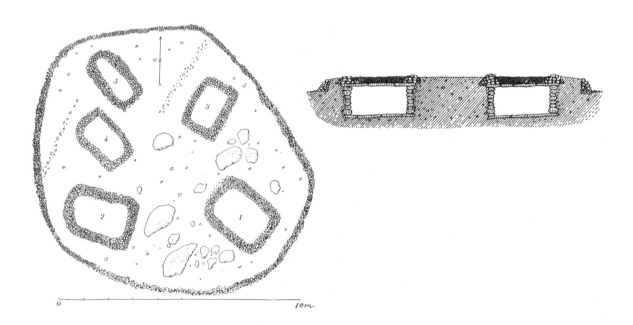

0   10m.

*Marajó ceramics, from Marajó
Island, Brazil. (From Hartt, 1885)*

(1911), and Hartman[31] all worked. C. V. Hartman's archaeological researches in Costa Rica are worthy of special note. A European-trained scholar, he was appreciative of grave-lot segregation and grave superposition. All in all, he was a careful fieldworker, and his well-illustrated and presented publications were outstanding for their time. Of all the South Americanists (if we include Costa Rica in this geographical assemblage), he was the best archaeologist, except for Uhle. In Brazil, there were excavations on the Amazon and in Brazilian Guiana by Derby (1879), Hartt (1871, 1885), Farabee (1921), Steere (1927), and

Goeldi (1900), and, farther south, Hermann von Ihering dug in the coastal sambaquis (Ihering, 1895). Inland, in Minas Gerais, argument continued over the Lagoa Santa crania.[32] Finally, we should mention Thomas Joyce's other book on South American archaeology as a whole. It appeared in 1912 and, like his *Mexican Archaeology* of 1914, was the first of its kind to attempt to give an archaeologic-ethnohistoric story of the whole continent. Based wholly on library and museum research, it is a remarkable and admirable summary of the state of archaeological knowledge for South America at the close of the Classificatory-Descriptive Period. Pertaining to an era when regional chronologies had not yet come to the fore as a prime goal of archaeological research, Joyce was largely concerned with interpretations of art and iconography and with attempting to understand the ideologies of Pre-Columbian cultures through this native imagery, as studied in conjunction with ethnographical and ethnohistorical sources.

THE DEVELOPMENT OF CONCEPTS AND METHODS

The rise of systematic archaeology, the beginnings of scientific geology, and Darwinian evolutionism—all European developments of the mid nineteenth century—were the stimuli that gave rise to the formal discipline of archaeology in America. The old mold of sheerly speculative thought about the antiquities of the past was broken. Carefully recorded description and classification of the phenomena of the past had begun, and typologies were developed; geographical distributions of the data were plotted; archaeological field techniques were greatly improved; a vastly greater amount of field exploration was carried out than ever before; and all of this was accompanied by a steadily growing professionalization of the discipline in an academic alliance with anthropology as a whole. Such was the positive picture. On the negative side, there was a failure to develop control of the chronological dimension of the data, especially through stratigraphy. The period also witnessed a decline, toward its end, in the evolutionary theory that had stimulated and informed its inception.

To turn to the positive aspects first, pioneer work on classification of stone artifacts in the Descriptive-Classificatory Period was carried out in North America by Charles Rau of the Smithsonian Institution.[33] Thomas Wilson (1899), Curator of the United States National Museum, also made contributions of this nature, as did Gerard Fowke (1896). Wilson's interests appear to have flowed naturally from his official position. The United States Congress was eager to make the Museum the primary repository for important and representative collections of native antiquities from all parts of the nation, and the Museum's curators had to devise schemes for the classification, exhibition, and storage of the collections. While this was a step in the right direction, it also led to a tendency to consider the specimens in isolated cross-cultural classes. That is, all stone axes, from all over the United States, were grouped together rather than being considered within a framework of culture complexes or units (Trigger, 1968b, p. 529). The culture-complex concept had not yet emerged with any clarity in American archaeology. Nevertheless, in spite of its limitations, artifact classification of the nineteenth century pointed the way toward systematic treatment and objective examination.

Classificatory advances were also made in the treatment of earthworks of the eastern United States, as may be seen by comparing the Squier and Davis 1848 report with that of Thomas' survey published in 1894. Such progress followed faithfully the directive of Joseph Henry's *Annual Report of the Smithsonian Institution for 1874* (1875, p. 335): "It is considered important to collect all possible information as to the location and character of ancient earthworks, which exist in various parts of the United States, with a view to classify them and determine their distribution in relation to special topographical features of the country as well as to different regions."

W. H. Holmes performed the outstanding typological and classificatory work of the period on the pottery of the eastern United States (Holmes, 1903). Holmes worked with the available literature and with hundreds of pottery collections, which, for the most part, bore only general geographical provenience. His monograph was a major substantive contribution, for it laid the groundwork of archaeological knowledge for ceramics for a large part of North America. In it, he went beyond previous studies, since, for the first time in the New World field, great attention was paid to minor stylistic differences in ceramic designs and forms and in the materials and inferred methods of their manufacture. These several criteria, taken in conjunction, enabled Holmes to identify several well-defined pottery regions within the eastern United States. American archaeologists had long been cognizant of geographical-cultural variation. At first, they had simply recognized that the archaeological remains of a certain arbitrarily defined region — as, for example, in *The Antiquities of Tennessee* (Thruston, 1890) — were different from those of another such region similarly selected. Holmes put this into systematic comparative perspective, and, in doing so, he participated in and contributed to the "culture area" formulations of Mason (1895, 1905) and Wissler (1914).

Good typological control of the archaeological data did lead to other conceptual advances in some instances. These were, however, relatively little developed by most scholars and would not become standard parts of archaeological thinking until the next period. For

MAP OF
NORTH AMERICA

example, the integrative concept of a specific *culture* was used frequently and effectively by Max Uhle, in Peru. Mills also employed it in Ohio (Mills, 1907). Yet, the concept remained vaguely defined in most of its substantive applications and not defined at all as an abstract methodological device. The broader integrative concept of *horizon style* was used very successfully by Uhle, who established the first American area chronology by this means. In this, as in many other things, Uhle was well ahead of his time; but he appears to have taken the horizon concept for granted, never applying this name to it nor trying to define it as a concept. The still more inclusive concept of *culture stage,* which combines both historical and evolutionary dimensions, was evoked by some writers of the Classificatory-Descriptive Period; but this followed along, more or less, with the European-derived Savagery-Barbarism-Civilization concepts of the day and was little more than an affirmation of faith in the doctrine of "psychic unity." The assumed developmental levels of culture were not tested against the real American data. Indeed, there was no way to do this without adequate chronologies, of which almost none existed.

There was some interest in use of functional explanations of the archaeological data. Squier and Davis (1848) employed a simple functional classification to the mounds and earthworks they investigated and classified, inferring function in a very general analogical way—burial places, building platforms, fortifications, and so on. There was considerable speculation about the way artifacts functioned, and there was even a measure of experimentation to test some of these speculations or hypotheses (Hough, 1916). More significantly, a very few archaeologists, notably Cushing among the Zuñi, tried to arrive at functional explanations of prehistoric artifact forms by comparing them with those of their presumed tribal descendants among living Native Americans (Cushing, 1886). Archaeologists of the period also showed some interest in the possible influences of natural environment on cultural development. This was usually with relation to site locations and resource utilization; or, in some instances, environment was seen as the real determinant of culture. In neither case, however, was there any systematic consideration of environment in archaeological studies that even vaguely resembled that of modern ecology.

As we have noted, the sheer quantity of archaeological work in North, Middle, and South America increased throughout the Classificatory-Descriptive Period. Museums, both in Europe and in the Americas, sponsored fieldwork to obtain specimens for display, and there was a growing interest in archaeological work on the part of governments in the United States and in Latin America. This led to the founding of new museums and participation in international expositions (such as the 1892

"Cultural Characterization Areas" on the facing page are based on archaeological data. I North Atlantic; II Georgia–Florida; III Middle, Lower Mississippi Valley; IV Upper Mississippi–Great Lakes; V Great Plains–Rocky Mountains; VI The arid region; VII California; VIII Columbia–Fraser; IX Northwest Coast; X Arctic Shoreland; XI Great Northern Interior; XII Northern Mexico; XIII Middle Mexico; XIV Southern Mexico; XV Maya Province; XVI Central America. (From Holmes, 1914)

Modern pueblo pottery-making as depicted by Cushing. (From Cushing, 1886)

Columbia Exposition in Chicago) and scientific congresses (such as the biennial Congress of Americanists, which began in 1875).

The general increase in archaeological interest and activity and the professionalization of the subject were intimately bound up with the academic development of archaeology, especially in the United States. Brinton founded a department for the teaching of archaeology and anthropology at Pennsylvania, and Putnam did the same at Harvard.

From the very beginning, American archaeology was in close alliance with the rest of anthropology. Actually, the links were first firmly forged in the Smithsonian Institution by J. W. Powell who, as chief of the Bureau of Ethnology, also instigated the mound and earthwork archaeological survey of Cyrus Thomas, who was in his employ. The obvious importance of a related archaeological-ethnological attack on the problems of Native Americans and their origins was a consequence of Thomas' mound survey and the demonstration that the earthworks had indeed been constructed by the forbears of the Native Americans. The physical anthropological study of skeletal material from the mounds was also found to be relevant to the solution of such problems, and this third major branch of anthropology was brought into the American alliance. All of this stands in notable contrast to the situation in the Old World, where the three disciplines tended to develop separately. Many of the differences between New World archaeology and Old World archaeology can be traced to this time and to this turn of events in the Americas.

American archaeology has undoubtedly benefitted greatly from this association with anthropology. Through this association, archaeologists have been made more aware of the structural variation of simpler cultures. It has also helped power a unified attack on problems of cultural history by a direct-historical approach from the ethnographic present into the archaeological past and has provided the archaeologist with a rich reservoir of information for ethnographic analogies pertinent for prehistoric situations. But, we think, there has also been a debit side to the alliance. The distrust of evolutionary thinking and the marked historical particularism of American anthropology forced the American archaeologist into a niche with a very limited horizon. The strength of archaeology is its perspective, in which it examines culture change and development through time. These were definitely not the objectives of the American archaeological-ethnological establishment as it emerged into the twentieth century.[34] As a result, archaeology enjoyed little esteem in the field of anthropology.

The rejection of cultural evolutionism in American anthropology began with Franz Boas and his students. Various reasons have been cited for this,[35] and we will not try to go into them here. It is, however, fair to note that, by the late nineteenth century, many of the claims of the evolutionists had become absurd. The most obvious instances of culture contact and diffusion were ignored; cultural similarity was explained by "psychic unity" operating within the severe constraints of uniform culture stages. Boas demanded a return to factual evidence and to what was to be called *historical particularism*. It was a salutary reaction, but, like many such, it was carried too far. One might have thought that American archaeology would have withstood this reaction, would have profited from an insistence upon firm evidence and then gone on with its essentially diachronic task. But it did not, and this we believe was owing to three factors. First, there was a lack of any well-documented long-term culture sequence in the New World. The Late Pleistocene claims of the Classificatory-Descriptive Period had not stood up to critical scrutiny. Thus, at the beginning of the twentieth century, there was no good evidence that the Native Americans had been in this hemisphere for any appreciable length of time. Second, there was no good support for significant or major culture change within the archaeological evidence that pertained to the Native Americans and their ancestors. And third, and closely related, there was no concept of microchange in culture and its importance. Uhle was the notable exception, as we have seen; but his influence, or the influence of the ideas he represented, was not to spread to the rest of the Americas until the beginning of the Classificatory-Historical Period. Culture change still had to be viewed in broad outline. The models were those of the Old World jump from Paleolithic to Neolithic or the social theorist's stage scheme of Savagery-Barbarism-Civilization. American archaeologists of the time did not think they could adduce evidence for such dramatic macrochange on the New World scene, and so they felt they were in no position to rebut the historical particularists.

These factors reveal that the weaknesses of American archaeology were as much responsible for the outcome of events as Boasian antievolutionism, if not more so. Without widespread use of the stratigraphic method, American archaeologists of the turn of the century were in no position to determine culture sequences and to develop any concept of small-scale cultural change through time; conversely, until such a concept could be appreciated, they would be slow to conduct stratigraphic excavations with this as a goal. Although some archaeologists were aware of the stratigraphic method, it was not widely utilized nor appreciated at this time in the Americas. Trigger (1980a, 1989) has argued that an anti-Native American ethnic bias on the part of North Americans in general caused archaeologists of that area to ignore the possibilities of long-term culture depth and change in the native archaeological record, and because of these biases the stratigraphic method lagged in its application.[36] While this interpretation is a beguiling one and deserves further examination, we are hesitant to accept it without more explicit evidence and substantiation. It should be noted that, during this time in the latter part of the nineteenth century, the lack of regular communication among the relatively few archaeological scholars—in annual scientific meetings, through major archaeological journals, or in academic lectures and discussions—impeded the dissemination of information about the merits of this important method.

All of these factors tended to be reinforced by an antievolutionary intellectual climate where a search for such change was hardly an important research target. In another score of years, American archaeologists would break out of this self-defeating circle. Ironically, Boas would be one of those instrumental in helping them do it.[37] For the time being, though, the loss of the evolutionary mode of thought also meant the loss of general problem orientation in American archaeology. Problems, such as they were, remained specifically historical. More general questions of development, function, and process were left alone. After the "stratigraphic revolution" of the Classificatory-Historical Period, American archaeology began to build a solid culture-historical foundation. On this foundation, it has since constructed, largely from its own resources, a new conceptual framework; and today there is a new alliance with anthropology. But this takes us far ahead of our story. Our immediate concerns now are the developments of the Classificatory-Historical Period.

NOTES

1. Among the useful general sources for this period are: Belmont and Williams (1965); Bieder (1986); Bernal (1980); Clewlow (1970); Fernandez (1980); Goetzmann (1967); Hallowell (1960); Haven (1856); Haynes (1900); Hinsley (1981); Kirbus (1976); Morgan and Rodabaugh (1947); Pollock (1940); Silverberg (1968); Thomas (1898); Willey (1968); Wilmsen (1965).

2. Haven (1856, p. 149), for example, could state unequivocally, in the beginning of the period, that there were no antiquities in the Oregon Territory. By the end of the period, such a statement would have been impossible.

3. Dunnell (1991), in contrast to Silverberg (1968), has argued that at least among the budding professional community, this controversy had been settled much earlier in the mid-nineteenth century and that few serious scholars supported the "lost race" view.

4. Kehoe (1989) views such statements as evidence of the "Whiggish" stance of this book. Nevertheless, however the nature of our discussion is characterized, the importance of the founding of the Smithsonian Institution cannot be dismissed or underemphasized in the history of American archaeology.

5. Whittlesey in Squier and Davis (1848, pp. 14–42).

6. An index (F. S. Nichols, 1954) is now available.

7. See McKusick's (1970, 1991) monograph on one particular society (the Davenport Academy of Sciences, Iowa).

8. See Meltzer (1985) and Hinsley (1981) for discussions of the Bureau of American Ethnology during this period.

9. The lack of adequate temporal typologies of artifacts led Thomas (1885, p. 70) to support his otherwise well-founded case by arguing against any great time-depth.

10. See Brew (1968) for a fuller discussion of the founding of the Peabody Museum.

11. Jones (1864); Wyman (1868b) and Schumacher (1873) even call the shell-mounds "kjökken-möddings" (kitchen-middens).

12. Even earlier, both Charles Lyell and F. W. Putnam (1883, 1899) expressed similar views; see also Dexter (1966a, p. 152).

13. For a biography of Putnam see Tozzer (1935).

14. Gibbs' (1862) "Instructions for Archaeological Investigations in the United States," in the *Annual Report of the Smithsonian Institution for 1861,* clearly shows these European influences.

15. Clewlow (1970); but see also Jennings (1968, p. 34).

16. See Schultz (1945) for further details on Hrdlička's career.

17. Trigger (1989, pp. 270–275) argues that the beginning of functional considerations of archaeological data in the Americas can be marked by H. I. Smith's work at the Fox Farm site and can be further traced through the research of scholars such as Parker, Webb, and Wintemberg. As we discuss in Chapter Four, although there certainly were a number of isolated examples of functional thinking in the decades prior to the late 1930s, functional analyses did not enter general archaeological consciousness until much later. Our argument here is similar to that presented below for stratigraphic excavation, which certainly was practiced occasionally prior to the early twentieth century, but did not become a regular part of archaeological fieldwork until after the research of Nelson and Gamio.

18. On general evolutionary grounds, Mills (1907) felt that the more complex-looking Hopewell culture was later than the Fort Ancient culture. He even tried to use some stratigraphic data to bolster this contention.

19. For background on Dall's life, see Merriam (1927).

20. Kehoe (1989) criticizes us for the small number of women cited in this history. In this connection, Nuttall is one of the very first women to have published in American archaeology. If the number of women cited herein is low — and it is obvious that it is — this should be attributed to the bias of the field up until very recent times rather than to the biases of the present authors. It also is of interest to note that of the post-1980 references added to this new edition, nearly one-quarter have female authors.

21. Tozzer, a student of Putnam's and an early Harvard Ph.D., trained a whole generation of students in Middle American archaeology (Phillips, 1955; Willey, 1988).

22. Bernal (1977) gives considerable detail on Mayanists prior to 1880.

23. Förstemann (1906; see Ian Graham, 1971). Joseph T. Goodman (1897, 1905) made similar discoveries, but it is not completely clear how independent these were of the work of Förstemann.

24. Landa (1864); see also Landa (1941) for an annotated translation by Tozzer.

25. See Rowe (1954) for a discussion of Uhle's career and influence. The significance of much of Uhle's work was not made known until Kroeber and others worked over the Uhle notes and collections a good many years later (Kroeber, 1925a, 1925b, 1926, 1927; Kroeber and Strong, 1924a, 1924b; Gayton, 1927; Gayton and Kroeber, 1927).

26. Uhle had formulated his chronology by 1900, but he referred to it again in later publications (1903, 1910, 1913a, 1913b).

27. Since Uhle's time, it has been recognized that the more probable center for the radiation of Tialnuanaco-like influences to coastal Peru was the site of Huari, near Ayacucho (Menzel, 1964).

28. Uhle went to Ecuador at the invitation of Jacinto Jijón y Caamaño, who was later to become the leading archaeologist of his country (see Jijón y Caamaño, 1914, 1920, 1927). Uhle was influential in this Ecuadorian scholar's development, as he was also in the rise to prominence of the Chilean archaeologist Ricardo Latcham (see Latcham, 1928a, b).

29. Rowe (1954), flyleaf quotation from Uhle.

30. Rowe (1954, Appendix A — Uhle lectures). Rowe's opinion of the influence of cultural evolutionary thinking on Uhle is not as favorable as ours.

31. Hartman (1901, 1907); see also Rowe (1959b) for an appraisal of Hartman.

32. See Mattos (1946) for bibliography on this.

33. Rau (1876); Rau (1879) also made some early observations on a tablet from Palenque, Chiapas, Mexico.

34. For these objectives, see Wright and others (1909, p. 114).

35. See Marvin Harris (1968). The Boasian attitude can also be seen in the evaluation of various archaeological luminaries by Robert H. Lowie (1956); see also Boas (1940). The degree to which antievolutionary attitudes inhibited the growth of interest in the stratigraphic method in archaeology is, however, disputed by J. H. Rowe (1975), who argues that Boas' first criticism of cultural evolution did not appear in print until 1896 and that the debate against evolutionary thinking did not begin in earnest until the 1909–16 period, when it was taken up by students of Boas. Hence, these attitudes came along too late to have stultified the acceptance of stratigraphic ideas, as these had been propounded by a few workers in the latter part of the nineteenth century. We are still unconvinced; however, as we have pointed out in our first edition, Boas deserves credit for being one of the instigators of the stratigraphic method in the Valley of Mexico.

36. Meltzer (1983, pp. 38–40) agrees with Trigger's argument, while taking issue with our discussion above. He contends that antievolutionary think-

ing entered the scene too late to affect the flat-line chronology view of the time. Meltzer also argues that the although personnel of the BAE were evolutionists, their approach was "grounded in a subliminal and denigrating stereotype of the Native American" (Meltzer, 1983, p. 40). While such may have been the case, we find it hard to believe that Powell would have — or just as importantly, countenanced — an anti-Native American bias. Moreover, we believe that Meltzer misunderstands our discussion, since we do not argue that anti-evolutionism caused the lack of time depth in Americanist thinking but rather that the lack of time depth subsequently weakened the ability of archaeologists to counter this anti-evolutionism.

37. Boas (1913) was one of those who encouraged Gamio to make stratigraphic excavations in the Valley of Mexico.

CHAPTER FOUR

The Classificatory-Historical Period:
The Concern with Chronology (1914–40)

Chronology is at the root of the matter, being the nerve
electrifying the dead body of history.

BERTHOLD LAUFER

A DEFINITION OF
THE PERIOD

The central theme of the Classificatory-Historical Period in American archaeology was the concern for chronology. The name of the period, *historical,* carries this implication, at least insofar as history is a time-ordering of events. We will consider the period in two parts: an earlier part, extending from 1914 until 1940, will be the subject of this chapter; a later part, from 1940 until 1960, will be dealt with in Chapter Five. The search for chronology prevailed in both the earlier and later parts of the period, but it was especially dominant in the earlier part. After 1940, other problems began to compete for attention.

Stratigraphic excavation was the primary method in the drive for chronological control of the data. It became a widely recognized part of American archaeology by the beginning of this period and in the next two decades spread to most parts of the New World. The principle of seriation was allied to stratigraphy, and also served chronological ends. Typology and classification, which had their systematic beginnings in the previous Classificatory-Descriptive Period, now became geared to stratigraphic and seriational procedures. Whereas earlier classifications of artifacts had been merely for the purposes of describing the material, they were now seen as devices to aid the plotting of culture forms in time and space. Besides artifact classifications, American archaeologists also began culture classifications. These, too, were strongly influenced by chronological considerations.

Beyond the immediacy of stratigraphic, seriational, and classificatory methods, the ultimate objectives of American archaeology in the

Classificatory-Historical Period were culture-historical syntheses of New World regions and areas. Some of these began to appear before 1940. For the most part, they tended to be mere skeletons of history — pottery type or artifact sequences and distributions. Some archaeologists did attempt to clothe these skeletons in more substantial cultural contexts. The old close relationship between American archaeology and ethnology led easily to the use of ethnographic analogies in interpretations of use and function in prehistoric cultures; and the interest in the relationships between culture and the natural environment that had its beginnings in the culture-area concepts of the ethnologists provided a base for cultural-ecological study. But, prior to 1940, these trends were barely in the making; only later did they come into prominence. Finally, the early part of the Classificatory-Historical Period was characterized by continued improvements of field methods and excavation. These refinements were, indeed, a necessary part of the stratigraphic method that so dominated the period. They were also a part of the recognition of the importance of a careful recovery of materials and features.

The stratigraphic method had been developed in European geology and adapted to European and Mediterranean archaeology. It was known in the Americas at least as early as the 1860s, and we have told how Dall, Uhle, and others carried out occasional stratigraphic excavations. These operations included observations as to the superimposition of the strata and, at least in a gross way, a recording of their artifactual and feature contents. But the method did not become widely popular, nor was it much used by those few who showed an awareness of it.

THE STRATIGRAPHIC REVOLUTION

The reasons for the delay in the acceptance of the stratigraphic method in American archaeology have been discussed in the preceding chapter: the inability of archaeologists of the time to find sudden and dramatic cultural shifts, setting one era or epoch off from another, later reinforced by a rejection of evolutionary thinking. Few American archaeologists seemed interested in problems of minor, gradual changes through time.[1]

Added to these reasons may have been others of a less philosophical, more immediately practical nature. Many American sites, especially those of eastern North America, did not lend themselves readily to stratigraphic digging. Refuse deposits were thin and without easily discernible physical strata. Artificial burial tumuli and other earthworks were not ideal for stratigraphic purposes. Their constructions were often complex; they contained redeposited materials; and their excavation demanded sophisticated digging and interpretative techniques that had not yet been applied or taught in American archaeology. The same disadvantages applied to the great mounds and pyramids of Mesoamerica and Peru. Deep refuse deposits did exist in some places, and, eventually, these would be disclosed; but for a time they went unnoticed. Thus, as we come up to the years just before World War I, little stratigraphic digging of consequence had been carried out in the Americas, and archaeological chronology was in its infancy.

The stratigraphic revolution began at about the same time in two areas—Mesoamerica and the North American Southwest. The two archaeologists responsible for the innovation were Manuel Gamio and N. C. Nelson. Both were young scholars who had been trained in the rising new discipline of anthropology. Gamio had been a student of Franz Boas at Columbia University; and Nelson had worked under Kroeber (a former Boasian disciple) at Berkeley. Significantly, Boas played a part in Gamio's stratigraphic work. In 1911, Boas had become one of the directors of a shortlived organization known as the International School of American Ethnology and Archaeology with offices in Mexico City. He, together with A. M. Tozzer and G. C. Engerrand, encouraged Gamio to conduct stratigraphic excavations in the Valley of Mexico to clarify and demonstrate objectively the sequence of Mexican Pre-Columbian cultures.[2] As far back as the 1880s, W. H. Holmes (1885) had observed that Aztec and earlier potsherds and artifacts were to be found in deep strata in the Valley of Mexico (Schávelzon, 1984), but Holmes made no detailed stratigraphic examination of this situation. In 1911, Gamio, along with the German scholar Eduard Seler, called Boas' attention to the archaeological zone of Atzcapotzalco, where pottery fragments were found in great quantity on the surface and in barranca collections. Some of these pertained to the Aztec civilization, others to Teotihuacan, and still others to a third, unknown complex. While it was generally taken for granted that pottery of the Teotihuacan style preceded that of the Aztec, the position of the third, unidentified style was in doubt. Boas, in response, suggested stratigraphic digging to resolve this problem of sequence.

Gamio began his stratigraphic work by sinking a 7.00 meter test pit into the Atzcapotzalco refuse. Ceramics and other artifacts were removed from arbitrarily chosen levels of the pit. These varied from as little as 20 cm. in thickness to as much as 60 cm. Cultural materials were found to a depth of 5.75 meters below the surface. Although the digging and provenience lots were by arbitrary depth, considerable attention was paid to the depositional nature of the debris and soil and to its physical strata. Aztec pottery was found rather superficially in the humus and dust of the two uppermost arbitrary levels; below this was Teotihuacan pottery, occurring in decomposed volcanic tufa down to a depth of about 4.15 meters; and, from this latter depth down to 5.75 meters, sherds of the unnamed ceramic group (tentatively referred to as the *Tipo de los Cerros*) were found in river sands and gravels, which overlay sterile clay. This unnamed ceramic group was, indeed, soon to be called the *Archaic* pottery of the Valley of Mexico. Subsequently, it would be referred to as *Preclassic or Formative* by a later generation of archaeologists. Gamio and his colleagues recognized it as similar to materials from Zacatenco and elsewhere, establishing an Archaic pottery horizon for the valley. The Atzcapotzalco stratigraphic evidence also supported the interpretations of a gradual transition from this Archaic horizon into that of the Teotihuacan culture. This interpretation of gradual cultural change appeared to be demonstrated by a mixture of both pottery styles in levels of intermediate depth as well as by the transitional nature of certain ceramic and figurine forms in these levels. No pottery counts were made, although a crude sort of quantification was attempted by weighing the potsherds from the various levels of the test pit. From this, Gamio drew some conclusions about relative chronological durations of the respective occupations and the densities of these occupations—a procedure of rather dubious value. The true significance of Gamio's work lay in the fact that he had established the basic archaeological sequence for central Mexico. Seler and other scholars had long worked in the region but had seen things from a descriptive, typological, and iconographical point of view. Although highly aware of ethnohistory, their perspective on the whole Pre-Columbian past was blurred and foreshortened. With Gamio's single pit, Middle American archaeologists began to appreciate time-depth and, better yet, to realize that something could be done about it (R. E. W. Adams, 1960).

Nelson's stratigraphy dates from three years after Gamio's, but his use and refinements of the method go much further.[3] His background is pertinent in helping us trace the spread of ideas in archaeological methods. In 1913, in an off-season during the period in which he was working in the Southwest, he visited Europe and the French and Spanish caves, where Obermeier and Breuil were conducting stratigraphic excavations. In fact, he aided in the digging of the Castillo Cave in Spain. By his own account, this experience made a strong impression on him (see Woodbury, 1960b). He had already had some experience with stratigraphic digging, in the California shell-mounds, under Kroeber's general direction and under the influence of Max Uhle (Nelson, 1909, 1910). Uhle, it will be recalled from our comments in the previous chapter, had attempted to excavate the San Francisco Bay shell-mounds stratigraphically and had put forward a culture sequence of their occupation. Kroeber had remained unconvinced of the value of the sequence in defining significant culture change, and this appears to have had a

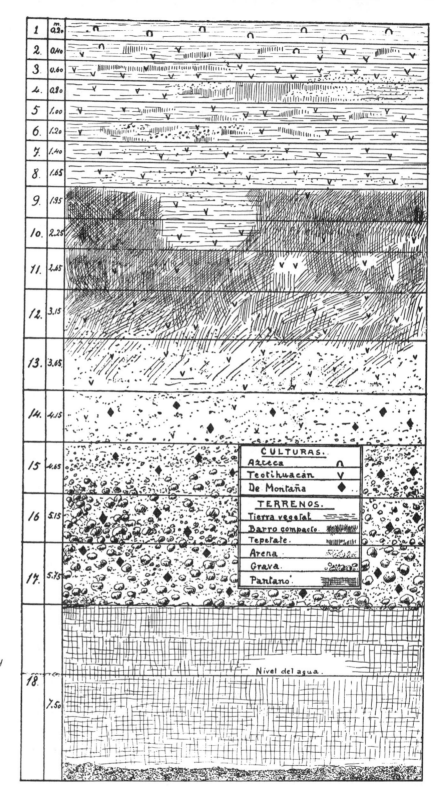

Cross-section diagram of Gamio's excavations at Atzcapotzalco, Valley of Mexico. Numbers of levels and metric depths at left. Soil strata indicated. The inverted U symbol stands for the presence of Aztec pottery; the V for Teotihuacan; and the solid diamond for Archaic pottery. (From Gamio, 1913)

dampening effect on Nelson's work or, at least, his interpretations.[4] But the European experience of a few years later must have turned his mind in this direction again. He returned to the United States and the Southwest between 1913 and 1915, determined to give the stratigraphic method another try. Some results were published as early as 1914, but it was not until 1916 that he made his stratigraphic findings known in an important journal article (Nelson, 1914, 1916).

To see Nelson's Southwestern work in proper perspective, it is necessary to go back a bit. When he began the surveys and excavations for the American Museum of Natural History in the Galisteo Basin of New Mexico, there was a substantial amount known about Rio Grande region archaeology. He had been preceded by Bandelier (1892) and Hewett (1906), and there was a general concensus of opinion "that the Rio Grande Pueblos underwent certain cultural transformations in prehistoric times" (Nelson, 1916, p. 161). Several pottery styles had been identified. These were known to be associated, respectively, with different kinds of Pueblo ruins. One of these styles was clearly associated with early European materials, and a fairly good guess could be made about the chronological order of the others. But, as Nelson said, tangible proof of this chronology was still wanting (Nelson, 1916, p. 162).

Nelson obtained this proof of chronology by stratigraphic excavations at a number of sites in the region, including San Pedro Viejo, Pueblo San Cristobal, and San Marcos. At several sites, superpositions of one pottery type over another were found, but a full sequence placing all the known pottery styles of the region eluded him at first. In some of the sites, Nelson noted that the superpositions were of styles in which the later was probably separated from the earlier by a hiatus—a hiatus in which, he reasoned, one or two of the chronologically unplaced styles of the region would probably fit. At Pueblo San Cristobal, Nelson finally found the deep refuse accumulation that gave him the stratigraphic order of all the Galisteo Basin pottery styles. The debris deposit was ten feet deep, and it was exposed in a creek bank where it had been cut by the stream and was near the Pueblo. It had been used as a place of burial. This fact was duly recorded by Nelson, who comments on the possible dangers of intrusions and disturbances that might confuse true stratification; however, he selected a spot where there were no visible disturbances or distortions in the near-horizontal bedding planes of the refuse. His photograph shows this bedding to be extremely thin and fine, with no clear physical strata of any thickness. Perhaps because of this, he excavated by arbitrary levels, one foot in thickness. The size of the excavation was a three-by-six-foot block.

Potsherds from each of Nelson's arbitrary levels were kept separately, and these sherds were classified and counted by level. No percentages were computed, but the numerical results were presented in a small table. Commenting on the vertical distributions of the sherd styles in this table, Nelson observed that corrugated and "biscuit" wares showed no significant top-to-bottom changes. In contrast, black-on-white types had their maximum occurrence at the bottom of the test and gradually diminished upward. So, the black-on-white style had died out during the occupancy of San Cristobal, or at least during the use of this particular rubbish dump. Early glaze wares had their inception deep in the refuse, reached a maximum of popularity in middle levels, and then diminished at the top levels. A paint-glaze combination style occurred only in the uppermost levels, and Nelson observes that, if the refuse had continued higher, this style, too, would have increased in volume. Obviously, he was thinking very much in terms of the unimodal life-curves of pottery styles and types that are today the stock-in-trade of the archaeologist.

The title of Nelson's 1916 article and the initial pages devoted to the stratigraphic presentation show that the author was aware of its innovative character, but he says nothing whatsoever about the employment of a new method or technique. This is also true of Gamio's article and Boas' contemporary comments about it. Thus, one might think that American archaeologists of *ca.* 1914 took the stratigraphic method for granted. But the published records of the time just do not bear this out. There is no record that Gamio had ever done any digging or observing that was comparable to the pit at Atzcapotzalco prior to that time. Nelson had had his California shelf-mound experience, but this did not involve frequency counts per level in the manner of the Galisteo analyses. We cannot but conclude that Gamio and Nelson had consolidated an archae-

Thickness of Section	Corrugated Ware (1)	Biscuit Ware (2)	Type I, Two- and Three-Color Painted Ware	Type II, Two-Color Glazed Ware			Type III, Three-Color Glazed Ware
			Black-on-White Painted Ware (3)	Red Ware, Black or Brown Glaze (4)	Yellow Ware, Black or Brown Glaze (5)	Gray Ware, Black or Brown Glaze (6)	Gray, Yellow, Pink and Reddish Wares, Combination Glaze-and-Paint Design (7)
1st. ft.	57	10	2	24	23	34	5
2d "	116	17	2	64	90	76	6
3d "	27	2	10	68	18	48	3
4th "	28	4	6	52	20	21	
5th "	60	15	2	128	55	85	
6th "	75	21	8	192	53	52	1 ?
7th "	53	10	40	91	20	15	
8th "	56	2	118	45	1	5	
9th "	93	1 ?	107	3			
10th "	84	1 ?	69				
= 8 in.	(126)		(103)				

Nelson's pottery type counts by level from the excavations in the Galisteo Basin, New Mexico. (From Nelson, 1916)

ological method, at least for the New World, despite the fact that neither claimed any credit for originality in doing so.[5]

Nelson's work led immediately to regional chronology-building. In the same article, he tells how he used this chronology of pottery styles in dating other sites from unit surface collections or from excavated collections from individual Pueblo rooms. In this work, he did not compute percentages or even tabulate frequencies but only noted occurrences or absences of chronologically diagnostic types. For the region, Nelson interpreted the steady, gradual stylistic change—as revealed in the San Cristobal stratigraphy and as suggested in the surface and room collection—as indicating a continuity of populations at the sites. Southwestern archaeology was on its way, with a field method and with hypotheses about cultural-sequence successions generated from this method.

The first Southwestern archaeologist to make use of the stratigraphic method on a large scale was A. V. Kidder (see Woodbury, 1973). A contemporary of Nelson's, Kidder had been trained under Tozzer at Harvard and had taken a course in field methods with the noted Egyptologist G. A. Reisner, one of the most modern archaeological excavators of the early twentieth century. Kidder began his work in the Southwest at about the same time as Nelson, and the latter, in two footnotes to his 1916 paper, records that Kidder's investigations on the Pajarito Plateau (Kidder, 1915) and at Pecos had confirmed his Galisteo pottery sequence. Kidder's dig at Pecos was to be the largest undertaking of its kind to that time in the Southwest, indeed in America north of Mexico, and it still stands as a major site operation.[6] The Pecos site, in the Upper Pecos Valley

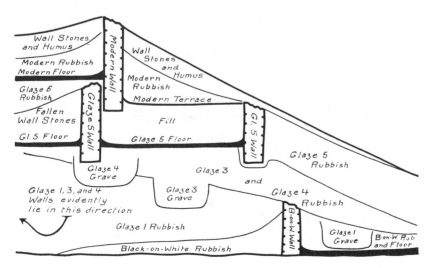

Cross-section diagram of refuse stratigraphy and building walls and floors, Pecos Ruin, New Mexico. The presence of ceramic styles in the refuse is indicated by black-on-white, Glaze 5, and so forth. (From Kidder, 1924, by permission Yale University Press, New Haven)

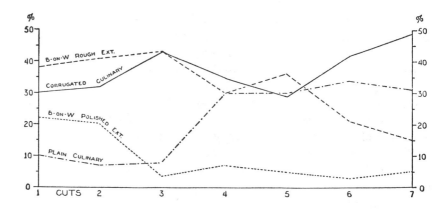

	Number of Sherds							Approximate Percentages						
Cut Number...	1	2	3	4	5	6	7	1	2	3	4	5	6	7
B.-on-w. polished ext. ...	63	65	20	28	9	10	12	22	20	6	7	5	3	5
B.-on-w. rough ext.	108	137	143	126	70	64	39	38	41	43	30	36	21	15
Plain culinary	30	23	27	129	59	106	78	10	7	8	30	30	34	31
Corrugated culinary....	82	104	141	144	58	129	127	30	32	43	33	29	42	49
Totals............	283	329	331	427	196	309	256	100	100	100	100	100	100	100

Table and graph showing sherds and percentage changes per type by level from Forked Lightning. (From Kidder, 1931)

of New Mexico, is actually composed of two ruins, Forked Lightning and Pecos Pueblo proper. As it turned out, Forked Lightning was the earlier settlement, dating back to Pueblo III times (*ca.* A.D. 1000), and, after its abandonment, the villagers apparently moved across the arroyo to a more defensible position. This move is believed to have occurred at about A.D. 1200. Pecos Pueblo was then occupied through the Pueblo IV Period (A.D. 1300–1700) and on into the early nineteenth century.

The refuse at these sites had been deposited adjacent to the living structures, and it had also been built over in successive room additions to the Pueblo construction. In some places, where debris had been thrown over old escarpments, it had accumulated to a depth of 20 feet. Kidder described the nature of this refuse, the probable history of its deposition, and his methods of excavation in great detail (Kidder, 1924, 1931). For the pure rubbish heaps at the edges of the site, initial trenches were first cut into these great piles to obtain deep profile exposures. Only selected sherds were saved and noted from these initial trenches; but, with these deep profile exposures as guides, more thorough and careful excavation then proceeded by natural or physical strata, and potsherds were assigned provenances according to such strata units. The profiles were carefully examined for signs of intrusion or disturbance, and places where these were observed were eliminated as locations for stratigraphic tests. In some instances, columns or blocks of refuse were isolated on two, three, or four sides to allow for a more rigorous examination for intrusions. In these instances, pegs and strings were used to mark off physical strata on all sides of the block for the convenience of the excavators.

The potsherds from these controlled Pecos provenances were classified and tabulated, and, in the final report, these tabulations were offered both as numbers of sherds per type per provenance unit and as corresponding percentages. These results were also expressed in linear graphs drawn for percentages of types per unit or level. In general, the Forked Lightning-Pecos ceramic history was much the same as that which Nelson had found in the Tano refuse heaps of the Galisteo Basin — a decline of black-on-white wares through time with an increase of glaze wares — and, in fact, Nelson's results were of aid to Kidder in the excavations at Pecos. No single test of Kidder's gave quite the whole chronological story, but the percentage frequency figures for the Forked Lightning strata pit were easily fitted onto the figures for the lower levels of the Pecos Pueblo excavations; the well-tested ceramic chronology derived from all of these excavations and analyses was then applied to the dating of between-floor and between-wall deposits in the more complex stratigraphic situations.

From the Pecos excavations, Kidder went on to extend and integrate his stratigraphic method into a regional strategy of cultural-chronological research. In his own words (Kidder, 1931, pp. 6–7), this strategy or plan of attack consisted of five steps:

1. Preliminary survey of remains in the region under consideration.
2. Selection of criteria for ranking those remains in chronological order.
3. Comparative study of the manifestations of the criteria to arrive at a tentative chronological ranking of the sites containing them.
4. Search for and excavation of sites in which materials may be found in stratigraphic relationship in order to check up on the tentative ranking and also to obtain a large number of specimens for morphological and genetic studies.
5. A more thorough resurvey of the area in the light of the fuller knowledge now at hand in order definitely to rank all sites and, if necessary, to select for excavation new sites which may be expected to elucidate problems raised during the course of the research.

In other words — (1) reconnaissance; (2) selection of criteria; (3) seriation for probable sequence; (4) stratigraphic digging; and (5) more detailed regional survey and dating of sites.

Before Kidder had concluded his work at Pecos, the stratigraphic method was being employed by others in the Southwest. Erich Schmidt made tests of this nature on the Lower Gila in 1925, publishing pottery-type frequency count and percentages, along with graphic representation of the results (Schmidt, 1928). He was followed in this tradition by other Southwestern archaeologists, including the Gladwins (Gladwin, 1928; Winifred and H. S. Gladwin, 1929, 1935; Gladwin and others, 1937), Haury (1937, 1936a, 1936b, 1940; also in Gladwin and others, 1937), Roberts (1929, 1931, 1932), and Martin (Martin, Roys, and Von Bonin, 1936; Martin, Rinaldo, and Kelly, 1940).

Outside of the Southwest, G. C. Vaillant, who had been a student assistant of Kidder's at Pecos, published his first detailed stratigraphic work on the Valley of Mexico in 1930,[7] refining and extending back further in time the knowledge of the Archaic or Preclassic cultures that Gamio had revealed in the bottom of his Atzcapotzalco test. In 1932, W. C. Bennett (1934) carried out similar tests at Tiahuanaco, Bolivia, a site known for its stylistic relationships to one of the horizon markers in

Pottery type designs and their changes through time as seen in the Snaketown (Hohokam subarea) sequence. (From Gladwin and others, 1937)

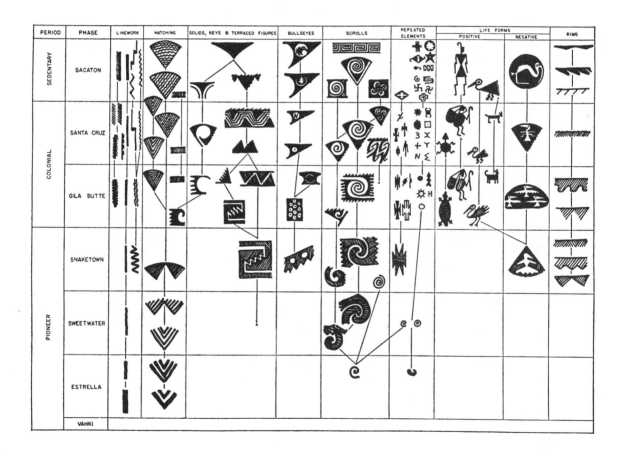

Uhle's early chronological scheme for the Peru-Bolivian area. H. B. Collins, Jr. (1937, 1940) and Frederica De Laguna (1934) developed an Alaskan Arctic chronology in Eskimo archaeology through combined uses of stratigraphy and seriation. And, in the latter part of the 1930s, detailed stratigraphic procedures became the vogue in the eastern United States, particularly in the Southeast under the leadership of Ford (1935, 1936, pp. 257–258), Webb,[8] and others.[9]

One interesting aspect of this American development of the stratigraphic method was the strong emphasis on metrical, as opposed to natural, stratigraphy. As we have seen, this metrical digging began with Gamio and Nelson. In commenting on the latter's work in the Galisteo Basin, R. B. Woodbury, an Americanist, states that Nelson added a refinement to the long-familiar principle of superposition by excavating in arbitrary and uniform metrical levels rather than depending on visibly separable strata.[10] On the other hand, the merits of metrical stratigraphy are questioned by many Old World archaeologists. Among these, Sir Mortimer Wheeler (1954, p. 53) argues that visible or natural strata are the only safe guides in excavating the events of the sequent past. Kidder appears to have been one of the few, or perhaps the only, American stratigrapher of the 1920s and 1930s who favored the natural as opposed to the metrical method. He states this very explicitly (1931, pp. 9–10): "In dividing the column (of refuse) into layers (preparatory to excavation) care was taken to follow a natural division, such as a layer of ash or charcoal, a hard-packed living surface, etc., rather than an arbitrary line. The resultant layers were not always of equal volume, nor did they have necessarily a uniform trend, but they did represent the actual structure of the column...." But his Americanist colleagues seem to have believed, or at least to have operated, otherwise. Schmidt, Haury, Vaillant, Bennett, Collins, and the eastern North American archaeologists all dug by metrical units. In so doing, in almost every case there was an awareness of the importance of physical strata as a part of the record of the past, and physical soil zones were correlated with arbitrary digging levels or provenance blocks on profile diagrams and in text discussion; however, the physical zone, stratum, or lens was rarely utilized as the provenance unit in artifact or pottery analyses.

The reasons for this difference between the American stratigraphic digging methods and the more frequent use of the natural or physical soil zone unit of digging in the Old World are, like the reasons for the delay in the acceptance of the method as a whole in the Americas, uncertain and open to speculation. To be sure, reasons have been given by some diggers. Haury (Gladwin and others, 1937, pp. 22–25) explains his preference for the arbitrary block-unit digging in the Snaketown refuse heaps by pointing out that this method gave him a more satisfactory vertical and horizontal control of the excavated materials than if he were to attempt to dig by following the numerous small and complexly bedded strata and lenses of the refuse. In this connection, he mentions that these natural or physical strata were too small and represented spans of time too brief to be of individual significance in determining the periods or phases of the refuse growth. Vaillant (1930, pp. 19–30) argues that the physical complexities of the Zacatenco site, in which refuse and semidestroyed architectural features were found over a hill slope, made physical strata digging impossible or inadvisable; and most of the other Americanists, when they comment on it at all, explain their preference for metrical stratigraphy in terms of the peculiarities of the formation of the deposits in question. We would also suggest that the widespread use of metrical stratigraphy in the Americas, and especially in the United States, reflects the lack of physically visible strata in many relatively shallow sites.[11] Finally, we would also say that, although we agree with Old World colleagues as to the limitations and hazards of metrical stratigraphy we do not see it as all bad. It is true that it can never be substituted for natural stratigraphy, but it can be used for further refinements within a framework of natural stratigraphy, and it can serve well in calibrating culture change in physical situations where it is the only kind of stratigraphy that can be employed.[12]

SERIATION

*S*eriation, in its simplest definition, is the arrangement of phenomena or data into series by some consistent principle of ordering. In archaeology, however, seriation is almost always concerned with time-ordering of the data. Other kinds of ordering, those reflecting geographical or functional variation in culture, are certainly possible, but seriations of this nature are relatively rare in archaeology.

Seriation is effected by taking into account the characteristics of the archaeological materials themselves and the differences among these characteristics. In this sense, the method is more uniquely archaeological than stratigraphy, the other prime method of determining relative chronology, for, whereas stratigraphy derives from the geological principle of superposition, seriation might be said to have its theoretical framework entirely in cultural history (Dunnell, 1970; Rouse, 1967).

Archaeological seriation has proceeded by observing two basic principles. One of these has been to assume that some kind of inevitable order guides culture change through time. Usually, this has been an evolutionary conception of simple-to-complex development, and such seriation has, accordingly, been referred to as *evolutionary seriation*. The second principle of seriation is by similarity, and hence is called *similiary seriation*

(Rowe, 1961). This means that the data units — the archaeological objects, groups of objects, or features of objects — are arranged in a series in accordance with their similarities, one to another; like is placed closest to like. The assumption behind this is that cultural change is gradual — at least within the same cultural tradition. The first and most notable example of evolutionary seriation in archaeology was Thomsen's ordering of the collections in the Danish National Museum on the assumption that the local culture had developed through a sequence of Stone, Bronze, and Iron Ages (Rouse, 1967; Daniel, 1950). In this case, subsequent archaeological research has validated this seriation many times over; however, other evolutionary seriations have sometimes been disproven by stratigraphic or absolute dating checks, so that the evolutionary principle of seriation cannot be considered as routinely valid archaeological procedure. On the other hand, the results arrived at by similiary seriation, when the method has been properly applied, have been uniformly reliable, being frequently confirmed by stratigraphy and various means of absolute dating. As a result, the similiary seriational principle is a widely accepted means of arriving at chronology — both in America and elsewhere — and, in fact, the word *seriation,* as now used, virtually always refers to similiary seriation. However, evolutionary and similiary principles have often been applied jointly. In American archaeology, a classic example would be Spinden's *A Study of Maya Art,* to which we have referred in the previous chapter. This work, published in 1913, utilized both evolutionary reasoning and similiary ordering of art forms to seriate chronologically Maya monuments and sculptures.

In tracing the rise and development of similiary seriation in the Americas, we should first record that it had become an accepted principle in European archaeology by the latter half of the nineteenth century. Worsaae's grave lot study of the 1840s utilized unit collections for comparison with each other and embodied the seriational idea (Rowe, 1962b). John Evans and others applied the similiary seriational principle to British data shortly after this. By the end of the century, the concept was well developed, especially as practiced and explained by Sir Flinders Petrie in Egypt (Rouse, 1967; Petrie, 1899, 1904). Petrie, we know, influenced Uhle, and this suggests one line of contact whereby the seriational principle may have spread to the New World. Of course, it is also possible, or even likely, that Uhle already was aware of the earlier European grave-lot seriational studies before he was familiar with Petrie's work. Another possible source for the spread of similiary seriation to the New World might have been Franz Boas. The "father of American anthropology" was German born and trained; he was probably acquainted with European studies of a seriational nature; and we know that he had made a kind of informal seriation of potsherd refuse from surface collections in the Valley of Mexico shortly before Gamio's stratigraphic excavations in the same region. In fact, the study of these collections, and the implications they held for chronology, were among the reasons that prompted Boas to urge Gamio to carry out his stratigraphic tests. In any event, it may well be significant that A. L. Kroeber, who was the first to demonstrate the effectiveness of similiary seriation for chronological ordering in the southwestern United States, was both a student and colleague of Boas as well as a close associate of Uhle.

Kroeber's paper on seriation, entitled "Zuñi Potsherds," was written in 1915, immediately upon the conclusion of the fieldwork on which it was based, and published in the following year (Kroeber, 1916). Together with the monograph by Leslie Spier, which appeared in 1917 and which we shall discuss later, it proved to be the viable beginnings for the propagation of the seriational method in New World archaeology. Kroeber describes his field operations as rather casual ones. He began collecting potsherds from the surfaces of Southwestern ruins as a kind of pastime on afternoon walks in the vicinity of Zuñi Pueblo, where he was primarily engaged in ethnological studies. In the course of these walks, he encountered eighteen abandoned site locations within a half-hour's hiking distance of the inhabited Zuñi Pueblo. At first, even before collecting specimens, Kroeber noted that some of these sites showed surface potsherds of a black-on-red style, whereas only white-slipped or black-on-white types were found on others. Eventually, he began systematic collection of sherds from the surfaces of all the sites. Concurrently with this, he read summaries of Zuñi history, and then he saw that those sites that were known to have been inhabited by the Zuñi peoples in the seventeenth century all showed predominantly red and black-on-red wares. In contrast, those sites with mostly white or black-on-white pottery were not recorded as having been inhabited in this early historical period. This established the red and black-on-red pottery complex at the upper or historical end of a postulated chronological series and the white and black-on-white pottery complex at the lower or most remotely prehistorical end of the series. Other sites displaying mixtures of black-on-red and black-on-white types were seriated, according to the relative proportions of these complexes, to intermediate chronological positions in this time-scale. Such a procedure led to the establishment of six subperiods, each marking a distinct segment of ceramic stylistic change (and time) on the seriated scale. The sequence was further confirmed by the steady decrease of a single pottery ware, corrugated, throughout the time-scale from the earliest to the latest subperiods.

Although Kroeber started this investigation by what is sometimes called *occurrence seriation* (Dunnell, 1970), in which only the presence or absence of the seriated units (the pottery complexes) were noted, he shifted his approach to *frequency seriation* in the course of the study, utilizing percentages of potsherds of the different types within the complexes to carry the refinements of the seriation in the six subperiods; his presentations of the data include tables listing sites and the percentages of the diagnostic pottery types found in each site collection. This frequency approach led him to conclude that the cultural history of the Zuñi region, insofar as it was represented by the eighteen sites in question, did not "represent two different migrations, nationalities, or waves of culture," as exemplified by the black-on-red and black-on-white pottery complexes, "but rather a steady and continuous development on the soil," as, for example, was implied in the gradual replacement of one group (or type) by another and the continuity throughout of the corrugated ware (Kroeber, 1916, p. 15). Kroeber concluded by saying that his sequence needed stratigraphy to substantiate it and that future studies of this kind should first be carried out on a similarly small regional basis before attempting multiregional comparisons and erecting more sweeping chronologies. In all of this, it is interesting to note that not once did Kroeber use the term *seriation.*

A longer and more detailed study of Zuñi region chronology by Leslie Spier (1917) followed immediately upon Krober's work. Spier, of course, was familiar with what Kroeber had done and also had spent three weeks in the field with Nelson in the summer of 1916. He devoted 30 pages of his report to a location and description of the ruins, which he included in his survey, along with a good site map. He referred to Kroeber's work as "associational seriation" based on "concurrent variations in associated constituents in the samples." This appears to be the first use of the term *seriation* in American archaeology. He also noted Nelson's stratigraphy and declared it his purpose to test both methods, cross-checking them against one another. One way he did this was to excavate stratigraphic pits in some of the same sites from which Kroeber had made surface collections. The results confirmed the surface collection seriations.

Of his own surface collection seriations, Spier (1917, p. 282) tells us:

> The first subgroup (of pottery collections) contains thirty-five samples from as many ruins. The wares are corrugated, black-on-white, black-on-red, and black-and-white-on-red. These samples may be arbitrarily ranked according to their percentages of corrugated ware from highest to lowest. The test of such a seriation as an historical series will lie in the observed seriation of the accompanying wares; for, when a group of three or more distinct, but mutually dependent, values are ranked according to some postulated sequence for one, and the other values are found to present serially concurrent variations, it may be concluded that the result is not fortuitous.

This is one of the best and most concise definitions of archaeological seriation in the literature. Spier supported his presentations of the data with tables and frequency graphs. He extended Kroeber's sequence substantially further back into the past with a second subgroup of pottery collections from other sites. In this second subgroup, there was again concurrent variation between corrugated ware and painted types, but Spier was aware that the concurrences and painted types were not the same as those for the first subgroup of sites. What this meant was that, in the second subgroup of sites, he had the earlier half of the corrugated-ware frequency curve, the half in which this ware was on the increase. The full and extended seriational sequence thus showed a complete life-curve for corrugated pottery, beginning with its inception at slightly more than 0 percent of the sherd sample, increasing to as much as 50 percent in mid-sequence, and dropping from this popularity peak to 0 percent again at the end of the sequence. In this life-span, the corrugated ware was first associated with black-on-white pottery types and then with black-on-red types. Spier concluded his report (1917, p. 326) with a statement in defense of seriation: "We have no reason to doubt that the samples of potsherds collected from successive levels of ash heaps present us with valid chronological indices. Why then cavil at the use of similar samples from the surfaces of ash heaps?"

Following Spier's work, seriation became standard archaeological procedure in the North American Southwest. It was utilized especially in site survey in connection with surface pottery collections and the relative dating of these. Nor was the similiary seriational principle altogether confined to pottery. Nelson (1920) applied it to Southwestern masonry types, and F. H. H. Roberts (1939) seriated Southwestern architectural forms in a time-sequence running from single-room pit-houses to multiroom above-ground pueblos. In this, Roberts was guided by architectural-pottery associations as well as by sequent similarity in building forms; however, this was in keeping with the general build-up of chronological knowledge within the Southwestern area. As more became known, it grew progressively easier to fit newly discovered data into a framework of existing information, with the results of stratigraphy and seriation cross-checking each other.

While the Southwestern archaeologists were operating with potsherd collections, and percentage frequencies of pottery types within these unit collections, a variant seriational procedure was being employed in Peru. This was a stylistic similiary seriation, in which individual pottery vessels were assigned to style groups, and then traits or features on the vessels were tabulated and plotted from group to group. This particular kind of similiary seriation had been done by Petrie in Egypt; and Uhle, perhaps through his knowledge of Petrie's writings, had made use of it in Peru. Uhle, though, published little in this regard that was explicit. It remained for Kroeber, together with some of his students, to make the Peruvian seriations explicit. This was done in a series of papers in the 1920s, in which Kroeber shifted from the potsherd frequency seriation he had pioneered in the Southwest to a grave-lot and stylistic approach that could be adapted to the Uhle collections. These collections came from a great many Peruvian cemeteries, and, fortunately, Uhle had carefully tabulated the specimens and determined their provenance by the grave-lot associations in which he had found them. The collections from the Ica Valley of the South Peruvian coast may be taken as an example of Kroeber's seriational treatment. W. D. Strong, then a graduate student at Berkeley, was the junior author.[13] The entire pottery vessel collection, numbering over 600 specimens, was classified by Kroeber and Strong into seven distinct styles. The grave-lot associations of these vessels offered clear clues to the chronological separateness of the styles: "In no case do the contents of one grave include objects of more than one style" (Kroeber and Strong, 1924a, p. 96). The main burden of the seriation, however, was not in the grave-lot units but in the nature of the styles themselves. Treating each of the seven styles as a unit, all the vessels assigned to a given style were then tabulated for traits of vessel form, uses of color or modeling treatment, and decorative design elements. From these tabulations, a similiary seriation was effected, whereby the seven styles were arranged in what was believed to be a chronological order. As one of the styles was recognizable as Inca, this gave an upper chronological end to the series; immediately preceding this was the Late Ica II style, so placed because it shared certain vessel form and decorative traits with the Inca style; Late Ica I preceded this on the basis of its similarities to Late Ica II; and the series was carried from here backward in time through the remaining four styles, which were also assumed to have been cultural phases.

Further Uhle collections from other Peruvian valleys were similarly studied by Kroeber and his associates. An interesting innovation in one instance was Strong's use of statistical coefficients of correlation in a seriational arrangement of styles (Strong, 1925). The materials in this case came from the Ancon Necropolis, and the statistical treatment verified the more usual observational analysis of pottery traits as well as the excavation notes of Uhle, who had detected some grave superpositions that served to indicate chronological ordering.

Stylistic similiary seriations in the manner of Uhle, Kroeber, and Strong were to be continued in Peru by John H. Rowe and his students, but these studies were not made until the 1950s and 1960s. The more immediate exploitation of the similiary seriational method followed the Southwestern surface sherd collection and type frequency model, and the archaeologist most responsible was James A. Ford, working in the southeastern United States.

At the beginning of the 1930s, Ford had worked with Henry B. Collins, Jr. in Alaskan archaeology. There, relative chronology had been worked out by a combination of stratigraphy and the association of prehistoric Eskimo villages with a series of old beach lines: the older ones farther inland, the younger ones progressively closer to the modern shore (Collins, 1937). This provided a chronological yardstick by which to arrange bone and ivory implements and ornaments in sequence and to study the gradual change in the forms and decorations of these artifacts through time. Although Collins' procedures were not initially seriational, they became secondarily so, and Ford was especially impressed with the gradualism of cultural change as registered in the rise and fall in popularity of types and styles.[14]

Ford carried this in mind when he returned to his home in the southeastern United States and obtained a post as an archaeological research associate with the Louisiana State Geological Survey. He did some stratigraphic digging in the middle 1930s, but his most important work of the period was a monograph on prehistoric village-site potsherd collections, which appeared in 1936. In the introductory pages to this work, Ford sounded the call for chronological information for the Southeastern area. He pointed out that archaeological sites of the area tend to be thin, lessening the possibilities for stratigraphy. To overcome this, he recommended a method of site survey and surface collecting and an approach to chronology that begins with the documented European historical horizon and works backward from there in time. He also concerned himself with a number of methodological questions. In arguing that change in ceramic styles will be gradual and generally uniform over the area of his survey, he noted that the area selected — the adjacent portions of Louisiana and Mississippi — is reasonably small and that within it the ceramic art must have been kept within fairly definite stylistic bounds. In other words, he attempted to define a ceramic or a cultural tradition and to recognize the necessity for such traditional boundaries as a prerequisite for similiary seriation, concerns we do not meet with in the literature on American archaeological seriation until several decades later.[15] He showed an awareness of some of the limitations of dealing with surface collections of potsherds alone, admitting that some deposits of pottery at a site might lie completely buried and therefore not be represented in surface collections. For the relatively thin Southeastern Native American village sites, he dismissed this, however, as being an unusual circumstance not frequently met with. In further concerning himself with the representativeness of random pottery surface collections, Ford made as many as three separate collections at some sites. Tabulating the difference between type percentages from one collection to another, he arrived at an average variation, which he subsequently observed is consistently smaller as the collections are larger. In sum, he makes a convincing case for his method.

In his substantive results, Ford defined seven ceramic complexes. Each complex is represented by the collections from a certain number of sites. Four such complexes can be designated as historical and, through geographical location of sites, documentation of historical site locations, and associations of glass beads and other early European trade items, these four complexes are identified, respectively, with the Caddo, Tunica, Natchez, and Choctaw tribes that occupied the Lower Mississippi Valley country in the sixteenth and seventeenth centuries. Three other complexes — Coles Creek, Deasonville, and Marksville — are regarded as fully prehistoric. Their chronological relationships in regard to the historical complexes and to each other are then arrived at by what is, in effect, *occurrence similiary seriation*. That is, some of the historical period complexes share some few types with the Coles Creek complex. Coles Creek and Deasonville are reckoned to be at least in part contemporaneous through the evidences of trade between the two; however, there is no typological overlap between Deasonville and the historical horizon complexes. Thus, Deasonville is presumed to have come to an end as a cultural or ceramic complex before Coles Creek died out. Finally, there is some typological overlap and similiary continuity between certain pottery design motifs running from Marksville through Coles Creek to Natchez. Here the reasoning is of the order of that employed by Kroeber and others in Peruvian stylistic seriations.

Two years later, Ford published an article on the applicability of a seriational method in the Southeast (Ford, 1938). Whereas, in the earlier monograph, he appears to have been groping his way toward such a method, it has now come clear in his mind. It remains, nevertheless, a rather sketchy outline. He seems to be speaking of occurrence rather than frequency seriation, although, in the monograph, he had made the statement that frequency, or quantitative, analysis of pottery types per collection was of major importance. Although Ford cites no specific bibliographical references in this second article, he lists titles, including a later retrospective work of Spier's on Southwestern stratigraphy (and seriation) (Spier, 1931) and Kroeber's famous paper "On the Principle of Order in Civilization as Exemplified by Changes of Fashion" (Kroeber, 1919). The latter is concerned with the configurations of gradual and rhythmic trends or curves of change — as illustrated by women's dress lengths — rather than with seriation proper; however, Kroeber's concepts undoubtedly reinforced Ford's thinking. In all this early work of Ford's, one has the impression that his methodology was largely self-discovered. Only later, as he became more sophisticated and better read in anthropology, did Ford begin to appreciate what he had achieved in the context of the anthropological and archaeological literature. A good many years later he brought out his more evolved frequency seriation (Ford, 1962).

If we confine ourselves strictly to the earlier part of the Classifica-tory-Historical Period, the most elaborate and refined similiary seria-tional procedures in American archaeology were those of Irving Rouse, published in 1939 in his monograph *Prehistory in Haiti, A Study in Method*. As the title implies, the intent of the book was essentially methodologi-cal; more strictly substantive treatments of the Haitian archaeological data were presented separately (Rouse, 1941). In formulating a time-scale for these cultures in the West Indies, Rouse was forced to rely primarily on seriation, deep stratified sites being lacking. Like Ford, he dealt entirely with ceramics. These were collections of sherds taken from a series of site excavations on the island. The sherds were grouped into twelve types, Rouse's *type* being more or less the equivalent of Ford's *complex*. On a more detailed level of typological examination were 51 *modes*. These modes pertained to vessel-form features (flat-topped rims), surface decorative elements (naturalistic ornamentation), or materials or conditions of manufacture, such as temper or firing. As such, the modes overlapped, to a degree, between types and provided a means of chro-nologically seriating the types. To demonstrate this seriation, Rouse selected eight modes that appeared to differ most in frequencies of occurrence from site to site. Percentages of occurrence were computed and graphed for these modes, and the site collections were placed serially by percentage trends. Time-direction to the seriation was given through the aid of very short stratigraphic sequences from some of the sites. In these seriations, Rouse worked on the assumption that all his ceramic data belonged to a single cultural-ceramic tradition, and he recognized that, without this assumption, seriation would have been impossible. The assumption was, indeed, borne out by the very clear continuity of many modes between his earlier Meillac and his later Carrier ceramic types. He was also specific about two other assumptions, that frequencies of modes varied independently and that each mode described a normal, or cyclical, frequency curve through time. Rouse felt that both of these assumptions were validated, respectively, by the fact that the graphed curves for changes in modal frequency were all some-what different and by the further fact that all such curves were unimodal.

Rouse's seriations were finer grained than Ford's, particularly in their use of the mode entity; but, perhaps more significant than this, Rouse was more conscientiously explicit in describing and explaining all his seriational operations in great detail. No other work in American archaeology up to that time—not even Spier's 1917 study—had shown such a self-conscious awareness of archaeological assumptions and procedures as *Prehistory in Haiti, A Study in Method.*

Typology and classification lie at the very core of archaeology; and our names, *Classificatory-Descriptive* and *Classificatory-Historical,* point up the difference in typological-classificatory procedures and goals for these two periods. Classification of the earlier period was, indeed, descriptive taxonomy. The diagnostic attributes or modes that were selected for definition of artifact types were chosen for what they indicated about the intrinsic nature of these artifacts. Beyond this, the goals of the typology were not stated. It was enough that the data of prehistory were being treated systematically, perhaps for a purpose no more philosophically profound than the arrangement of items in a museum case. Toward the end of the Classificatory-Descriptive Period, the dimension of geography did creep into classificatory studies. Although the initial operations were descriptive, students like Holmes observed that certain pottery and artifact types did have certain geographical distributional correlates. But this was as far as it went.

TYPOLOGY AND ARTIFACT (POTTERY) CLASSIFICATION

With the introduction of chronology into the data in the Classificatory-Historical Period, archaeologists were forced into more finely detailed and formally defined typologies to plot their data on the time-chart properly. As Rouse has said, such types were clearly historical as opposed to being merely descriptive.[16] Such historical taxonomy dominated the period, especially its earlier part. Not until after 1940, when concerns of context and function began to share the archaeological stage with chronology, did other kinds of artifact classifications appear (Rouse, 1960).

But to go back to the beginning of the Classificatory-Historical Period we see some studies that might be described as transitional between purely descriptive classification and classification designed to aid in chronology-building. S. K. Lothrop's two-volume monograph *Pottery of Costa Rica and Nicaragua* would be an example. Written in 1920–21 and published in 1926 after some revisions, it was based on a museum examination of some 3,500 to 4,000 pottery vessels. These specimens had come from graves excavated by amateurs and without provenance data, except of a general geographical sort. Realizing these deficiencies in the data, Lothrop knew he was limited primarily to descriptive treatment; however, he could do some gross geographical-distribution studies, and, hopefully, he might make comparative studies with reference to adjoining areas, such as Mesoamerica, which would give clues to chronology. Indeed, he was able to do this after a fashion by noting the presence of certain Maya Old Empire (or Classic) elements on some of his Costa Rica-Nicaragua polychrome pottery of the Nicoya style, and he also saw central Mexican (Toltec and Aztec) relationships to other Nicoya pieces (Lothrop, 1926; pp. 392-417). Still, developing a chronology in this manner was a risky business, and Lothrop left the matter with the final observation that, although considerable time-depth must be represented in the Costa Rica-Nicaragua collections, any regional chronology would have to be developed through fieldwork on and in the ground.[17] In retrospect, it seems likely that similiary seriation might have been a help in working out chronology for Lothrop; however, he makes no mention of the possibility.

Lothrop's actual classification procedures are discussed in less than two pages (1926, pp. 105-106). He established ware groups: polychromes, intermediates (two colors), and monochromes. Within a group—the polychromes, for example—he had named wares (Nicoya Polychrome), each defined by decorative motifs and techniques, and sometimes he divided these wares into subwares. But Lothrop's attention really focused on the individual specimen rather than the class or type. There are no statistical or numerical treatments of the data, either as whole vessels or as attributes of vessels.

It remained for the archaeologists in the southwestern United States to take the lead again, this time in devising types geared for chronology. As such, these pottery types were the logical outgrowths of stratigraphic and seriational methods on potsherds. The potsherd, by its very nature, became a kind of tab, a statistical unit highly adapted for counting and manipulation; and, as a result, chronological advances in the Southwest were rapid. However, the whole methodology had a feedback that was not altogether happy. The potsherd grew steadily farther away from the whole pot, from the larger cultural context, and from the people who made the pottery. A reaction was to set in against this some years later, but, for the time, such potsherd archaeology represented the vanguard in American studies.

One of the earliest, ablest, and most indefatigable exponents of such Southwestern pottery classifications was H. S. Gladwin, working from a private-foundation archaeological-survey base in southern Arizona. Together with Winifred Gladwin, he began a series of publications in 1928 that outlined a procedure for site description and designation, potsherd collection, and pottery classification and nomenclature.[18] This was followed, through the 1930s, by other publications that described and illustrated pottery types in handbook fashion (W. and H. S. Gladwin, 1931; Haury, 1936b; Sayles, 1936). Not unduly concerned with methodological or theoretical questions, the Gladwins went directly to the substantive matter at hand, the description of the types. As a consequence, there is much that is implicit and little that is explicit in their operations. Nevertheless, it is clear that they regarded pottery styles as sensitive indicators of culture change and viewed the potsherds as keys to spatial-temporal variation in culture. Along with their Southwestern colleagues,[19] they saw the necessity of keeping the pottery type as a unit that could be easily manipulated. Thus, in type naming, "it was also decided to omit, as far as possible, designations which introduce factors of time or comparison, since their use injects elements which later might require correction" (W. and H. S. Gladwin, 1930). Biological taxonomy served as a guide in establishing a binomial system of pottery type designation. Thus, the color combination or surface treatment of the pottery became the *genus* name (for example, black-on-white) with a geographical locality as the *specific* name (for example, Tularosa). Type descriptions were published in a set format, with name, vessel shape, designs, type site, geographical distribution, known cultural affiliations, and chronological data (Colton and Hargrave, 1937). The "biological" taxonomy, with its possible implications, was disturbing to some archaeologists, and a distinguished physical anthropologist of the time made the caustic observation that "potsherds don't breed." Nevertheless, the procedure had great usefulness and flourished. The essential thing was that the pottery types were commonly agreed-upon units that the archaeologists could examine in space and time with relative ease, and it is unlikely that any but the most unsophisticated conceived of pottery manufacture and development as constrained by the analogue of biological parenthood. To be sure, lines of development leading from one pottery type to another were plotted on the culture time-charts (Colton and Hargrave, 1937, p. 4), but these were recognized as the best available convention for diagraming the spread of cultural ideas through space and time. The limitations of the procedure and the model were not in their genetic implications but in the abstraction from context and overall barrenness. In spite of this, a structure of type, space, and time was erected in the Southwest, which has remained unequaled in its detail and refinement in any other archaeological area of the Americas.

As in the case of stratigraphy and seriation, historical typology moved to the eastern United States from the Southwest in the 1930s, and the archaeologist deserving most of the credit for this was, again, J. A. Ford. Previously, what had been descriptive types in the area were beginning to be recognized as being chronologically indicative. Such categories as *Hopewellian pottery, Woodland pottery,* and *Mississippian pottery* were a part of archaeological discourse in the 1920s and 1930s. Ford's real contribution, over and above this, was to present pottery typology as a part of the package of stratigraphy-seriation-typology, which made possible regional chronologies first in the Southeast and then in the Ohio Valley-Upper Mississippi area. In his seriational and survey monograph of 1936, Ford first made the case for the pottery type as the measuring device of cultural variation in space and time (Ford, 1936); but it was in a conference report on Southeastern pottery classification and nomenclature that he set down his most unequivocal statements on this theme: "The inadequacy of the procedure of dividing pottery into "types' merely for the purposes of describing the material is recognized. This is merely a means of presenting raw data. Types should be classes of material which promise to be useful as tools in interpreting culture history."[20] And, continuing to drive home the case for the definition of types as historical tools, he goes on to say that pottery types must be defined as combinations of all discoverable features — paste, temper, methods of manufacture, decoration, etc. — and "by this [sic] criteria two sets of material which are similar in nearly all features, but which are divided by peculiar forms of one feature (shell contrasted with grit tempering, for example) may be separated into two types if there promises to be some historical justification for the procedure" (Ford, 1938). In other words, there is to be no formal splitting of types, unless this demonstrably correlates with spatial or temporal difference (Krieger, 1944). The necessity of selecting a set of mutually exclusive features to serve as the primary framework of the pottery classification was emphasized, and, as the classification was usually to be applied to sherds, such features would most advantageously be those pertaining to surface finish and decoration. The resultant nomenclature was binomial and much like that of the Southwest. For example, *complicated stamped*, a surface treatment, was the type genus, and the geographical site name, *Swift Creek*, was the specific designant in the type *Swift Creek complicated stamped*. The first Southeastern area pottery type descriptions of the sort were published in the *Newsletter of the Southeastern Archaeological Conference* in 1939.[21]

Elsewhere in the New World, such historical typology was much less formal. In Middle America in the 1930s, Vaillant gave descriptive names to *wares* and *types*. Some of them remained as little more than descriptive types; others, which he dubbed *marker types*, were truly historical, in that they carried his sequence story in the stratigraphy.[22] Bennett's typology at Tiahuanaco was similar, and some of his categories were meaningful chronologically (Bennett, 1934). Both Vaillant and Bennett tended to look upon the pottery complex or the pottery period as a whole. That is, certain forms and features characterized a period, in contrast to another period. This way of conceiving the data was also expressed in R. E. Smith's Uaxactun work in the Maya Lowlands (Smith, 1936a, 1936b, 1955). There, the physical nature of the site, with refuse deposits sealed off and separated from other deposits by plaster floors and stone architectural features, led to a ready utilization of architectural or building periods as a chronology. Pottery complexes were then associated with these periods. As a result, there was less attention to the life-span of the individual type, and frequencies of occurrence were much less important in chronology-formulation than in the Southwest or Southeast.

In his 1939 monograph, Irving Rouse introduced the *analytical* type into American archaeology. Here, the emphasis was on attributes or modes rather than on the artifacts themselves, and it was an archaeological attempt to analyze the procedures and intent of aboriginal manufacture. Although typology still had chronology as an objective—and Rouse, as we have already noted, was much concerned with seriation—there were now the new goals of context and function.

The other main classificatory interest of the early Classificatory-Historical Period was in culture classification. This had no real forerunner in the preceding period. Apparently, some spatial-temporal control over the data was a necessary prerequisite to culture-classificatory thinking. Certainly, it is consistent with this that the first culture-classification scheme appeared in the Southwest. This was the *Pecos Classification*, which derived, especially, out of the early work of Kidder.

In 1927, a meeting of the leading archaeologists then working in the Southwestern area was called at Pecos, New Mexico. The objective of this Pecos Conference was to formulate a general classificatory scheme that would facilitate communication among archaeologists working on related problems (Kidder, 1927). Chronology was foremost in the minds of those present. They wanted a chronological classification of Southwestern cultures that would be generally applicable for the area as a whole. Kidder had already made a beginning along these lines in his first synthesis of the area published three years before (Kidder, 1924), and his concepts and terminology largely prevailed at the conference.

The earlier peoples of the Southwest of which archaeologists then had record were the preceramic Basketmakers of the "four corners" country of the adjacent portions of Arizona, New Mexico, Utah, and Colorado. Thus, the chronology of the Pecos Classification began with the Basketmakers. Believing that they had not yet found the earliest beginnings of this tradition, the conference group designated their earliest period Basketmaker II, leaving room for an undiscovered Basketmaker I. Basketmaker II peoples lived in pit-houses and practiced agriculture. So did their descendants of Basketmaker III, but the latter period was further characterized by the appearance of pottery. Subsequent changes in architecture, community arrangement, pottery

CULTURE-CLASSIFICATION SCHEMES

styles, and other artifacts were marked as the diagnostics of the succeeding Pueblo I–V Periods, the last two periods bridging, respectively, from Pre-Columbian to the early historical horizons and from historical to modern Native American pueblo villages. The Pecos Classification has stood the test of later archaeological research. Some modifications have been suggested (see Roberts, 1935, 1937), and tree-ring dates have given it a greater precision. The accuracy in dating, however, raised theoretical problems, for it became apparent that the Pecos *periods* were perhaps better described as *stages*. For instance, some Southwestern regions were seen to have achieved a Pueblo III or a Pueblo IV condition, as this was marked by architectural styles, before other regions; and the Gladwins, among others, made the criticism that the Pecos Classification was a yardstick of cultural development rather than a scale of time (W. and H. S. Gladwin, 1934). This problem of time-lag from region to region, and the fact that the Pecos Classification was better adapted to the northern or Basketmaker-Pueblo (Anasazi) portions of the Southwest than to the southern Hohokam and southeastern Mogollon territories, led the Gladwins to propose another kind of culture classification.

The Gladwins' culture classification was a direct outgrowth of their site-survey and pottery-classification approaches. In 1934, they published *A Method for the Designation of Cultures and Their Variations*. The title of this short paper is revealing. The Gladwins saw the problem as essentially one of nomenclature. As in their classifications of pottery, there seems little concern about the implications of their genetic-chronological scheme. Using the analogy of a tree, the basic and most fundamental grouping in their culture classification was designated the *root*. These roots were the major cultural divisions of the Southwest, as these were conceived of at that time: the *Basketmaker* (later to be called *Anasazi*), the *Hohokam*, and the *Caddoan* (later designated *Mogollon*).[23] Roots were then seen as subdividing into *stems*. These were assigned regional names, such as *San Juan* or *Playas* (of the Basketmaker Root). Stems were similarly split into still more reduced cultural units called *branches*, and these branches were also designated by geographic terms – *Chaco* or *Kayenta*, for example. The final subdivision was that of the branch into a *phase*. These, too, were given geographical names – *Jeddito*, *Puerco*, and so forth. The phase was the actual working archaeological unit. Phases were defined by comparing site or component remains with other site or component remains and establishing such a unit on the basis of a very high degree of culture-trait similarity.

Although the Gladwin classification was primarily one of cultures, grouped by their relative degrees of culture-trait similarity, space and time were given consideration. The root, stem, and branch formulations all involved geographical territory as well as culture forms. The temporal dimension was given implicit recognition by the genetic model of the scheme: that is, roots, by their very nature, preceded stems, and stems preceded branches. Of course, the further implications of this were a kind of monogenesis of Southwestern cultures: as archaeologists worked backward in time, or down the "tree," they would be discovering fewer and fewer cultural ancestors. Such a monogenesis, while a possibility, was by no means demonstrated for the Southwest. In other words, the scheme had built into it one of the kinds of things it should be designed to test. Actually, as it worked out, these more basic levels of the classification caused little practical difficulty. Sites were dug or surveyed; they or the components within them were classified into the working units, the phases; and these phases were arranged in explicit regional chronologies by stratigraphy and seriation. Modifications of the Gladwin scheme are used today in the Southwest, although in these current uses the rigid genetic structure has been largely dropped, leaving the phases and the regional sequences as the main operational features. Although such regional sequences gave archaeologists closer chronological control over their data than the reference frame of the Pecos Classification, the Gladwin scheme lacked the area-wide generalizing usefulness of the Pecos chronology.

If we refer to the Pecos Classification as *evolutionary-chronologic* and to the Gladwin scheme as *genetic-chronologic*, then a third culture-classificatory arrangement is probably best designated as *genetic-taxonomic*. This is the *Midwestern Taxonomic Method*, which was widely in vogue in the middle western and eastern United States in the 1930s and 1940s. Its principal proponent was W. C. McKern, and it is sometimes referred to as the *McKern Classification;* however, the system was first outlined by a conference group of midwestern United States archaeologists in 1932 and subsequently revised by conference in 1935 (McKern, 1939). It was thus in formulation at more or less the same time as the Gladwin scheme.[24] The Midwestern Taxonomic Method deliberately eschewed the dimensions of space and time in the mechanics of its classification; nevertheless, we think that it would be fair to say that it would not have been devised except in a general climate of archaeological opinion where great stress was being laid on chronology. The difficulty was that, in the midwestern and eastern United States, archaeological chronology seemed precluded by the apparent lack of deep refuse sites suitable for stratigraphy. The research of subsequent decades would show that this was not altogether true; however, as of 1930, few such sites had been discovered. In addition to this problem of no stratigraphy, there was another condition that prepared the way for the Midwestern Taxonomic Method. This was the presence of a great number of archaeological collections, available in museums or in private hands. These had been gathered over the years from site surfaces and from excavations. Most of the work had been done by amateurs, and, in many cases, there was little provenance information other than site or regional location. Still, such materials were a resource for the prehistory of the area, and a way would have to be found to deal with them. What was needed was a scheme that would give some order to these data. The Midwestern Taxonomic Method was a response to these combined circumstances and needs.

The Midwestern system operated solely with the cultural forms themselves — that is, with typology. Classification began with the unit of the culture complex, as this complex could be recovered from the artifacts and features of an archaeological site. Such a unit was called a *component*. In most instances, the component was a site, although, in those few cases where stratification did obtain, the component might be a level within a site. Such components were then grouped into *foci*, the first and lowest classificatory step on the genetic-taxonomic ladder. Components of a focus shared a very high percentage of trait similarities. Foci, in turn, were classified into *aspects*, the next higher bracket in the system where there was still a substantial trait sharing. The next genetic-taxonomic level was the *phase*. At this level, traits held in common diminished in number from those of the aspect level. Phases were then classed into *patterns* on very broad cultural criteria. For instance, in the eastern United States, it was generally conceded that, among the prehistoric pottery-making cultures, there were only two patterns, the Woodland and the Mississippian. The cultural characteristics of the former were semisedentary territorial adjustment, cord-marked or other surface-roughened pottery of subconoidal form, and stemmed or notched chipped stone points. In contrast, the broad Mississippian diagnostics were sedentary living, incised or modeled pottery of varying vessel shapes, and small triangular projectile points. Finally, the highest classificatory bracket in the Midwestern system was the *base*, a level on which distinctions were to be made between horticultural pottery patterns and those lacking farming and ceramics.

Neither McKern nor the other proponents of the Midwestern scheme were turning their backs permanently on space and time, the two indispensable dimensions of cultural history. In fact, the basic assumption of the system was that formal similarity reflected shared cultural origins and cultural history. Thus, history was implicit in the method, if covert. McKern and his colleagues felt that, once the classification had become reasonably complete, it and the archaeological cultures that composed it could then be placed in spatial-temporal perspective by studies directed to these ends. In opposition to this view were those archaeologists working in the southeastern United States, where a promising beginning had been made with stratigraphy and seriation. These researchers were impatient with a strictly taxonomic method, which, in their opinion, merely slowed down the march toward the ultimate goals of cultural history. Viewed with hindsight, this argument was resolved in a way that might have been anticipated. As more became known about Eastern archaeology, especially from the standpoint of chronology, the debate over the merits and limitations of the Midwestern method began to recede. Gradually, taxonomic categories were given chronological dimension.[25]

The Pecos, Gladwin, and Midwestern Classifications all developed within the context of working field archaeology, but one other culture-classification scheme comes from theoretical ethnology. This is the system of the Austrian *Kulturkreislehre* school.[26] It has had only limited application in American archaeology, and our reference to it will be brief. Its theoretical assumptions are those of worldwide culture spread, either through migration of peoples, diffusion, or both. Certain definable culture complexes, or *kreise,* have thus been spread. In the course of this, the complexes have frequently been modified by trait loss, addition, or alteration. A time-lag factor has operated in these spreads, so that a complex will not describe a horizon of the same absolute dates in all parts of the world where it is found; nevertheless, the original relative time-positions that culture complexes had in their hearth of origin often will be maintained in remote areas to which they have spread. As early as the 1930s, José Imbelloni, in Argentina, was a proponent of the approach in New World physical anthropology and, to some extent, in archaeology.[27] Later, O. F. A. Menghin, the European prehistorian working in Argentina, treated American archaeological data from this point of view.[28] But, except for some students of Menghin's and Imbelloni's, the *Kulturkreislehre* method has not had wide appeal for Americanists—either as a scheme for local New World culture classification or as a means of demonstrating interhemispheric diffusions. The majority of American archaeologists, although much concerned with diffusion and migration as processes, are unwilling to see them built into a classification scheme.

At several places, we have mentioned the close alliance of American archaeology and ethnology. One of the most important ways in which this association has been expressed is in what has come to be called the *direct-historical approach* to archaeology. Very simply stated, the direct-historical approach means working back into prehistoric time from the documented historical horizon. In archaeology, it involves sites where Native American groups are known to have lived in early historical

THE
DIRECT-HISTORICAL
APPROACH

times, so that the excavation of these sites reveals artifact complexes that can be associated with identifiable tribes or ethnic groups. The archaeologist may then find other sites in the region whose artifact complexes show stylistic overlap with the historically identified complexes but whose origins or beginnings go back to prehistoric times.

The term *direct-historical approach* seems to have been first used in a formal designatory way by W. R. Wedel (1938); however, the basic principle behind it is almost as old as archaeology. It was used by the Spanish explorers in Middle America and Peru in the sixteenth century when they identified certain living Native American groups with earlier monuments; Cyrus Thomas and F. H. Cushing employed the approach, albeit in a limited way, in their respective mound and Southwestern Puebloan studies; and it is the principle that linked Kroeber's prehistoric potsherd seriations to the historical and modern Zuñi sites. The direct-historical approach was also followed by A. C. Parker in New York State as early as 1916, when he investigated Native American village sites and

Strong's classification of Plains cultures in accordance with the Midwestern Taxonomic Method. Strong, however, has arranged the classification in a chronological ordering – a procedure not a part of the Midwestern system. (From Strong, 1935)

Suggested Cultural Classification for Certain Nebraska (and Colorado) Sites

Basic culture	Phase	Aspect	Focus	Component
Mississippi	Upper Mississippi	Nebraska	Omaha	Rock Bluffs, Gates Saunders, Walker Gilmore II.
			St. Helena	Butte, St. Helena, etc.
	Central Plains	Upper Republican	Lost Creek	Lost Creek, Prairie Dog Creek, etc.
			Sweetwater	Sweetwater, Munson Creek, etc.
			Medicine Creek	Medicine Creek
			North Platte	Signal Butte, III, etc.
		Lower Loup (Protohist. Pawnee?)	Beaver Creek	Burkett, Schuyler, etc.
		Lower Platte (Historic Pawnee)	Columbus	Horse Creek, Fullerton, Linwood, etc.
			Republican	Hill, etc.
	Woodland	Iowa "Algonkian"	Sterns Creek	Walker Gilmore I
Great Plains	Early Hunting	Signal Butte II(?)	Signal Butte	Signal Butte II
		Signal Butte I	Signal Butte	Signal Butte I
		Folsom	Northern Colorado	Lindenmeier (Colo.)

related them to historical Iroquoian tribes (Parker, 1916; see also Wintemberg, 1928, 1936, 1939). Later, W. A. Ritchie continued Parker's work in developing the prehistoric sequences for the region that were antecedent to the historical Iroquoian and Algonquian cultures (Ritchie, 1932, 1938). Collins pioneered the approach in the Southeast, and Ford followed his lead (Collins, 1927; Ford, 1936; Stirling, 1940). But it was W. D. Strong who gave the greatest impetus to the direct-historical approach with his important monograph *An Introduction to Nebraska Archaeology* in 1935.[29]

Strong, assisted by W. R. Wedel, began with a rich background of historic-site documentation that had been assembled by ethnologists and amateur archaeologists.[30] They excavated historical Pawnee sites and the closely related protohistoric-period sites of the same tribe. From these, they went on to dig the fully prehistoric sites of the region. This and subsequent research (Wedel, 1936, 1938, 1940; Strong, 1940) laid the firm groundwork for Plains archaeology, with its prehistoric Upper Republican, protohistoric, and historic Pawnee cultural sequence in Nebraska. The chronological and ethnohistorical aspects of the work were further enhanced and dramatized by the striking cultural changes that Strong was able to demonstrate in the development of this tradition of Plains cultures. Riverine horticulturists were seen transformed to horse nomads in the span of the late prehistoric-to-historic centuries (Strong, 1933). The potential of the approach for cultural interpretation and the examination of culture change was obvious. Strong's "Nebraska archaeology" became a model for this kind of archaeology, as the method was then carried to other American areas in the late 1930s and after.

The direct-historical approach is quite properly termed an *approach*, not a *classification*. At one time, J. H. Steward posed it in opposition to the Midwestern Taxonomic Method as an alternative and better way of doing archaeology (Steward, 1942). But there is no real conflict between the two on methodological grounds. The Midwestern scheme is taxonomic and comparative; the direct-historical approach is a method for investigating specific cultural histories.[31] It was to be the latter, however, that led into functional interpretations of archaeological cultures.

Stratigraphic and seriational methods, pottery and artifact typology, culture-unit classification, and the direct-historical approach were all employed during the early Classificatory-Historical Period in American archaeology for the eventual reconstruction of cultural history. The term *reconstruction of cultural history* may be interpreted to mean a good many different things, and the connotations placed upon it by archaeologists

AREA SYNTHESIS:
THE GOAL

in the Modern Period are not quite the same as those of 50 years ago; but, to most New World archaeologists of 1940, the goal of such reconstruction, or certainly an intermediate goal, was the *area synthesis*. Such a synthesis was usually little more than an ordering of the archaeological remains of a given area in a spatial-temporal framework. The essence of this ordering was the archaeological *chronology chart*, a diagram arranged with chronological periods in a vertical column and geographical subdivisions across the top, so that the various culture units (phases, foci) could be placed in their appropriate boxes. By 1940, a number of such American area charts could be drawn with reasonable confidence. In the North American Southwest, the time column could be calibrated in absolute years, thanks to *dendrochronology* (tree-ring dating); and, for parts of Middle America, absolute chronology was provided by the Pre-Columbian Maya calendar. Elsewhere, relative chronology still prevailed. Besides the Southwest and Middle America, large-scale area syntheses had been attempted in Peru, the eastern United States, Alaska, and the West Indies. In addition to these areas — all of which correspond more or less to the culture areas of the ethnographer — there were others in which archaeological chronologies had been begun on limited regional bases but had not yet been extended in area-wide fashion.

Pre-Columbian Peruvian pottery, a Recuay style vessel with negative-painted decoration. (Courtesy of the Berlin Staatliche Museum)

A Moche style effigy vessel. Both this figure and the Recuay style vessel date from what Uhle designated as his Early Period (now referred to by archaeologists as Early Intermediate Period). (From the Peabody Museum, Harvard University)

We have already observed (Chapter Three) that the first American area archaeological synthesis actually preceded the Classificatory-Historical Period. This was the achievement of Max Uhle, who pieced together a Peruvian area chronology—from stylistic seriation, the horizon-marking effectiveness of the Tiahuanacoid and Inca styles, and occasional stratigraphic data—as early as 1900. For a while, little was done with the Uhle synthesis. He was followed in Peru by J. C. Tello and P. A. Means. These were both able scholars, but they were as much interested in ethnohistory and Inca ethnology as in archaeology, and neither presented his archaeological conclusions with adequate supporting evidence. Tello's reconstruction of the Peruvian past paid little attention to the Uhle chronological scheme. Instead, he saw the rise of Peruvian civilization from the point of view of upper Amazonian origins.[32] Means was more influenced by Uhle. For instance, he utilized the concept of a Tiahuanaco horizon;[33] however, he was not a field archaeologist, and he did nothing to verify or disprove the Uhle chronological structure.

The leading proponent and chief conceptualizer of the Uhle synthesis was Kroeber. As already noted, he made detailed seriation studies on the Uhle collections in the 1920s and also carried out field explorations in Peru in the same decade. In 1927, he published an important article, "Coast and Highland in Prehistoric Peru," In this, he summarized Uhle's work and his own investigations, commented on the Tello and Means schemes, and went on to outline what he considered to be the major problems of Peruvian archaeology. He conceived of these mainly as the clarification of chronological relationships. Subsequently, following the excavations of W. C. Bennett (1934, 1936, 1939) and Rafael Larco Hoyle (1938–40, 1941) in the 1930s, Kroeber visited Peru once more, traveling over the country, reviewing sites and collections, and conferring with a number of young colleagues who were then digging in the country. The result of this visit was the short monograph *Peruvian Archaeology in 1942* (Kroeber, 1944). In it, he accepted Larco Hoyle's and Tello's early dating of the Chavin culture and placed Chavin as another major horizon style in the Peruvian area synthesis. In addition to the substantive chronological summary, the Kroeber 1942 synthesis is also noteworthy for its first clear definition of this concept of the *horizon style*.

As might be expected, the North American Southwest was not far behind Peru in chronological synthesis. In 1924, Kidder published *An Introduction to the Study of Southwestern Archaeology*. In this, he mapped nine subdivisions of the Southwestern area[34] and then treated the archaeology of each in accordance with a chronological scheme of: (1) Basket Maker; (2) Post-Basket Maker; (3) Pre-Pueblo; and (4) Pueblo. These generally correspond to the periods of the Pecos Classification, which was to be devised in the 1927 Conference, a few years later. Basket Maker was to become Basketmaker II, the prepottery but horticultural beginnings of the Southwestern sequence as it was then known; Post-Basket Maker was changed to Basketmaker III, the modified Basketmaker culture, which possessed pottery; Pre-Pueblo, with its small above-ground structures and relatively simple pottery, was more or less synonymous with Pueblo I in the later Pecos Classification; and fully developed Pueblo corresponded to the periods of Pueblo II, III, and IV. Kidder prefaced his detailing of the archaeology with a short chapter on the modern pueblos. This described something of their life-ways and history, and it also offered suggestions as to just how the various Puebloan groups may have descended from the earlier prehistoric cultures. Most of Kidder's archaeological information came from the northern regions and from the Rio Grande. For other parts of the Southwest, such as the southern deserts, little more could be offered in

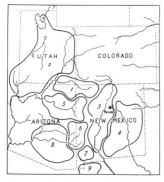

Southwestern cultural areas (or regions) following Kidder's 1924 synthesis. (1) San Juan; (2) Northern Peripheral; (3) Rio Grande; (4) Eastern Peripheral; (5) Little Colorado; (6) Upper Gila; (7) Mimbres; (8) Lower Gila; (9) Chihuahua Basin. (From Kidder, 1924)

1924 than a description of "red-on-buff" pottery and some of the adobe architecture.

In spite of its limitations, Kidder's *Introduction* marked the coming of age of the Southwest as an archaeological area. New work could be fitted into a spatial-temporal structure, and such a structure pointed the way to progress. Great advances were made in the 1930s. One of these was methodological and interdisciplinary. A. E. Douglass, the astronomer, had long been studying Southwestern tree-ring growth patterns as an aid in research on sunspot cycles. Beginning with living trees, he also extended his search for materials into archaeological Pueblo ruins, which had preserved wooden timbers. By 1929, he had built up two long tree-ring sequences. One ran back from the present, through the historic, and into the late prehistoric Pueblo periods; the other was a floating chronology, which pertained to some as yet unassigned segment of the prehistoric past. In the summer of 1929, timbers were found in certain prehistoric ruins in eastern Arizona that allowed Douglass to close the gap between his two tree-ring chronologies. The result was a means of accurate year-to-year dating, which could be applied to those Southwestern ruins located in the northern regions of the area where the proper trees and tree-growth circumstances permitted. A beam specimen, of either preserved wood or charcoal, was simply compared against the master tree-ring chronology and placed at that point where its patterns of ring growth (large or normal year rings contrasted with small or drought year rings) indicated a match (McGregor, 1941, pp. 69–85; Bannister, 1963). By the middle 1930s, Southwestern chronology for the northern and northeastern regions could be quoted in absolute time. Thus, it became known that Basketmaker II antedated A.D. 500; Basketmaker III fell between 500 and 700; Pueblo I, between 700 and 900; Pueblo II, between 900 and 1100; Pueblo III lasted from 1100 to 1300; and Pueblo IV lasted from 1300 to 1600 (McGregor, 1941, p. 322). One of the things this exact dating did was to make the archaeologists aware of the time-lag factor in cultural diffusion and spread, and this pointed up the fact that the periods of the Pecos Classification were really stages of cultural development rather than absolute time-periods. With chronology held as an extra-cultural constant, archaeologists could now ponder rates of cultural spread and culture change, where previously they had only culture change itself as a measure of time.

The other advances were in sheer substantive knowledge. The Gladwins and their cohorts opened the southern Arizona Hohokam cultural division of the Southwest through the systematic chronological-distributional work that has been noted in our discussions of stratigraphy, seriation, and classification. Haury and Martin did the same for the Mogollon country. Hohokam was seen to have ties to Mexican cultures, and Mogollon could be linked to both Hohokam and to Anasazi (the new name for the Basketmaker-Pueblo cultural continuum). In general, the area was proving to be more culturally diverse than had been thought.

New area syntheses of the 1930s attempted to take this cultural diversity into account. Roberts did this in two summary articles (1935, 1937), and H. S. Gladwin offered another overview in the concluding monograph on the Snaketown excavations (1937, vol. 2). When J. C. McGregor brought out his book-length *Southwestern Archaeology* in 1941, he had to make accommodation for still more regional diversity as well as for chronological expansion. It was now clear that a hunting-collecting *Cochise culture* had preceded the Basketmakers and the other early

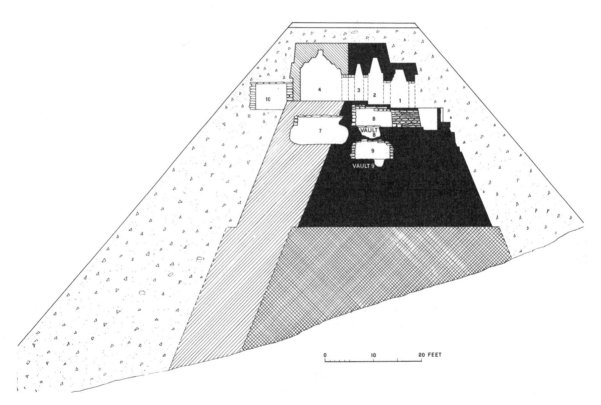

Cross-section drawing of a pyramid, Holmul, Guatemala. This Maya Lowland building was excavated by Merwin in 1912, and it is important in Maya archaeology because of its architectural stratigraphy (which was not made known until 1932). The outer casing of the pyramid dates as Late Classic; that portion of the interior structure with the corbelled-vault rooms dates as Early Classic; the earliest building phase, without vaulted buildings and with tombs 8 and 9, dates as very late Preclassic. The pottery from these tombs was the first from the Maya Lowlands to be identified as similar to Spinden's Archaic pottery from the Valley of Mexico. (From Merwin and Vaillant, 1932)

Southwestern farmers by several thousand years.[35] McGregor (1941, p. 67) even suggested a new Southwestern-wide area chronology, with a period terminology that was intended to capture the salient characteristics of each period; however, he did not use the scheme in his actual data presentation but reverted instead to the more conventional subareal chronologies of Anasazi, Hohokam, Mogollon, and Patayan.

In Middle America, there had been some chronological ordering in the Maya Lowlands prior to 1914. This had been made possible by the translations of Maya calendrical inscriptions and the correlations of these calendrical dates with those of the Christian calendar. Although there was some debate as to just how these correlations should be made, the result was a "floating chronology" almost 600 years in length, which fell somewhere in the first millennium A.D.[36] Unfortunately this important means of dating was limited to the Maya lowlands, where such inscriptions were found. Elsewhere in Middle America, there was little in the way of chronology. There was, of course, the Valley of Mexico, where a gross relative chronology had been begun by Gamio, but this was the only exception. Spinden's handbook on Mexico, the best synthesis for the Mesoamerican area in the 1920s, suffered from this lack of regional chronological information (Spinden, 1928). Although an admirable summary, and one that went beyond sheer description in his concept of an Archaic culture, the attempts to order the various Mesoamerican cultures chronologically were far wide of the mark. Forced to operate wholly by conjecture, he surmised, for instance, that Classic Maya civilization had preceded that of Teotihuacan and Monte Alban—placements that have not withstood the tests of further research.

In fact, even as early as the late 1920s, G. C. Vaillant was beginning to question Spinden's chronological ordering. Vaillant's own experience in the Valley of Mexico, his work with Maya pottery, the Carnegie Institution's recent diggings in the Maya lowlands (Ricketson and Ricketson, 1937; J. E. S. Thompson, 1939) and highlands,[37] and Alfonso Caso's explorations at Monte Alban in Oaxaca[38] all combined to suggest significantly different interpretations from those offered by Spinden. Vaillant had actually begun such a synthesis in 1927 in an unpublished Ph.D. dissertation (Vaillant, 1927). He went further along these lines in a 1935 article, and, in 1941, he gave his ideas detailed expression in his book, *Aztecs of Mexico*.[39] In this book, he offered an area-wide period terminology. He reserved the bottom-most bracket on the time-chart for undiscovered Paleo-Indian cultures. For the next period, advancing in time, he changed Spinden's name of *Archaic* to that of *Middle Cultures*, in recognition of the very likely possibility that they were not the earliest on the Mesoamerican scene. Vaillant then applied the names *Full Independent Civilizations* and *Late Independent Civilizations* to what are today the Early and Late Classic Periods. For the Postclassic, Vaillant used the name *Mixteca-Puebla Period,* after the dominant culture of that time. A spatial-temporal organization of the data was beginning to take shape. With the perspective of 50 years, we see that the most significant changes have been the downward chronological extension of the Middle (or Preclassic) cultures, the realization of the importance of the Olmec among these, and the identification of Tula, rather than Teotihuacan, with the Toltecs. Of course, radiocarbon dating, which was not available to Vaillant, has deepened the time-scale for the Middle (or Preclassic) cultures well below the 1941 estimate of 200 B.C.

In the eastern United States, a purely taxonomic synthesis, in the manner of the Midwestern Taxonomic Method, had been published by Thorne Deuel in 1935. Some regional syntheses dealt with chronology, such as those of Parker and Ritchie in New York (Parker, 1922; Ritchie, 1938), Strong's in Nebraska (Strong, 1935), and Setzler's in the northern Mississippi Valley (Setzler, 1940). But the first large-scale spatial-temporal organizations of prehistoric Eastern data followed in the wake of the extensive federal-relief-supported surveys and excavations of the 1930s. These were carried out throughout the area by various government-financed agencies—WPA, NYA, CCC, and the TVA authority—through cooperative organizations, including the National Park Service, State Park Services, museums, universities, and other sponsoring groups. Such projects were especially numerous in the southeastern United

Archaic or Middle Culture figurines from Central Mexico. (These are more commonly referred to now as Preclassic or Formative Period.) Heights (from left to right): 10.3 cm., 13.2 cm., 11.5 cm. (From Vaillant and Vaillant, 1934)

States (Quimby, 1979; Haag, 1985). Total numbers of workmen employed aggregated into the thousands, and many young, newly graduated archaeologists obtained their first on-the-job training as crew supervisors in these federal programs. Laboratory analyses frequently went hand-in-hand with field-excavation activities, and there was frequent intercommunication among these archaeologists. One formalized aspect of this sharing of data and ideas was the formation of the Southeastern Archaeological Conference, with its initial meeting at Ann Arbor, Michigan, in 1938, but with subsequent meetings in the various southern states.[40]

J. A. Ford and J. B. Griffin were major figures in bringing about the first area-wide synthesis, which owed so much to these intensive archaeological efforts of the 1930s. In 1941, Ford, with G. R. Willey (Ford and Willey, 1941) published an Eastern-area chronology and culture-classificatory scheme, devised somewhat after the fashion of the Southwestern Pecos. Instead of employing the period concept, however, they referred to stages, or *sloping horizons.* Virtually nothing was known of Late Pleistocene occupations in the East at this date (although there was important information from the western Plains), so this stage was omitted from the Ford-Willey synthesis. They began with the *Archaic,* a term then used in some regions of the eastern United States to refer to preceramic, presumably nonfarming cultures.[41] On the extensive chronology charts, Ford and Willey gave no indications as to the origin point or direction of movement of Archaic cultures; but, for the first of their pottery-making stages, which they called Burial Mound I (Early Woodland and Adena cultures), the direction of cultural diffusion (and perhaps population migration) was plotted as from south-to-north. Similarly the innovative influences and peoples on the succeeding Burial Mound II (Middle Woodland and Hopewellian cultures), Temple Mound I (Early Mississippian), and Temple Mound II (Late Mississippian) stages were all thought of as coming from somewhere in the South (ultimately from Mesoamerica) and then spreading up the Mississippi Valley and its tributaries. The scheme was more all-embracing and ambitious than the Pecos chronology. It not only covered more territory and more cultural variation, it took on the task of describing the diffusional dynamics for the area. This last was speculative, and it is now clear that the picture Ford and Willey sketched was much too simple. The East was not an empty area, or a low-level culture zone, which was then filled by successive movements of people or diffusions of ideas from Mesoamerica. Archaic culture has since been demonstrated to have great time-depth, regional variation, and richness; and we know that subsequent developments in the East must have owed as much to this heritage as they did to exotic intrusions. Also, the estimates that Ford and Willey applied to their chronology have been shown by radiocarbon dating to have been ridiculously late, especially for the earlier stages of their scheme. Nevertheless, the chronological-developmental order of the synthesis proved correct, as did most of the specific culture-unit assignments associated with it. A few years later, J. B. Griffin (1946) was to publish another general chronological scheme for the East, using the Archaic-Woodland-Mississippian terminology for his periods and being much more cautious about the directions of cultural diffusion.[42] Together, these two syntheses provided the larger chronological framework for archaeological discourse about the East for the ensuing decades.

In the Arctic, a number of archaeological excavations (Mathiassen, 1927; Jenness, 1928; De Laguna, 1934; Collins, 1937) oriented to problems of chronology laid a basis for area synthesis. Several syntheses or partial syntheses appeared prior to 1940 (Jenness, 1933; Birket-Smith, 1936; Mathiassen, 1934), but Collins' (1940) summary of that data was perhaps the most successful and may be taken as a summary of what was known at the end of the early part of our Classificatory-Historical Period. In it, he postulated an original Eskimo culture being brought across the Bering Strait from Asia at some unknown time in the past. From this beginning, he conceived of a splitting-off of a Dorset culture of the East, a Kachemak Bay I development of southern Alaska, an Aleutian Islands branch, and an Old Bering Sea culture. The Birnirk, Punuk, and Thule cultures later developed out of the Old Bering Sea culture. Thule first spread eastward and then, on a very late prehistoric horizon, spread back to the West to give a uniformity to all modern Eskimo/Aleut/Inuit cultures of the Far North. Collins' dating estimates on most of this have turned out to be

Chronology chart from Ford and Willey's synthesis of eastern North American archaeology. Successive stages are indicated with time-lag slope following the authors' interpretations of the direction of diffusion of traits. Culture phrase names are shown, and the small numbers in circles refer to individual sites. (From Ford and Willey, 1941)

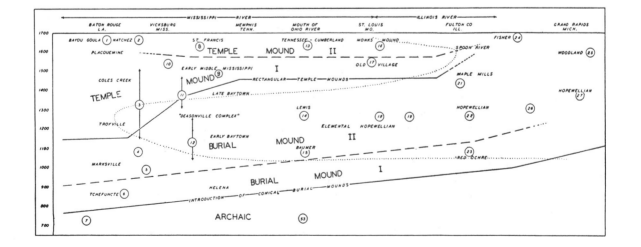

fairly accurate. The basic Eskimo culture has been pushed back to the third millennium B.C. in the form of Denbigh, and there now are clues to much earlier Eskimo or Denbigh-like cultures as far east as Greenland. Still older lithic cultures have also been discovered in the Arctic. But the picture as seen by Collins in 1940 gave a secure nucleus around which further chronological-distributional findings could be formed.

In the West Indies, Rouse's Haitian investigations provided a core of chronological information around which he constructed a general sequence for most of the Greater Antilles by a series of comparisons (Rouse, 1939). In California, the excavations in the Sacramento Valley began chronology for this area (Heizer and Fenenga, 1939; Heizer, 1941). For the rest of North America in the 1914–40 period, archaeological chronology was still in the future. This was also true for most of South America.[43] In spite of the considerable systematic work that had been carried out by the Argentines and Chileans, there was still little or no chronological ordering for these countries.[44] An exception was in far-southern South America, where J. B. Bird had revealed a long sequence going back to a Late Pleistocene horizon and continuing forward in time to the historic period (Bird, 1938, 1946b). This Strait of Magellan sequence was to be most important to American archaeology, for it showed that humans had reached the southern extremity of this hemisphere at a relatively early time. How early was not known then, but subsequent radiocarbon dates for Bird's earliest period have placed it in the 9000–8000 B.C. range.

Although area synthesis was the overall goal in the early Classificatory-Historical Period, some attention was also paid to interareal relationships. These could hardly be called *syntheses.* At best, they were attempts at cultural correlations, usually with an eye toward chronology. Many of them focused attention on occasional long-distance similarities in odd pottery forms or designs that suggested some sort of prehistoric culture contacts.[45] Some brought linguistic affiliations and possible movements of people into the argument to bolster similarities in the archaeological record (Lothrop, 1940). Some viewed the data quite critically and made every effort to plot diffusion or trade within believable chronological limits (Phillips, 1940; Brew, 1940). Lack of absolute chronological control was a major stumbling-block in examining or testing these hypotheses for contact (Kroeber, 1940, Table XI). It was obvious that there had been currents of influence running from Middle America north to the southwestern United States as well as to the Mississippi Valley, but the questions of when, what, and how eluded the archaeologists (Kroeber, 1930; Kidder, 1936).

INTERAREAL
CONSIDERATIONS

Actually, the most interesting and fruitful of all of these attempts to correlate or in some way integrate the data of two or more American areas was Spinden's Archaic hypothesis. First enunciated in 1917 (Spinden, 1917) and further elaborated in his handbook of 1928, the Archaic hypothesis had both chronological and developmental implications. Spinden had been inspired by the results of Gamio's Valley of Mexico excavations, which had revealed a simpler culture underneath the re-

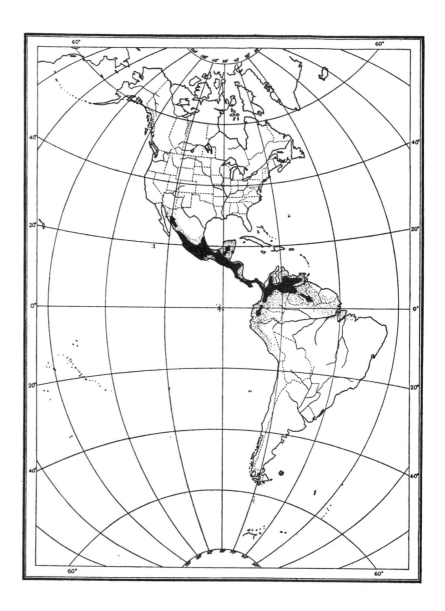

The distribution of Archaic culture in the Americas as conceived by Spinden. (From Spinden, 1917)

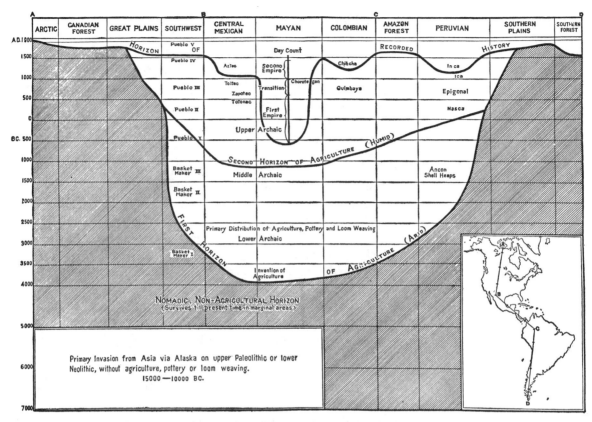

Spinden's conception of the development of Pre-Columbian civilizations. The establishment of Archaic culture defines the base or floor of the white loop. Spinden dated the primary invasion of the Americas from Asia, via the Bering Strait, at ca. 15,000–10,000 B.C. This was probably a sheer guess on his part, but it indicates that not all Americanist thinking on this matter was following Hrdlička's shortened chronology. The Figgins Folsom discoveries, which validated a late Pleistocene presence of humans in the Americas, were published in 1927. Spinden was probably not aware of them when he prepared the manuscript for his 1928 Handbook, from which this diagram is taken. (From Spinden, 1928)

mains of the more elaborate Teotihuacan civilization. This culture had competently made pottery—hand-made pottery figurines—and was further characterized by deep village refuse and evidences of farming. Spinden noted that similar pottery and figurines were found in other parts of Mesoamerica, and this suggested to him that the later civilizations of Mesoamerica—Teotihuacan, Maya, Zapotec, and so forth—were the regionally specialized developments arising from a common American village farming base, which he called the *Archaic*. Further considerations led him to see signs of the Archaic in the American Southwest, in Peru, and Argentina. In other words, this Archaic was a kind of American Neolithic. Having its origins in the Valley of Mexico, it had spread outward to other parts of the hemisphere from this center and was, in this sense, a historically interrelated phenomenon. But its significance was also as an evolutionary stage in the rise of New World civilization. Vaillant, among others, took issue with Spinden (Vaillant, 1934). As cultures contemporaneous with the Valley of Mexico Archaic began to be revealed in other parts of Mesoamerica, it became obvious that many of these had quite complex or sophisticated traits that were not found in the supposed "mother culture" of the Valley of Mexico Archaic. Gradually, it became clear that Spinden's Valley of Mexico Archaic was a relatively late phase in the development of the Archaic, or Preclassic, and that the story of these early, presumably basic, farming cultures was infinitely more complex than he had imagined. In spite of this, Spinden had been on the right track. Certainly, it was on this general time-level of the Archaic, or Preclassic, farmers that many fundamental ideas of New World cultures, including agriculture and pottery-making, were transmitted from one to another. Further, such a basic farming condition was also a developmental prerequisite to later cultural elaborations and civilizations.

In concluding our brief comments on interareal relationships, this seems an appropriate place to make even briefer comments on the concern with interhemispheric contacts. By this, we do not refer to the ancient Bering Strait crossings of Paleolithic people from Asia to the Americas but rather the possibilities of contacts between later Old World cultures and those of the New. As noted, this was a major theme of archaeology in the Speculative Period, and these concerns persisted into later periods, where they were treated both speculatively and objectively. Only the latter treatment needs mention here. We have already remarked on the *Kulturkreislehre* classificatory approach and have indicated how it was geared to interhemispheric migration-diffusion studies between the Old and New Worlds. Another less programmatic but equally systematic approach was that of Erland von Nordenskiöld. He compiled lists of similar traits from Asia and the New World (Erland von Nordenskiöld, 1921, 1931). Many of these were of definite Pre-Columbian provenance. Some may have been accidental convergences; others possibly could have been brought by early immigrants on a Paleolithic-Paleo-Indian level; but others, such as the technique of lost-wax casting of metals, were of a complexity that suggested later contacts. Nordenskiöld was cautious in his presentations, pushing no particular claims. For the most part, the temper of American archaeologists of the time on this issue was "wait and see."[46]

We left Late Pleistocene human studies in the Classificatory-Descriptive Period in a state of doubt and confusion. Various finds had been put forward as being of great age—some on the basis of rather general similarity to European Paleolithic implements and some because of apparent association with Pleistocene fauna or geological strata—but none of these finds could be validated as being truly ancient. The breakthrough came in 1926, when J. D. Figgins discovered chipped stone projectile points and extinct bison remains in a geological context of undisputed Late Pleistocene age at Folsom, New Mexico (Figgins, 1927). The stratum in which the artifacts and bones were found was a deeply buried clay layer, which represented a former water hole, apparently a site where the ancient hunters killed the large herbivores when they came there to drink. The projectile points of the Folsom site were of highly distinctive form, lanceolates with incurved bases and flutings of the sides. After the Folsom discovery, similar points were found under similar Pleistocene conditions and with extinct faunal associations in the Clovis-Portales region of New Mexico (Howard, 1935) and at Lindenmeier, Colorado (Roberts, 1935b).

Thus, by 1940, the case for Late Pleistocene humans in the Americas had become established. The accepted wisdom of the relatively late entrance of humans on the New World scene, which had dominated the thinking of the earlier decades, had fallen. Age estimates were still geological guesses, generally ranging from 15,000 to 10,000 years. Since

CONSIDERATIONS OF THE EARLY PEOPLING OF THE AMERICAS

Folsom point and extinct bison ribs in situ. Folsom, New Mexico. (From the Peabody Museum, Harvard University)

Excavations at Lindenmeier, Colorado, in 1937. (From E. N. Wilmsen)

Fluted Folsom points and knives from the Lindenmeier site. (From the Smithsonian Institution)

then, radiocarbon dates have shortened this somewhat for Clovis-Folsom, although not by very much. Distinctions in typology and differential ages of the various early complexes were then only vaguely discerned. Writing in 1940, Roberts made no formal separation between the Folsom and Clovis points (Roberts, 1940). Another point, the Yuma, which had fine flaking but no fluting, was thought perhaps to be somewhat later than Folsom. Other early artifact complexes were also known by 1940, including those of Sandia Cave (New Mexico), Gypsum Cave (Nevada), Signal Butte (Nebraska), Clear Fork (Texas), Mojave and Pinto Basin (California), and Cochise (southern Arizona).[47] The antiquity of these was implied by typology, geological or faunal associations, cultural stratigraphy, or combinations of these. In the next three decades, some would be validated, some rejected, and others continued in a limbo of debate. Patterns in affiliation, distribution, and chronological placement would emerge; but, as of 1940, it was still too early for this.

The improvement of field methods and techniques continued unabated into the Classificatory-Historical Period. The necessities of stratigraphy furthered this, for one thing, but the more spectacular field innovations in the 1914–40 period were in the excavation of features. In Middle America and, to some extent in the Southwest, what might be thought of as feature digging or architectural digging developed from the nature of the remains themselves. The stone-covered pyramids or plaster-gravel floors of Middle American sites made themselves known to the uncovering spade in an unambiguous fashion (see Ricketson and Ricketson, 1957); they were easy to follow. Southwestern pueblo walls and floors were similar. But, in the eastern United States, it was more difficult. Earthen mounds and houses made of wood or thatch left much less in the way of definite outlines. Archaeologists had to proceed more cautiously, if they wanted to obtain a proper feature record. At first, this was done by arbitrary control points—surveyed grids, benchmarks, and the like, from which features were measured and plotted as the excavation proceeded. Burial mounds were sectioned by five-foot slices, and cross-sectional mound profiles were drawn at these intervals (see Cole and Deuel, 1937). In some instances, this probably provided an adequate record, but, in others, it soon became obvious that much in the way of former surface features—either from sub-mound levels or from various buried mound surfaces—was either being lost or was being made extraordinarily difficult to recover by a subsequent piecing together of a series of small vertical-slice records.

FIELD METHODS
AND TECHNIQUES

A partially excavated Maya temple. The building is the famous E-VII-Sub, a late Preclassic stucco-faced pyramid at Uaxactun, Guatemala. The Carnegie Institution archaeologists who excavated it in the late 1920s (Ricketson and Ricketson, 1937) removed the overlying fill of the badly damaged later pyramids, which had been built over it, to reveal the earlier building. This kind of architectural digging, by peeling or cleaning hard-surfaced structures, was typical of Middle American archaeology of the period and still is. (From the Peabody Museum, Harvard University)

Clearly, a peeling technique, like that long used in the Old World, in the Middle East, or, to a degree, in Middle America or the Southwest, was called for, and this was soon widely employed in the North American East.[48] Clay house floors, temple floors, or special building floors were carefully scraped, with diggers following lines of soil color and texture. Old post holes were revealed, sometimes filled with charred burned posts, sometimes marked only by a dark smudge of earth where the wood had decayed (a *post-mold*). Entries, fire-basins, and other features were disclosed. These not only gave a better record for the field notebook, but it made possible photographs that offered the viewer or reader a much better idea of the feature in question than even the most painstaking descriptions. There was nothing very profound or brilliant about any of this, except that it was to the archaeologist's advantage to uncover the disjointed fragments of the lost past in such a way that they could be as fully rearticulated into their original condition as possible. At this lowly and mechanical level, these were the first steps on the way to the recovery of context, function, and, hopefully, an understanding of culture process.

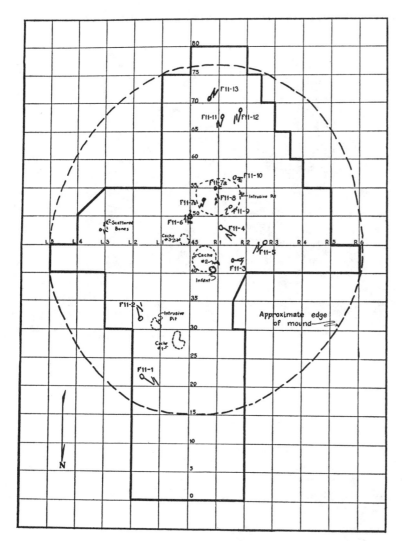

Field map of a mound excavation in Illinois showing the five-foot grid and burial and other features. Such a plan was available at the close of mound-slicing operations (Reprinted from Rediscovering Illinois by Cole and Deuel by permission of the University of Chicago Press. Copyright 1937.)

Mound excavation in the southeastern United States — beginning the profiling or slicing of a mound. (From De Jarnette and Wimberly, 1941)

The technique of drawing soil profiles of a mound with portable string and frame grid (see Webb and De Jarnette, 1942).

Excavation of a Pre-Columbian house structure in Tennessee, possibly a temple or chief's house. It was situated on the top of a flat-topped mound. The construction technique of small poles set in slit-like trenches has been disclosed by the peeling or scraping excavation technique, in which differences in soil texture and color have been very closely followed. A fire basin can also be seen near the center of the building. (From the Department of Anthropology, University of Tennessee, Knoxville)

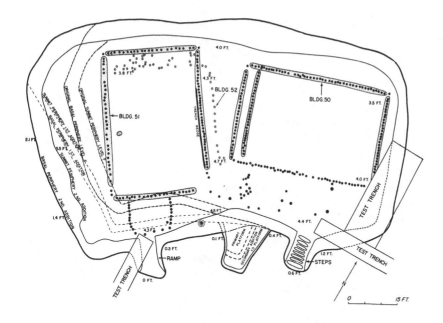

Map of structure plans, as indicated by post-molds and other features, on mound platform. (From Hiwassee Island *by Lewis and Kneberg, reproduced by permission of The University of Tennessee Press. Copyright © 1970 by The University of Tennessee Press.)*

T his first part of the Classificatory-Historical Period continued strongly in the scientific tradition of the previous period. Facts were gathered and systematized, and care and exactitude were beginning to be stressed in field and excavation procedures. Speculation and theory were considered more or less synonymous and were to be eschewed by the respectable members of the archaeological establishment. The amateur was still very much a part of the scene; indeed, public interest in archaeology was growing, especially in the United States; but, in both the United States and Canada, amateurs were beginning to be brought under the eye of the professional.

As we have emphasized throughout this chapter, the motif of this first part of the Classificatory-Historical Period was the establishment of archaeological chronologies. Regions or areas of greater chronological knowledge could be contrasted to those for which data were few, and strategies of continuing research were planned with this in mind.

The massive federal-relief-supported archaeology of the 1930s foreshadowed (and probably suggested) the government and industrial-supported salvage archaeology that followed the Second World War. In

APPRAISAL OF TRENDS

a sense, a trend continues from this period into the conservation and resource-planning archaeology of the Modern Period. Although most of the federal archaeology of the 1930s was conceived as a form of welfare or economic relief during the Depression years, an attitude was beginning to be established. Archaeology was a part of the national scene, something that deserved to be supported from public funds. Even more specifically, some particular federal programs of the 1930s, those of the Tennessee Valley Authority in Tennessee and Alabama, had from their inception a conscious salvage objective. Thousands of archaeological sites were to be inundated through new dam constructions, and swift action on the part of archaeologists was necessary. Credit is due to many of them of that period, especially W. S. Webb, for their part in saving the prehistoric heritage of this part of the Americas. The model was also constructed for the River Basin salvage programs of the 1940s and 1950s. Although this specific series of events pertains only to the United States, salvage archaeology has subsequently been a part of efforts throughout most of the Americas.

By 1940, the stage was set for the archaeological boom that followed in the decades after the close of World War II. Archaeology, however limited in its intellectual perspectives as it may appear from hindsight, had begun to put its house in order by developing a descriptive and historical methodology. The field had become more a part of the public consciousness. Precedents had been set for governmental involvement in the United States and Canada. In Latin America, archaeology was seen as a powerful tourist attraction in many countries—especially Mexico, Guatemala, and Peru—and research benefitted from governmental funds diverted to archaeology to promote this purpose. Everywhere, higher education and university education was expanding, and interest in archaeology was a part of this more general expansion. More individuals would now come into the field of American archaeology; more research would be carried out; and with this would come new questions and new attitudes about the subject.

NOTES

1. See Rowe (1962a, pp. 339–400); but see also Rowe (1975) for a different explanation. See also Kroeber (1909).
2. Gamio (1913); Boas (1913); Tozzer (1915). J. A. Graham (1962) observes that Engerrand, who was trained primarily as a geologist, had just returned to Mexico from Europe, where he had seen recent geological and archaeological excavations, and that it is possible that he passed these ideas along to Boas.

3. See Spier (1931); Woodbury (1960a, 1960b). It should be emphasized, again, that neither Gamio nor Nelson was the first to observe and record cultural superposition in archaeological sites. In the Southwestern area alone, other archaeologists, including Richard Wetherill (see Prudden, 1897), J. W. Fewkes (1912), and Byron Cummings (1910), had made these superpositional discoveries prior to Nelson's or Gamio's work; however, in none of these instances was gradual cultural change plotted by means of stratigraphy. See also Rowe (1975) and Wissler (1921). The latter describes the background to Nelson's work, but we do not see this work as a break with evolutionary thinking, as Rowe does.

4. Uhle's work of 1902 was published in 1907. Kroeber's negative opinion of the results came out in 1909. See Rowe (1962a, pp. 399–400).

5. The importance of chronology seems not to have been stressed in American archaeological writings until after this. An important exception was Edward Sapir's (1916) call for "time perspective" in aboriginal American studies, and, although this article was to have an influence on the course of American archaeology, it was written by a linguist and ethnologist for a more general anthropological readership. Later, in the 1920s and 1930s, there were some retrospective reflections on the importance of chronology—and stratigraphy—in American archaeology (see Tozzer, 1920, 1927; Spinden, 1933); these were more enthusiastic than those of *ca.* 1914.

6. Kidder (1924, 1931). The 1931 report was written in collaboration with C. A. Amsden. For a new biography of Kidder, see Givens (1992).

7. Vaillant (1930, 1931, 1937). Kroeber (1925c) attempted stratigraphic digging in the Valley of Mexico Archaic sites in 1924. He had little success with sequence in the digging, but, through seriation of several site collections of pottery, he was able to establish a rough chronology of complexes or phases.

8. Webb and De Jarnette (1942) is the best published example; however, W. S. Webb's influence on Southeastern excavations dates back to the 1930s.

9. A very "stratigraphy-conscious" article is one by Willey (1939).

10. Woodbury (1960a, 1960b). Uhle's (1907) California shell-mound digging had been by natural strata.

11. See Heizer's (1959, p. 282) comments and see also R. H. Thompson's (1955) review of Wheeler (1954).

12. For further details of stratigraphic excavations, see Heizer (1959, pp. 214–343).

13. Kroeber and Strong (1924a). Other publications in this series of studies based on the Uhle collections include Kroeber and Strong (1924b); Kroeber (1925a, 1925b, 1926); Strong (1925); Gayton (1927); Gayton and Kroeber (1927).

14. Personal communication from J. A. Ford to G. R. Willey in the later 1930s.

15. For example, as expressed by Rouse (1967) and Dunnell (1970).

16. Although Rouse (1960) was writing a good many years later, his distinction can certainly be applied in retrospect.

17. Such chronologies were not established until many years later (see M. D. Coe and Baudez, 1961, and Baudez, 1963).

18. See Winifred and H. S. Gladwin (1928a, 1928b, 1930). It should be pointed out, however, that the binomial system of pottery taxonomy was formulated, as a scheme, in the First Pecos Conference on Southwestern Archaeology, held at Pecos, New Mexico, in 1927 (Kidder, 1927).

19. Winifred and H. S. Gladwin (1930). These pottery type procedures were further formulated in the Southwestern conferences, at Pecos again in 1929 and at Gila Pueblo, Arizona, in 1930 (Hargrave, 1932).

20. Ford (1938). Although Ford is best described as the editor of this report, there can be little doubt, in view of the phraseology and idea content, that this and the following quote are directly from him.

21. These first type descriptions were prepared by W. C. Haag.

22. Vaillant (1930, 1931). Vaillant's pottery figurine classification was formal and structured but essentially descriptive.

23. The Gladwins were generally careful not to place linguistic or ethnic tags on archaeological complexes (Winifred and H. S. Gladwin, 1934). The *Caddoan Root* designation was a temporary and unfortunate exception.

24. Winifred and H. S. Gladwin (1934). Shetrone, as early as 1920, proposed that Ohio Valley culture complexes should be recognized and classified according to their typologies (see Griffin, 1959). A comparative discussion of the Pecos, Gladwin, McKern, and Colton Classifications may be consulted in McGregor (1941, pp. 57–68).

25. However, as Trigger (1989, p. 192) points out, "the Midwestern Taxonomic Method, while struggling for classificatory objectivity and quantitative precision, perpetuated the pessimistic views about the Indians' capacity to change that had characterized American archaeology during the nineteenth century."

26. The classic work on the *Kulturkreislehre* school is Graebner (1911), but there is an informative review of the school and its approach in Kluckhohn (1936).

27. His best summary statement on the method and his views of it were published a little later (Imbelloni, 1945).

28. See Menghin (1957). The author of *Weltgeschichte der Steinzeit* (1931) did not begin work in the Americas until after World War II.

29. Strong (1935). See also Strong (1927) for combined ethnological and archaeological research done under Kroeber's encouragement at the University of California. Steward (1937) also wrote along similar lines under Kroeber's influence.

30. Especially the amateur archaeologist, A. T. Hill.

31. Strong (1935) expressed some regret that his Nebraska work had been done before the Midwestern scheme had been promulgated, and he attempted to fit his cultures into this scheme, as shown here. This added little or nothing to Nebraska cultural history and left him open to criticism that this mingling of space-time ordering and strictly formal classificatory ordering violated the principles of the Midwestern Taxonomic Method.

32. Tello's early general works were published in 1923 and 1929. A later synthesis of 1942 follows along the same lines, although by this date Tello was able to bring the Chavin concept into sharper focus. Previously, it had been a part of a larger, vaguer construct called *Archaic Andean* culture.

33. Means's great work was published in 1931; however, his interpretation was fairly well set as expressed in an article published in 1917.

34. He called these *areas*. They would correspond to what are now more usually referred to as *regions* within a major culture area (Willey, 1966–71).

35. Sayles and Antevs (1941); but the Cochise culture had been brought to the attention of other Southwestern archaeologists in the 1930s.

36. As of that time, there were two Maya-Christian calendrical correlations, the 11.16.0.0.0 (also known as the *Goodman-Thompson-Martinez Correlation*), and the 12.9.0.0.0 (also known as the *Spinden Correlation*). See J. E. S. Thompson (1937). Radiocarbon dates favor the 11.16.0.0.0 correlation, which would place the Classic Maya dates in the span of about A.D. 270–890; the 12.9.0.0.0 correlation would move this chronology back by about 260 years.

37. See Kidder (1940) for a summary.

38. See Caso (1938) for one of the later preliminary reports on Monte Alban.

39. Vaillant (1941, pp. 1–27, Table I). See also the chronological chart (Table X) in *The Maya and Their Neighbors*, C. L. Hay and others (1940), which was prepared by Kroeber, in conjunction with Vaillant.

40. This organization still thrives and is the principal annual meeting for southeastern states archaeologists; it continues to issue a series of *SEAC Newsletters* (see Bibliography).

41. This is a quite distinct usage of the term from that applied by Spinden (1928).

42. Griffin also deserves great credit in any history of the development of archaeology in the area for his role as a catalytic agent. As director of the Ceramic Repository of the University of Michigan in the 1930s, he traveled widely during the days of federal-relief archaeology, visiting working laboratories of various field projects and offering comment especially on interregional ceramic comparisons and relationships (see V. Jones, 1976).

43. An exception would be Linne's (1929) Panamanian work, which made some suggestions of sequences.

44. See, for example, the summary articles by Márquez Miranda (1946a, 1946b); Lothrop (1946); Casanova (1946); Aparicio (1948); Willey (1946); Serrano (1946). Bird's (1946a) article on northern Chile, based on his own stratigraphic digging (Bird, 1943), is an exception.

45. For examples, Kidder II (1940) or Vaillant (1932).

46. Gladwin (1937, Volume 2 of the Snaketown report) was one notable exception. He felt that the Old World contacts with New World later cultures were clear and strong. Contrast his views with those of Kidder (1936).

47. See Roberts (1940) for bibliographical references to these various complexes.

48. See Webb and De Jarnette (1942) or Lewis and Kneberg (1946). Although the dates on these particular reports are slightly later than 1940, much of the fieldwork on which they are based was done in the 1930s.

The Classificatory-Historical Period: The Concern with Context and Function (1940–60)

Archaeology . . . is always limited in the results it can produce.
It is doomed always to be the lesser part of anthropology.

E. ADAMSON HOEBEL

A DEFINITION OF
THE PERIOD

The somewhat depressing quotation above, taken from the writings of a leading American ethnologist of the time, is a fair statement of how anthropology as a whole regarded archaeology in the Classificatory-Historical Period. Ethnology and social anthropology were considered to be the places where the main bastions of theory and wisdom were located. Archaeology was definitely peripheral. Any attempt on the part of the archaeologist to contribute to the larger problems of cultural understanding was met with an astonishment like that in the classic case of the talking dog; it was not what the dog said that was so amazing but the fact that the dog could say it at all. Most archaeologists accepted their marginal position and second-class status with becoming humility; only a few were restive. The latter were willing to admit that "archaeology is always limited in the results it can produce," but they were also inclined to inquire if ethnology did not also have its limitations. Might not an archaeological study of the cultural succession of material objects over a long and otherwise unrecorded span of time reveal to us things of importance that even the most omniscient of living informants could not disclose to an ethnologist? Why, indeed, should archaeology be "doomed always to be the lesser part of anthropology?" Perhaps it had a potential as yet unrealized. Such, in any event, were the seditious thoughts in the minds of some archaeologists, who were also encouraged by a few sympathetic ethnologists to ask such questions. These thoughts and questions were to lead to a critical reexamination of the aims and procedures of archaeology and the instigation of some new experimental trends that were to characterize the latter half of the Classificatory-Historical Period.

These new experimental trends concerned context and function — and hinted at process. They did not replace the prevailing preoccupation of the Classificatory-Historical Period, which remained firmly set in chronological ordering. The dissatisfactions, stirrings, and experiments were portents of the future. The decades from 1940 to 1960, we think, are appropriately contained within the definitions of the Classificatory-Historical Period, but it was also a time of ferment and transition.

The new contextual-functional approaches are considered under three headings in our discussions. The first of these headings or categories takes as its theme the proposition that artifacts are to be understood as the material relics of social and cultural behavior. Earlier attempts had been made to ascribe use or function to archaeological artifacts, but the difference in the 1940–60 period was in the close attention paid to context in arriving at functional inferences.

A second contextual-functional approach is that of settlement patterns. It was felt that the way humans had arranged themselves upon the landscape, with relation to its natural features and with relation to other people, held important clues for archaeologists in their understanding of socioeconomic adaptations and sociopolitical organizations.

The third approach, relating to the other two, is that of the relationships between culture and natural environment. That is, it involved humans and their resource base. While sometimes referred to as *cultural ecology* in the 1940–60 period, it was generally something less than the ecosystem approach of more recent years.

In the search for context and function, these methodologies were abetted and further stimulated by scientific aids from other disciplines. Geological findings became steadily more important to archaeology; botany and biology were keys in furthering cultural-natural environment studies and in tracing out the histories of domestication; material analyses of all kinds, in chemistry, metallurgy, and physics, allowed for greater insights into the processes of artifact manufacture as well as for identifications of sources of raw commodities. Above all, radiocarbon dating provided absolute dates for archaeologists, and this had important repercussions in freeing them from their overwhelming concern with chronology and their means for obtaining it and allowing them to turn their attention to other aspects of cultural history and development.

As we have noted, these new trends and interdisciplinary borrowings in no way stifled the conventional archaeological tasks of constructing spatial-temporal syntheses for New World regions and areas. After World War II, the number of archaeological investigations in the Americas increased significantly, and the great majority of these investigations were directed to the goal of chronology-building. Old sequences were corrected or refined, and new ones were established in regions heretofore unexplored. The concepts of *horizons* and *traditions* were formulated and widely used. These were historical constructs concerned primarily with the occurrences of styles or technical features in space and time and in the establishment of diffusional or genetic connections between such forms. At the same time, they attempted to reconstruct or elucidate the circumstances of these relationships and, in this way, linked strictly historical with functional objectives.

The latter half of the Classificatory-Historical Period also saw the formulation of archaeological syntheses that went beyond the historical and functional and added to these the dimension of cultural evolutionary process. Such syntheses, with their cross-cultural or comparative orientation, were harbingers of the search for process and explanation that became so important after 1960.

THE FIRST DISSATISFACTIONS

The first signs of dissatisfaction with the limited goals of chronological ordering in American archaeology appeared in the late 1930s. The earliest was William Duncan Strong's essay, "Anthropological Theory and Archaeological Fact," published in 1936.[1] In it, he challenged archaeologists and ethnologists to work in concert to understand cultural development and change. The year before, Strong had given eloquent testimony to the pertinence of ethnology in his direct-historical approach to Nebraska archaeology. He advocated that archaeologists look to ethnology for theoretical leads as well as strictly factual information.

Paul Martin also sought the theoretical collaboration of archaeologists and ethnologists. In his summaries and conclusions to two Southwestern archaeological site reports in 1938 and 1939, he went beyond the suggestions of Strong by using Redfield's concept of *folk culture* to explain variation in the size, form, and contents of prehistoric Pueblo ruins.[2]

Neither Strong's nor Martin's "dissatisfactions" were put forward as such. Rather than pointing out the error of old ways, they were indicating new paths that might be explored. Instead, it was left to the ethnologists to criticize the archaeologists. One of those to do so was Julian H. Steward, who teamed with the archaeologist F. M. Setzler in bringing out an article called "Function and Configuration in Archaeology."[3] By that time, Steward had published a major ethnological monograph on the native tribes of the North American Great Basin (Steward, 1938) and had also carried out and published archaeological research in the same area (Steward, 1937a). Therefore, he was familiar at first hand with both of these aspects of anthropology. In their essay, Steward and Setzler took the position that most American archaeologists were so immersed in minutiae that they never came to grips with the larger objectives of archaeology. In their opinion, these objectives should be the same for the archaeologist as for the ethnologist: an understanding of culture change as well as a geographical-chronological plotting of its manifestations. Archaeologists should try to see their particular cultures in general perspective as well as detailed perspective. For example, they should ask questions about the subsistence base as well as about the form of arrowheads or the designs on pottery. They should seek information on the sizes of the human populations through examinations of subsistence potentials and settlement-pattern studies. In the preceding year, Steward had published an article — now a classic — with the title "Ecological Aspects of Southwestern Society," in which he had drawn together archaeological and ethnological settlement data in demonstrating a thesis on cultural-environmental interaction in the North American Southwest (Steward, 1937b). All in all, the tone of the Steward-Setzler article, although not severely polemical, was definitely critical of the way archaeology was being practiced in the Americas.

A much more caustic statement on the condition of American archaeology was made by Clyde Kluckhohn in "The Conceptual Structure in Middle American Studies" (1940; see also Kluckhohn, 1939), published in the 1940 Festschrift volume *The Maya and Their Neighbors* in honor of the "dean" of Maya studies, Alfred M. Tozzer (Hay and others, 1940). Most of the articles in the volume were by Mesoamerican archaeological specialists, and most were solidly in the traditions of the early Classificatory-Historical Period. Kluckhohn, although an ethnologist-social anthropologist, had done some archaeological work (Kluckhohn and Reiter, 1939). At that time, he probably would have agreed with the statement that archaeology was "the lesser part of anthropology," but he would also have insisted that it need not be. This, in fact, was what his article was about. He asks some of the same questions that Steward and Setzler had put: What are the objectives of archaeology? To what ends are data gathered and presented? He felt that most Middle American archaeologists, scholarly and expert as they were, had a tendency to wallow in detail for and of itself alone. In addition to this, the field seemed pervaded with a fear of theory. In fact, in the American archaeological lexicon of the 1930s — for Middle America as well as elsewhere — the word *theory* was a pejorative synonym for *speculation*. In Kluckhohn's words (1940, p. 47): "Ask an archaeologist to set forth and justify his conceptual scheme. It is an induction from my experience that the betting odds are enormous against this having even occurred to him as a problem." And (1940, p. 51), "But while one may agree wholeheartedly with him [Strong, 1936] that anthropology '. . . is a broad, historical science concerned with the relationship of cultural and biological factors through time and space,' one must insist in the same breath that the conceptual tools for determining this relationship have very largely yet to be forged." (See also Sabloff, 1982a).

In brief, Middle American archaeology—and American archaeology as a whole—operated without explicit theoretical or conceptual formulations. This meant that theory was often implicit and unexamined. Assumptions about such things as cultural stability, the mechanics of diffusion, monogenesis or polygenesis, and the relationships of race, language, and culture went untested, although they were passed along as common coin. Kluckhohn felt that Middle American archaeology, or any archaeology, had two choices in conceptual direction. One of these would be historical, in the sense of following out and recreating unique events in their particularity. The other alternative would be scientific, or comparative—namely, a consideration of the data with an eye toward examining trends and uniformities in cultural development and process.

He contended that Middle American archaeologists had never faced up to this choice. He saw most of the scholars in the field to that time as being essentially involved in historical particulars. He cited Vaillant and Kidder as having had interests that verged on the scientific, although, in his opinion, neither of them had followed through with systematic research or expositions of conceptual means. Kluckhohn voiced a preference for the scientific course. While he admitted that there was an argument that the two approaches might be looked upon as sequent phases of planned research, he leaned toward the belief that data collected for historical purposes would seldom be serviceable for scientific purposes.

CONTEXT AND
FUNCTION:
ARTIFACTS AS
BEHAVIOR

The early complaints about the state of archaeology shared two basic themes. One of these concerned the need for archaeologists to translate their findings—the material remains with which they dealt—into cultural behavior. The other theme was that the archaeologist should be alert to cultural process. In the latter part of the Classificatory-Historical Period, the first of these themes claimed primary attention. The second, the consideration of cultural process, was to receive some implicit recognition, but there was little explicit concern until the 1960s.

The translation of artifacts (as this term may be used in the broadest sense) into social and cultural behavior proceeded through attempts to recreate the contexts of the past and to elucidate the functions of the material remains of those contexts. By *context*, we mean here the full associational setting of any archaeological object or feature: its position on or in the ground and its positional relationships to other objects and features. With these data, archaeologists order their materials, relating them to *assemblages* or *complexes,* which ostensibly have cultural significance, and they may also relate these materials to natural environmental settings. Our definition of *function* is of the broadest sort. We mean both use and function, as these terms have been defined by cultural anthropologists (Linton, 1936). This subsumes the way artifacts and features were made and used by a vanished people and the meanings that they once had for these people.

Context and function may be viewed either synchronically or diachronically. Both views are necessary. However, in the latter part of the Classificatory-Historical Period, the emphasis was on the synchronic view. In part, this was a reaction against the strong diachronic emphasis on pottery sequence chronicles that still dominated archaeology; in part, it was a reluctance to view cultural development in an evolutionary manner. It was only after 1960, when the goal of cultural process became an important one in American archaeology and evolutionary thinking had reemerged, that there was a shift to a diachronic consideration of context and function.

Obviously, the functional implications of archaeological artifacts are as old as antiquarian interests. The recognition of a human-made stone object as an axe carries with it connotations of behavior, and we have mentioned functional classifications of this sort in the Classificatory-Descriptive Period. It is difficult, therefore, to pinpoint in time a first usage for this kind of functional analysis; however, we feel that it is fair to say that such efforts did not begin to be programmatic and emphasized in American archaeology until the late 1930s. The monograph on eastern North American archaeology, *Rediscovering Illinois,* by F. C. Cole and Thorne Deuel, published in 1937, was one of the earliest full-dress attempts.[4] In this work, the authors followed the procedure of listing all the discovered archaeological traits on any *site component* (a single occupation site or a level within a multiple occupation site) under functional categories, such as *Architecture and House Life, Agriculture and Food-Getting,* or *Military and Hunting Complex.* Traits were so classified, depending on their form, appearance, and the contexts in which they were found. The innovation seems a slight one, but it had the advantage of keeping the investigators thinking in terms of these activities rather than simply in terms of the objects themselves. It also began to forge an implicit link between ethnographic behaviors and ancient ones.

Cole and Deuel offered no rationale for this kind of presentation, simply taking it for granted that artifacts imply behavior, but Martin, to whom we have already referred as one of those first to question conventional archaeological procedures, did provide such a rationale in his 1938 monograph. Martin began by observing that culture cannot be considered as the physical objects (artifacts) themselves, nor can it be the generalized resemblances existing among sets of such objects (types). Instead, he felt it referred to patterns of social behavior, which were based on a body of meanings held by a society and transmitted by tradition. Assuming this, he then goes on to ask if typological variation in artifacts can be assumed to indicate a corresponding variation in culture. His reply, based on observations from ethnological instances, is positive. In his words: "This conviction is obviously based on the proposition that in a primitive society, for every variation in style of artifacts there is, within limits, a corresponding variation in the meanings which they have to their makers. If the proposition is true, it further follows that, subject to the same limits, the degree of variation in artifacts through time is indicative of a corresponding degree of variation in that part of the culture to which they pertain" (Martin, Lloyd, and Spoehr, 1938; see also Martin, 1974).

Irving Rouse, writing at about the same time as Martin, had a similar conception of culture and the artifact. His 1939 monograph, *Prehistory in Haiti, A Study in Method* (cited in Chapter Four) had been one of the first attempts to devise a typology that would be sensitive to functional as well as chronological factors. In it, Rouse states: "Culture cannot be inherent in the artifacts. It must be something in the relationships between the artifact and the aborigines who made and used them. It is a pattern of significance which the artifacts have, not the artifacts themselves."[5] However, Rouse seemed to differ with Martin, and with some other archaeologists, in that he saw artifacts as reflecting the behavior involved in their manufacture but not the behavior involved in their use. His view of the artifact—as of 1939—was as more or less an isolate, with an emphasis on the form and material rather than on the context of its associations.

It was John W. Bennett who realized the functionalist implications of Martin's and Rouse's writings. In 1943, he published an article, "Recent Developments in the Functional Interpretation of Archaeological Data,"[6] in which he reviewed some of the same writings we have discussed here and formally proposed the concept and term *functional archaeology*. In addition he referred to archaeological uses of the concept of *acculturation*, by T. M. N. Lewis and Madeline Kneberg in Tennessee (1941) and by Dorothy L. Keur (1941) in the southwestern United States. He also mentioned Waldo R. Wedel's work in cultural and environmental interaction studies in the Great Plains (Wedel, 1941), seeing the importance of this line of research and its obvious functional dimension. A year later, Bennett himself, published on this same general theme in a paper, "The Interaction of Culture and Environment in the Smaller

Societies," (J. W. Bennett, 1944b), in which he employed both archaeological and modern sociological data to make a case for environmental pressures on cultural forms.

Bennett was also much interested in the use of the social anthropological concept of a *religious cult* to explain the function and use of certain copper and shell artifacts found throughout the southeastern United States on a Late Pre-Columbian time-level. These artifacts, from their nature and appearance and from the contexts in which they were found, were most readily interpreted as ritual paraphernalia, quite probably the symbols of status and power. That almost identical pieces were found in sites as distant from each other as Etowah, Georgia, and Spiro, Oklahoma, in sites of otherwise quite different regional cultures, and almost always in large mound or ceremonial sites, had suggested to A. J. Waring, Jr. and Preston Holder[7] that they were dealing with the material remains of a widespread, interregional and intercultural cult. As Bennett (1943, p. 213) said, the Waring-Holder analysis "embraces ethnological data, general sociological concepts of religious organization, and other functional criteria." It demonstrated that both *microcontext* (paraphernalia found in obviously important graves) and *macrocontext* (presence of similar paraphernalia or objects in comparable site contexts in major sites throughout the Southeast) could be used together to arrive at highly logical functional interpretations. Twenty years later, archaeologists would not have been satisfied to stop here and would have attempted to go on from this interpretation to devise tests for it; but, in the early 1940s, it was a significant step forward.

Another macrocontextual study of about this time was Ralph Linton's "North American Cooking Pots" (1944). This was an armchair article but one based on long experience with the data in question from both archaeological and ethnological points of view. In brief, his thesis was that the Woodland elongated and pointed-bottomed pot with a roughened exterior surface was a vessel primarily adapted to the slow boiling of meats and that its functional relationships were with peoples whose primary subsistence was that of hunting. This was supported by ethnological observations, by archaeological observations and inferences about subsistence practices, and by the complementary negative evidence that peoples who were basically agriculturists made and used quite different pottery. The study is a nice example of a combination of formal artifactual properties and broad-scale contextual setting as a means for functional elucidation.

Bennett also wrote a kind of macrocontextual study, "Middle American Influences on Cultures of the Southeastern United States" (1944a). This was a topic that had been approached in more conventional diffusionist ways by other authors,[8] essentially by trait comparisons. Bennett's approach was also comparative, but he tried to narrow the range of expectations in diffused traits by considering the functional implications of the trait, the context from which it was derived, and the context into which it could have been introduced and accepted. The last qualification was the key. He hypothesized that certain Mesoamerican features would have been readily accepted into the lower-threshold cultures of the southeastern United States, whereas others would have been rejected no matter how many times they would have been made available. Bennett's attempt was an early and trial one; unfortunately, it has not been followed up by those interested in Mesoamerican-Southeastern connections.

Two macrocontextual and functional studies appeared in Peruvian archaeology in the 1940s. In one of these, "Interpretations of Andean Archaeology," Wendell C. Bennett (1945) posed some interesting questions about traditional persistences of artifactual and technical traits and their probable linkages with different kinds of sociopolitical orders. Again, this idea was never carried further, either by the original author or others. The other article, "A Functional Analysis of 'Horizon Styles' in Peruvian Archaeology" by Gordon R. Willey (1948), was directly stimulated by John W. Bennett's writings. Willey endeavored to identify the sociopolitical or religious characteristics of Chavin, Tiahuanaco, and Incaic stylistic horizons by examining the cultural contexts (nature of artifacts, settlements, and overall patterns of distribution) of these horizons. The *horizon* concept, as we shall show later, was basically a historical device; however, it was also possible to look at it from a functional point of view.

By 1948, functional concerns were thus a minor but noticeable element in American archaeology. This foreknowledge did something, although not much, to prepare the way for Walter W. Taylor's *A Study of Archaeology* (1948). This was the first monographic critique of American archaeology, and it embodied a programmatic outline of archaeology for the future that was contextual and functional. Taylor had been working on these ideas for his doctoral dissertation as early as the late 1930s and early 1940s. Significantly, he wrote his dissertation at Harvard where Kluckhohn, who was then writing his own critique of Middle American archaeology, influenced his thinking. Taylor submitted the thesis in 1943 and revised it for publication after World War II.

Taylor began by noting the same ambiguity in the aims of American archaeology that Kluckhohn had stressed—namely, the indecisiveness as to whether historical or scientific (anthropological) goals are to be pursued. He defined history or historiography as "projected contemporary thought about past actuality, integrated and synthesized into contexts in terms of cultural man and sequential time" (Taylor, 1948, pp.

34–35). In contrast, cultural anthropology "is the comparative study of the statics and dynamics of culture, its formal, functional, and developmental aspects" (Taylor, 1948, p. 39). According to Taylor, archaeology became historiography when it went beyond *antiquarianism* (the securing of isolated and unrelated artifacts and data of the past) and mere *chronicle* (the arrangement of these objects and data in chronological sequences) to integrate the data of the past into a cultural context. Such a context refers to all the affinities among the data as these may be expressed in spatial associations or in quantitative or qualitative values. After such a reconstruction of context, the archaeologist may then go on to comparative studies about the nature and workings of culture in the formal, functional, and developmental aspects mentioned previously.

Taylor thus saw historiography and cultural anthropology as two sequent phases of a research procedure, in contradistinction to Kluckhohn, who had advocated one approach or the other. Taylor also saw the reconstruction of cultural context as a part of historiography or the historical operation. A functional interpretation of this reconstruction (or model) would then be the anthropological study, which would follow. Although other archaeological writers of the time are not clear or explicit on this point, there seems to have been a general tendency (as one can judge from the statements of Strong, Steward, Martin, and others) to lump together everything that went beyond typology and bare sequence or chronicle into the newer functional archaeology. Thus, such functional archaeology embraced the reconstruction of contexts, inferences as to use and function, and attempts to say something about process. These are obviously interrelated but, nevertheless, analytically separable concerns. As we have said, the decades of 1940–60 saw the focus of attention on the first two objectives, and Taylor's monograph had this emphasis.

Taylor devoted much of the book to a fine-grained critique of the writings of the prominent archaeologists of the Classificatory-Historical Period. Kidder, who had been a leader in the stratigraphic revolution and was the foremost Americanist of the time, was especially singled out for attack as representative of the conventional archaeology. According to Taylor (1948, p. 67), "When Kidder writes theory he often talks historiography and anthropology. When he directs field work and publishes reports he talks comparative chronicle." In his more detailed argument, Taylor held that no picture of past life had been reconstructed from any of Kidder's excavations, nor did he use his data to analyze or discuss functional matters. His nearest approach to either had been in his studies of the pottery from the Pecos, New Mexico, ruin, but even here the main objective was that of identifying cultural influences from other regions of the Southwest rather than looking at the significance of the pottery in the total culture of the Pecos site. Taylor notes that Kidder is aware of such possibilities and that he raises questions about the relationships between pottery decorative motifs and other Puebloan art but that he had done nothing to follow up these questions. He concludes (1948, p. 48): "If such problems had been attacked with regard to the nature and interrelations of pottery within Pecos itself, Kidder would have been 'doing' historiography, at least of the ceramic complex. If he had then proceeded to compare his findings with similar findings from other sites or areas with the intent of abstracting the regularities between the two sets of [ceramic] data, he would have been 'doing' cultural anthropology. As the matter now stands, he has done neither."

Kidder's Maya studies, and the program of the Carnegie Institution in the Maya field, were also attacked, especially for their failures to seek out or even be concerned with the data of settlement patterns and their implications. For instance, after thirty years of research, Taylor complained, there was still no real information or informed opinion on the degree to which the Lowland Maya centers were or were not urban phenomena; there were virtually no archaeological data on ordinary Maya dwellings; little or nothing was available on ancient Maya food habits. Pottery, as in the Southwest, had been employed in the reconstruction of chronicle or bare sequence, not in the reconstruction of use and function.

In Taylor's opinion, most of the archaeologists then practicing in the United States or anywhere in the Americas were as much at fault as Kidder. This included such men as Thompson[9] in Maya studies, Haury[10] and Roberts[11] in the Southwest, and W. S. Webb[12] and J. B. Griffin[13] in the eastern United States — to name only a few of those Taylor took issue with.

As might be expected, Taylor's praises were reserved for those few functional attempts from the 1940s that we have reviewed: Martin, Wedel, J. W. Bennett, Lewis and Kneberg, Waring and Holder.[14] He also noted that some archaeologists, including Kidder, wrote occasional statements that revealed both an interest in and insight into contextual and functional archaeology but that these writings were usually quite slight and often brought out in journals other than the standard professional ones, as though the authors were mildly ashamed of such excursions into popularization. This, we think, was an apt observation, for at that time, such forays away from recognized and approved procedures were considered unsound, and the archaeologist who went too far in this direction was suspect.

In concluding, Taylor was at pains to lay out what he considered to be an improved approach for American archaeology, one designated in his terms as the *conjunctive approach*. By this, he meant the drawing together, or the conjunction, of all possible lines of investigation on a specified archaeological problem. To chronicle and intersite relationships would be added close contextual intrasite study, with attention given to both the artifacts and features in themselves and to their relationships with all other artifacts and features. Such relationships would be sought not only in spatial or physical associational dimensions but in possible functional and systematic ties. For example, an archaeologist in a pottery study might look at the changing relationships between the numbers of jars to those of bowls. A drop in the numbers and percentages of large jars might indicate a decline in the need for water storage and thus, in turn, prompt the investigator to turn to other types of evidence to see if there had been a climatic change with possible increases of precipitation. Or, if warfare is suggested by fortified sites, the archaeologist should be alert to the possibilities of increases in the numbers of projectile points or other artifacts suitable for weapons. Nor should the archaeologist ignore cultural patterns for which no apparent functional correlates can be found. Taylor cites, as an example, the complete lack of symmetry in Coahuila Cave basketry designs, and he contrasts this with the concept of *regularized decorative wholes*, which dominates the designs of the San Juan basketry several hundred miles to the north of Coahuila. These decorative differences cannot be explained by either the basketry materials or the weaving techniques, which are the same in both regions. It is a fundamental difference in cultural patterning not readily understood. What does it relate to functionally? Maybe we will never find out, but it is the kind of datum to be borne in mind by the investigator.

Speculation, Taylor stoutly maintained, was not only justified in archaeology but required. It was the very life of the discipline, for, if archaeology was to investigate the nonmaterial aspects of culture through its material ones, it must have recourse to hypotheses (Taylor, 1948, p. 157):

> With the proper and sensible proviso that conclusions are based on "the facts at hand" and are subject to revision in the light of fuller and better data, it is a premise of the conjunctive approach that interpretations are both justified and required, when once the empirical grounds have been made explicit. Why has revision been such a bugbear to archaeologists? Other disciplines are constantly reworking their hypotheses and formulating new ones upon which to proceed with further research. When these are found to demand modification and change they are altered. Why should archaeology assume the pretentious burden of infallibility?

Not surprisingly, Taylor's monograph was not happily received by the archaeological establishment. Some members of that group were inclined to shrug it off angrily as nonsense; others, who had chafed under the narrow restrictions of conventional archaeology, may have had secret resentment at not having had Taylor's courage; still others, including some of those most pointedly attacked, felt that they had been reprimanded for failing to do what they had *not* set out to do. That is, Taylor's goals were recognized as admirable but believed to be beyond the "data strength" of American archaeology at that time. Spatial-temporal and taxonomic systematics had to be carried farther before contextual and functional archaeology could have any real chance of success. Or so ran one argument.[15]

In spite of the immediate negative reaction from a large part of the archaeological profession, Taylor's words were not forgotten. A decade and a half later, some of them were echoed in the New Archaeology of the Explanatory Period. More immediately, they helped keep alive the interest in context and function for some archaeologists in the 1950s.[16]

As one looks back on all of this some forty years later, the debate does not seem surprising. American archaeologists had been striving, since the end of the nineteenth century, to get the house of prehistory — as represented by the monuments and artifacts of antiquity — into some kind of typological, spatial, and temporal order. They had devoted their careers to this job — and it was still continuing. Taylor's critique seemed unwarranted, and there was initial resentment; but, after this anger had died down, there was a quiet acceptance of many of his ideas.

One important aspect of the concern with context and function that drew attention after 1950 was in artifact typology. Between 1914 and 1940, artifact typology (and especially pottery typology) was geared almost wholly to problems of chronology. Ford and others referred to typologies in terms of their "usefulness" in this regard (Ford, 1938; see also Krieger, 1944). If types were not "useful" in effecting chronological separations in the material, they were considered essentially worthless, as subjects of little more than sterile exercises in description. Such a view was, of course, in keeping with the narrowly limited definition of archaeology as being concerned with chronological ordering and little else. From this position, it was logical to conceive of the type as being something imposed on the data by the classifier. However, if one wished to broaden the goals of archaeology to include function and context as well as chronology, then the artifact had other things to tell us. With this outlook, the imposed type, which was merely a concept of the archaeologist, would be of little service. Instead, the archaeologist should be looking for the types, or mental templates, that were once carried in the minds of the original makers and users of the artifacts. As we have seen, this approach to typology appeared in the late 1930s, with Martin's insistence on the artifact as a registration of past cultural behavior and Rouse's similar premises. Taylor, in his launching of the *conjunctive approach,* devoted a chapter of his book to typology and classification and took a comparable position. He reasoned that, for the proper recreation of cultural context, the typologist should make every effort to discover or recapture the types as these once existed in the vanished culture. In this way, the lines of a debate on typology were drawn between those predisposed to see the artifact type as something imposed on the data and those who saw it as something to be discovered within the data.

In this debate, Ford championed the type as an imposed or designed construct of the archaeologist; A. C. Spaulding led the attack on behalf of those who saw it as discovered. The controversy started with Ford's publication in 1952 of "Measurements of Some Prehistoric Design Developments in the Southeastern States." It concerned Lower Mississippi Valley ceramics and comparisons drawn between these and similar styles in northwest Florida and northeast Texas. Relative chronologies existed in all the regions involved and for the most part were based on individual site stratigraphies with percentages of types per level computed in unimodal frequency curves. Such frequencies were compared from site to site and region to region. By his term and concept of

A percentage frequency chart from a Lower Mississippi Valley archaeological excavation, in which pottery types are graphed by level. The graphs approximate unimodal curves. This is a typical chart following J. A. Ford's procedures. (From Ford, Phillips, and Haag, 1955)

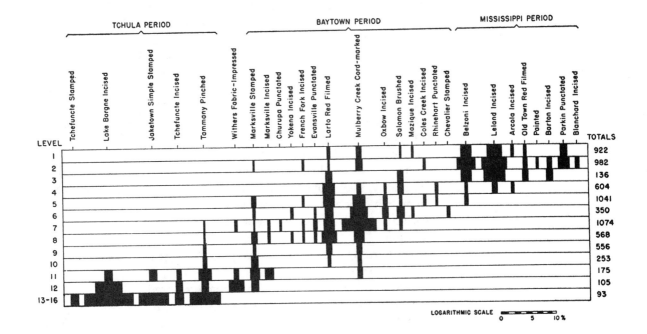

The chart on the facing page is a stylized presentation of unimodal curves representing pottery type frequencies, with illustrations of vessels of each type. This particular chart attempts to correlate ceramic sequences from northeast Texas, Louisiana, and Florida. (From Ford, 1952)

measurement, Ford was referring to relatively gradual changes, accretions, and losses in pottery design motifs and elements and the correlation of these with relative time and with geographical space. That is, form (the designs), time, and space were the variables, and observations on their covariance were called *measurements.* In his introduction to the monograph, Ford took exception to Taylor's insistence on the importance of the reconstructed context and a determination of function (Ford, 1952, p. 314): "If a clear and complete reconstruction of all possible details of man's unrecorded history in all parts of the world is the primary goal of modern archaeology, then we have merely refined the ancient curio and fact-collecting activities of our predecessors and still can only beg that our studies be tolerated for esthetic purposes." His feeling was that archaeology should march more rapidly from its concern with chronology to become a "science of culture" and "to provide basic data for a close examination of general principles, of causes, speed, inevitability and quantitative aspects of culture change over long periods of time" (Ford, 1952, p. 318). Such basic data, in his opinion, were offered in his 1952 article.

Spaulding's highly critical review (1953a) took issue with much of this. To him, the tone of the monograph, particularly the use of the word *measurements,* gave a specious scientific precision to the operation. Although in this work Ford had not pressed his opinion that types were imposed or created by the archaeologist—in effect, arbitrary units sliced out of the reality of the continuum of evolutionary change—there was just enough of this philosophy in it to provoke a highly negative reaction from Spaulding. The latter had a very different concept of the type, and this he set down in an article published in the same year as his review of Ford. In "Statistical Techniques for the Discovery of Artifact Types,"[17] Spaulding proposed that culture did not evolve as an even, constant flow; instead, it was characterized by "clusterings" or "irregularities," by sudden spurts and relatively static periods. These clusterings, in Spaulding's view, could be discovered by statistical analyses—analyses that would show just how various traits or trait modes had been truly associated.[18] Such clusterings were discovered types, and, because of their reality, they would tell the archaeologist a great deal more about human behavior and culture change than those types that purported to be arbitrary segments sliced out of the continuum of a uniform cultural evolution.

The Ford-Spaulding debate was joined along these lines with several exchanges in the professional journals (Ford, 1954a, 1954b, 1954c; Spaulding, 1954a, 1954b, 1960). The debate centered on the nature of the type and of culture change. What was also being argued—although this did not surface as such—was the basic purpose or purposes of the

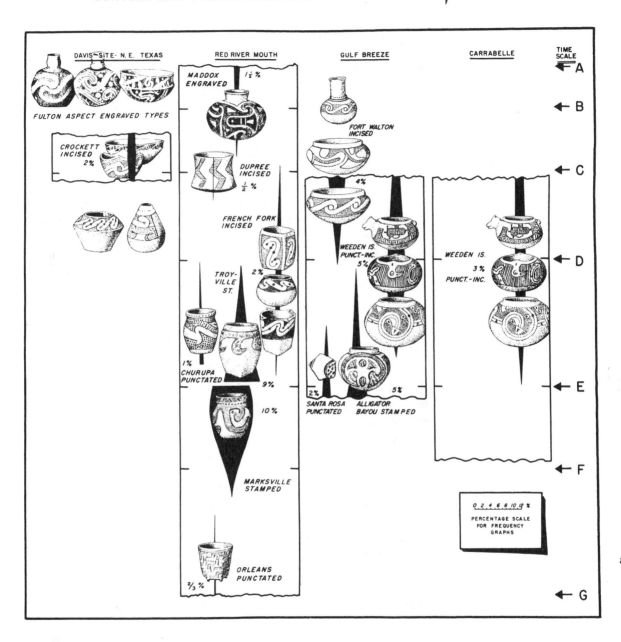

typology and the classification. If these purposes were those of chronological ordering and no more, Ford's imposed or designed types were sufficient. Certainly, they had been subjected to considerable empirical testing in this regard and had not been found wanting. But if, in addition to chronological control, the archaeological objectives also included an appreciation of cultural context and function, it would appear that Spaulding's statistically "discovered" types were more appropriate. Beyond these considerations lay the question of which kind of type was more suited to the elucidation of culture change or process. Ford, as we have pointed out, wanted to go swiftly from chronological ordering or chronicle to process. In the final pages of his "Measurements" article, he gives us the distillate of these processual findings.

We question whether or not Ford has, in any effective way, come to grips with process. Has he told us anything about the "general principles" or the "causes, speed, inevitability, and quantitative aspects of culture change," as these were listed in his introduction? He has perhaps told us something of general principles. Cultural forms evolve from like cultural forms; change tends to proceed by gradual modifications – at least in the pottery types Ford had under examination. But it is highly doubtful if we have come any closer to an understanding of the other aspects of change. The concluding statement to the monograph is, rather, a description of the formal, observable aspects of stylistic change in pottery. Except for possible diffusional influences, we have no inkling of cause. It is our opinion that the archaeologist will be best placed for the study of process by a preliminary consideration of context and function – and, as follows from this, by a typology that is best geared to serve these ends. The leap from chronological ordering to process is too great to be negotiated successfully. The functionings of culture have to be understood as preliminary to causal explanations. Again, these comments carry us ahead of our story, and we shall come back to them in the next chapter; however, it is worth emphasizing that Spaulding was a forerunner of many of the concerns about cultural variability that came to be emphasized in the following decade.

The majority of American archaeologists, or at least those who were immediately concerned with pottery typology, tended to side with Spaulding in the Ford-Spaulding debate. At least, most of them became explicit in maintaining that types were, indeed, cultural realities and that they could be discovered by statistical or other proper analytical approaches.[19] As the 1950s moved into the 1960s, the issues of the Ford-Spaulding debate receded and were replaced by a new argument, which was joined by those who preferred a "taxonomic" or "type-variety" classification (Wheat, Gifford, and Wasley, 1958; Gifford, 1960; Sabloff and Smith, 1969) versus those who favored an "analytical" or "modal" approach (Rouse, 1939, 1960; Lathrap, 1962; Wright, 1967; Dunnell, 1971). Both of these schools conceived of types as models that once existed in the minds of the makers and users of the objects concerned, and, as such, both kinds of types were suited to contextual and functional problems in addition to their chronological purpose. The question now became which approach was more effectively designed to study cultural change. The debate continues and probably will continue for some time; but it is fair to say that a choice depends very largely on the kind of change and degree of change the archaeologist is attempting to delineate.

To leave typology and return to the wider aspects of the "artifact as behavior," we can observe continued interest in and concern with context and function throughout the 1950s. Some of this was expressed in writings that showed the archaeologist's increasing self-consciousness concerning the objectives, theories, and methods of his discipline.[20] The book *Method and Theory in American Archaeology* by Gordon R. Willey and Philip Phillips is perhaps the best-known example of such writings. Originally issued as two journal articles in 1953 and 1955, it came out in final revised form in 1958 (Phillips and Willey, 1953; Willey and Phillips, 1955; Willey and Phillips, 1958). Its first part is devoted to methodological and procedural matters, incorporating the general trend of the thinking of the times.[21] The authors conceive of archaeological research on three operational levels: (1) observation (fieldwork), (2) description (culture-historical integration), and (3) explanation (processual interpretation). They define *culture-historical integration* as "almost everything the archaeologist does in the way of organizing his primary data: typology, taxonomy, formulation of archaeological units, investigation of their relationships in the contexts of function and natural environment, and determination of their internal dimensions and external relationships in space and time" (Willey and Phillips, 1958, p. 5). As defined thus, culture-historical integration very clearly includes both spatial-temporal ordering and context and function. Willey and Phillips then go on to say that, although archaeologists have sometimes used explanatory concepts, such as acculturation, diffusion, and stimulus diffusion, they have largely been concerned with specific and limited cultural situations, with no attempt to draw generalizations. "So little work has been done in American archaeology on the explanatory level that it is difficult to find a name for it. The term 'functional interpretation,' which has gained a certain amount of currency in American studies . . . is not entirely satisfactory . . . [and] we have substituted here the broader 'processual interpretation'" (Willey and Phillips, 1958, p. 5). According to this view, historical integration (which subsumes context and functional interpretation) should precede the search for process.

In the 1950s, however, the distinction between contextual-functional and processual interpretations was not always clearly made nor understood. Although in the 1958 quotation cited above, Willey and Phillips did separate the two, their earlier 1953 article did not (Phillips and Willey, 1953; see also Willey, 1953a). In another article published in the same year,

Willey addressed himself quite directly to the matter of process in attempting to understand culture contact phenomena. This article, "A Pattern of Diffusion-Acculturation" (Willey, 1953d), used a comparative approach in analyzing the circumstances surrounding the apparent implantation of foreign colonies in the territory of another culture. From this analysis, Willey thought he saw a similar sequence of events or cause-and-effect relationships: (1) a period of different cultures existing side-by-side; (2) an interval of dominance by the foreign invader; and (3) a final fusion or synthesis of the two cultures, in which certain traits of the invading culture (elements of politico-religious symbolism) persisted. This same theme was expanded and refined in a 1955 seminar "An Archaeological Classification of Culture Contact Situations" held under the auspices of the Society for American Archaeology (Lathrap, 1956). The principal result of the seminar was, as the title implies, a classification that described different types of contact between two distinct cultures. One category of these (which included Willey's "cultural colonization" model of the earlier article) was designated as *site-unit intrusion;* the other, *trait-unit intrusion.* The seminar group avoided claims of explanation or cause, either in the specific examples chosen to illustrate their several types of culture contact or in comparative generalization; however, the possibility of cause-and-effect generalizations being drawn was implicit in the whole seminar venture and in the final sentence of their report: "In culture contact situations, we can, for example, look for factors influencing the results of contact under different circumstances, taking advantage of the fact that we can observe the before, during, and after with equal perspective" (Lathrap, 1956, p. 26).

Another seminar in the same 1955 series, "An Archaeological Approach to the Study of Cultural Stability," (R. H. Thompson, 1956) was more ambitious in its consideration of process and cause than the one on culture contacts. In this seminar, emphasis was on *in situ* culture change or lack of change through time; and the participants sought to define and classify types of culture change by conceiving of these as *tradition segments.*[22] Criteria of the definitions were in the diachronic configurations of the segments rather than their particular culture contents. For example, configurations were seen as *direct* (essentially unchanging cultural continuity) or *elaborating* (increasing complexity of the tradition through trait addition) — among other types. Although the steps leading to such a classification involved a consideration of cultural contexts and function, just as in the type definitions of the culture contact situations of the other seminar, the main interest was centered on the framing of hypotheses about causal factors or processes involved in the shaping of the *tradition segments.* These factors included such things as environment, demography, diffusion from other cultural traditions, and the cultural heritage of the tradition under consideration. The causal reasoning of the seminar was inferred from what was generally known in anthropology and cultural history at large (for example, large or increasing populations would tend to result in "elaborating" tradition segments).

This interest in process within the framework of culture stability-instability examination was one of the main themes of a regional archaeological monograph by Robert Wauchope, who had been one of the members of the cultural stability seminar. The monograph, to a very large extent, is a site excavation and survey descriptive presentation on northern Georgia (Wauchope, 1966); however, it includes a twenty-page section on cultural process. Although not published until 1966, the monograph was in preparation in the late 1950s and reflects the thinking of the period.[23] At the same time, Wauchope was going well ahead of most of his contemporaries of the late 1950s in attempting to quantify culture change (largely in pottery types) on a 1:100 scale and in appraising such things as "technical versus esthetic change" and "peasant versus urban change." In commenting on technical versus esthetic change, he noted that the Georgia data do not support an often-stated anthropological assumption that technology changes more readily than art. For the peasant versus urban model, insofar as it could be applied to the Georgia data, he felt these data tended to substantiate greater and more rapid rates of ceramic change at the urban or urban-like pole. He comments, from this Georgia viewpoint, on broad developmental trends in cultural growth that have been suggested by other archaeologists and anthropologists.[24] Some of these trends, regularities, or laws find possible confirmation in the Georgia data; others do not. Throughout, the tone is cautious, the mood clearly experimental. How far can archaeological data and methods go toward checking anthropological assumptions concerning cultural development (these mostly drawn from evolutionary theory), and how far can they pioneer in these directions on their own? These are the questions asked, but, on the whole, no answers are given.

Other archaeologists who were thinking and writing along these lines in the 1950s include J. B. Griffin, L. S. Cressman, and J. B. Caldwell.[25] Like Wauchope, Willey and Phillips, and the seminar participants, they all saw the approach to process to lie in cross-cultural comparisons, and in this they all tended to move from the specific to the ever-widening generalization.

Although the decades 1940 to 1960 had been characterized by an increasing realization of the importance of context and function, there was a tendency on the part of the archaeologists writing at that time to slight these aspects of prehistory when they transferred their attention to trends, regularities, and laws. There was, perhaps, a too-ready search for universals, however much this was accompanied by cautious back-tracking, and too little attention to an examination of the actual mechanics of process, as these might be observed in contextual-functional settings. Wauchope and Caldwell (the latter in his *Trend and Tradition in the Prehistory of the Eastern United States,* 1958) were perhaps better in this regard than the others, and, to some extent, their work foreshadows the archaeological views of process that were to appear in the 1960s.

Up to this point, we have talked of context and function under the rubric of the artifact as behavior, construing this in the broadest sort of way. There are, however, two significant contextual-functional approaches from the late Classificatory-Historical Period that also helped to focus attention on process and that deserve some separate comment here. These are the *settlement pattern* and the *culture and environment* approaches.

SETTLEMENT PATTERNS

Prior to the 1940s, archaeologists paid little attention to settlement patterns in the Americas. They prepared site maps and sometimes were concerned about site locations with reference to terrain features, but there had been no studies that emphasized the disposition of ruins over sizable regions or the arrangement of features within a site. In 1946, however, Steward encouraged Willey to make settlement survey and analysis his part of the combined Virú Valley (Peru) investigations.[26] The Virú Valley fieldwork went forward during most of 1946, and, in 1953, Willey brought out his *Prehistoric Settlement Patterns in the Virú Valley,* the first monograph-length treatment of regional settlement patterns.[27]

Detailed maps were prepared of all sections of the valley; aerial photographs were used extensively in mapping; on-the-ground investigations checked mapping; and observations were made on building and architectural features. The dating of sites was worked out through excavations by other members of the Virú Valley party, plus J. A. Ford's analyses of surface sherd collections. The Virú Valley had been originally chosen because it was moderately well known archaeologically and lay in the Peruvian North Coastal zone, for which a preliminary ceramic sequence was already available. The Virú Valley diggings and surveys corrected and refined this sequence, and Willey's settlement study would have been impossible without it; however, the central objective of the settlement investigation was context and function. How did the different communities of the Virú Valley interrelate and function on the successive time-planes, or culture periods, of the Virú Valley sequence?

Willey defined settlement patterns as "the way in which man disposed himself over the landscape on which he lived. It refers to dwell-

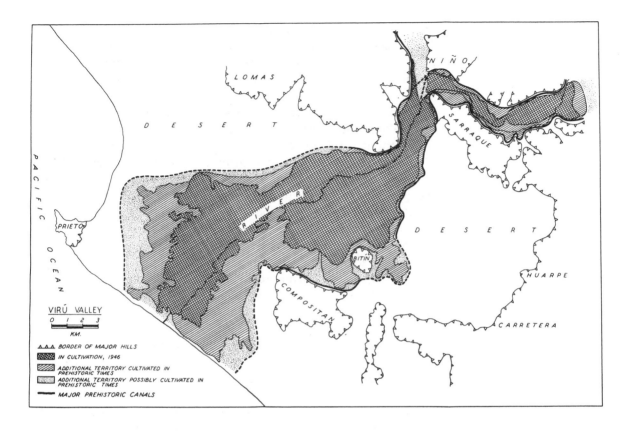

ings, to their arrangement, and to the nature and disposition of other buildings pertaining to community life. These settlements reflect the natural environment, the level of technology on which the builders operated, and various institutions of social interaction and control which the culture maintained. Because settlement patterns are, to a large extent, directly shaped by widely held cultural needs, they offer a strategic starting point for the functional interpretation of archaeological cultures" (Willey, 1953b, p. 1). In the last sentence, Willey revealed a certain ambiguity between function and process, for "widely held cultural needs" implies a basis for ready cross-cultural comparisons; the study, though, is essentially one of *in situ* context and function.

Most of the Virú Valley settlement monograph is substantive presentation. The author acknowledges the experimental nature of the work, but such comments are confined to little more than a page. Archaeological sites and features are presented by cultural phases or periods. A rather gross functional classification of sites further orders the presentation. There are *dwelling sites,* divided into those that showed exposed

Map of the Virú Valley showing areas in cultivation in modern times, in contrast to those under irrigation and cultivation in prehistoric times. The plotting of canals and garden sections was one of the principal aspects of the Virú settlement pattern survey. (From Willey, 1953b)

architectural foundation arrangements and those that were simply refuse hillocks; *pyramid mounds*, of apparent ceremonial or public function;
pyramid-dwelling-construction complexes, or sites that seemed to combine
public-ceremonial and dwelling functions; *cemeteries*; and *fortifications*.
The period presentation is followed by a chapter that considers the
development or evolution of the various functional classes of sites. That
is, dwelling-sites or *politico-religious structures* (such as pyramids) are
traced through the some 1,500 years or more of the Pre-Columbian
occupancy of the Virú Valley. A section on *community patterns* follows,
in which the author attempts to show how different kinds of sites were
integrated into overall patterns of living at the different time-periods. A
chapter on settlements and society is the most boldly theoretical, with
inferences drawn from settlement to population sizes and to sociopolitical organization; however, even here, Willey was exceedingly cautious
and did not advance the numbers and kinds of hypotheses that he might
have. A final chapter is a more conventional archaeological one — at least
for the early 1950s — which compares the Virú Valley settlement types
with those of other regions of Peru, insofar as this was possible with the
limited data then at hand.

The reaction to the Virú Valley work was, in general, favorable, if
mildly so. The completely nonpolemical tone aroused no hard feelings;
the massive substantive presentation was eminently respectable, even if
a reader might be wary of the short theoretical forays. It was not
immediately followed up in Peru, although it was to be within a decade.[28] Willey shifted his interests to the Maya area in the 1950s and in

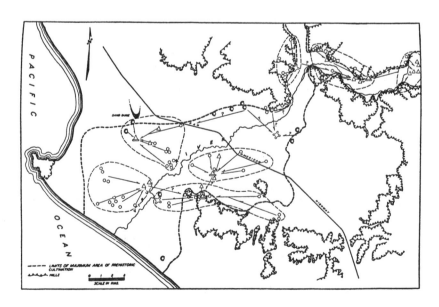

*Map presenting ideas about
community hierarchies and
interactions during the Huancaco
Period (Moche culture) in the
Virú Valley, Peru. (From Willey,
1953b)*

1954 began a settlement-pattern investigation—combined with more standard archaeological operations—in the Belize Valley (Willey and others, 1965). Archaeologists of other New World areas showed an interest in the approach by participating in a symposium on the settlement-pattern theme in 1954, the results of which appeared in 1956 (Willey, 1956). Willey, who edited the volume, provided only a very brief introduction and failed thereby to give the book the theoretical setting and purpose that it needed. Some of the contributors limited themselves to rather cautious descriptions of sites and site distributions; others addressed themselves somewhat more to context and function; but two papers—one by William T. Sanders on central Mexico and another on the Lowland Amazon by Betty J. Meggers and Clifford Evans—went daringly beyond this to talk about process and cause.

Another joint effort, essentially on a settlement-pattern theme, was also published in 1956. This was the result of another of the 1955 Seminars in Archaeology and was entitled "Functional and Evolutionary Implications of Community Patterning" (Meggers, 1956). The seminar group established a series of community types, for both sedentary and nomadic peoples, and then enquired into the functional and evolutionary aspects of these types. The approach was broadly comparative, being both world-wide in scope and concerned with ethnographical as well as archaeological data. As the title implies, the results were seen as both functional and evolutionary, thus moving beyond function to process. This was clearly the most advanced (in the sense of being theoretically oriented) use so far made of settlement data.

Whereas the seminar report was framed in the rather broad evolutionary terms and reasoning that, whether acceptable or unacceptable, were familiar to anthropologists and archaeologists, another theoretical treatise on settlement patterns was more controversial. This was K. C. Chang's "Study of the Neolithic Social Grouping: Examples from the New World" (1958). The title is not altogether revealing, as Chang drew upon extensive Old World ethnographical information in establishing correlations between social-organizational and settlement types on a Neolithic level. He then took these correlations and applied them to archaeological settlement data in the New World—in Mesoamerica, Peru, and the North American Southwest. Chang concluded by suggesting "that it should be the archaeologists's first duty to delimit local social groups such as households, communities, and aggregates, rather than to identify archaeological regions and areas by time-spacing material traits, since cultural traits are meaningless unless described in their social context" (Chang, 1958, p. 324). This was a bold call for the preeminence of the social dimension in archaeological study—a pushing forward of the settlement-pattern approach as the first order of archaeological business. Some archaeologists demurred (Nicholson, 1958; Rouse, 1968, Chang, 1968); and we are not inclined to follow Chang all the way on this procedural argument (Willey, 1958b); still, it is all too clear in retrospect that American archaeology was for a long time hampered by its failure to come to grips with the social settings of the cultures that were being studied and to realize that an awareness of settlement patterns is a first step in this direction (Trigger, 1963, 1967, 1968a; Chang, 1958; Sears, 1961; Mayer-Oakes, 1961; Millon, 1967; Sanders, 1949, 1962; Naroll, 1962).

In retrospect, we are inclined to think that it is at this point in the history of American archaeology that the subject shifted from its elitist orientation to one that can be best described as middle class (see Patterson, 1986, for a somewhat different view). Beyond this, we would now go so far as to say that settlement pattern study is almost a mandatory first step in any archaeological investigation concerned with the processes of social and political change in prehistoric societies.

CULTURE AND ENVIRONMENT

In the latter part of the Classificatory-Historical Period, an attempt was also made to place archaeological cultures in their appropriate natural environmental settings. This was, in part, a reaction to the strong antienvironmentalist tone of American anthropology, which, under Boasian leadership, had proscribed environment as a possible explanatory factor in the development of culture. This is not to say that environment was completely overlooked by archaeologists; it was usually described but thought of as having at best a permissive or passive role in conditioning culture. This philosophy is especially clear in A. L. Kroeber's "Cultural and Natural Areas of Native North America" (1939). Occasionally, some archaeologists would regard environment in a more active or causative sense as a catastrophic agent. For instance, a major drought, an earthquake, or even artificial environmental imbalances were conceived of as destroying a culture, as in the case of the fall of Classic Maya civilization (Sabloff and Willey, 1967). But in all of these cases, a holistic view of culture and environment in an interacting, systemic relationship was lacking. Culture and environment were regarded as two separate entities. The holistic approach, which is the true ecological approach, was not to be a part of American archaeology until a few years later.[29] What did develop in the latter part of the Classificatory-Historical Period, and which went beyond the very simple descriptive treatments of the environment that had been current, was the attitude that the environmental setting of any culture should be studied as thoroughly as possible to reconstruct an appropriate prehistoric environmental context, which in turn would allow for functional interpretations.

Such concerns in environmental archaeology in America had a much earlier inception in European prehistory, and American archaeologists undoubtedly were influenced by these pioneer Old World studies. For instance, in Scandinavia, an interest in environmental reconstruction can be traced well back into the nineteenth century, and, in Great Britain, Sir Cyril Fox, O. G. S. Crawford and Grahame Clark had long been working along these lines. The Europeans had been stimulated in all of this by German and British geographers, and we would also surmise that the lack of a strongly intrenched antienvironmentalist school of thought, as in America, allowed for earlier European considerations of the environmental factor.[30]

With relation to the matter of the reconstruction of past environments for contextual-functional interpretations, June Helm has said that, by the end of the 1950s, "the ecologically contextual study had become an established model in American archaeology" (Helm, 1962, p. 361). Although not agreeing with her use of the word *ecology* in this particular context, we would agree that the functional emphases of the period did include, as would seem logical, considerations of environmental setting. Such considerations took the form of attempts to reconstruct environments and diets of ancient cultures and relied heavily on data and techniques from the natural sciences. The cultures involved in these studies were most often hunting and gathering ones, which tended to leave meager artifactual remains.[31]

Typical of these important early attempts at environmental reconstruction was the work of Waldo R. Wedel on the Great Plains of the United States. Wedel attempted to put native subsistence activities in the context of environment, especially the former climatic environments of the Plains (Wedel, 1941, 1953). Another example was the study by Emil W. Haury and his associates at Ventana Cave, Arizona. Haury utilized the knowledge and skills of geologists and other natural scientists in a major prehistoric environmental reconstruction (Haury and others, 1950). A similar synthesis of archaeological, geological, paleobotanical, faunal, and pollen studies was carried out by Frederick Johnson at the Boylston Street Fishweir site in Massachusetts.[32] Still other instances of archaeological-environmental studies of the period are to be seen in the writings of J. D. Jennings, W. G. Haag, and G. I. Quimby.[33] Also worthy of special mention are a series of investigations on the California shellmounds pioneered by E. W. Gifford (1916) and later continued by R. F. Heizer, S. F. Cook, and other colleagues.[34] They reconstructed the diet of the ancient shell-mound dwellers, and, with some ingenious formulas based on weight and quantities of midden debris, arrived at site population estimates. But, in all these studies, as we have said, the goal was that of the descriptive creation of an environmental context, with little or no concern with environment as a systemic causative factor in cultural development.

The conception of environment as a determinative force in the rise and growth of cultures went well beyond the contextual-functional environmental reconstructions and moved American archaeological interests in the direction of cultural evolution. The environmentalist perspective must be considered as an important trend of the late Classificatory-Historical Period. Environmental determinism and cultural evolution had been jointly submerged in American anthropological thinking at about the turn of the century. Now, in the mid-twentieth century, we see them reemerging together. The major focus on this reemergence was in the study of the complex cultures of the New World, those usually referred to as the "civilizations" of Mexico and Peru.

The principal figure in the environmental-evolutionary trend was Julian H. Steward. We have already commented on this ethnologist-social anthropologist's influences on American archaeology, particularly with reference to settlement-pattern research; his contributions in the realms of what he was to call *cultural ecology* and *multilinear evolution* were to be even greater.[35] Basically, Steward called for the archaeologist to compare specific cultural sequences in specific environmental settings in order to look for developmental regularities. He hypothesized that particular aspects of the environment would influence what he called the *core* elements of a culture. These core elements were essentially technological ones. In other words, different kinds of environments would influence the nature of technological adaptations, which in turn would influence and condition other aspects of culture. For the first time in many decades, an American anthropologist was saying that environment could determine cultural adaptation.

Although Steward's overemphasis on the role of the core in cultural development and his lack of a holistic or true ecological view of culture and environment can be criticized,[36] he had a major and salutary influence on American archaeological theory. His 1949 article "Cultural Causality and Law: A Trial Formulation of the Development of Early Civilizations" was a bold attempt to put his theoretical ideas into practice (Steward, 1949a); and his 1955 collection of essays, *Theory of Culture Change,* was especially influential (Steward, 1955b). Following the lead of the Sinologist Karl Wittfogel (1957), he also stimulated research on the role of irrigation in the rise of civilization. In South American studies, his "Circum-Carribean" hypothesis not only engendered lively debate but produced constructive rebuttal (Steward, 1947, 1948a; Rouse, 1953b, 1956, 1964a; Sturtevant, 1960).

There were also other important figures in the environmental and evolutionary trend in the late Classificatory-Historical Period. Pedro Armillas, a Spaniard who emigrated to Mexico, brought a materialist point of view to bear on the problems of the rise of urban civilization in the Valley of Mexico, quite independently of Steward. He, too, was especially interested in the role of irrigation and helped to inculcate a similar interest in a number of Mesoamerican archaeologists, including W. T. Sanders.[37] Angel Palerm and Eric Wolf, the latter a student of Steward's, also concentrated their efforts on investigating the correlations between differing Mesoamerican environments, agricultural techniques, and the development of civilization (Palerm, 1955; Wolf and Palerm, 1955; Wolf, 1957). A slightly modified version of Wittfogel's hydraulic hypothesis became a working premise for many of these workers and later helped give rise to a number of fascinating ecological studies in the 1960s.

While Steward's influence, direct and indirect, was strongly felt in the 1950s, that of another American ethnologist-social anthropologist, Leslie A. White, was delayed until the 1960s. Even though his *Science of Culture* was published in 1948, American archaeologists did not follow up his theories to any great extent until the following decade.[38] One student of his, however, Betty J. Meggers, was an exception to this. She produced several important theoretical papers in the 1950s, all of marked evolutionary orientation (Meggers, 1954, 1955, 1957). Her article "Environmental Limitation on the Development of Culture" argued for the deterministic nature of environmental influences, discussing and categorizing various types of environment which would be conducive, in varying degrees, to the rise of civilization or which would preclude this condition. This 1954 article was heavily criticized at the time it was written (W. R. Coe, 1957; Hirschberg and Hirschberg, 1957; Altschuler, 1958), but, while it may have been in error in specific examples, it also offered some important insights (Sabloff, 1972; Ferdon, 1959). Moreover, much of her fieldwork, in collaboration with Clifford Evans, was designed to test evolutionary and environmentalist hypotheses (Meggers and Evans, 1957; Evans and Meggers, 1960).

To conclude, concern with the role of environment with regard to culture began to increase during the latter part of the Classificatory-Historical Period. An understanding of ancient environments was a readily recognizable need, fully consistent with other contextual-functional emphases in American archaeological studies. Beyond this, a consideration of environments was seen as essential to an understanding of the development of culture by those few archaeologists who had begun to quest

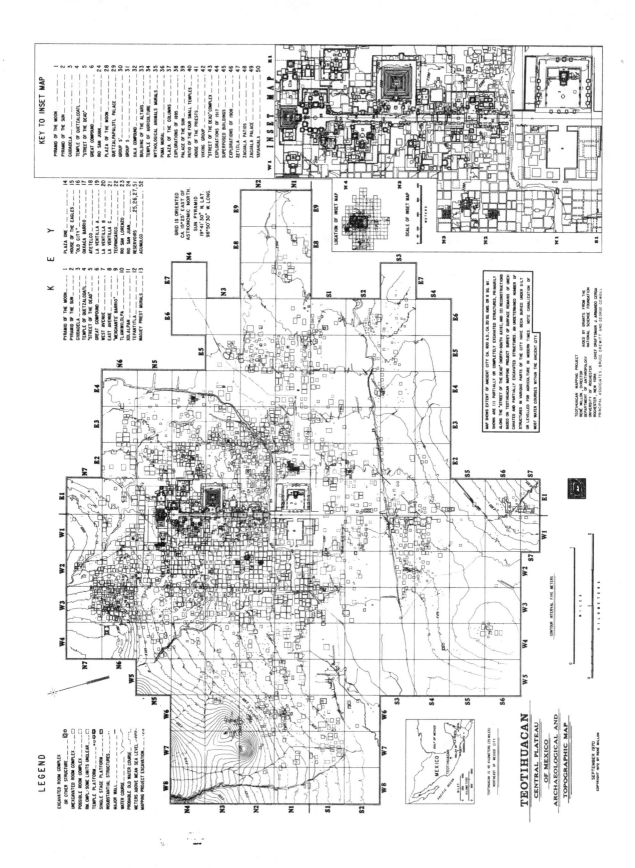

LEGEND

EXCAVATED ROOM COMPLEX
OR OTHER STRUCTURE
UNEXCAVATED ROOM COMPLEX
POSSIBLE ROOM COMPLEX
RM CMPLC - PLAN UNCLEAR
TEMPLE PLATFORM
SINGLE STAGE PLATFORM
INSUBSTANTIAL STRUCTURES
MAJOR WALL
WATER CHANNEL
WATER COURSE
PROBABLE OLD WATER COURSE
METERS ABOVE MEAN SEA LEVEL
MAPPING PROJECT EXCAVATION

KEY

PYRAMID OF THE MOON	1	PLAZA ONE 14
PYRAMID OF THE SUN	2	HOUSE OF THE EAGLES 15
CIUDADELA	3	"OLD CITY" 16
TEMPLE OF QUETZALCOATL	4	OAXACA BARRIO 17
"STREET OF THE DEAD"	5	ATETELCO 18
GREAT COMPOUND	6	LA VENTILLA A 19
EAST AVENUE	7	LA VENTILLA B 20
WEST AVENUE	8	LA VENTILLA C 21
"MERCHANTS' BARRIO"	9	TEOPANCAXCO 22
TLAMIMILOLPA	10	RIO SAN LORENZO 23
XOLALPAN	11	RIO SAN JUAN 24
TEPANTITLA	12	RESERVOIRS 25,26,27,51
MAGUEY PRIEST MURALS	13	ACUIMULCO 52

GRID IS ORIENTED
CA. 15°25' EAST OF
ASTRONOMIC NORTH.

SUN PYRAMID
19°41'30" N. LAT.
98°50'30" W. LONG.

KEY TO INSET MAP

PYRAMID OF THE MOON	1
PYRAMID OF THE SUN	2
CIUDADELA	3
TEMPLE OF QUETZALCOATL	4
"STREET OF THE DEAD"	5
GREAT COMPOUND	6
RIO SAN JUAN	24
PLAZA OF THE MOON	28
QUETZALPAPALOTL PALACE	29
GROUP 5	30
GROUP 5'	31
XALA COMPOUND	32
TEMPLE OF AGRICULTURE	33
BUILDING OF THE ALTARS	34
MYTHOLOGICAL ANIMALS MURALS	35
PUMA MURAL	36
PLAZA OF THE COLUMNS	37
EXPLORATIONS OF 1895	38
PALACE OF THE SUN	39
PATIO OF THE FOUR SMALL TEMPLES	40
HOUSE OF THE PRIESTS	41
VIKING GROUP	42
"STREET OF THE DEAD" COMPLEX	43
EXPLORATIONS OF 1917	44
SUPERPOSED BUILDINGS	45
EXPLORATIONS OF 1908	46
ZETILLA	47
ZACUALA PATIOS	48
ZACUALA PALACE	49
YAYAHUALA	50

INSET MAP

LOCATION OF INSET MAP

SCALE OF INSET MAP

MAP SHOWS EXTENT OF ANCIENT CITY CA. 600 A.D. (CA.20 SQ. KMS. OR 8 SQ. MI.)
SHOWN ARE (1) PARTIALLY OR COMPLETELY EXCAVATED STRUCTURES, PRIMARILY
ALONG THE "STREET OF THE DEAD" (NORTH-SOUTH AXIS), AND (2) RECONSTRUCTIONS
BASED ON TEOTIHUACAN MAPPING PROJECT SURVEYS OF SURFACE REMAINS OF UNEX-
CAVATED AND PARTIALLY EXCAVATED STRUCTURES. NOTE ABSENCE OF
STRUCTURES IN VARIOUS PARTS OF THE CITY HAVE BEEN BURIED UNDER SILT
OR LEVELLED FOR AGRICULTURE IN MODERN TIMES. NOTE CANALIZATION OF
MOST WATER COURSES WITHIN THE ANCIENT CITY.

TEOTIHUACAN MAPPING PROJECT
RENÉ MILLON, DIRECTOR
DEPARTMENT OF ANTHROPOLOGY
UNIVERSITY OF ROCHESTER
ROCHESTER, NEW YORK

AIDED BY GRANTS FROM THE
NATIONAL SCIENCE FOUNDATION
CHIEF DRAFTSMAN J. ARMANDO CERDA
PRINCIPAL ASSOCIATES, BRUCE DREWITT AND GEORGE COWGILL

TEOTIHUACAN

CENTRAL PLATEAU
OF MEXICO
ARCHAEOLOGICAL AND
TOPOGRAPHIC MAP

SEPTEMBER 1970
COPYRIGHT 1972 BY RENÉ MILLON

CONTOUR INTERVAL FIVE METERS

MILES

KILOMETERS

TEOTIHUACAN IS 40 KILOMETERS (25 MILES)
NORTHEAST OF MEXICO CITY

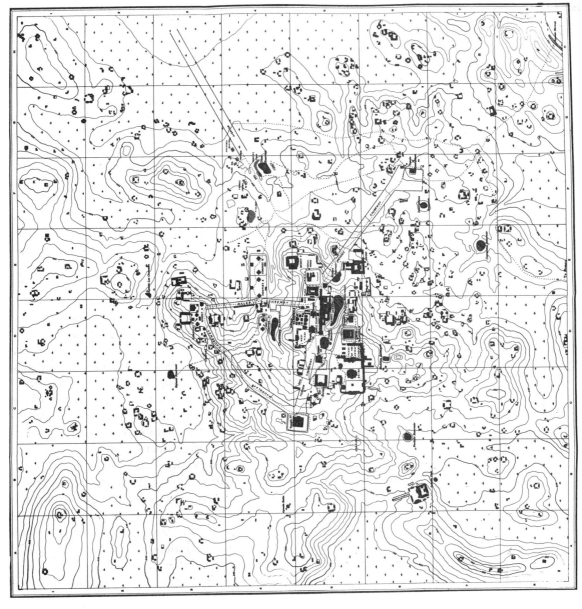

(above)

Plan of the great Pre-Columbian city of Teotihuacan, Valley of Mexico, with inset at right showing detail of the center of the city. This reduced version illustrates the immense care taken by René Millon and associates in mapping the urban zone at Teotihuacan as one step in their study of the processes of urbanism at this important site. From such detailed settlement-pattern studies, the archaeologists have estimated that, at its zenith, Teotihuacan had a population of over 100,000. All plans in the drawing are drawn to the same scale. (From Millon 1973, by permission)

(right)

A settlement-pattern map of the major ceremonial center and outlying ruins at Tikal, Guatemala. The area shown measures 4 × 4 km. (From Carr and Hazard, 1961)

for the causes of culture change. As Frederik Barth, a social anthropologist, said, after noting that the invention of radiocarbon dating would obviate the necessity for American archaeologists to concentrate all their energies on matters of chronology, "It can no longer be the archaeologist's ultimate ambition to make chronological charts of cultures.... The only way the archaeologist can contribute to the general field of anthropology is by asking questions of *why*, for which a general framework is needed. One simple and directly applicable approach is that of ecologic analysis of cultural adaptations, treating problems of relationship of the ecologic area, the structure of the human group, and its cultural characteristics."[39] But Barth's call would not be answered on any scale for more than a decade. Only a beginning had been made in the 1950s in the fight for the reintroduction of environmental concerns to archaeology and anthropology. As late as 1958, it could be stated that "archaeologists too often leave their ecology in the ground, due to interest in artifacts and ignorance of techniques for observing and interpreting ecological evidence" (Meighan and others, 1958, p. 131). But "ignorance of techniques" was not the primary reason. American archaeologists all too often lacked a clear understanding of the goals of their research and did not always know at the time they excavated what kinds of data would be needed to understand the nature of the cultural development at a particular site or in a particular region. It would only be with the clarification of the goals of archaeology in the Modern Period that the fragmented *environmental* concerns of the 1940s and 1950s would become the holistic *ecological* concerns of the 1960s. The prime element in this clarification of archaeological goals would be the reintroduction of the concept of *cultural evolution*. This reintroduction would not become sophisticated and effective until after 1960. We have, however, referred to some of the initial attempts to apply evolutionary theory in connection with cultural-environmental relationships, and later in this chapter we will return to other trial formulations of evolutionary concepts in the 1950s. For the moment, though, let us consider other matters as we move forward with the course of our history in the late Classificatory-Historical Period.

SCIENTIFIC AIDS
FROM OTHER
DISCIPLINES

One of the most significant developments of the latter part of the Classificatory-Historical Period was American archaeologists' increasing awareness of new inventions or possible applications of various scientific techniques.[40] To the popular mind, which tends to view scientific change phenomenologically, new awareness of scientific techniques is often considered revolutionary (Daniel, 1950, p. 287). That is, it is often felt that, with the advent of the 1950s, American archaeology suddenly added a scientific tool to its regular equipment and became a radically changed discipline. This, however, was not quite what happened. Although new dating techniques, and particularly radiocarbon dating, did have an immediate impact on American archaeology, techniques from other disciplines had only just begun to affect archaeology in the New World; and, although archaeologists began to use a host of new scientific aids, they were not prepared conceptually to use them in holistic combination or in ways that would affect significantly the kinds of data they were unearthing. Certainly, the necessity for an interdisciplinary approach was recognized in the Americas by the 1940s, and various scientific studies often formed descriptively impressive but generally neglected appendices to site reports. There were even some brilliant uses of scientific techniques in reconstructing the cultural histories and cultural contexts of individual sites, but these had the effect of supplements to already existing methodologies and seemed to do little to develop new ones.

As might be anticipated, the most widely used scientific aids were those that could be employed in chronology-building. These led to both relative and absolute dating refinements. Of all these, the most revolutionary was W. F. Libby's radiocarbon or carbon-14 method. It was devised in the late 1940s, and radiocarbon tests were made available to archaeologists in all parts of the New World during the 1950s. The method operates on the principle that the radioactive carbon of the atmosphere is, and was, absorbed by all living organisms. This absorption ceases at their death, and decay, with loss of radiocarbon, then begins at a steady and predictable rate. By testing the remains of such organisms found archaeologically — such as pieces of charred wood or bone — for their residual amounts of radiocarbon, they could be dated on an absolute scale. If such remains were found in firm association with other cultural materials, and had not been reused, then the cultural remains in question could be dated absolutely (Libby, 1955; Willis, 1969).

Radiocarbon dating had a great impact on many areas of American archaeology. For example, it showed once and for all that early settlers had reached the North American continent more than 10,000 years ago.[41] It also helped archaeologists to fill the Archaic gap between the migratory Late Pleistocene groups and the later sedentary cultures in several parts of North America (Willey, 1968a). In the Great Basin, radiocarbon dating enabled J. D. Jennings to erect a 10,000-year-long sequence for the migratory bands of that harsh area and to hypothesize the existence of a long-lasting Desert culture (Jennings, 1957, 1964). In Middle America, the enigmatic Olmec culture was shown to antedate the Classic Maya civilization by many centuries (Drucker, Heizer, and Squier, 1959), and its great significance as regards the development of civilization in Middle America and in general was finally realized. The list could go on and on, but suffice it to say that radiocarbon dating had a major influence on the ordering and lengthening or shortening of numerous cultural sequences throughout the Americas.

Radiocarbon dating also helped to set the stage for the following Modern Period in several interrelated ways. First, it helped establish full cultural sequences, so that the archaeologist could look at the evolution of culture in a more precise manner than before. Second, it gave an

Radiocarbon laboratory with view of combustion train from the conversion of sample to pure carbon dioxide. (From MASCA, The University Museum, University of Pennsylvania)

absolute time-range to the various sequences, so that rates of evolution in differing or similar environments, cultural conditions, and so on could be studied. Third, it helped archaeologists to compare cultures at a single time-period and therefore enabled them to look at and hypothesize about a variety of factors that caused differences or similarities among these cultural systems. Although for a time some archaeologists were sceptical of the accuracy and exactness of radiocarbon dating (Willis, 1969; Allibone, 1970) continued refinements and improvements in the technique have resulted in a steadily growing confidence in the method. Today, there is a general consensus that radiocarbon dating has been a very major contribution to the development of archaeology in general and in the New World in particular (Taylor, 1978).

Although radiocarbon dating was the most important chronological aid in the 1940–60 era, other absolute and relative dating procedures were pursued. Among these, dendrochronology, to which we have referred in the preceding chapter, was carried to new refinements, resulting in southwestern North American culture sequences being the most finely calibrated in the New World (Bannister, 1969). Other chemical and physical methods and techniques used in dating include paleomagnetism or archeomagnetism, obsidian hydration, and fluorine analyses of bone.[42] Geological dating, essentially of a relative nature, also enjoyed many advances in the late Classificatory-Historical Period. Through the efforts of Kirk Bryan, Ernest Antevs, and others, associations of cultural materials with geological strata and glacial deposits and relations to climatic sequences were all used to give approximate dates or to help in the interpretation of the stratigraphy of a number of archaeological sites, especially Late Pleistocene sites. The sites that were dated by these two scientists included such important ones as Lindenmeier (Colorado), Ventana Cave (Arizona), Leonard Rockshelter (Nevada), and Bat Cave (New Mexico).[43] Some geological dating was also accomplished, as Heizer has pointed out, through glacial varve sequences (although this technique was more successful in Europe), changes in shoreline levels, and rates of stream-channel meandering, dune migration, or travertine deposition (Heizer, 1953, pp. 6–14). Fisk's work on the changing channels of the Mississippi River was especially useful to archaeologists working at sites bordering this long river (Fisk, 1944; Phillips, Ford, and Griffin, 1951).

Dating was not the only subject for which American archaeologists looked for help, although it was the most important one. In their contextual concerns, as we have already noted, they turned to geological, zoological, and botanical sciences for aid in climatic and dietary reconstructions. Attention was also paid to technical studies of artifacts through the use of such techniques as spectroscopic analysis. With relation to pottery, Anna O. Shepard's work is an outstanding example (Shepard, 1956; see also Bishop and Lange, eds., 1991); the same can be said for the geologically oriented analyses of such scientists as Howel Williams (H. Williams, 1956; H. Williams and Heizer, 1965). However, when compared in sophistication and in quantity to such analyses in the Modern Period, this early work was small indeed (Brill, 1971).

Aerial photography and electronic detecting are two other techniques that deserve mention. The former was used to good advantage in Peru as early as 1931 by the Shippee-Johnson Expedition (Shippee, 1932) and in the later 1940s in the Virú Valley (Ford and Willey, 1949), as well as in the Southwest.[44] But again, aerial photography did not come into its own in relation to site survey and discovery until the 1960s. The same can be said for detecting devices. One only has to contrast the early and very limited use of mine detectors by C. W. Meighan at Drake's Bay, California (Meighan, 1950; Rowe, 1953, pp. 912–913) with the later sophisticated employment of a variety of such devices to see the difference (Aitken, 1969; Rainey and Ralph, 1966).

In addition, as noted earlier in our discussion of artifact types, there was a growing interest in statistics in the Classificatory-Historical Period. The earlier-mentioned works of Brainerd, Robinson, and Spaulding are good examples of this interest (Brainerd, 1951; Robinson, 1951; Spaulding, 1953b, 1960). But it was not until the Modern Period that

Aerial photography is an aid in detailed mapping as well as in site location and discovery. This aerial photograph shows the Chimu city of Chan Chan of the northern coast of Peru, where aerial photography played a crucial role in the detailed mapping by the Chan Chan Project. (From Services Aerofotografico Nacional, Peru)

Low-altitude photograph of an archaeological excavation in the Pueblo-type ruins of Casas Grandes, Chihuahua, Mexico. (From The Amerind Foundation, Inc., Dragoon, Arizona)

American archaeologists began to take advantage of the new computer advances that had already begun to affect other disciplines.

Thus, the late Classificatory-Historical Period saw a gradual increase in the attention paid to developments in other disciplines that could offer aids to archaeological research: physics, chemistry, the natural and biological sciences, and mathematics. In a somewhat helter-skelter fashion, more and more American archaeologists became aware of the advantages of these aids and began to experiment with them on their own or to consult appropriate experts. Our very brief discussion here has touched on these various aids only lightly; but their importance is, we think, obvious. By the 1960s, their acceptance became general practice; and, moreover, a conceptual structure was erected after that date that enabled the archaeologist to integrate and to point these aids toward particular research goals.

THE CONTINUED
CONCERN WITH
CHRONOLOGY AND
SPACE-TIME
SYNTHESIS

So far in this chapter, we have devoted our attention to innovations in archaeological goals and procedures; however, as we have stated, the preponderance of archaeological research carried on during the 1940-60 period was of the traditional kind, oriented toward the building of chronological sequences. We cannot hope to summarize or even comment on more than a sampling of the results of this work here. The best we can do is to touch on some of the highlights. In so doing, we will extend our coverage forward to include the decade of the 1960s. This takes us into the Modern Period, with its significant changes in theoretical outlook and methodology, which we will deal with in the next chapter; however, much of the work of the 1960s, with its continued emphasis on the schematics of space-time synthesis, does not differ in kind from that of the preceding period.

In reviewing this latter part of the Classificatory-Historical Period, a first consideration of consequence is that there was a great burgeoning of archaeological interest and activity following World War II. This was especially true for the United States, but it also occurred in most other American countries. In the previous chapter, we have referred to government support of archaeology as a federal economic relief measure in the United States in the 1930s, and, in this connection, we commented on some of the salvage aspects of this work. In 1945, such salvage work was inaugurated on what was to be a growing scale as an adjunct to federal flood-control projects. Through the intervention of a committee of professional archaeologists (see Johnson and others, 1945), and with the sympathetic help of some legislators, the U.S. Congress was persuaded to set aside funds for such research. Subsequently, salvage archaeology, both under federal and private contracts, expanded rapidly into all parts of the United States throughout the 1940s and 1950s.[45] A second United States governmental venture (or series of ventures) that was to have an impact on archaeological interest and research was the planning, preparation, and publication of sets of handbooks relating to the Native Americans. These were compilations, by leading authorities, of physical anthropological, ethnological, and archaeological information. They provided research data baselines that served to indicate regions and directions for further research. These handbooks followed in the tradition of the first *Handbook of American Indians North of Mexico*, which was brought out early in the twentieth century by the Smithsonian Institution (Hodge, 1907–10). This was an ethnographic and ethnological compendium with very little archaeological data; but, in the 1940s, the Smithsonian, under its Bureau of American Ethnology and the editorship of Julian H. Steward, published the much more extensive *Handbook of South American Indians*, which contained substantial archaeological sections (Steward, 1946–50). In the 1950s, government financing also made possible the preparation of the multivolume *Handbook of Middle American Indians,* which incorporated even more extensive archaeological syntheses.[46] This, in turn, was followed by plans and preparation for a giant ethnological-archaeological *Handbook of North American Indians,* once again undertaken by the Smithsonian Institution.[47] All these handbooks have served, or will serve, as archaeological summaries, stimuli, and bases of departure for further research. In the United States, a third governmental boost to archaeology was the financial support for field research channeled through the Social Sciences Division of the National Science Foundation. Beginning in the 1950s, this organization put millions of dollars at the disposal of private institutions for archaeological research in all parts of the world, and particularly in the Americas.

To this governmental support within and from the United States can be added various privately endowed archaeological operations and governmental and private research programs by the Canadian and Latin American governments and private institutions and individuals in these countries.[48] The post-World War II period also saw a renewal of work by Danish archaeologists in the American Arctic and by European and Japanese archaeologists in Middle and South America.

All of this contributed enormously to our substantive knowledge of the New World's past. On the Late Pleistocene level, we now have hundreds of important sites, where previously the reliable discoveries numbered less than a dozen. Radiocarbon dates gave firm chronological structure to an area of investigation that previously had had only the most general sort of estimates. By the mid 1960s, it had become apparent that an early fluted projectile point horizon could be documented for the North American High Plains and parts of the Southwest *ca.* 9500–8000 B.C. Two periods appeared distinguishable within this horizon, an earlier Clovis and a later Folsom. Clovis or Clovis-like points had a much more widespread North American distribution, being found at various places in the eastern half of the continent. Datings on these eastern finds were not as secure, either through geological contexts or radiocarbon determinations, as those of the West; but the general interpretation was that early hunters of the terminal Pleistocene had spread over most of North America with a Clovis-like technology and that later point forms had evolved from the Clovis into a number of separate regional point styles, including Folsom, Plainview, Midland, Yuma, and Eden in the West and such types as Suwannee and Dalton in the East. This evolution could be dated to the Early Post-Pleistocene, lasting until about 7000 B.C., plus or minus 500 years.[49]

A major Late Pleistocene debate was carried on over the possibilities of a pre-projectile point or pre-bifacial-flaking horizon or occupancy of the New World, some authorities arguing for the reality of such a relatively crude technological era in the Americas and others insisting that humans first came to the Western Hemisphere from Asia only at about 10,000 B.C. and with a heritage that allowed them to develop rapidly the Clovis-type hunting gear (Krieger, 1964; Haynes, 1964). A Paleo-Indian or Big-Game Hunting horizon (the names applied to the Clovis and related point technologies) had been established for the Far West as well as the rest of North America,[50] and related materials from South America were recognized as marking an approximately contemporaneous horizon for that continent. However, finds from both Mexico and Peru, of the order of 20,000 to 18,000 B.C., raised the still highly controversial issue of whether humans had come to the New World well in advance of the 10,000 B.C. date-line and whether these earliest immigrants had possessed a simple flint technology that lacked bifacially flaked projectile points (Mirambell, 1967; MacNeish, 1969, 1970).

The era from about 7000 B.C. until about 2000 B.C., generally referred to as the time of the Archaic cultures, became increasingly well documented after 1950. Subsistence economies varied from land game-hunters to fishers, shellfish-gatherers, and seed-collectors. This was interpreted as a time of notable population increases and relatively stable, if still semisedentary, patterns of life. Some technological continuities can be traced from earlier times. Projectile point forms, for instance, show gradual modifications from the early hunting modes of the terminal Pleistocene and Early Post-Pleistocene into the Meso-Indian or Archaic types; however, there can be no doubt but that major changes in life-style had occurred. This is reflected in various tool types adapted to new food-getting techniques. Ground stone artifacts, which had been absent or extremely rare in the earliest American cultures, had become common. These changes of the 7000–2000 B.C. period came about in various ways but characterized all parts of the Americas from which there were available archaeological data (Willey, 1966–71; Jennings, 1968, 1974).

On later time-levels, chronological control, through more stratigraphic work and through radiocarbon dating, provided the underpinning for areal syntheses, and systematic chronological investigation was pushed into areas and regions that had been only sketchily known before World War II. In South America, the well-established Peruvian area chronology was extended back in time through coastal shellfishers and minimal horticulturists to earlier hunters and gatherers. In the well-preserved refuse of deep midden sites, the transition from plant-collecting and shellfish-gathering to incipient cultivation and on into established farming was traced in both the food remains themselves and in the artifactual complexes associated with them.[51] The settlement pattern studies on the coast, already referred to, led on to an interest in the rise of Pre-Columbian urbanism in the area (Rowe, 1963). Considerable attention was also paid to the *horizon style* concept and to the way this had been applied in Peruvian studies. More refined analyses of the Tiahuanaco horizon, which Uhle had conceived of so many years before, gave greater insight into the actual origins of this powerful style and the mechanisms of its spread to other parts of Peru (Menzel, 1964). In the same way, the earlier Chavin horizon was more closely scrutinized through new excavations at Chavin de Huantar and elsewhere (Lumbreras, 1971; Patterson, 1971); and Peruvian archaeologists were made aware of a whole early period of pottery development, chronologically intermediate between the Chavin horizon (*ca.* 900 B.C.) and the late preceramic cultures (terminating at *ca.* 1800 B.C.).[52] In keeping with the relatively advanced state of Peruvian culture-sequence control, no less than four general books of area synthesis were published on Peru between 1949 and 1967.[53]

Other South American areas, while considerably behind Peru in the amount of archaeological research carried out in the spatial-temporal organization of the data, came along swiftly in the decades between 1940 and 1970. Important stratigraphic work was carried out in Ecuador by Clifford Evans, Betty J. Meggers, and Emilio Estrada in the 1950s and 1960s, and Meggers brought out a general synthesis of the area in 1966.[54] Archaeological sequences in that country revealed a long history of pottery-using cultures, with ceramics beginning even earlier here (*ca.* 3000–2500 B.C.) than in Peru or Mesoamerica. In Colombia, Gerardo Reichel-Dolmatoff, a French-trained archaeologist with a European background, took the lead in stratigraphic archaeology in that country, and he, too, climaxed his efforts with a general book.[55] To generalize, the archaeological cultures of Ecuador and Colombia, as well as those of Lower Central America,[56] exhibited marked regional differentiation, with a bewildering variety of ceramic styles. For the most part, they lacked the impressive public works or great buildings of Peru or Mesoamerica; the trend toward urban patterns of life was not as far advanced, nor were there good archaeological evidences (or ethnohistoric data) that would suggest phenomena of the order of the Inca or the Aztec states or empires. At the same time, many regions of this "Intermediate Area" (so named for its geographical position between Peru and Mesoamerica) showed archaeological signs of dense populations and, throughout, a high level of craft development (especially in pottery and metallurgy).

Archaeological synthesis had been begun in the Caribbean area in the late 1930s, with Rouse's studies of the West Indies, and, in subsequent years, he expanded and refined it[57] From the West Indies, he moved to the mainland, where, in conjunction with J. M. Cruxent, he extended his overall Caribbean chronological scheme to embrace the

Monumental stone sculpture from San Agustin in southern Colombia, height above 90 cm. Only after World War II did archaeologists begin to learn enough about this fabulous site to date such monuments in a relative chronology. (From the American Museum of Natural History)

Pottery figurine of the Chone type from the Ecuadorian coast. (From Estrada, 1957)

several archaeological regions of Venezuela (Rouse and Cruxent, 1963). Farther south, in tropical lowland South America, were Meggers and Evans, who began by establishing a long ceramic sequence at the delta of the Amazon.[58] A few years afterward, D. W. Lathrap initiated a program of excavation and survey in the Upper Amazon Basin that provided crucial information for linking Amazonian ceramic styles with those of Peru and Ecuador (Lathrap, 1958, 1970, 1971). Another scholar in Amazonian archaeology in the 1960s period was the German-Brazilian P. P. Hilbert, who did a number of excavations in the Middle Amazon (Hilbert, 1968; see also Roosevelt, 1991). Systematic knowledge in the East Brazilian Highlands and along the Atlantic Coast was pushed forward rapidly in the 1960s by a cooperative program of Brazilian and North American archaeologists organized and guided by Meggers and Evans.[59] Here, along the coast, the cultures of the Brazilian *sambaquis,* or shell-mounds, were found to date back to the third and fourth millennia B.C. and to exhibit an Archaic way of life and a conservatism comparable to that of some of the Meso-Indian, or Archaic, shell-mound cultures of the North American Atlantic and Pacific littorals. This Archaic type of existence was succeeded some time in the first millennium A.D. by cultures of an Amazonian tropical agricultural pattern, presumably carried into eastern Brazil by expanding Tupian tribes (Lathrap, 1970).

In northwestern Argentina, A. R. Gonzalez began intensive and detailed stratigraphic studies at various cave sites in the San Luis and Cordoba Provinces and also took the lead in the chronological organization of what was generally thought of as the Argentine *Diaguita region.*[60] Gonzalez was also the first to attempt a chronological integration of Northwest Argentine and North Chilean archaeological sequences based on scientific ceramic trait comparisons (Gonzalez, 1963). Farther south in Argentina, the Austrian prehistorian O. F. A. Menghin was active in studies of Late Pleistocene humans in the 1950s.[61] He has been followed by a number of younger Argentine scholars who have continued these interests (Bormida, 1968; Cigliano, 1962). But later ceramic cultures of the Parana-Paraguay River system, the Pampas, and Patagonia have received little attention, and chronological ordering here has advanced little beyond the stage reached in the 1940s. In far southern South America, J. B. Bird's earlier work of the 1930s was followed up by the French archaeologists J. M. Emperaire, Annette Laming-Emperaire, and Henri Reichlen (1964), who confirmed and refined Bird's findings and also provided new information and chronological data on the early peoples of the Chilean Archipelago.

The 1940s to the 1960s brought the archaeology of Mesoamerica to a point where a variety of contextual-functional and processual problems could be formulated and attacked from a firm data base. One

A stone sculpture in the Olmec style, representing a man holding an infant were-jaguar, height 55 cm. (From Michael D. Coe)

significant discovery was the substantial antiquity of the Olmec art style and the Gulf Coast sites in which it was so well represented (Stirling, 1943; Drucker, 1952; M. D. Heizer, and Squier, 1959; M. D. Coe, 1968a, b; Bernal, 1969). Another notable series of advances were made in Maya hieroglyphic studies. In 1950, the leading Maya glyphic scholar, J. E. S. Thompson, brought out his compilation, *Maya Hieroglyphic Writing: An Introduction,* a systematic review of our knowledge of Maya writing to that date (Thompson, 1950). However, other scholars thought Thompson's approach to translation too conservative and limited. Among these were the Russian, Yuri Knorozov (1967),[62] who advocated a phonetic approach to the glyphs through the known Maya languages, Heinrich Berlin (1958), who defined and discovered the "emblem glyph,"[63] a key step in the political hieroglypic textual translations which were to follow in the subsequent decades, and Tatiana Proskouriakoff (1960), whose translations and interpretations of glyphic texts and iconography began to revolutionize our understanding of ancient Maya political structure and royal lineages. In addition to the advances in the understanding of Maya writing, substantial progress had been made on early Zapotecan glyphs and calendrics by the Mexican authority, Alfonso Caso (1946). The spectacular urban dimensions and functions of the site of Teotihuacan would be still another kind of discovery.

The great La Venta pyramid. Upon clearing by archaeologists, this mound was revealed to have a conical fluted form, a most unusual shape for a Mesoamerican structure. Made of earth, it is the largest mound of the Olmec ceremonial center of La Venta, Mexico. La Venta is believed to have flourished ca. 1200–800 B.C. (From Robert F. Heizer and the National Geographic Society)

The site had been known to archaeologists for many years, but it was not until the 1950s and 1960s that its true physical nature and its former widespread influences in commerce and politics on the Mesoamerican scene were realized and appreciated (Millon, 1967; Sanders and Price, 1968). Yet another discovery would be the clarification of the relationships between the Classic Lowland Maya civilization and other Mesoamerican cultures during the Late Classic Period (A.D. 600–900) (Jiménez Moreno, 1959). Some discoveries involved new data on agriculture, such as those of MacNeish in Tamaulipas and in southern Puebla, where, in both instances, the archaeologists found long preceramic sequences associated with the slow transition of plant-gathering to plant cultivation (MacNeish, 1958, 1967, 1974). Parts of Mesoamerica still lacked adequate exploration and chronological systematization — Guerrero and West Mexico would be examples — but, on the whole, the area became one of the best known, albeit the most complex, of the New

Aerial photograph of the huge urban site of Teotihuacan. (From Millon 1973, by permission)

World. The conception of it as a culture area was tacitly accepted as early as the late nineteenth century, and the Spinden and Vaillant area syntheses of 1928 and 1941 helped to establish this conception still more. In 1943, Paul Kirchhoff addressed himself directly to this question of Mesoamerica as a culture area or culture sphere, with the implications that such an entity was, in effect, a culture-area-with-time-depth and not the "flat," synchronic culture area of the ethnographers (Kirchhoff, 1943). This was followed by a number of area syntheses. Some of these were essentially historical and descriptive;[64] others combined both historical and evolutionary perspectives (Armillas, 1948; Bernal, 1959; Sanders and Price, 1968).

In North America, the southwestern United States, in which archaeological systematics were most developed prior to 1940, continued to be a center of intensive research. One obvious problem was that of southern relationships of the cultures of the area, and a number of archaeologists, including C. C. Di Peso, concerned themselves with this (Di Peso, 1963; Di Peso and others, 1956; Schroeder, 1957, 1965). Questions of migrations or diffusions between Mesoamerica and the Ho-

A reconstruction drawing of the Classic Maya ballcourt (ca. A. D. 600–800) at Copan, Honduras. This drawing is the work of T. Proskouriakoff, a member of the Department of Archaeology of the Carnegie Institution of Washington, an organization that undertook much important work in the Maya area from 1914 to 1958. (From the Peabody Museum, Harvard University)

Excavated and partially restored pyramid of the Maya site of Tikal, Guatemala. Compare this photograph with the figure on page 72, which was taken more than a half-century earlier (From William R. Coe, Jr., University Museum, Philadelphia)

hokam and Mogollon regions were still debated, although the evidence that was coming in suggested that both processes were at work at different times and places (see Reid and Doyel, eds., 1986; Minnis and Redman, eds., 1990: Section V). Another problem was that of the antecedents of the Puebloan and Desert farmers; but now the chronological gap between Late Pleistocene peoples and these pottery-agricultural cultures was filled by Archaic-type discoveries (Irwin-Williams, 1968). As might be anticipated in view of the relatively advanced state of Southwestern distributional and dating studies, the area had been one of the main centers for contextual-functional and processual inquiries. We have already referred to some of these and will come to them again in the next chapter.[65]

Eastern archaeology had farther to go than the Southwest to come abreast in space-time ordering. As of 1971, it still lagged a bit, but great progress had been made. As in the Southwest, and elsewhere in the New World, the Archaic era was brought into focus.[66] The origins of many elements in the Adena-Hopewellian cultures remained somewhat mysterious—including the beginnings and importance of agriculture in the East—but a much more sophisticated appreciation of the nature of Hopewellian culture replaced the earlier taxonomic conception of it (Caldwell, 1959, 1964). A great many regional monographs were published,[67] in addition to the hundreds of site reports, although there were no book-length syntheses of the East as a whole.[68] As in the Southwest, a good many studies were concerned with context, function, and process. These studies rested on fairly adequate regional or site data bases, although, for much of the East, fundamental spatial-chronological information was still sparse. A very large amount of fieldwork was carried out in the river valleys of the Plains, most of it in connection with the salvage programs, and this made possible such a general book as Wedel's on the Plains area (Wedel, 1961; Lehmer, 1971).

Archaeology in the Far West of the United States and Canada enjoyed a great boom in the 1940–70 decades. Previously, there had been little or no sequence information from these areas. This includes California, the Great Basin, and the Northwest Coast and Plateau.[69] The cultures of these areas did not come within the American agricultural orbit but followed modes of subsistence comparable to those of the Meso-Indian or Archaic cultures down to historical times. The chronological groundwork done in these areas provided archaeologists with frames of reference for studying the generally gradual changes in these cultures, especially in relation to the natural environmental settings.

In the North, Subarctic archaeology had its beginnings in these recent decades, and the data from there have posed a number of interesting problems as to origins and directions of influence. Arctic (and, at

Cross-sectional diagram of the main plaza, temples, and other structures at Tikal, Guatemala. This diagram shows the complexities of large architectural excavations. (From William R. Coe, Jr., University Museum, Philadelphia)

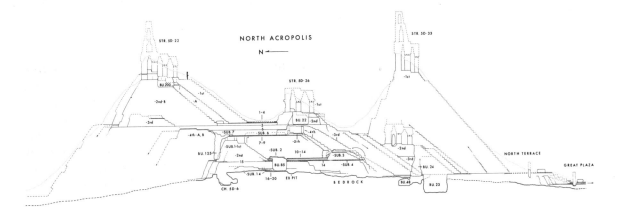

Detailed natural stratigraphy in Danger Cave, Utah. (From J. D. Jennings)

one remove, Asiatic) influences are seen intermixed with those from North American Archaic cultures (MacNeish, 1964b). In the Arctic proper, the good beginning made by Collins in Eskimo chronology was continued by Larsen and Rainey and by Giddings and Anderson.[70] Cultures immediately antecedent to "classic" Eskimo ivory-using ones were linked to a widespread Arctic Small Tool tradition, embracing complexes all the way from the Cape Denbigh in the West to Sarqaq in Greenland. This tradition, with its emphasis on flint microblades, is

clearly of Asiatic Mesolithic derivation. A still earlier horizon, the *Paleo-Arctic*, also has Asiatic affinities, but they are less well defined.

Interareal syntheses, some of them of continental or hemispherical scope, began to appear in considerable numbers in the latter part of the Classificatory-Historical Period and on into the 1960s. Some of these were primarily chronological and descriptive. The Martin, Quimby, and Collier book on the archaeology of America north of Mexico, *Indians Before Columbus*, published in 1947, was of this nature. It offered a factual and chronologically ordered account of archaeological findings (with some attempts at contextual-functional presentations) in a series of

Irrigation canal excavation at the Hohokam site of Snaketown in southern Arizona. This site, the source of much of the archaeological knowledge of the Hohokam culture, was excavated by Gladwin and Haury in the 1930s. Sections of the site were reexcavated by Haury in the early 1960s. (From the Arizona State Museum. Photo by Helga Teiwes.)

regional and areal sequences. Little or no attempt was made to break down area compartmentalization, either by plotting lines of diffusion or by viewing the data in accordance with broad developmental patterns of stages (Martin, Quimby, and Collier, 1947). Salvador Canals Frau's two books, *Prehistoria de América* and *Las Civilizaciones Prehistoricas de América*, which appeared in Argentina in 1950 and 1955, were hemispheric in scope.[71] While utilizing some broad diffusional categories, of a highly speculative sort, they did not differ greatly (except in their lack of precise control of the data) from the Martin-Quimby-Collier effort. The huge compendium *Manual de Arqueología Americana* by the Spanish Americanist José Alcina Franch was prepared in 1958, although not published until 1965.[72]

Radiocarbon dates, which began to pour in during the 1950s, enabled the archaeologists to cross-date culture sequences from one area to another. This aided in both diffusional and developmental perspectives (Wauchope, 1954; Willey, 1955a, 1955b, 1958) and resulted in New World syntheses that were expressed in both historical and developmental (evolutionary) terms, often with a blending of the two. The developmental or culture-stage principle was utilized by Willey and Phillips in their 1955 article and 1958 book.[73] This outlook owed much to Julian Steward's earlier articles on South American cultural evolution or development (Steward, 1947, 1948b, 1949b). It was employed by Steward and Faron in a combined archaeological-ethnographical summary volume on South America (Steward and Faron, 1959) and used by Sanders and Merino in a concise 1970 volume on the New World as a whole (Sanders and Merino, 1970). We shall return to the developmental stage classifications of New World cultures later, in a more theoretical context.

A more strictly historical outlook is seen in the volume by H. Marie Wormington, on *Ancient Man in North America*, which is concerned only with Pleistocene and Early Post-Pleistocene cultures (Wormington, 1957), in George Kubler's *The Art and Architecture of Ancient America: The Mexican, Maya, and Andean Peoples* (Kubler, 1962), which examines the New World civilizations from an art history point of view, and in the archaeological articles in a book by R. F. Spencer and J. D. Jennings, *The Native Americans* (Spencer, Jennings, and others, 1965).

Two other books of the period are collections of articles by various regional specialists. One of these, *Aboriginal Cultural Development in Latin America: An Interpretative Review*, edited by Meggers and Evans and published in 1963, deals with Middle and South American archaeology as of that date; the other, *Prehistoric Man in the New World*, edited by Jennings and Norbeck and published in 1964, runs from the Bering Strait to Cape Horn in its coverage. Both are fundamentally descriptive-historical, although summary articles by Meggers and Bernal, respectively, essay some stage concepts.

Two other syntheses are those of Jennings, *Prehistory of North America*, which appeared in 1968 and covers America north of Mexico in a combined developmental stage-historical organization, and of Willey, *An Introduction to American Archaeology*,[74] a two-volume treatment of the entire New World published in 1966–71, which follows a historical-genetic scheme. Such works were designed primarily as college textbooks and general references; but they also served the purpose of formalizing the discipline and were one more sign of American archaeology's coming of age.

The only major American work of synthesis of the era that could be considered an example of doctrinaire diffusionism was James Ford's *A Comparison of Formative Cultures in the Americas*, published in 1969, in which he attempts to explain the first appearances of ceramics and a number of other Neolithic-level traits in North America as a result of their diffusion from an original hearth in northwestern South America. The scheme is an involved one, incorporating what Ford called an initial

Area and chronology chart showing the development of major cultural traditions in North America. (From Willey, 1966, Vol. 1, An Introduction to American Archaeology, reprinted by permission of Prentice-Hall, Inc., Englewood Cliffs, New Jersey)

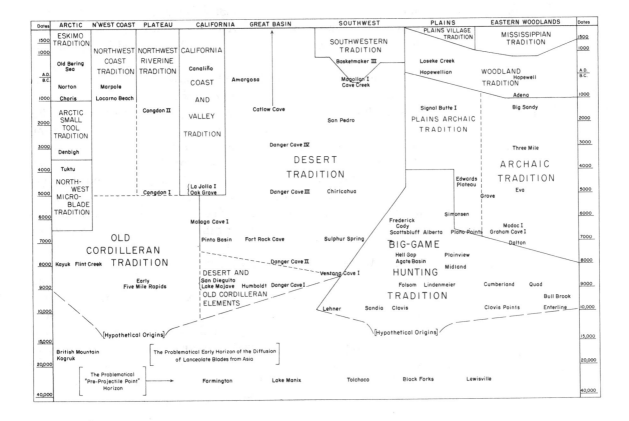

"Colonial Formative" diffusion and a later "Theocratic Formative" wave (characterized by ceremonial center constructions). In many ways, it is comparable to Spinden's Archaic hypothesis, although Ford worked with much more chronologically controlled data.

While the tradition of American culture history as an essentially self-controlled one, without important contacts or relationships to the Old World, continued to dominate the thinking of most archaeologists, some new points of view about this appeared in the late Classificatory-Historical Period and then in the 1960s. Of course, Old World-New World relationships on a Paleolithic-New World early hunting level had always been a respectable line of inquiry, although very little had been done about it. Through the 1960s, the subject remained largely speculative; however, with Russian discoveries in Siberia being made available in English translations, a number of clues for connections emerged (for example, Rudenko, 1961). The significance and interpretation of these varied, but the consensus of Americanist opinion in the 1970s was that Levallois-Mousteroid techniques, by whatever slow and circuitous diffusion, were transferred from Asia to the Americas and may well have provided the bifacial-flaked blade technology that eventually gave rise to the early American Clovis and related industries.[75] Somewhat better documented has been the case for Asiatic Mesolithic traits spreading or being carried to the New World across a Bering land bridge in later millennia to form the bases for Arctic and Subarctic techniculture prior to the appearance of the more typical Eskimo complexes. These last, too, were generally seen as incorporating Asiatic traits.[76]

More dubious and debatable have been the claims for Trans-Pacific relationships between Asia and America in relatively Late Pre-Columbian times. The Austrian ethnologist-archaeologist Robert von Heine-Geldern had long been the spokesman for the importance of such diffusions in the rise of the New World Mesoamerican and Peruvian civilizations, and he continued to argue his case in the 1950s and 1960s (Heine-Geldern, 1954 1959a, 1959b, 1966). Generally, American archaeologists were not convinced, citing difficulties in finding the proper Asiatic antecedents with the proper dating and arguing for the more likely possibility of independent development and evolution.[77] Nevertheless, there is a haunting similarity about such things as Shang and Chao bronzes of China and the more or less contemporaneous Chavín stone sculptures and ceramics of Peru — just to name a single example — and, although the trend of American archaeology in the late 1960s and 1970s was away from long-range diffusionistic explanations and more convinced of *in situ* evolutionary forces in cultural development, it was still fair to say that these questions had not been finally resolved — nor have they been resolved as of 1990.

Ecuadorian Valdivia and Japanese Jomon pottery. a–d, g are Japanese sherds; e–f, h–i are Ecuadorian sherds. (From B. J. Meggers and C. Evans)

One of the most compelling arguments for Trans-Pacific contact was put forward in the late 1950s and into the 1960s by the late Ecuadorian archaeologist Emilio Estrada in collaboration with Meggers and Evans. All three had worked in coastal Ecuadorian archaeology, where the Valdivia ceramic complex, dating to *ca.* 3000–2500 B.C., was discovered by them as the earliest pottery of the area (Meggers, Evans, and Estrada, 1965). This Valdivian pottery is of relatively simple vessel forms, although competently made, and it features incised and other surface-plastic decorative motifs. Its resemblances to pottery of about the same age from the Japanese Jomon shell middens is startling, and the three archaeologists hypothesize that Jomon fishermen, carried out into the Pacific currents, eventually landed in coastal Ecuador, where they introduced the trait of pottery-making to other fishers and shellfishers who were on a more or less comparable technological level to themselves. The majority of American archaeologists have not been convinced;[78] some have (Ekholm, 1964; Ford, 1969); and others still assume a wait-and-see attitude (Willey, 1966–71, Vol. 2, chapter 5).

HISTORICAL AND
DEVELOPMENTAL
CONCEPTS

The main methodological innovations of the late Classificatory-Historical Period were, as we have said, in the realm of contextual and functional interpretations. Some historical concepts were also developed during this time and deserve special mention. They are most fittingly referred to here, because they were concepts that were invented and employed in connection with the cultural area and chronological syntheses — which we have just reviewed — and because they all have processual dimensions and appropriately serve as transitions in theory and method between the late Classificatory-Historical Period and the Modern Period. These concepts are the *horizon style*, the *cultural tradition* (in its various guises), and the *culture stage*. The first two are fundamentally historical in their properties — that is, they relate primarily to cultural description and spatial-temporal locations — however, both are also secondarily concerned with process, in that certain kinds of human behavior must be invoked to explain their existence. The third, the culture stage, has primary referents in both history (chronology) and process (cultural evolution). Such stage appraisals led, naturally, to cross-cultural comparisons. We have already noted some of these in connection with cultural-environmental relationships, but the comparisons were wider in scope than this.

Although we are treating these concepts here, apart from our previous discussions of context and function, it should be recognized that horizon styles, cultural traditions, and culture stages were very much a part of the widening interests in the nature of the prehistoric record and of archaeologists' attempts to enrich that record and to understand it.

The horizon-style concept was formalized by Kroeber in 1944 (p. 104). He defined the *horizon style* as "one showing definably distinct features, some of which extend over a large area, so that its relations with other, more local styles serve to place these in relative time, according as the relations are of priority, consociation, or subsequence." The three major Peruvian horizon styles, which were recognized at that time and which subsequent research has further confirmed, were the Chavin, Tiahuanaco (Tiahuanaco-Huari), and the Inca. Kroeber also suggested two other horizon styles, the negative-painted and the white-on-red (Willey, 1945); but, as these are characterized by technical (kinds of paintings) rather than stylistic or iconographic features, the name *horizon markers* might be more appropriate in their case. Functionally, the dis-

semination of a highly complicated iconography and the spread of a simple ceramic painting technique may have quite different implications (Willey, 1948). The horizon-style and horizon-marker concepts are now standard features of American archaeological procedure, although the way they are applied and their utility has occasioned some discussion.[79]

The concept of the tradition was introduced into Peruvian archaeology by Willey in 1945 as a kind of counterpoise to Kroeber's horizon style. Whereas the latter emphasized the dissemination or diffusion of a complex of traits or elements (a style) over a relatively large geographical area in a short span of time, the former emphasized the persistence of certain cultural traits or elements in the same area over a relatively long span of time. In his article, Willey dealt with a particular class of tradition, the pottery tradition, and, defined it as follows: "A pottery tradition comprises a line, or a number of lines, of pottery development through time within the confines of a certain technique or decorative constant. In successive time periods through which the history of ceramic development can be traced, certain styles arose within the tradition. Transmission of some of these styles during particular periods resulted in the formation of a horizon style; other styles in the continuum of the tradition remained strictly localized" (Willey, 1945, p. 53).

The tradition, then, as the word implies, had reference to "traditional" or time-persistent ways of doing things—in the particular instances discussed for Peru, of making pottery. It was a historical-genetic concept and as such related, in its fundamental approach, to culture-classification schemes like the Gladwins', which had been proposed for southwestern North America during the earlier half of the Classificatory-Historical Period (W. and H. S. Gladwin, 1934). Goggin broadened the tradition concept in applying it to whole cultures in Florida (Goggin, 1949).

The tradition concept was also related to that of the culture area or the culture-area-with-time-depth. Kirchhoff did not apply the term *tradition* to his Mesoamerican area definition, but he might well have done so (Kirchhoff, 1943). W. C. Bennett did in his definition of a Peruvian culture-area-with-time-depth, or in what he called the "Peruvian Co-Tradition" (Bennett, 1948). Martin and Rinaldo (1951) followed Bennett's lead, both in concept and terminology, in defining such a co-tradition for the southwestern United States. This latter usage occasioned a reply by Rouse (1954), who questioned their application and definition of the co-tradition concept. According to Rouse, the co-tradition was intended by Bennett to be more than just a culture-area-with-time-depth. It was, rather, a culture area in which all the lines of cultural development could be traced back to one single line—a monogenetic conception (see also Rouse, 1957). However, it is probably fair to say that this rather special definition of the co-tradition concept is not one employed by most American archaeologists, who still tend to think of it as the more loosely structured culture-area-with-time-depth.

As to the term *tradition* itself, there has been no clear concurrence of opinion on just how it should be defined. Some archaeologists prefer to use it in the more restricted sense of Willey's Peruvian pottery traditions; others would see it as something considerably more inclusive.[80] Still other archaeologists have come up with similar, although not entirely identical, historical concepts. J. R. Caldwell's Hopewellian interaction sphere is one of these.[81] He refers to a series of regional cultures linked by a common participation in some elements of culture (mortuary ritual and paraphernalia) but not in others. As such, the interaction sphere, a highly useful way of looking at the obvious results of trade and other forms of intercommunication and common cultural bonds, partakes of some of the properties of both a tradition (in the broader sense of the definition) and a horizon style.[82]

The culture-stage concept, as we know, has an early history in archaeological and anthropological studies, going back to the early Danish Stone, Bronze, and Iron Age formulations and to the more anthropologically oriented evolutionary scheme of Savagery-Barbarism-Civilization.[83] This kind of classification was reintroduced into American archaeology by Julian Steward. His experience in editing *The Handbook of South American Indians,* with its vast array of archaeological and ethnological cultures and the necessity for organizing these into some kind of meaningful overall pattern, was undoubtedly a conditioning factor in Steward's thinking, although one must also take into account his earlier culture-and-environmental and evolutionary studies in the North American Great Basin (Steward, 1938). Steward's views on culture stages and cultural evolution are expressed in his *Handbook* (Steward, 1948a, 1949a) articles as well as in the organization of the *Handbook* itself, in which his major culture types, which to a large extent could be blocked out as culture super-areas of that continent, were, in effect, stages.[84] Steward went from these to his better-known article "Cultural Causality and Law: A Trial Formulation of the Development of Early Civilizations" (Steward, 1949a), to which we have already referred in our discussion of environmental factors in cultural development and evolution. Still another article of Steward's, "A Functional-Developmental Classification of American High Cultures" (Steward, 1948b), forecasts the more detailed Willey-Phillips stage scheme of a few years later (see also Willey, 1950).

The Willey-Phillips historical-developmental interpretation of New World prehistory, appearing first as an article in 1955 and then in 1958 as part of *Method and Theory in American Archaeology,* was clearly influ-

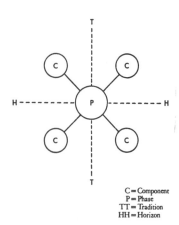

C = Component
P = Phase
TT = Tradition
HH = Horizon

Diagram showing the relationships between horizons and traditions and culture components and phases. (From Method and Theory in American Archaeology *by Willey and Phillips, 1958, by permission of The University of Chicago Press. Copyright 1958.)*

enced by Steward and also by an outline that had been propounded very briefly by A. D. Krieger at a 1952 symposium.[85] Beyond this, it should be recognized that prototypes for such a scheme had for a long time been a part of the more or less routine archaeological area syntheses in the Americas. The Southwestern Pecos Classification had periods that were also stages, because the criteria for these did not appear at the same time in all parts of the area (Kidder, 1924, 1927). The Ford-Willey chronology for the eastern United States recognized that the major periods of the area were best described as stages (Ford and Willey, 1941). A number of the Peruvian area chronologies, devised shortly after the Virú Valley program, are also stage schemes, for the criteria by which the periods were established (esthetic florescence, imperialism, conquest, and so forth) were not fully synchronous for all parts of the Peruvian area.[86] The same is also true of the Armillas chronology for Mesoamerica (Armillas, 1948). Thus, there were numerous area models for Willey and Phillips to use; they simply projected the model for the whole New World. Their scheme, as it finally appeared, comprised five major New World stages (Willey and Phillips, 1958). In chronological and developmental order, these were: (1) Lithic (Paleo-Indian and other Late Pleistocene beginnings in the Americas); (2) Archaic (Post-Pleistocene hunting-collecting adaptations); (3) Formative (the village agricultural threshold and/or sedentary life); (4) Classic (beginnings of urban development); and (5) Postclassic (the imperialistic states). Whereas Lithic cultures were defined as being entirely extinct, it was argued that many existing or historic New World societies (those of northern and far western North America and of southern South America) had remained on an Archaic stage level. Similarly, most agricultural or horticultural peoples of the New World were conceived of as having tarried on a Formative level. Only in Mesoamerica and Peru were the Classic and Postclassic stages admitted to have existed.

The Willey-Phillips interpretation met with considerable interest, for it raised again the idea of cultural evolution, which for so long had lain dormant in American archaeology. Much of the comment was critical, for, to some archaeologists, such developmental or evolutionary schema were rejected on principle (Swanson, 1959; Miller, 1959). Others, while in general theoretical agreement, felt that the Willey-Phillips criteria for the proposed stages were not wisely selected (McKern, 1956; Evans and Meggers, 1958). Still others suggested modifications or variant schemes (Hester, 1962; Rouse, 1964c). But, most importantly, evolutionary thinking had been rejuvenated, and this ferment of ideas was to form the transition from the late Classificatory-Historical Period into the Modern Period.

SUMMARY

The twenty years between 1940 and 1960 were transitional years in American archaeology, falling between the rather lean space-time systematics of the immediately previous years and the radical claims and optimism that were to come in the 1960s. Changes were occurring that led from an archaeology concerned almost wholly with limited descriptive history to one involved in richer historical contexts and processes. In effect, history was being expanded from its minimal archaeological definition of a chronicle of potsherds, artifacts, and buildings to a definition embracing social behavior and cultural institutions as these were viewed in the contexts of settlement pattern arrangements and natural environmental settings. There were, expectably, variations from one American region to another as to how these changes proceeded, but we think it fair to say that the question of function[87] was the innovative idea of the day. These attempts to view past cultures as living situations were to help prepare the way for studies that addressed the underlying causes of culture change. We can broadly characterize this shift as moving from questions of "how" to questions of "why."

The last two decades of the Classificatory-Historical Period also saw the rise of large-scale archaeological syntheses, and this period was characterized by a trend from what was essentially a descriptive-historical orientation to a historical-developmental orientation. The theoretical bases for these syntheses were not very clearly set out. Some of them were primarily diffusionistic—that is, culture-historical; others were more developmentally inclined — that is, evolutionary. Such theories did not explain culture change, but the organization of the data prepared the archaeologists to address questions of change. More importantly, perhaps, an attitudinal transition was taking place. Archaeologists were beginning to sense that their discipline could be made to tell much more about the past than they once expected it could, and this difference in attitude set the stage for the New Archaeology.

NOTES

1. Strong (1936). It is undoubtedly significant that Strong, although primarily an archaeologist, had published in ethnology (Strong, 1927).
2. Martin, Lloyd, and Spoehr (1938); Martin and Rinaldo (1939); J. W. Bennett (1943); and, more recently, a retrospective view by Martin (1974).
3. Steward and Setzler (1938). This article was published in *American Antiquity;* this journal, founded in 1935, was a signal event in the growth of American archaeology.
4. Cole and Deuel, 1937. B. G. Trigger (1974), in a review of the first edition of our book, objected to

this selection as a marker for the beginning of serious interest in context and function, noting the writings of the Canadian archaeologist W. J. Wintemberg as having had such concerns prior to this date (see Wintemberg 1928, 1936, 1939; also see Trigger, 1989, pp. 270–275 for his discussions of the early functional writings of Smith, Parker, and others). This is true, but, as we already have discussed in Chapter 3, we adhere essentially to our original date-line. Certainly, for most American archaeologists, the idea does not seem to have caught on intellectually until the late 1930s and afterward. As to Trigger's (1989, p. 273) intriguing suggestion that the early isolated examples of functional interpretation "constituted a more serious effort to infer human behavior from archaeological remains than did the ethnographic trait lists of the 1930s and 1940s," it is not clear at all to us that the functional studies of the 1930s and 1940s, many of which went beyond trait lists, were a less serious effort than those of earlier times. Thus, we cannot completely agree with Trigger (ibid; emphasis ours) that "the classificatory orientation of the Midwestern Taxonomic Method, and of chronological studies generally, *suppressed* a professional interest in the behavioural interpretation of archaeological data in North America for a longer period than Taylor (1948, p. 91) or Willey and Sabloff (1980, p. 134) have believed." It appears to us that the changes in American cultural anthropological thinking occasioned by Radcliffe-Brown's teaching at the University of Chicago (which at the time was a major training ground for archaeologists) and, to a lesser extent, by Malinowski at Yale University, were more arguably important *positive* influences than the Midwestern Taxonomic Method was a *negative* influence in this regard.

5. Rouse (1939, p. 16). Rouse was a student of the ethnologist Cornelius Osgood, who was much interested in material culture typology from both ethnological (Osgood, 1940) and archaeological (Osgood, 1942) perspectives.

6. J. W. Bennett (1943). Bennett received his graduate education at the University of Chicago, where Radcliffe-Brown, an influential proponent of the functionalist approach, had taught. In this connection, R. S. MacNeish (1975) has raised the point that our first-edition narrative of such events neglected the general graduate student and younger-generation archaeological ferment of the late 1930s and early 1940s, especially that radiating from the University of Chicago. We willingly concede the importance of that institution and its Department of Anthropology to the intellectual development of those times; however, in a formal history, one must largely rely on written and published works rather than on "who said what to whom" in informal conversations and argument, however stimulating or significant such conversations may have been.

7. Waring and Holder (1945); their ideas were known in Southeastern archaeological circles before that time.

8. Vaillant (1932); Phillips (1940). Later, however, Vaillant (1940) did consider Mesoamerican-Southeastern relationships in a functional light.

9. Representative works: J. E. S. Thompson (1939, 1940).

10. Representative works: Haury (1934, 1940).

11. Representative works: Roberts (1929, 1931, 1939).

12. Representative works: Webb and De Jarnette (1942); Webb and Snow (1945).

13. Representative work: Griffin (1943).

14. Taylor (1948, p. 170) was quite positively influenced by the British archaeologist Grahame Clark (1939, 1940).

15. Willey (1953a); however, Willey was influenced by Taylor in his pursuit of the Virú Valley settlement studies (Willey, 1953c). See Woodbury (1954) for a critical review of Taylor.

16. See Willey, 1977.

17. Spaulding (1953b). Earlier uses of statistics in American pottery studies (Strong, 1925; Willey, 1943; Brainerd, 1951; Robinson, 1951) had been primarily concerned with chronological ordering.

18. George Cowgill (1977, p. 327) argues that we have misrepresented Spaulding's 1953 statements

by confusing *formal analysis* with *form-time* analysis. It is true, as Cowgill states, that Spaulding best explicates the relationships between culture change through time and the nature of typology in a later (Spaulding, 1960) article; however, to our way of thinking, Spaulding's position on change through time is implicit in his 1953 statement, and this seemed and still seems to us to be the crux of his debate with Ford.

19. R. H. Thompson (1958); Rouse (1953a, 1960); Wheat, Gifford, and Wasley (1958); and the Peruvian studies of Rowe (1962c) and his associates (Menzel, Rowe, and Dawson, 1964), in which attempts have been made to relate form and meaning in art. On the Ford side of the argument, see a statement by Brew (1946).

20. The best example of this is an article by A. C. Spaulding (1960).

21. See Spaulding (1957) and Swanson (1959) for critical comments.

22. For the culture *tradition concept,* see Willey (1945) and Goggin (1949).

23. There are very few post-1960 references cited in Wauchope's bibliography, and none that could be said to pertain to the New Archaeology of the 1960s. Binford (1968a, p. 14), for example, notes that Wauchope's definition of cultural process differs from that accepted in the 1960s.

24. Griffin (1956) and Cressman (1956) are among the archaeologists; Kroeber (1948); White (1949), Goldschmidt (1959); and Sahlins and Service, eds. (1960) are among the ethnologists-social anthropologists.

25. For Griffin and Cressman see note 24; see also Caldwell (1958).

26. See Willey (1946b) for an early summary and description of the Virú Valley project; subsequent publications on the project, in addition to Willey (1953c) are: Strong and Evans (1952); Bird (1948); W. C. Bennett (1950); Collier (1955); Ford (1949); Ford and Willey (1949); and Holmberg (1950). A retrospective reference is Willey (1974).

27. Willey (1953c); however, O. G. Ricketson, Jr., had been concerned with Maya settlement size, in connection with population estimates, and this work forms a chapter of the Uaxactun site monograph (Ricketson and Ricketson, 1938).

28. D. E. Thompson (1964a, 1964b), a graduate student of Willey's, did a settlement survey of the Casma Valley; see also Patterson and Lanning (1964). More recently, D. J. Wilson (1988) has brought out an impressive settlement pattern study on the Santa Valley.

29. Vayda and Rappaport (1968); it is noteworthy that Steward's "cultural ecology" did not really embrace a holistic, truly ecological approach.

30. See Daniel (1950, pp. 302–308) for a concise historical discussion of environmental concerns in European archaeology. See also Crawford (1912, 1921); Fox (1923, 1932); and Clark (1936, 1952, 1953, 1954). The general lack of influence on American archaeology by cultural geography is noted by Haag (1957) and surely was a factor in the differences in development between European and American archaeology. However, a few individual geographers, such as Sauer (1952), have had some influence on the discipline.

31. As Meighan (1959, p. 404) has stated, "The study of archaeology may be seen as largely a natural science when dealing with the earliest or simplest technological levels, whereas as cultures become more complex, the archaeologist may utilize more and more of the humanities."

32. Frederick Johnson (1942, 1949). For recent summaries of the contributions of this type of interdisciplinary study, see Brothwell and Higgs (1969).

33. Jennings (1957); Haag (1957); Quimby (1954, 1960a, 1960b); see also Helm (1962) for additional references.

34. Cook (1946, 1950). Heizer (1960) offers a full discussion and numerous references; see also Heizer (1955).

35. See Manners (1964) for further discussions of Steward's role in the development of American anthropology.

36. See Vayda and Rappaport (1968) for criticisms of Steward's work.

cle by Willey (1960b), which follows an evolutionary organization, and one by Armillas (1956), which does so in part.

74. Willey (1966–71). For a briefer historical treatment, see Willey (1960a). See also two general syntheses by Schobinger (1969) and by Bosch-Gimpera (1971).

75. See Bushnell and McBurney (1959) for a negative view; see Müller-Beck (1966) or Chard (1963) for positive ones. A survey of the question is also in Griffin (1960).

76. See the Arctic references in note 70.

77. See Phillips (1966). An article by Clair C. Patterson (1971) presents a strong argument against the Trans-Pacific diffusion of metallurgical techniques (casting, gilding, and so forth) to Peru from Asia as Heine-Geldern (1954) had argued. See also Riley and others (1971) for articles presenting both sides of the issue.

78. See Rowe (1966) for a strong negative reaction.

79. See Parsons (1957) and Meggers and Evans (1961) for some specific applications; see also Willey and Phillips (1958, pp. 29–34) and Rouse (1955).

80. Willey and Phillips (1955, 1958); R. H. Thompson (1956); Caldwell (1958); Willey (1966–71).

81. Caldwell (1965). The British archaeologist Christopher Hawkes (1954) has defined what he called a *diffusion sphere*, which is similar to the interaction sphere, although not quite the same.

82. The "Southeastern Ceremonial Complex" or "Southern Cult" data of Waring and Holder (1945) might be subsumed under the interaction-sphere concept, although the horizon-style definition might also apply.

83. See our comments in Chapter One. See also Harris (1968, p. 28) and Clarke (1970, pp. 4–14), as well as Morgan (1877).

84. The later book by Steward and Faron (1959), which was based on the *Handbook*, expresses this even more clearly.

85. Published in Tax and others (1953, p. 247).

86. See Strong (1948); Willey (1948); Larco Hoyle (1948); Bushnell (1956). The Uhle-Kroeber Peruvian horizon scheme, which we have described in Chapter Four, did not have these stage qualities; and Rowe's (1960) chronology for the area derives directly from theirs.

87. The term *function* is used here in a broad way, subsuming both use and function. R. C. Dunnell (1978) has emphasized the differences between *style* (the effective vehicle for the tracing of culture history) and *function* (the principle of data organization in what he has called "cultural reconstructionism"). Dunnell sees cultural reconstructionism as coming to the foreground in American archaeology in the late 1930s and 1940s, especially in North America, where archaeology had roots in anthropology and ethnology. While cultural reconstructionism complements cultural history, it operates with quite different principles. He also argues, as we have, that a successful transition to processual archaeology must build on functional or cultural reconstructive archaeology.

CHAPTER SIX

The Modern Period:
New and Continuing Ways of Explaining
and Understanding the Past (1960–1992)

This is the way of histories; that as they came closer to
the present and future, the errors of proportion become
greater; so does the writer's subjectivity.

BRIAN ALDISS

A DEFINITION OF
THE PERIOD

Any attempt to view what we call the *Modern Period* in historical
perspective is most difficult. The events are too recent, the time is
still upon us. Nevertheless, we must make this period—the three decades between 1960 and 1992—a part of our history of American archaeology. Not to do so would be to fail in one of our most important
objectives to see the developments of the immediate present in relation
to those of the past.

In our first edition (1974), we devoted only a single chapter to the
period after 1960. Then, in the second edition (1980), we expanded this
to three chapters. We were, at that point, we think, becoming too
obsessed with the present. It was a disproportionate history. Here, in this
third edition, we have returned to a single—if long—chapter. We must
also explain our change of the name of the period in this third edition.
Previously, we had designated it as the Explanatory Period. Now, in
light of some of the developments of the last decade or so, we have
changed this to the more non-committal term, Modern Period. In selecting this term, we should specify that we use it in the very ordinary
chronological sense. We are in no way evoking "modernism" as opposed
to "post-modernism" or entering into that epistemological debate (see
Harvey, 1989). We have done this because we feel that the goal of
explanation—in the strict sense of the explanation of process in past
culture change—is too limiting. The course of American archaeology
over the past thirty years, while still much involved with such explana-

tion, has shown other concerns which also must be considered as a part of the recent history of the discipline.

One of the major hurdles in analyzing the intellectual trends of the Modern Period is to avoid perceiving them in an overly rigid manner. Would it thus be preferable to view the past three decades as a linear sequence from the traditional archaeology to New or Processual Archaeology, Postprocessual Archaeology, Critical Archaeology, Interpretive or Hermeneutical Archaeology, Cognitive-processual Archaeology, and so on? We firmly believe that such a linear stance would be mistaken because elements of these approaches are present today and their underlying themes have been part of the intellectual scene for the Modern Period, as well as in preceding periods. After all, thirty years or so is a relatively short stretch of time, and given the large quantity of recent theoretically oriented articles, it would be easy to err in attempting to argue that one trend was rising while others were falling. Likewise, it would be easy to fall into the trap of acting like pollsters who do not reveal their sampling techniques, so that readers would not be sure if intellectual historians were presenting accurate readings of the pulse of contemporary archaeology or simply indulging in wishful thinking.[1] It has recently been argued, for example, in relation to one aspect of the period:

New Archaeology was a reform movement launched by a handful of archaeologists in departments of anthropology in North America in the mid-1960s. It rose to a peak of intellectual vogue in the late 1960s and early 1970s, and gradually faded in popularity in the mid-1970s. (Gibbon, 1989, p. 1)

We believe that given the limited time frame and broad intellectual ferment of the Modern Period to date, trying to judge the popularity of various intellectual trends with method and theory articles, chapters, and books as the data base can be hazardous at best, because there seems to be a wide gulf between what a limited number of scholars are saying the field is (or should be) doing and the kinds of research currently underway or recently published. Indeed, this may always have been the case in archaeology. In any event, it thus seems preferable, at this juncture when our perspective is so short, to examine the various intellectual trends that have characterized the field during the Modern Period and look at their historical roots, as well as their interconnections of opposition, rather than attempting to chart their waxing and waning in some deterministic linear fashion.

As previously, we begin the chapter with the thesis suggested near the close of the preceding one—that the reemergence of evolutionary concepts in the late 1950s, after long years of disfavor, prepared the base for the *New Archaeology* of the 1960s. We then examine this New Archaeology, its links with the past, and its innovations, especially those that can best be summed up under the term *Processualism;* the employment of systems theory and the concept of the ecosystem; the use of statistics and the role of the computer; deductive reasoning and the positivist philosophy of science; attitudes about ethnographic analogy in archaeological interpretation; an emphasis on cultural variability; various problems of archaeological operation; and some selected case examples of early New or Processual Archaeology from the 1960s. After this, we continue with the further consolidations and broadenings of New Archaeological procedures and theory. This is followed by a consideration and a selective review of the influences which New Archaeological thinking has had upon the course of American archaeology over the past three decades, by what we have designated as "mainstream accommodations" to the New Archaeology. We then take up the essentially critical reactions of the British and American Postprocessual Archaeologists to the New Archaeology.

THE NEW ARCHAEOLOGY

In the mid-1950s, when Willey and Phillips published their scheme for New World prehistory, cultural evolutionism was still largely proscribed in American anthropological circles.[2] For a long time, Leslie White had been its only protagonist.[3] Julian Steward, as we have seen, joined the issue in the late 1940s and 1950s with a brand of evolutionary theory that seemed somewhat more immediately pertinent to the problems of archaeology. Willey and Phillips were familiar with numerous culture sequences in the New World, and they could also see beyond the particulars of these sequences to realize that the story carried in them was the story of the rise of civilization. At the same time, they were also aware of the many areal and regional peculiarities of American Pre-Columbian history and its complex cross-currents of diffusion. They shied away from anything that seemed to them to be deterministic or that would readily *explain* the series of stages by which they viewed the New World past (1958, p. 200): "The method is comparative, and the resulting definitions are abstractions which *describe* culture change through time in native America. The stages are not formulations which *explain* culture change [original italics]." They were, therefore, hesitant to use the word *evolution* because of what seemed to them to be its deterministic and causal implications. They felt that explanation must lie in a complex interplay of diffusion, cultural-environmental interaction, demographic change, "homotaxis in a true evolutionary sense," and psychological factors (Willey and Phillips, 1958, pp. 70–71). Throughout, they showed

Leslie A. White, 1900–1975. (From the Michigan Historical Collections, Bentley Historical Library, University of Michigan)

a disinclination to separate evolution from history. In one sense, Willey and Phillips were obviously right; process was not to be plucked easily from the matrices of history. At the same time, their refusal to recognize their approach as an evolutionary one—even if no more than a preliminary step in the arrangement of the data—was a hesitancy in keeping with the antievolutionary attitudes of the times.[4]

Much more direct evolutionary statements than those of Willey and Phillips were also made by a few other American archaeologists in the 1950s. Perhaps significantly, these were people who had been more influenced by White than by Steward. Betty J. Meggers was one of these. We have already referred to her 1954 paper on natural environment as a limiting factor in cultural growth, in which she combined a cultural-environmental approach with evolutionism. In 1955, in an article entitled "The Coming of Age of American Archaeology," she defended evolutionary theory against the criticisms of the historical particularists by arguing, "Its validity stems from the fact that observable conditions can be more easily understood and more simply explained if the law is assumed" (Meggers, 1955, p. 121). Observing that the main trends in social anthropology between 1930 and 1955 had been in the direction of psychological explanations of cultural phenomena, she pointed out that archaeologists, particularly in their area schemes of developmental stages, had been moving toward evolutionary explanations. Referring to the social anthropologist Hoebel's statement about archaeology being the "lesser part of anthropology," Meggers (1955, p. 120) goes on to add: "The strides that have been made [in archaeology] in recent years indicate that far from being a handicap, there is considerable advantage in being forced to deal with culture artificially separate from human beings." In other words, a concept of cultural evolution came easy for the archaeologist, given the nature of his or her data; in contrast, the cultural anthropologist Leslie White had to arrive at it by a more difficult intellectual route.

More substantively, Meggers (1956) made a signal contribution as a participant and editor of the symposium group that produced the paper on community patterning referred to in the previous chapter in our discussions of settlement-pattern studies. In this work, the basic evolutionary assumptions of progress through improved subsistence and the greater survival value of sedentary as opposed to nomadic life were made at the outset—definite explanatory and causal statements that go beyond anything offered by Willey and Phillips. These assumptions were then examined cross-culturally to arrive at a stage scheme of settlement or community patterning applicable to the Americas and beyond.

At the close of the 1950s and the 1960s, a number of writings appeared on evolutionary theory or on applications of it to specific

Julian H. Steward, 1902–1972. (From Mrs. J. H. Steward)

substantive problems. J. A. Ford, G. I. Quimby, and W. G. Haag—all former students of White's—were among the authors. Ford's field researches had long been guided by evolutionary precepts; these now became even more explicit (Ford, 1962). Quimby (1960a) used Nasakapi and Eskimo data—both archaeological and ethnological—in combining White's evolutionary perspective with environmental determinism to attempt to explain the nature of northeastern North American cultures. Haag, in a critical review article, "The Status of Evolutionary Theory in American Archaeology," offered a definition of evolution for archaeologists: "Evolution is change in form and function through time of material culture and any bodily acts, ideas, and sentiments that may be inferred therefrom" (Haag, 1959, pp. 96–97). He went on to say that evolution had long been a part of American archaeology, but essentially on a subconscious level.

Willey, in an article published in 1960, moved somewhat farther toward an evolutionary outlook by stating that the processes of cultural evolution are selective ones and that, through these, humans promote their survival and fulfillment. He cautioned, however, that the courses by which this comes about are not "programmed by laws of inevitably" and further observed that, while technical-environmental adaptations seem easy to plot on a historical-evolutionary scale, those of the ideological realm (art) are not.[5]

Old World archaeological and evolutionary influences also began to make themselves felt in American archaeology at about this time. Robert J. Braidwood, although who, like Willey, was somewhat hesitant to conceive of cultural evolution as a process outside of specific historical contexts, had viewed Near Eastern prehistory in an evolutionary light (Braidwood, 1948, 1952). He, like most other Near Eastern archaeologists, had been influenced by the archaeological and evolutionary writings of V. Gordon Childe.[6] In 1959, he traced the history of evolutionary theory in archaeology in a summary article, focusing attention mainly on the Old World, but with some references to the New, and showing how Darwinian concepts as applied to culture had changed from the early De Mortillet usages to those of Childe and others (Braidwood, 1959).

A former student of Braidwood's, Robert Adams, brought Old World and Americanist ideas about cultural evolution even closer together by researching in Mesopotamia and Middle America and directing his attention in both areas to the quantum advance from temple-centered societies to those of the urban states. In his "The Evolutionary Process in Early Civilizations" (1960), Adams was critical of Steward and Wittfogel, arguing that causal relationships cannot be established by stage definitions and cross-cultural comparisons alone. He challenged single-explanation hypotheses, such as Steward's (see, for instance, 1949a) belief that population pressure led to warfare or Wittfogel's (1957) insistence that the administrative requirements of large-scale irrigation produced the despotic state. The only way to avoid self-contained causal theories, in Adams' view, was to recognize the complexity and interdependence of events leading up to major stage transformations and to present these to the greatest possible range of historical detail. He recognized no inherent opposition between cultural-historical integration and evolutionism. Adams called for two things, one of which we have referred to before. This is the necessity for contextual-functional analysis as an intermediate step between chronological ordering and processual understanding. The other, which is implicit but not explicit in Adams' writings, is systemic analysis—the only way in which the "complexity and interdependence of events," in Adams' terms, may be viewed in their proper relationships to one another.

Adams' major work along these lines—and one in which he followed up his call for full historical and contextual detail—is his brilliant *The Evolution of Urban Society: Early Mesopotamia and Prehispanic Mexico* (1966). In it, he traces with great care the parallel evolution of two societies, one in the Old World and one in the New World, from kin-based farming villages to stratified, politically organized states. While Adams rejected any single-principle explanation of cultural evolution, Steward (1966, p. 730) in reviewing his work, felt that "the author has documented the incipiency of crop improvement, better utilization of microenvironments, and increased specialization and interdependency of local population segments as the new processes or trends that led to state institutions." Certainly, by 1966, the date of the publication of Adams' book, it was the outstanding example of the cross-cultural comparative approach to an understanding of cultural evolution, the only such attempt in which there had been a microanalysis of the archaeological (and ethnohistorical) data bearing on the cases at hand.

By the late 1960s, a change had taken place in American archaeology. There had been a tacit acceptance of cultural evolution. Any representative sampling of the then recent American archaeological literature, with its strong reliance on the ideas of White and Steward and the younger cultural evolutionists among the social anthropologists, such as Sahlins, Service, and Fried, bears this out. For example, in the four issues of the journal *American Antiquity* that were published in 1971, there was a total of 16 references (in 21 articles) to the theoretical works of these five men. A decade earlier, the four issues of the 1960–61 volume contained only two references to Steward (in 28 articles) and none to any of the other four authors. This swift and quiet change is one of the most interesting phenomena of the Modern Period.

As we have seen, the theory of cultural evolution was generally anathema as late as the 1950s. The factors bringing about the change are not altogether understood, but they were probably multiple. The general trend toward a more scientific approach in all the social sciences (and even some of the humanities) was undoubtedly one of them. Another very significant factor was the change in the political climate in the United States. In the 1940s and 1950s, it was common for the spectre of Marxism to be raised by antievolutionists in the heat of argument.[7] Given the political tenor of the time, the implications of such an association should not be underestimated. The 1960s, on the other hand, saw a somewhat more realistic appreciation of the relationships between evolutionary theory and political dogma, which may have made evolutionary thinking more palatable.

In addition to these factors, perhaps the most basic reason for the change was generated within archaeology itself. If archaeology, by its very nature, is concerned with chronology, and if chronology is the dynamic dimension of evolution, then it should come as no surprise that evolutionary theory should at last establish itself in archaeology. The Classificatory-Historical Period was a story of the successes of chronological ordering. Toward the close of that period, while American social anthropology was still largely ruled by the antievolutionists and functionalists, evolution came quietly into archaeology through comparative considerations of the long precise chronological sequences of cultural change that had been developed in the years between 1914 and the late 1950s. Without this well-documented chronological ordering, we doubt very much that the theoretical exhortations of White or Steward would have moved American archaeologists. But the hard and indisputable facts of chronology, particularly when revealed by the methods of stratigraphy, were too much for the literal-minded archaeologists to ignore. They were convinced that culture did indeed change through time and that this change was not altogether random. That such a condition for the acceptance of evolutionary theory was self-generated within archaeology seems borne out by the fact that this same acceptance did not occur in social anthropology.

Although the revival of evolutionary theory in the late 1950s prepared the way for the advances of the Modern Period, this revival by itself did not constitute the beginnings of that period. Its inception is placed a few years later, for the Modern Period is most meaningfully characterized by what has been called the *New Archaeology*. This name does not tell us much, other than that it differed from the archaeology that preceded it, and so we must attempt a definition of the New Archaeology.

Our definition will be seen in clearer perspective if we first describe certain attitudes that provided a background for the rise of the New Archaeology. To begin, it was a product of anthropological archaeology, of young archaeologists who, as graduate students, had been partly trained by social anthropologists as well as archaeologists. Their central concern was the elucidation of cultural process. Although there had been, as we have seen, a certain amount of talk about the necessity for archaeologists to come to grips with cultural process in the late Classificatory-Historical Period, this had remained — like the proverbial concern about the weather — just talk, no one had done much about it. The "New Archaeologists" felt that the time had come for a serious attack on questions of process. Second, the New Archaeology was (and to some extent still is) pervaded with a great optimism about the possibilities of success in processual explanation and in arriving at "laws of cultural dynamics" (Binford, 1968a, p. 27; although see Redman, 1991, for a less optimistic view). A third attitude held that archaeology, in its revelation and explanation of cultural process, could be made relevant not only to the rest of anthropology but to the problems of the modern world as well.

Let us turn from this background to a more specific definition of the New Archaeology in its approaches. In service of the goal of understanding culture change, the New Archaeologists advocated a number of related changes in traditional archaeological practices. They espoused an evolutionary approach; a systems view of culture that emphasized cultural variability and its systemic organization; an ecosystemic perspective that was concerned with the links between cultures and their environments; the statistical control of such links and variability and attention to sampling techniques that would permit generalizations about the variability; and a general "scientific" approach that stressed explicitness of assumptions, problem-orientation and structured research strategies, hypothesis testing (particularly in the deductive-nomological form), and a positivist philosophical position. Some of these tenets of the New Archaeology, as we shall see, had greater impacts on the field than others. Yet the overall program had a profound affect on the practice of American archaeology that can still be felt today.

If this brief statement may serve as a minimal definition for the American New Archaeology — and if this New Archaeology marks the threshold of our Modern Period — just when and where did the synthesis take place? To what extent were the important elements of the New Archaeology present before 1960, our dividing line between the Classificatory-Historical and Modern Periods? In reviewing a collection of essays, edited by Sally R. Binford and Lewis R. Binford and published in 1968, as a representative expression of the New Archaeology, Walter W. Taylor, Jr. (1969, p. 383), has challenged the contention of "newness":

> A full discussion of a very similar overall approach to our discipline has been in print since 1948 (W. W. Taylor, *A Study of Archaeology*). The systematic view of culture has been a basic premise of American anthropology, including archaeology, certainly since Malinowski, if not since Boas, and as for Binford's other tenets, I can point to passages in *A Study of Archaeology* covering each of them, even that of testing hypotheses.... What the Binfords have produced in this book is not an exposition of the theory and practice of a new perspective but an explicit restatement of an old one, with some new and modern additions, together with some very pertinent, cogent, stimulating examples of archaeological research resulting from it.

But Binford (1968a, p. 27) feels quite differently about it, observing:

> Despite a recent statement that one should not speak of a "new archaeology" since this alienates it from the old . . . we feel that archaeology in the 1960s is at a major point of evolutionary change. Evolution always builds on what went before, but it always involves basic structural changes.

Who is correct? This is not simply a dispute over intellectual credit but a question about the way ideas are formed, synthesized, and propagated. A rereading of Taylor's *A Study of Archaeology,* to which we have referred at considerable length in the previous chapter, will verify his contention that some of Binford's tenets were, indeed, present in what he advocated. One of the fundamentals of Taylor's "conjunctive" approach was full contextual recovery of the data of prehistory, which is surely related to the New Archaeologist's insistence on as complete recovery of all the variability in the archaeological record as possible. Taylor's claim to hypothesis-testing through deductive reasoning is also borne out in several places in his text. Nor can it be denied, as Taylor insists, that a systemic view of culture had been held by the anthropological functionalists since the 1920s.

What then, are the differences between Taylor's position of 1948 and that of the New Archaeologists of the 1960s? We would argue that three features characterize the latter but not former: (1) a cultural-evolutionary point of view; (2) a systemic model of culture, which incorporates this evolutionary point of view; and (3) a battery of new methods, techniques, and aids that were not available in 1948.

An examination of Taylor's book reveals that it does not embody a cultural-evolutionary outlook. It is probable that Taylor was influenced in this matter by Kluckhohn, whose opinions in the 1940s, at least on this point, were very much those of the traditional antievolutionist position of the main body of American social anthropology.

As to a systemic view of culture, it is our opinion that, unless such a view is informed by an evolutionary outlook, it is severely limited as a means of observing and understanding culture change. Although the functionalist position conceives of culture and society systemically, it does so either in the manner of what systems theorists would refer to as a *mechanical equilibrium model,* which, like a clock, has no internal sources of change, or it does so by means of a model in which all feedback is negatively reinforcing, thereby maintaining the *status quo.* Such models are not ideal for sociocultural study. More pertinent for this purpose are "complex adaptive models," which allow for positive and negative feedback and which are self-informing and adaptive (Clarke, 1968, Chapter 2). Such models, when viewed in diachronic perspective, reveal an evolutionary trajectory of culture change. The New Archaeologist has been concerned essentially with such models and with their evolutionary potential, and in this we would see a significant difference between Taylor's 1948 systemic perspective and that of the 1960s. In making this observation, it is only fair to point out that, in 1948, systems theory had made little or no impact on the social sciences. This advance of the New Archaeology owes much to similar advances in ecology, geography, and sociology.

From 1948 until the 1960s, archaeologists drew upon new methods, techniques, and aids from the sciences. For example, the computer began to revolutionize the systemic approach in archaeology. Sheer quantitative control resulted in qualitative differences in what archaeology could and could not accomplish, and materials analyses of all kinds opened up new investigative leads that were not conceived of in 1948. From a philosophical point of view, such new methods are less important in distinguishing between the conjunctive archaeology of the late 1940s and the New Archaeology of the 1960s than the essential ideological differences, which lie in the more recent applications of cultural-evolutionary theory and systems theory—and in their synthesis.

The archaeologist responsible for this synthesis, which made the New Archaeology possible and which marks the threshold of the Modern Period, is Lewis R. Binford. The term New Archaeology was first used, in its modern sense, by Joseph R. Caldwell in a 1959 article.[8] This admirable paper contains many of the elements we have been discussing, but it does not draw these elements together and outline the methodological guidelines in the way that Binford was able to do in his 1962 essay, "Archaeology as Anthropology." In this and a series of important papers in the 1960s,[9] Binford was able to absorb the rising tide of evolutionary and environmentalist thinking of the late Classificatory-Historical Period, along with the more vocal dissatisfactions about the traditional descriptive-chronological goals of American archaeology, and to synthesize these with a systems outlook and deductive reasoning. He combined all of this with polemic force in pointing to the inadequacies of existing archaeological theory and method, and he formulated a coherent program for archaeological research with goals that were attractive to the coming generation of research students.[10] For all of this, he deserves great credit in any history of American archaeological thought.[11]

We have defined the New Archaeology by what we consider to be its four basic characteristics: cultural-evolutionary theory, a systemic view of culture and of culture and the environment, an emphasis on cultural variability and its control through statistical sampling, and a general scientific approach. The reemergence of evolutionary theory in American archaeology has already been discussed. In addition, it should be noted that the evolutionary position of most New Archaeologists—although not always overtly formulated—in practice assumes the technical-economic realm of culture to be the primarily determinative one in change, with the social and ideational realms changing in secondary relation to it. This marks a distinct difference from that of the historical-developmental stage approach of Willey and Phillips, where no attempt was made to pinpoint causality. Let us now take a look at systems thinking in archaeology.

First, we must recognize that the revival of evolutionary thinking and the introduction of systems models in archaeology are systemically related and that these, in turn, are also systemically related to the development of environmental concerns into ecological ones and to the growing use of computers in archaeological research. Utilization and development of each of these approaches have had ramifications for the others. The development of the New Archaeology cannot be understood without consideration of the growth of these innovations in the context of a burgeoning intellectual trend toward more scientific research.

The initial push toward a systems viewpoint in American archaeology can be traced to Binford's path-breaking 1962 article, "Archaeology as Anthropology," which we have mentioned previously. Following Leslie White, Binford directed archaeologists' attention to the subsystems of culture, particularly the major cultural subsystems: the technological, social, and ideological. He stated that the artifactual assemblages relevant to these subsystems must be identified and their functional contexts elucidated. The archaeologist would then be able to study the changing structural relationships between these assemblages and their subsystemic correlates. In this manner, the archaeologist could move toward the goal of understanding the evolution of cultural systems.

However, although Binford clearly had a systemic conception of culture, he lacked, at least in 1962, a systemic, holistic view of cultural systems in relation to their environments. Binford (1962, p. 218) cites with approval Steward's methodology of cultural ecology and points out that it "certainly is a valuable means of increasing our understanding of cultural processes." But, if Binford was not to champion immediately both a systemic view of culture and a systemic view of culture and environment, others were soon stimulated to combine the two viewpoints.

As we stated in the preceding chapter, in relation to environmental studies, the key conceptual change that marks the Modern Period has been the change from a linear model — environment influences culture — to a holistic or systemic one — human populations seen as parts of ecosystems (Hardesty, 1971; Vayda and Rappaport, 1968). Early movements toward a holistic view of the human-environment interaction can be seen in William T. Sanders' (1956) concept of the "symbiotic region" as applied to prehistoric Central Mexico and the search for the origins of New World agriculture by Richard S. MacNeish, first in Tamaulipas, Mexico, and then, most importantly, in the Tehuacan Valley of Mexico (1958, 1964a, 1967). But, on the whole, although much of the ecological research of the 1960s was a quantum step above the early work of the Classificatory-Historical Period in both theoretical and methodological sophistication and use of modern ecological concepts, the *overall* conception of most archaeological projects still lacked a holistic view. A good example would be the research into the prehistoric ecology of the Upper Great Lakes region of North America, which produced the excellent full-scale monographs by Yarnell on the flora and by Cleland on the fauna of the region in addition to fine excavation reports, including one by McPherron in the New-Archaeological tradition.[12] However, the very fact that separate faunal, floral, and archaeological monographs were produced is indicative of the failure to integrate these research efforts and their results into a comprehensive whole at that time.

The individual most closely identified with the conceptual shift in environmental studies to a holistic approach and the relationship between humans and their environments is Kent V. Flannery.[13] Certainly, Flannery should be singled out as the leader in establishing the ecosystem as the basic model for viewing the adaptive changes between humans and their environment. His work represents the logical advance beyond the theoretical foundation laid by Binford.[14] In particularly, the work of Flannery and his colleagues in the Valley of Oaxaca, Mexico is one of the best available examples of the new approach.[15]

Although the ecosystem concept has only recently become known on the American archaeological scene, it has a much more respectable antiquity in ecological studies. It was first used as far back as 1935 by Tansley, and its place in ecological research was secured with the publication of the first edition of Eugene Odum's classic *Fundamentals of Ecology* in 1953.[16] It is important to note, though, that Marston Bates' article "Human Ecology," which appeared in the same year as part of the encyclopedic *Anthropology Today,* and presumably was widely read at the time, did not discuss the ecosystem concept (Bates, 1953).

Basically, the ecosystem can be defined as the interactions, involving energy and matter, between one living population (such as humans) or all living populations (an ecological "community") of an area and the nonliving environment (F. C. Evans, 1956; Odum, 1963, pp. 3–4; Boughey, 1971). By adopting the ecosystem model into their research, American archaeologists provided a framework for their investigations with clearly defined units and boundaries, unified their models with those of other scientists, and permitted the quantification of their materials. The advantages of the ecosystem strategy are many, and the future possibilities for studying the processes involved in the evolution of ecosystems (with the focus on human populations) are unbounded.[17]

A further conceptual advantage, beyond viewing culture internally as a system and externally as a part of a larger ecosystem, has been the realization by archaeologists of the compatibility of these viewpoints and that of general systems thinking in the sciences. Building on ideas first advanced by such brilliant thinkers as Bertalanffy and Weiner, a systems outlook soon emerged.[18] The applicability of this perspective to the New Archaeological scene of the Modern Period was quickly realized, although it was just as quickly realized that the systems perspective

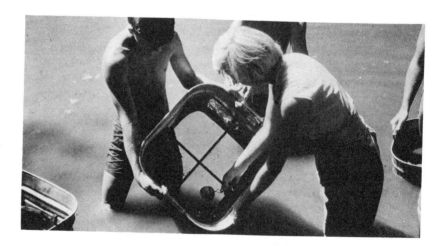

Advances in ecological theory are reflected in and abetted by advances in field techniques. One such technique is the flotation of organic particles from midden debris in order to recover plant and food remains. (From Stuart Struever)

was heuristically more useful than the "theory." Again, one of the leaders of this new advance was Flannery. His 1968 article "Archaeological Systems Theory and Early Mesoamerica" was an especially clear landmark statement.[19] The most detailed discussion of the utilization of systems thinking in archaeological research, however, came not from an American but from a British archaeologist, David Clarke, who was one of the first to adopt a multidisciplinary systems framework, and his *Analytical Archaeology* is easily the most ambitious early effort in this area. It was another testament of the growing international communication among archaeological scholars that characterized the 1960s[20] and has gained momentum throughout the Modern Period.

The viability of a general systems approach to archaeological problems and its growing acceptance during the 1960s could be illustrated by the fact that, in 1969, Frank Hole and Robert F. Heizer felt compelled to rewrite their leading textbook, *An Introduction to Prehistoric Archaeology*, which had first been published only three years previously, to include a section on general systems theory. However, their revision pointed up a major problem facing American archaeology in the Modern Period: the disjunction between theory, on the one hand, and method and practice on the other. Much of *An Introduction to Prehistoric Archaeology* treats of the methods and results of an "old" archaeology, which are difficult to correlate with the new theoretical slant of the text involving a systemic outlook. But the same point could be scored against many of the writings of that time and since. There was then and still remains a need to develop new conceptual tools for the study of culture process (Binford, 1965).

There is, however, one reason to be optimistic about the successful follow-through of systemic concepts in archaeology. This is the fact that archaeologists now have available to them a sophisticated technological tool: the computer.

It can be argued that, without the increasing application of various satisfactory techniques and the use of computer programs, many archaeological ideas would remain pipe-dreams, while others would not even have been conceived. Of particular note in terms of recent advances are the means for data storage and retrieval now available and the statistical tools for chronological ordering, artifact classification, the unbiased sampling of sites, and multivariate analyses of past cultural patterns.[21] With the ready availability of computer facilities at many universities, these latter kinds of studies can easily be executed. Significantly, in terms of the development of American archaeology, they make possible the kinds of analyses that Binford outlined in 1962 in his discussion of artifact assemblages and the systemic inferences that should be made about their patterning in archaeological sites. One additional advance in computer utilization that deserves mention is the use of computer simulations as a means of advancing systems analyses.[22]

It is important to realize, nevertheless, that use of the computer, like the various scientific techniques discussed in the preceding chapter, cannot in and of itself revolutionize American archaeology. As William A. Longacre (1970, p. 132) had said, "Statistical techniques are not magical." Statistical techniques and computer programs are simply tools that can be used profitably by archaeologists. The results of studies that utilize these tools will be as progressive as the archaeological research strategy in which the tools play a role and as progressive as the archaeologist's knowledge about the parameters of, and the assumptions behind, the applicability of the tools.[23] However, archaeologists who will not use statistical and computer analyses, out of dislike, distrust, ignorance, or perhaps fear of mathematical manipulation, will cut themselves off from an integral part of modern archaeological methodology.[24]

The growing use of statistics, aided and abetted by computer applications, was also related to a rising concern with sampling in archaeological research. The attention to sampling was in turn related to a new emphasis on cultural variability that emerged from the systems view of culture (see Winters, 1969, for an early application of this view). If it were accepted, as New Archaeologists argued it should be, that cultural systems and their constituent subsystems were not homogeneous, then it followed that scholars could not readily generalize from one arbitrary part of a site to a whole site or from one site to a larger region. It clearly was not acceptable anymore to just excavate a test pit or two and use such work to talk about the overall site. Yet, on the other hand, it usually was not feasible or practical to excavate or collect from a complete site or area. Therefore research strategies had to be devised which effectively sampled a site or region so that justifiable statistical generalizations could be made.[25]

The introduction of the "interaction sphere" concept in the eastern United States to replace the older Hopewell culture construct is a good early example of the replacement of a traditional homogeneous concept with one that attempted to show how variability in economic specialization was regionally organized. The interaction sphere concept also was used to argue that a Hopewell "culture" did not diffuse from a center in southern Ohio to a large array of centers over a wide area (what Binford, 1965, lambasted as the "aquatic" view of culture with traits "flowing" in a cultural "stream" from one center to another) but that various centers interacted differentially with different goods (and embedded symbols) being manufactured and traded to various villages.[26]

Such anti-diffusionism was in keeping with the New Archaeology's general emphasis on internal cultural change.

As we shall discuss below, the concern with controlling variability through rigorous sampling strategies was subsequently wedded to burgeoning settlement pattern studies to produce sophisticated regional studies of cultural development in such areas as the eastern United States, the Greater Southwest, and Mesoamerica. It also helped deal a final blow to the older elitist biases in the Maya Lowlands, since what had previously been viewed as elite "ceremonial centers" came to be seen as complex urban centers operating in regional environments.[27]

We have considered cultural evolutionary theory, systems analysis, ecology, variability, sampling, and quantitative methods in the service of understanding cultural processes, but these were not the only pillars of the New Archaeology. Perhaps the most significant—and arguably the most effective—part of the New Archaeologists' agenda was the attempt to make the discipline more "scientific." They saw a number of aspects of archaeological research that needed to be changed in order for scientific rigor to be brought to the field. Certainly, the drive towards increased quantification was closely linked to this scientific program, as was the growing sophistication of physical and chemical analyses of archaeological materials (see Brill, ed., 1971; Tite, 1972; Fleming, 1976; R. E. Taylor, 1976, 1978; and R. E. Taylor, ed., 1976, for some early examples). Among the most important trends initiated in the 1960s in service of the program were emphases on explicitness and problem orientation.

Traditional culture-historical archaeology was built on a series of assumptions—some common sense, others not—that over time came to be treated as dogmas. In the American Southwest, for example, it was once assumed that with the development of the pueblos, people lived a fully sedentary life. Therefore, any lithic scatters were automatically dated to the Archaic Period when a more migratory hunter and gatherer lifeway prevailed. This assumption has subsequently been shown to be unfounded (see, for example, Upham, 1984; see also Cordell, 1984). As another example, in the Maya area, it was assumed that the ancient Maya exclusively practiced slash-and-burn cultivation as the historic and modern Maya did. Again, this assumption—and all its implications relating to population density and sociopolitical organization—has been shown to be untenable (see Harrison and Turner, eds., 1978; Sabloff, 1990). Methodologically, there also were a myriad of assumptions relating, for instance, to artifacts such as ceramics or lithics and to rates of change.

New Archaeologists argued that such assumptions had to be made explicit and carefully examined. Research strategies had to be clearly formulated, and the archaeological problems that the investigator was studying and hoped to solve had to be stated prior to the commencement of fieldwork. Thus, it was not considered sufficient for archaeologists to say that they were digging a mound because it was the largest in the area or the most "interesting." At the very least, in this regard, the New Archaeology helped add a degree of rigor in research that had often been lacking before the Modern Period.

Philosophically, the push towards a more scientific archaeology was made within a positivist context. We follow Merrilee Salmon (1992) in broadly defining positivism as "the view that *knowledge* of the world is obtained only through applying the scientific method to experience obtained through our senses." Although many New Archaeologists did not consciously promote a positivist position when they argued for explanations for their social science that would be the same as those of the natural sciences and would produce valid laws of cultural processes, others quite clearly advocated positivism.

The latter argued that archaeology must adopt a positivist philosophy of science and employ the explanatory procedures that are an integral part of this philosophy. These procedures are deductive in nature and have as their object the confirmation of "covering" or general laws.[28] As Albert C. Spaulding (1968, p. 34) said, "The view which I find convincing is attractively simple: there is only one kind of serious explanation, the nomological or covering-law explanation." The principal philosopher of science who championed such a view and was most often cited by New Archaeologists is Carl Hempel. In particular, Hempel's advocacy of deductive-nomological explanation in his 1966 book *Philosophy of Natural History* and the equation of explanation with prediction were forcefully advanced by many New Archaeologists such as Patty Jo Watson, Steven LeBlanc, and Charles Redman in their 1971 book *Explanation in Archaeology: An Explicitly Scientific Approach.*

The New Archaeologists who promoted a positivist philosophy rejected both the view that there is a separable philosophy of history with its own explanatory methods (*cf.* Dray 1967) and the argument that absolute laws of history that explain all cases cannot be discovered. Other forms of explanation, including probabilistic procedures, were not seen as valid, nor were Hempel's own changing views ever carefully considered by the New Archaeology.[29] Moreover, problems caused by the lack of a body of established archaeological theory from which hypotheses could be deduced were not carefully considered. These difficulties engendered a huge amount of controversy that often seemed to create more heat than light.[30] To some critics, the New Archaeology and deductive-nomological explanation mistakenly became nearly one and the same.[31] To our mind, however, the emphasis on the importance

Patty Jo Watson. (Photo by John Sheets; from the Center for Advanced Study in the Behavioral Sciences, Stanford, California)

of hypothesis testing was the crucial component of the New Archaeology, not one particular form of it.

The appearance of *Explanation in Archaeology: An Explicitly Scientific Approach* appears to have marked the end of the first phase of the New Archaeology when its basic tenets were presented and detailed and the beginning of the second or operational phase, to be discussed below, which emerged in the early 1970s with the growing concern about the pragmatic and uniquely archaeological problem of finding the most secure ways of linking past behaviors with material remains. Intellectual developments in the past two decades lead us to the opinion that the impact of this important volume was more in the area of its subtitle – *An Explicitly Scientific Approach* – than its main one – *Explanation in Archaeology*.[32]

Of all the aspects of the early New Archaeology, it is in the area of general concern with adding more rigor in research and analysis, that the New Archaeology – to our mind – has been most successful. Even for those archaeologists today who operate as if Willey and Phillips' *Method and Theory in American Archaeology* had just been written and suspiciously regard much of the non-culture-historical writing of the past three decades as little more than hot air, the importance and value of an explicitly scientific approach has been widely recognized and appreciated as a means of moving from the traditional evaluation of *people* to evaluations of *ideas*. While, as we have seen, there has been and still is a great deal of controversy and disagreement about the specific form of hypothesis testing advocated in *Explanation in Archaeology*, the call for explicitness, problem orientation, and hypothesis testing in service of the general goal of reaching broad understandings of culture change remains as vibrant and relevant today as it was twenty years ago, if not more so, especially in the face of recent demands for a nihilistic archaeology ruled by methodological relativism, which we will discuss shortly. The broad achievement of these particular goals of the New Archaeology is, we believe, one of its most enduring contributions.

Our consideration of the early phase of the New Archaeology should go beyond discussion of theoretical principles and include at least a sampling of archaeological researches that were held up by New Archaeologists as exemplars of the new approach. Most of these case studies were presented in short articles, usually more or less balanced between substantive and theoretical presentation. There were a few monographs; but, importantly, a number of major projects were initiated that embodied the goals and orientations of the explanatory approach and were known from partial publication or from preliminary statements. We

SOME
ARCHAEOLOGICAL
RESEARCHES OF
THE 1960S

must, of necessity, be brief and selective in our summary of this research. It is, for the most part, rather difficult to classify under convenient categories of discussion, but we will attempt to do so. In general, archaeologists asked questions about function and the nature of cultural change, and these questions then drifted into the social and ecological dimensions of culture. One such kind of question was concerned with the recognition of individual and class-status differences, as these were revealed by archaeological data, especially the data of mortuary practices. Another kind of question was directed to prehistoric residence patterns and their implications for kinship, as these were inferred in artifactual, architectural, and settlement information. Other questions involved cultural-environmental interrelationships or ecosystems and matters of subsistence. Still others, and perhaps the most exciting, inquired into the complexities of cause that lie behind those fascinating "quantum leaps" in human history that are sometimes called the *agricultural revolution*, the *urban revolution*, or the appearance of *complex societies*.

We will begin with those studies that were concerned with status differences in society. Quite fittingly, one of these was summarized in Binford's classic 1962 article. In this research, Binford was interested in explaining some peculiar variables in the prehistoric record of the Wisconsin Great Lakes region, especially with reference to an archaeological manifestation known as the *Old Copper Culture*. The study is of particular interest, for in it Binford incorporated Leslie White's views on cultural evolution, a general systems theory approach, and a deductive line of reasoning in testing the hypotheses he made about the Old Copper Culture. This Old Copper Culture (Wittry and Ritzenthaler, 1956) was known to be from the Archaic Period in date, but it was unique within eastern North America in its possession of tools and weapons hammered out of nuggets of surface copper. The problem posed by the Old Copper Culture was that its metal technology did not persist — at least in the form of heavy tools and points — into the later cultures of the area; instead, these later cultures had reverted to stone implements. This appeared to contradict the evolutionary principle that more efficient tool types always succeed those of less efficiency. Binford questioned the efficiency of these copper tools, citing White's energy potential theory of cultural evolution, and argued that the time needed for collecting surface copper and for making the artifacts greatly reduced this presumed efficiency. He went on to suggest that these particular implements, rather than being essentially utilitarian, were "socio- technic" items that functioned as achieved status symbols in an egalitarian society. A number of lines of evidence were developed to support this hypothesis. To begin, the total cultural setting did, indeed, indicate that the Old Copper Culture, and the North American Archaic in general, had had an egalitarian social setting. Beyond this, the copper implements were relatively rare, were not of highly esoteric forms, and were virtually always found in graves. All these things seemed to point to a symbolic function in a relatively simple society. That is, they were not common enough to have been general tools, but they were readily recognizable as symbolizing hunting, fishing, and woodworking activities. If they were symbols, the particular status an individual had achieved in the culture was not passed on to his descendants but ended at his death and was "taken with him" to the after life. From a strictly technological standpoint, copper apparently was not prized highly enough for the culture to have developed mechanisms for retaining the metal within the sphere of the living and using it to refashion new tools. The failure of copper tools to be perpetuated in the later Woodland cultures of the region could be taken to mean that these societies had moved away from the egalitarian norms of the Archaic, a supposition reinforced by the considerably more elaborate features of these cultures as revealed by archaeology. Whether or not Binford's explanation continues to stand as the correct one, he is quite right in saying that "only within a systemic frame of reference could such an inclusive explanation be offered" (Binford, 1962, p. 224).

The great potential of burial and mortuary data for social inferences about past societies is an obvious one, although it had long been neglected in American archaeology. William H. Sears was one of the first to elucidate it in his 1961 article "The Study of Social and Religious Systems in North American Archaeology." Subsequently, Binford (1971) has examined the subject at greater length and in worldwide perspective in "Mortuary Practices: Their Study and Potential."[33] This latter article is one of a symposium volume on the subject (Brown, 1971), which includes three Americanist papers on burials and their associations as these are seen at the respective sites of Etowah (Georgia), Moundville (Alabama), and Spiro (Oklahoma) — three of the greatest town-and-ceremonial center sites of the southeastern United States area. All the authors were able to draw a number of inferences from their data in the deductive manner that Binford employed in his Old Copper Culture study. From Etowah, Lewis H. Larson, Jr. (1971), suggested a convincing social stratification as reflected in differences between mound and village interments. The remains in the mound appeared to be those of an upper class whose paraphernalia, duplicated with individuals of different age groups, is best interpreted as badges or symbols of office or class. For Moundville, Christopher S. Peebles (1971, p. 68) had somewhat comparable findings and interpretations. "The model suggested from the archaeological remains is one of a completely ranked and functionally specialized politico-religious organization as part of this cultural system." Actually, Peebles dealt with data from a number of other sites and through statistical treatments of his data was able to indicate, within a high degree of probability, such entities as local communities, local centers, and a regional center, the last being the apparent capital of Moundville. Peebles' paper is as much methodological example as substantive report, and this is even more true of James Brown's (1971) on Spiro. Both archaeologists used ethnographical data from historical source material on Southeastern Indian tribes as comparative checks on their archaeological findings, but there was also a conscious effort on the part of both to operate wholly within the archaeological realm in their primary considerations of the data and all the relationships among these data. Brown did this in an especially formal manner. His objectives were to construct models for both archaeological (Spiro) and ethnological (Natchez, Choctaw) cultural systems and to compare these on a structural rather than a specific-culture-content basis. These attitudes toward the use of ethnographical data in analogy will be referred to again below, for they are very much a part of the New Archaeology.

Another use of burial data in social-dimensional interpretation was that of William L. Rathje (1970) as set out in his paper "Socio-Political Implications of Lowland Maya Burials: Methodology and Tentative Hypotheses." Rathje examined the changes through time (from Late Preclassic to Late Classic, *ca.* 300 B.C.–A.D. 900) of Maya burial customs (amounts and nature of grave goods, nature of tomb or grave) as these related to age and sex and settlement location (ceremonial center, village hamlet) to make a strong case for a gradually increasing rigidity in class stratification. In a later paper, he was able to incorporate his mortuary subsystem into an overall cultural-system model that offered an explanatory hypothesis for the collapse of Maya civilization (Rathje, 1973).

Social organization, as reflected in residence patterns, was another theme that attracted the attention of a number of younger scholars in the 1960s. A leader in this research was James J. F. Deetz. Deetz actually began his research along this line in the late 1950s, and these culminated in a doctoral dissertation submitted in 1960. His well-known work, a monograph, *The Dynamics of Stylistic Change in Arikara Ceramics,* was based on the earlier thesis and was published in 1965.[34] In it, Deetz analyzed a series of ceramic collections obtained from house ring excavations in sites documented as protohistoric-to-historic Plains Arikara. These analyses were made on a fine-grained attribute basis, and the numerous associations of these pottery decorative attributes, with each other and with house features, were provided through computer programming and analyses. It was Deetz's hypothesis that pottery decorative attributes would cluster in a distinctly nonrandom fashion in matrilocal households and that there would then be a trend from non-random to random as matrilocal residence broke down. Deetz's ceramic sequence through time bore out this kind of change, and the pottery change, in turn, appeared to correlate with a change from large to small house types. Supporting ethnohistorical information—that it was the Arikara women who made the pottery and that matrilocal residence quarters were larger than those of simple patrilocal families—provided the basic underlying assumptions for the study. Viewed as a whole, the two simultaneous aspects of change (in pottery and in house size) would seem to bear out Deetz's hypothesis; however, he adds, with caution, that, although this suggests a systematic relationship, it does not offer unequivocal proof (Deetz, 1968a).

These concerns with prehistoric residence patterns, social organization, and social interaction were also seen in the writings of William A. Longacre, James N. Hill, Robert Whallon, and Mark Leone. Longacre and Hill working in Southwestern Pueblo sites in eastern Arizona, defined room and other architectural functions through statistical and materials analyses of pottery, artifacts, and pollen residues. The search of rooms or features of archaeological sites for artifacts or other data that might help identify the former purposes of these architectural remains is not new to archaeology, but a systematic examination of all recovered data to this end marked a departure from previous practices.

Longacre (1968; see also 1964, 1966), working with pottery design attributes in the manner of Deetz, showed two major clusterings of these attributes in two distinct architectural assemblages of the same Puebloan site. That each of these assemblages had its own *kiva*, or ceremonial chamber, suggested their original corporate nature. On the assumption that women of the culture made the pottery (extrapolated from ethnographical analogies from the same general region), these data, as in Deetz's Arikara work, argued for matrilocal residence and probably matrilocal clans. Of wider interest in Longacre's observations of this site in its general context is the fact that it marked a time in Southwestern prehistory in which small, apparently single-kin unit villages were being replaced by larger communities, such as the one he investigated. This congregating of formerly dispersed populations into larger multiunit sites can, in turn, be correlated with the onset of climatic stringencies that rendered the total environment less hospitable.

After making a formal classification of the Pueblo site's features, Hill (1968) then phrased a series of expectations or propositions that should be borne out by the analyses, if his hypotheses about the functions of the various types of rooms and features were valid. Thus, "the large rooms should contain a wider variety of materials than are found in other room-types, since the largest number of different kinds of activities were presumably performed in them. Or, "the small rooms, in addition to containing only a small number and variety of artifacts and manufacturing debris, should contain reasonably large quantities of the remains of stored food crops—especially corn and squash. . . . This evidence should be in the form of corn cobs, seeds, or pollen."[35] Hill's hypotheses about the original usages of rooms and features were inspired by ethnographical analogies with historical and modern Hopi and Zuñi practices. These were largely confirmed by his tests, although a few were not, suggesting that there had been some unexpected changes in site and feature functions in the thousand-year-long prehistoric-to-historic cultural continuum in the Puebloan Southwest.

Whallon's (1968) studies of ceramic collections from prehistoric Iroquois sites in New York showed a high degree of attribute clusterings by site, which, on the assumption that women made the pottery, tended to bear out the Deetz thesis of matrilocal residence for such archaeological situations.[36] In the Iroquois case, such residence is, indeed, known from the slightly later historical horizon. On an intersite basis, Whallon also discovered that, through time, there was an increasing stylistic uniformity in pottery within each site. This, he postulated, corresponded with an increasing lack of control between sites (a trend verified from other lines of evidence), which resulted in a kind of ceramic decorative inbreeding.

An intersite study in the Southwest by Mark Leone (1968) operated with the hypothesis that increasing dependence on agriculture led to community economic autonomy and to "social distance" between communities. Dependence on agriculture was determined from the variability of tools used in a village, and social distance was measured by the evidence for greater or lesser endogamy within a village. This latter condition was appraised by differences in design and color attributes of pottery found in the village—a principle of the Deetz, Hill, Longacre, and Whallon studies. Both variables were found to co-vary positively, supporting Leone's thesis. This particular research, broader in scope than the previous ones, was very obviously aimed at deriving cultural law, which in this case might be stated as follows: unless other conditions (such as trade or major invasions) intervene, Neolithic-level economies result in community autonomy and in social distance.

Whereas mortuarial customs and settlement and artifactual patterning have afforded variables by which to infer social status, residence and kin relationships, culture and environment interrelationships obviously have been the crucial ones in economic and demographic inferences. We are, to some extent, drawing artificial lines here, for the purposes of presentation, since all these things are linked systemically. This linkage was indeed an important intellectual thrust of the New Archaeology.

However, some research can be identified as definitely ecological; on the Mesoamerican scene, both W. T. Sanders and R. S. MacNeish have been pioneers in this regard. Sanders' (1956) interests along this line began as early as the 1950s, and his Teotihuacan Valley (a branch of the Valley of Mexico) survey was carried out over many seasons, with interim reports (Sanders, 1962, 1965) and with the first of a series of final reports published in 1970 (Sanders and others, 1970). The survey carried out by Sanders and his colleagues was, for the time, extraordinarily thorough. All this is especially interesting, because Manuel Gamio (1922) had conducted another great survey almost fifty years before in the Teoti-huacan Valley. Both Gamio and Sanders were interested in the full range of human occupance of the valley; the two reports serve as a measure of the shifts in problem emphasis, theoretical concepts, and methods that took place in American archaeology and anthropology in the interven-ing decades. In brief, Sanders views culture as a complex of adaptive techniques to the problems of survival in a particular geographical region. Although such adaptations may be primarily in the field of technology and subsistence, these are systematically linked to all other aspects of culture. He looks at environment not only as a permissive-re-strictive factor in cultural development but, in the sense that it limits choice, as a directive factor. His view of the total ecological system is one that contains three semiautonomous systems — culture, biota (flora and fauna), and physical environment. Each of these "functions on the basis of discrete and separate processes"; yet, there is interaction among them, and this interaction "is one of the dominant stimuli that produces change in the cultural system" (Sanders, 1965, p. 193). Sanders' ambitious objec-tives were thus to explain the changes that took place in the Valley of Teotihuacan in ancient peoples' adaptations to their environment and all the systemic effects that this technology-subsistence-environmental interaction produced. Although Sanders' materialist-deterministic slant has been criticized by some Mesoamerican colleagues, there is general consensus that his interpretations, to date, go a long way toward eluci-dating cultural process in the Central Mexican Uplands from *ca.* 1000 B.C. to modern times.

MacNeish's attention has been directed to the threshold of village agriculture — the beginnings of settled life based on cultivation in Mesoamerica. He began this work in the dry caves of Tamaulipas in the late 1940s and 1950s, where he demonstrated the early stages of maize domestication in preceramic, essentially food-collecting, contexts (Mac-Neish, 1958). Later, he shifted his geographical focus farther south into the heart of Mesoamerica, exploring cave and open sites in the Tehuacan Valley in the Mexican state of Puebla. Here, he was able to push the first appearances of maize back to *ca.* 5000 B.C., at a time when that plant was

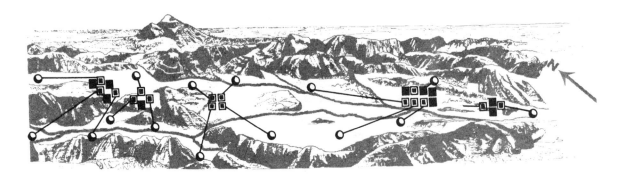

Diagram showing relationships between seasonal communities and subsistence scheduling in the Tehuacan Valley of Mexico. The Coxcatlan and early Abejas phases here represented are later preceramic complexes. Community pattern: semisedentary macrobands that had wet-season fall camps▣, or annual camps▤, but often separated into dry-season microband camps◖. (From MacNeish, 1964a, Science, 143, Fig. 7, copyright 1964 by the American Association for the Advancement of Science, Washington, D.C.)

either wild or in the very earliest stages of domestication. By bringing a variety of disciplines from the natural sciences to bear on the problem, and by an imaginative plan of attack, MacNeish provided a number of community-interaction models based on analogies to historic peoples in the Great Basin, each representative of a different time-level and each diagramming the subsistence-settlement-pattern relationships. Thus, "semisedentary macrobands" lived in wet season fall camps, exploiting certain types of wild plant foods and carrying on a limited amount of plant cultivation. Such macrobands then split up into "dry season microbands," which followed other food-getting pursuits for that period. At a certain point in time (*ca.* 1500 B.C.), this kind of semisedentary living was superseded by the establishment of the first permanent villages and little ceremonial centers (MacNeish, 1964a, 1967; Byers and MacNeish, 1967–76).

In a different environmental context — the Pacific Coast of Guatemala — Michael D. Coe and Kent Flannery (1964, 1967) made a similar ecosystem study involving the varied but integrated exploitation of a number of microenvironmental niches, as these bear on the problem of the first permanent villages in that region.

Turning his attention to the Mexican Highlands, and drawing upon MacNeish's work and his own in the Valley of Oaxaca, Flannery then went beyond subsistence-settlement diachronic models to offer an explanation of the detailed processes involved in these changes. This article, "Archaeological Systems Theory and Early Mesoamerica," published in 1968, is to our thinking, the best example of the archaeology of the Modern Period produced during its first decade. Drawing upon both archaeological and ethnological information, Flannery reconstructed the "procurement systems" (actually subsystems of an overall subsistence system) of the late (*ca.* 5000–2000 B.C.) preceramic and preagricultural phases of the Mexican Uplands. These procurement systems included the gathering of the maguey plant, cactus fruits, and wild grasses and

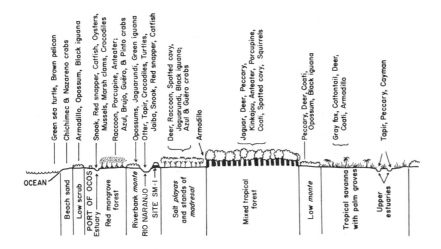

Diagrammatic representation of microenvironments and food resources available to the early inhabitants of the Pacific coast of Guatemala. (From Coe and Flannery, 1967)

the hunting of deer and other animals. Such procurement activities were regulated by nature's seasonality and by culture's scheduling. As Flannery (1968a, p. 79) says:

> Seasonality and scheduling . . . were part of a "deviation-counteracting" feedback system. They prevented intensification of any one procurement system to the point where the wild genus was threatened; at the same time, they maintained a sufficiently high level of procurement efficiency so that there was little pressure for change. . . .
>
> Under conditions of fully achieved and permanently maintained equilibrium, prehistoric cultures might never have changed. That they did change was due at least in part to the existence of positive feedback or "deviation-amplifying processes. . . ."
>
> These Maruyama (1963, p. 164) describes as "all processes of mutual causal relationships that amplify an insignificant or accidental initial kick, build up deviation and diverge from the initial condition. . . ."
>
> Such "insignificant or accidental initial kicks" were a series of genetic changes which took place in one or two species of Mesoamerican plants which were of use to man. The exploitation of these plants had been a relatively minor procurement system compared with that of maguey, cactus fruits, deer, or tree legumes, but positive feedback following these initial genetic changes caused one minor system to grow out of all proportion to the others, and eventually to change the whole ecosystem of the Southern Mexican Highlands.

This, in a nutshell, is one of the most stimulating hypotheses about the immediate causes of the agricultural revolution in the Mexican Highlands of the fifth to third millennium B.C. that has been offered. At the time of its publication, more than any other single short paper, it pointed to the great potential of the New Archaeology to provide explanations of cultural developments.

Other ecosystem researches that deserve mention were those of Stuart Struever (1968a), working with Woodland cultures in the Illinois Valley; of Ezra Zubrow, in his consideration of "Carrying Capacity and Dynamic Equilibrium in the Prehistoric Southwest" (1971); and an examination by Binford (1968c) of "Post-Pleistocene Adaptations" on a worldwide basis, with the development of a series of hypotheses about the stage-threshold crossings from Paleolithic-to-Mesolithic and from the latter to village agriculture.

The ecosystem model and ecological explanations were applied by some American archaeologists to that other great transformation of human history, the shift from simpler agricultural societies to civilizations. With such a model, they saw a sequence of events in which a technological improvement in dealing with the environment—specifically, canal irrigation—so increased food production that population boomed. This, in turn, created other greater economic capacities and needs, and all these demographic pressures and other complexities eventually gave rise to the state and civilization.[37] Others, while admitting the importance of all this, were not convinced that the triggering mechanism necessarily always lies in an ecological relationship and preferred to see a greater role assigned to ideology.[38] Still others offered explanations that involved a complex systemic interplay of trade, ideology, and social prestige as offering the most convincing model of the rise of civilization and the truly complex society or state.[39] In all of this, there was the question of definitions as well as the arguments about process. What is the meaning of the elusive term *civilization?* Although some authorities were willing to apply the name to such early elaborate ceremonial-center-oriented cultures as Olmec or Chavin, others preferred to associate the term and concept with the rise of formal urbanism as at Teotihuacan. The longterm program of René F. Millon and associates (1967, 1970) in the mapping and close-up functional study of the great Teotihuacan site was of real importance in turning archaeologists' attention to these problems and providing basic data for their solution.

One major branch of American archaeological research deserves separate mention here in view of its sudden upsurge in the 1960s. This is called *historical archaeology* or *historic-sites archaeology.* These terms refer to the subject matter of Post-Columbian times, involving either native peoples, Europeans, or both. As in Europe, the historical-archaeological field was cultivated for a long time; but, in the Americas and especially

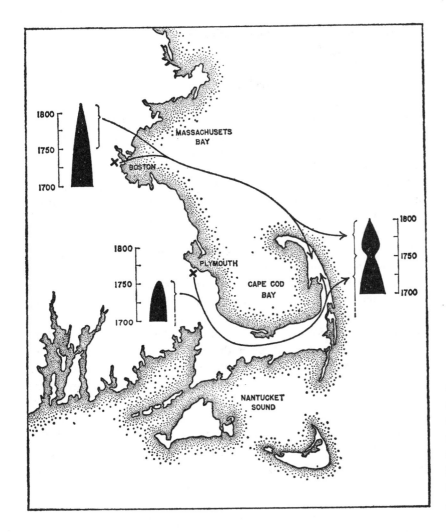

Changes in tombstone style in eastern Massachusetts during the eighteenth century. James Deetz's use of historical archaeology to test archaeological assumptions and hypotheses has been one of the important advances of the Modern Period. (From Deetz, 1968b)

in the United States, it has only recently come to claim its proper share of attention in the Modern Period.[40] Most American historic-sites archaeologists were primarily interested in historical particulars, but the influences of the New Archaeology have also made themselves felt. For example, the work of Deetz and Dethlefsen (1965, 1971; see also Deetz, 1966) on New England grave stones gave archaeologists an excellent methodological check on seriational procedures. In fact, according to Deetz (1968b), one of the great values of historical archaeology lies in just this ability to examine archaeological methods and theories in contexts of verifiable historical control and, in so doing, to refine concepts and procedures and to understand better the processes of cultural change (see Schuyler, 1970).

CONSOLIDATING
AND BROADENING
THE NEW
ARCHAEOLOGICAL
AGENDA

Given the rhetorical vehemence with which the New Archaeology was introduced in the 1960s and early 1970s, there should be no surprise that the reaction by some to the processual agenda was equally strong. We will examine this counterattack later in this chapter. What is perhaps more surprising is the number of archaeologists who just ducked the crossfire and continued their research with little explicit recognition of the many intellectual currents swirling around them. But, as we shall see below, even those scholars who tried to carry on with business as usual were influenced by the exhortations of the New Archaeologists.

In the wake of the changes of the 1960s, it was commonplace for many American archaeologists to remark that the discipline had undergone a revolution and that a new theoretical structure or paradigm (as defined by Kuhn 1962) had replaced the traditional one. But, despite the pervasiveness of this viewpoint, it seems to us that at best the revolution is still in its initial phase. Only time will tell if it ever will be successful. It is too early to make predictions—or to celebrate the demise of processual archaeology, as some critics would have the field believe. Clearly, the clock cannot be turned back to 1960, as some polemicists seemingly would like to see (for example, see Courbin, 1989). The writings of the 1960s persuasively showed the traditional structure to be too narrow, too untheoretical in its smug pragmatism. Moreover, the new outlook of the Modern Period has opened new possibilities to archaeology. There was—and still is—great promise and some demonstrable results. American archaeology was able to tell a better story than it had done previously—better in a behavioral sense and in the sense of providing a richer context of past life. Beyond this, optimistically, was the still greater promise of higher-order explanations of cultural change. But, by the mid-1970s, a number of reflections and questions about this progress began to surface.[41]

The New Archaeologists proved not to be complacent after their polemical successes, so that even in the New Archaeology camp, ideas did not remain static, thus allowing the New or Processual Archaeology to show considerable resiliency in the past two decades in the face of numerous attacks (see R. Watson, 1991). Various weaknesses and inadequacies of the initial program were soon recognized by its practitioners. It was further realized that these problems were exacerbated by the failure of the New Archaeology to provide the breakthroughs in scientific understanding of broad cultural processes that some may have been led to believe would happen almost immediately. During this time, as the New Archaeology began to cope with these perceived problems, several important new trends emerged. Let us turn to a brief examination of these new directions. One of the initial problem areas facing archaeologists who wished to translate the new perspectives into solid archaeological achievements involved the boundaries of the field. How was the field to be defined, and on what kinds of information and questions could it most profitably focus its attention?

Several archaeologists at the University of Arizona—William Rathje, J. Jefferson Reid, and Michael Schiffer—have argued for a totally non-traditional view of archaeology (Reid, Schiffer, and Rathje, 1975). As Schiffer (1976, p. 4) states: "The subject matter of archaeology is the relationships between human behavior and material culture *in all times and places* [italics ours]." In effect, these scholars would define archaeology as the science of material culture. An oft-cited, innovative example of this broad definition is the ongoing Tucson Garbage Project, which was conceived in the early 1970s by Rathje and his associates and already has produced some fascinating results (Rathje, 1974, 1978; Rathje and Harrison, 1978; Rathje and McCarthy, 1977). But is their research archaeology? Certainly, aspects of the Garbage Project are clearly archaeological in nature. As Rathje and McCarthy (1977, p. 285) note: "Hopefully Garbage Project studies will make a contribution toward supplanting the role of general sociocultural glosses within archaeological interpretation with quantitative models of adaptive strategies, pieced together from the garbage of both past and present." However, their definition of the project indicates other aspects of their work. They view the Garbage Project "as a new form of social science research in contemporary societies *and* [italics ours] as a method of refining traditional archae-

Laboratory sorting in modern archaeology. A scene of the work of W. L. Rathje's Garbage Project in Tucson, Arizona. Rathje is standing at right. (From W. L. Rathje, The Garbage Project, University of Arizona, Tucson)

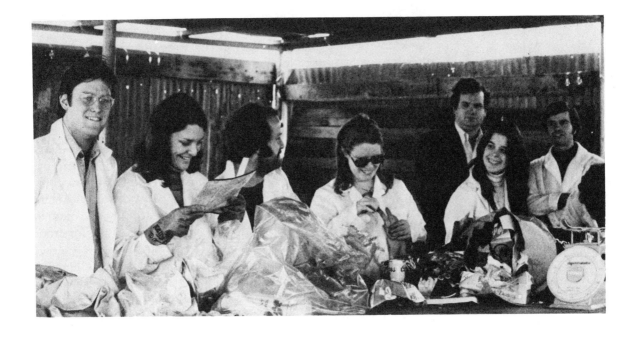

ological interpretation" (1977, p. 285). Is "the new form of social science" to be considered part of archaeology or a separate pursuit? Some archaeologists have expressed fears about such expansion of the horizons of contemporary archaeology (see Trigger, 1978, p. 14) and how these new concerns may dissipate the strength of archaeology in the future. It is not clear to us that it is in the best interests of archaeology in the long run to become the "science of material culture." Currently, however, we believe that many American archaeologists would feel better and safer with Charles Redman's (1973, p. 20) definition: "today's archaeologist is a social scientist who studies human behavior and social organization by analyzing artifacts of past human activities." Even though the idea of science of material culture pushes archaeology into new areas of research, ultimately it seems to downplay or eliminate some of archaeology's nonmaterial concerns. Redman's definition, however, is not as limiting as the "material culture" definition, and it addresses archaeology's most traditional concerns: human beings and their cultural behavior in the past.

Another suggestion has been made by Gumerman and Phillips (1978), who believe that, with all of archaeology's borrowing from a variety of disciplines, it would be better to view it as an autonomous "technique" rather than a traditional subdiscipline of anthropology. Again, although Gumerman and Phillips make several good points about the limiting nature of archaeology's anthropological connections, we feel that the understanding of cultural process is a uniquely anthropological concern and that American archaeology would do best, at present, to strengthen rather than weaken its anthropological ties. As Frank Hole (1978, p. 152) has so well put it: "It seems to me that whatever directions we may take in method, theory, technique, era or area, we must keep in mind the central idea that we are dealing with and trying to understand the human experience."

As interesting as this definitional question is, to our mind, the most significant intellectual development of the second phase of the New Archaeology is related to the problems of making the initial processual agenda operational. If archaeologists were to gain better understandings of culture change, they had to deal with their unique resource, the archaeological record, more effectively than had previous scholars. Pragmatically, the question of how archaeologists could overcome the limitations of the archaeological record came readily to the forefront. Instead of passively accepting the premise that the partially preserved record placed researchers in a tight straightjacket as to the kinds of cultural questions they could feasibly investigate, archaeologists began to explore ways of overcoming such obstacles. Michael B. Schiffer (1976, p. 12), for example, while asserting that "archaeological remains are a distorted reflection of a past behavioral system," argued that this situation need not lead to a dead end, because, as he went on to say, "the cultural and non-cultural processes responsible for these distortions are regular; there are systematic (but seldom direct) relationships between archaeological remains and past cultural systems."

In a series of influential publications, Schiffer has emphasized two types of formation processes of the archaeological record.[42] These are natural formation processes (*n-transforms*) and cultural formation processes (*c-transforms*). An example of the former would be that, all things being equal, pollen is preserved and bone is destroyed in acidic soil; an example of the latter would be that the "more butchering of an animal at a kill site, [the] fewer bones [that] will be carried back and discarded at the base camp or village" (Schiffer, 1976, p. 15 and p. 21). Although Schiffer argues that such transforms should be termed "laws," it perhaps would be preferable to call them "interpretations" or "generalizations," since they are partial explanations at best. A descriptive correlation between, say, artifact size and weight and place of discard does not completely explain the discard activity. Nevertheless, whatever one wishes to label transforms, it is obvious that they are an essential foundation for attempts to build a theoretical understructure of the processes of change in past cultures.

Paying attention to formation processes significantly changes archaeologists' approaches to their field data. It gives them a different perspective when they attempt to assign meaning to the archaeological record. As Lewis Binford (1976b, pp. 295–296) has stated:

> The self-deception that one can (1) make contemporary observations, (2) use contemporary ideas of relevance to classify these observations, (3) accurately project these contemporary facts into the past through stratigraphic or carbon 14 procedures, (4) and obtain "culture history" is a fallacy. It results (in) a projection of the present into the past. Only when historical meaning is given to our contemporary observations does one offer a tentative "culture history." Such ideas must be evaluated and it is in this role that scientific procedures are crucial. Historical interpretations are not more securely made than any other type of interpretation. This "self-deception" is a general "fossil director" for the products of traditional archaeologists.

It is precisely in attempts to give meaning to the archaeological record that what we consider *the* most critical problem of the Modern Period, from both practical and philosophical points of view, lies. Disagreements about the nature of the inferences made—and the inferential procedures used—in interpreting the archaeological record that researchers study today are at the heart of much of the argumentation that has characterized methodological and theoretical discussions in the past three decades. We have referred to American archaeology's close linkage with ethnology and ethnography throughout its history. The interrelationships of the data of prehistory and ethnohistory were the crux of Cyrus Thomas' attack on the Moundbuilder versus Native American problem. The direct-historical approach pointed the way to specific ethnic identifications of archaeological complexes in the Classificatory-Historical Period, and Strong, Steward, and others called for more systematic and intensive uses of ethnographic analogy in the functional and contextual interpretations of archaeological data. As American archaeology moved into the Modern Period, ethnographic analogy retained a vital role. We have seen, for example, its uses in the ceramic-social-organizational studies of Deetz, Longacre, and others. In general, a positive attitude toward ethnographic analogy is still held by many or most American archaeologists, who see in such specific historical analogies the only way of reconstructing the particularistic qualities of past cultures. At the same time, ethnographic analogies — or certain uses and limitations of them — have come under attack during the Modern Period. To put this debate in proper perspective, it is necessary to first say something about analogy in archaeology in general.

To begin, analogy in archaeology is the mode of inference by which the residues of human behavior are translated into the original terms of that behavior (insofar as possible). It is the first step in archaeology. Hypotheses about the past cannot be framed without it, nor can inductive or deductive reasoning be brought into play to test these hypotheses until the analogies have been made. There are two kinds of analogy available to the archaeologist. One of these is the kind to which we have just referred — specific historical analogy, or what is more commonly called *ethnographic analogy*. It operates within a specific historical context — for example, the continuum of the Southwestern Puebloan cultural tradition in North America from prehistoric to historical times or the Teotihuacan-Toltec-historical Aztec continuum of central Mexico. Such specific historical or ethnographic analogy stands in contrast to the other kind of analogy: general comparative analogy. General comparative analogy is also ethnographic, in the sense that its points of reference are located in observed human behavior, but its interpretations of the past are projected through broadly comparative and essentially universalistic observations and generalizations about human cultural behavior rather than being derived from the narrow confines of a specific historical context.[43]

In an article entitled "Major Aspects of the Interrelationship of Archaeology and Ethnology," K. C. Chang (1967b) has discussed these two kinds of analogy in some detail and has emphasized the vital importance of ethnographic analogy to the archaeologist. In a commentary on Chang's article, Binford (1967a, 1968b) has taken a somewhat different view.[44] He argues that to rely wholly or even primarily on such specific historical analogies is to limit archaeologists seriously in their abilities to see the past in processual terms—as the raw material for the eventual formulation of cultural laws. Binford is not opposed to all uses of ethnographic or specific historical analogy. His position is, rather, that it is useful as an adjunct in archaeological interpretation and as a pool of information to be drawn upon in framing hypotheses about particular past cultures; it cannot, however, be considered an essential key to explanation of process. The latter, he says, must be approached by archaeologists on their own terms, meaning through the uses of general comparative analogy.

In contrast to Binford's position, Keith M. Anderson (1969, p. 138) has written, "Careful analysis and comparison of archaeological remains, the use of vigorous analytical techniques, and statistical manipulation may lead to precise definition of significant and comparable technological elements. However, these techniques do not, by themselves, interpret prehistory. Such interpretation depends upon ethnographic analogy." And, very directly addressing the New Archaeology, he also states: "Knowledge of systemic relations between components of technology and the rest of culture is necessary to make inferences concerning the use of particular artifacts. However, there are limitations to the exactness of a systemic model."

As we see it, much of this disagreement over the value of ethnographic or specific historical analogy derives from a difference in emphasis on the objectives of archaeology. If one favors a reconstruction of a specific past, with interpretations of the functions of artifacts found in a Southwestern Pueblo ruin or the meaning of gods of the Teotihuacan murals, then Anderson is correct. Such interpretations must derive from ethnohistory or ethnographic analogies. But, if instead one eschews the reconstruction of the past as the prime goal of archaeology, as Binford does, then specific historical analogy is much less important and indeed can be quite limiting. However, we cannot accuse either Chang or Anderson of a disinterest in process.[45] Nor would we be satisfied with an archaeology that was entirely particularistic. But we would not completely go along with Binford's (1967a, 1968a) assertion that archaeologists today are self-sufficient within their discipline to formulate verifiable hypotheses to explain archaeological observations. At least, we question whether these hypotheses would necessarily be very pertinent or meaningful. Is the perspective of technical-ecological interaction sufficient to explain all that it is important to know about past cultures? We would say not. In dealing with specific historical applications,

Anderson (1969, p. 38) puts it well: "Logical analysis of form depends as much on perception of the object, which is conditioned by cultural background, as by any universal principles."

These attempts to arrive at a greater understanding of past behavior through analogy lead us to consider still other archaeological uses. One important example pertains to comparative rather than specific historical analogy, and a prime example is Flannery's (1968b) employment of a Burmese Shan-Kachin model of trade exchange and social interaction to explain what transpired between the Pre-Columbian Olmec and ancient Oaxacans of Mesoamerica. Here, the type of analogy is what Willey (1977) has dubbed "specific comparative." The two cultural situations, the ethnographically known Burmese one and the archaeological one from Mesoamerica, were in no known way historically related to one another. The model was applied, because the cultural and sociopolitical types and certain elements of the geographical and resource situation seemed similar—so much so, that a similarity in behavior and culture process was predicated. The procedure, of course, has its limitations, but it has the advantage of citing observable cultural and social interaction—specific as to time and place—rather than creating a model based on general comparative knowledge. In other words, specific comparative analogy relates a past culture to an integrated cultural system and thus its use can be expected to bring archaeologists to look more closely at the complex interrelationships between individuals and their culture than is the case with a "bits-and-pieces" approach.

Considerations of analogies took a new direction in the 1970s. While the New Archaeologists had forcefully argued against the traditional mode of linking the archaeological record and past behavior by stipulation or assumption, they had not been correspondingly clear about how meaning should be rigorously given to the record. Binford (1983b, pp. 9–17) has written that as a result of his exchange with the authors of this volume (Sabloff and Willey, 1967; Binford, 1968d) on the question of the "collapse" of classic Maya civilizations, he came to realize that his original views of explanation had been too narrow. While criticizing us for interpreting "the facts of the archaeological record by intuition, analogy, convention, speculation," Binford (1983b, p. 10) did not yet have a more productive procedure to replace traditional methods and fell prey on occasion to the same practices (his speculations on how to verify that an invasion had taken place, for example) he was objecting to in our article.

In arguing against our position which he characterized as a procedure by which "the past was to be described by intuitive, traditional, and humanistic means, and then explained in processual terms," Binford subsequently came to understand that "The very act of inferring the past

Lewis R. Binford. (From Lawrence
Straus)

from archaeological observations was a central problem in processual
archaeology" (1983b, p. 10). Furthermore, Binford realized that analogical procedures that derived interpretation of the record in part from the
record itself and then were tested against the record were inherently
circular.[46] Thus, Binford and his colleagues began to further develop

ideas about how best to give meaning to the archaeological record with particular emphasis on ethnoarchaeological or actualistic studies as the key procedural elements. Ironically, as we discuss below, Binford's analogical arguments in turn have been criticized by the Postprocessualists as being circular and subjective.

Binford has termed the search for meaning in the archaeological record the building of *middle-range* or *bridging theory*.[47] Archaeologists, he argues, must try to understand what conditions of past systems could have produced the patterns uncovered in archaeological field research. In other words, links must be forged between the past dynamics of these systems and the currently visible static record. Such bridges can be built, Binford maintains, by studying the links between statics and dynamics in ethnographic ("actualistic") or historic situations and then drawing analogies to the links between the statics of the archaeological record and the dynamics of the prehistoric past. Thus, if material "signatures" of cultural activities can be delineated in ethnographic situations, for example, then it may be possible to find similar signatures in the archaeological record and, by analogy, link them with ancient activities.[48] Binford considers the examination of the links between statics and dynamics *middle-range*, because "we seek to make statements about the past in order to evaluate ideas we may hold about the conditions that brought about change and modification in the organization of dynamics occurring in past living systems" (1977, p. 7). In other words, not only must archaeologists learn *how* the archaeological record was formed, but they must try to explain *why* a dynamic system of the past produced the static archaeological record of today (the middle-range theoretical exercise in the assignment of meaning).[49] It should be emphasized that "middle-range" refers to the bridging aspect of theory-building, which serves to link the statics of the archaeological record to general propositions about the cultures that produced it, and *not* to the nature of such theories. Middle-range theories can vary from very specific, particularistic statements to quite broad ones with general significance, depending on the kinds of building blocks the archaeologist needs to formulate and test general archaeological hypotheses.

The first attempts at middle-range theory began to be published in the late 1970s. For the most part, they were the work of Binford and his students and associates. The prime example concerns the research carried out among the modern-day Nunumuit of Alaska. (Binford, 1976a, 1978a, 1978b; Binford and Bertram, 1977; Binford and Chasko, 1976). This ethnographical work was undertaken not to provide simple analogies to past activities of hunters and gatherers but to help begin the construction of middle-range theory. One aspect of this research focuses on a currently used Nunumuit hunting stand known as the Mask site (Bin-

The Mask site, a Nunamiut hunting stand and its environmental setting. (From L. R. Binford)

A closeup view of the Mask site hunting stand. (From L. R. Binford)

ford, 1978a). In his study of the Mask site, Binford suggests that, contrary to the view that where there are generalized work spaces in which a number of activities take place, organizational data will be obscured for the archaeologist, there are, instead, several interacting variables that do produce recognizable distribution data. Although he is not yet able to construct a middle-range theory to explain the dynamics of hunter-gatherer organization that lead to the spatial patterning of camp activities seen in the archaeological record, he does offer ideas as to how such a theory might be created. Among these are the suggestions that the degree to which activities are carried out in different spots is at least partially conditioned by the way their execution could interfere with other activities and that scheduling concerns in executional and bulk properties of manufactured items and incidental debris from their production "would condition the degrees of functional specificity among activity areas on a site" (Binford, 1978a, p. 360).

In addition, a number of articles in the volume *For Theory Building in Archaeology* (Binford, 1977) illustrate some of the potentially productive pathways for the development of middle-range theory. An example is Rosalind Hunter-Anderson's study of house form and its causes. Arguing that mobility is not the important determining factor, she (Hunter-Anderson, 1977, pp. 304–305) cites three variables as critical: (1) "the number of living or role aspects a structure is designed to harbor"; (2) "heterogeneity of the activities performed by the units sharing the house"; and (3) "the volume of associated materials and facilities." Even

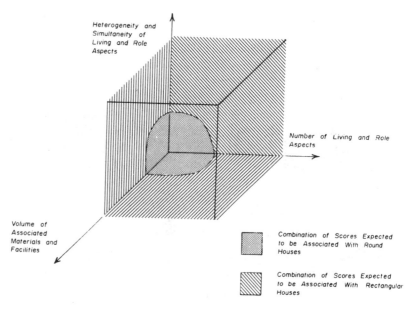

Heterogeneity and Simultaneity of Living and Role Aspects

Number of Living and Role Aspects

Volume of Associated Materials and Facilities

Combination of Scores Expected to be Associated With Round Houses

Combination of Scores Expected to be Associated With Rectangular Houses

Three-dimensional model of the effect of number of living and role aspects, heterogeneity and simultaneity of living and role aspects, and the volume of associated materials and facilities on house form. Higher values make rectangular house form more likely. An illustration of an effort at middle-range theory building. (From Hunter-Anderson, 1977, copyright by Academic Press, New York)

though Hunter-Anderson is unable to explain why certain values of a set of particular variables are correlated with a particular shape, she has paved the way for future theory-building that will specify conditions as to living units per house, sequentially performed activities therein, and volumes of facilities.

These early examples of attempts to construct middle-level theory generally were drawn from research on relatively simple societies. Variables relating to function and use appear to be fewer than would be the case in, say, an urban-type situation; or, at least, they appear more directly and easily traceable in the archaeological record. Theory-building deriving from studies of more complex ancient societies has more often been of the higher-range or general sort. Are the two unrelated, essentially separate operations? Should archaeologists concentrate on one rather than the other? And, considering the difficulties experienced by these promulgating explanatory theories about such things as the rise and fall of civilizations, should archaeologists, temporarily at least, ignore general theory-building in favor of such things as formation processes and middle-range theory? Binford firmly, and to our mind correctly, argues that the concerns over middle-range and upper-level or general theory should not be divorced. He rhetorically queries (1977, p. 7):

> Why do I suggest that the development of general and middle-range theory must proceed hand in hand? Simply because, in the absence of criteria of relevance, we may waste much time in developing middle-range theory concerning the dynamic significance of certain static facts that prove to be irrelevant to the evaluation of our ideas about the general determinant processes that promote change and diversification in living systems. The field must advance as a whole.[50]

By the 1970s, the term *cultural evolution* had lost much of its Whitean meaning to most archaeologists and became a more generalized synonym for *cultural process* or *culture change*. Thus, Binford (1972, p. 106) states, "We may generalize that we can identify the operation of evolution at the living systems level when we can demonstrate structural change."

In commenting on White's and Steward's continuing influence on evolutionary theory, it is probably fair to say that their strong emphasis on technological determinism has been transcended by many writers (Service, 1975; Flannery, 1972a, among others); however, many New Archaeologists, including Binford (1972, pp. 108–109) would see environment, or an environmental-technological interrelationship (ecological adaptation), as the crucial factor in evolutionary change. But, as we shall see, others have viewed this position as too limiting in its explanatory potential.

Current research in several areas that owes much to earlier concerns of White and Steward include historical archaeology,[51] the rise of agriculture, and the growth of the state. One of the most interesting developments in archaeological thinking about the growth of complex societies has been the increasing sophistication in the search for possible processual regularities. Examples of this research have been given in our previous discussions on the rise of the Pre-Columbian city. Flannery's review article "The Cultural Evolution of Civilizations" (1972a), to which we have referred, was an attempt to lead the way in applying a systems framework to more traditional explanations for the rise of the state. He terms such traditional single-cause explanations *socio-environmental stresses*. He believes that there are universal processes and mechanisms that are selected in differing cultural-historical situations by particular socioenvironmental stresses. From Flannery's perspective, to comprehend the evolution of complex societies, archaeologists must study how certain processes, mechanisms, and socio-environmental stresses are systematically articulated. He singles out the understanding of the processing of information and information flow—that is, the mechanics of processing, the people involved, and the kinds of information that are transferred—as crucial in studying how past cultural systems achieved statehood (Flannery, 1972b). Clearly, Flannery believes that future systemic explanations of the evolution of the state will be much more complex than some of the important texts on cultural evolution by Service (1962), Fried (1967), or Sanders and Price (1968) would indicate.[52]

As we have also seen above, the questions of the rise of food production and its implications for the transition from a nomadic hunting and gathering way of life to sedentary agriculture have been of keen interest for New World archaeologists. Recent research in Mesoamerica and Peru have enabled them to approach these questions with greater precision. Arguments about underlying causes for the change from hunting-collecting to farming still continue. The factor of population growth and pressure as a cause has received special attention, but the hypothesis remains unproven and, indeed, as we have seen, difficult to test. After careful review of the available archaeological and botanical data from many parts of the world, Flannery (1973) reached the cautious conclusion that gaining an understanding of the processes that lead to the rise of agriculture will be a much more difficult task than many archaeologists seem to believe and that the pathways that led to domestication in various Old and New World regions may have differed. After discussing the rise of domestic seed crops, he somewhat pessimistically concludes that (1973, pp. 307–308) "since early farming represents a decision to work harder and to eat more "third choice' food, I suspect that people did it because they felt they *had* to, not because they *wanted* to. Why they felt they had to we may never know, in spite of the fact that their decision reshaped all the rest of human history." Whether Flannery's pessimism will be proved remains to be seen.[53] Nevertheless, the whole problem of agricultural beginnings will probably never suffer from lack of interest and will continue as a focus for the testing and formation of general theory.

Fred Plog's *The Study of Prehistoric Change* (1974) is another example of concerns with general theory in the 1970s. As Plog (1974, p. ix) notes: "I am convinced that what archaeologists have to offer as social scientists is an understanding of long-term change." In attempting to explain the Basketmaker-to-Pueblo transition in the American Southwest, Plog formulated a general growth model from which he hoped to explain

The Hay Hollow Valley in Arizona, where Fred Plog tested his general growth model on the Basketmaker-Pueblo transition. (From L. R. Binford)

specific instances of change, such as the Basketmaker-to-Pueblo transition. Although his analysis is far more sophisticated than previous studies, Plog still is unable to test conclusively either a general or a specific explanation, as he readily admits.

However, in the past decade, Processual Archaeologists have continued to develop their interest in cultural evolution, while becoming more specific in their model building and hypothesis testing.[54] As Allen W. Johnson and Timothy K. Earle, in a recent book on *The Evolution of Human Societies*, state (1987, p. vii): "Theories of sociocultural evolution are not popular at the moment in anthropology. But we feel that this turning away from evolutionism, after a period of creativity a generation ago, is not warranted by the evidence."

Some of the most interesting research in this regard is on the rise of complex societies. While scholars working on this question still use terms such as "chiefdom," they have moved beyond standard evolutionary typology to concentrate on the local processes that led to complexity (see Earle, 1987; Drennan and Uribe, eds., 1987; Earle, ed., 1991). They frequently use regional scales in their studies as can be seen, for example, in the productive research in the highlands of Colombia, the Valley of Oaxaca, and the Basin of Mexico.[55]

A part of the Valle de la Plata, Colombia survey zone showing house terraces on the ridge to the left. (From Robert D. Drennan)

Robert Dunnell has promulgated a different view of the role of evolutionary theory, a view that has yet to gain wide acceptance. In a series of publications, Dunnell (1980, 1982, 1988, 1989a) has forcefully argued that archaeology should utilize modern Darwinian evolutionary theory directly without treating culture as a separate conceptual entity and should examine how artifacts in the broadest sense are affected by selection (also see Rindos, 1984, 1989; Leonard and Jones, 1987).

It is important to note that most of the processual research of the Modern Period has adopted materialist approaches that owe much to earlier Marxist thinking,[56] especially in the emphases on the political economy, socioeconomic exploitation, and class conflicts. However, the Marxist bases of these approaches are usually not acknowledged and dialectical modes of thought are rarely employed (but see Patterson and Gailey, eds., 1987, especially the article by Carole Crumley, 1987; also see Saitta, 1989). Furthermore, the use of Marxist insights is almost never linked to the modern political side of Marxism (see Patterson 1989). More explicit use of Marxist concepts can be seen in the neo-Marxist studies that emphasize the ideological aspects of culture more than materialist ones. These latter approaches fall into Postprocessual modes of thought, which on one hand call for a relativist position, while still trying to privilege a Marxist one. Such approaches will be treated below in our consideration of Postprocessualism.

In sum, New or Processual Archaeology, in its second phase, remains a potent and viable intellectual force in the Americas. Although relatively more concerned with *how do we know* questions than before, it has not lost sight of *why* questions. Important advances have been made on the latter front, although a unifying theoretical structure still eludes the field. As a result of the intellectual stimulation of the rhetoric of the 1960s, important progress in archaeological knowledge of the American past has been made in recent decades, and clearer insights into factors leading to complex human developments have been achieved. Faced with a number of challenges in the 1970s and 1980s, the New Archaeology has continued to be viable and dynamic.

In the three preceding sections we have set forth the ideas and the procedures of the New Archaeology and have offered examples of how they have directly influenced Americanist research. But it is also our strong belief that over and beyond this direct influence, the philosophy of the New Archaeology has caused a profound attitudinal change in the discipline of American archaeology. This change is reflected in a greater concern with problem definition in research planning and in the linking

MAINSTREAM
ACCOMMODATIONS
TO THE NEW
ARCHAEOLOGY

of the goals of the understanding of cultural process with those of understanding cultural history. Most American archaeologists see no conflict in this, and their practices of the past thirty years reveal such partial, covert, or even subconscious accommodations to the tenets of the New Archaeology. In this way, the cultural focus of the New Archaeological revolt of the 1960s soon entered and came to compose the mainstream of American archaeology by the end of the 1970s.

During this time we have seen a tremendous amount of archaeological research over all parts of the Americas. Indeed, the volume of work over this period is probably greater than all of that from previous times. Thus, the examples described in this section are necessarily selective, but we believe they are representative in showing a continuity of "older" (culture-historical) research interests combined with "newer" (processual) concerns that clearly emerged in the 1970s. We have tried to span widely over subject matter, geographical areas, and chronological periods.

Let us begin with the earliest chronological bracket, the Pleistocene presence of humans in the New World. Although it is still a matter for debate (Haynes, 1967; Irwin-Williams, ed., 1968b; MacNeish, 1971; Bryan, 1973, 1978; Dincauze, 1984; Adovasio et al., 1983; Guidon, 1986; Dillehay, 1989; Meltzer, 1989; Dillehey and Meltzer, eds., 1991, among many others), immigrants from northeast Asia may have entered the New World about 15,000 to 20,000 years ago or perhaps even earlier; but it was not until some time later — ca. 10,000 to 8,000 B.C. — that the sites and artifacts of the early American inhabitants began to take on the more readily recognizable patterns and forms which archaeologists have traditionally labeled as the *Paleo-Indian stage*.[57] Some of the best examples of behavioral and functional reconstructions of Paleo-Indian society have been provided through the analyses of animal kill sites on the North American Great Plains. In the Olsen-Chubbuck Site (Wheat, 1967) in eastern Colorado, some 200 bison skeletons were found, along with diagnostic late Paleo-Indian projectile points and knives, in the confines of a now-filled narrow arroyo. The animals had been driven into the arroyo, where they had toppled over and trampled on each other. Those in the eastern, and deeper, end of the ravine had been speared by the hunters and prevented from escaping. Other hunters had presumably driven the animals into the natural ditch-trap. Since most of the bison skeletons were found facing south, the archaeologists reasoned that they had been pursued from the north; this deduction allowed the further fine-point reconstruction that the wind on the day of the hunt had been from the south, giving the animals no scent of their impending destroyers. Another detail, from the osteological study of the animals, was that the age of the bison calves was but a few days, thus placing the date of

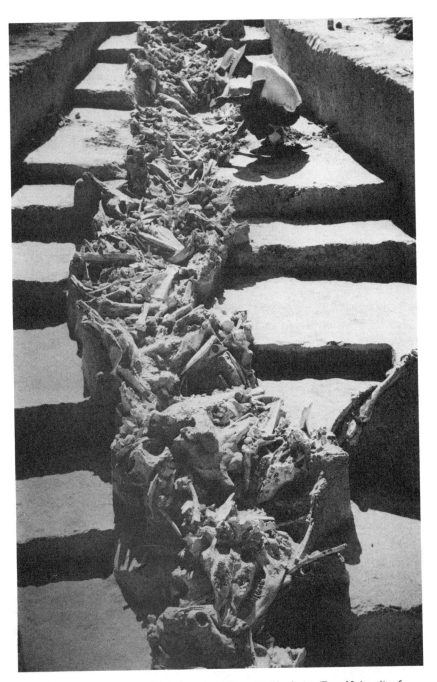

Bison bone remains as excavated in ravine trap at Olsen-Chubbuck site. (From University of Colorado Museum, Joe Ben Wheat photo)

the kill in late May or early June. Some of the Olsen-Chubbuck animals had been taken out of the arroyo and completely and systematically butchered; others, left in the arroyo, had been only partially cut up. Flint knives for butchering were present at the site, as were numerous scrapers, the latter allowing the inference that hide preparation had been carried out at the site. From the ethnographical knowledge that a Plains Native American could complete the butchering of a bison in an hour, and from estimates of the amount of meat taken from the kill, the excavator, J. B. Wheat, reasoned that 100 people might have done the job in half a day. A minimum of 150 persons could have made use of the meat by eating it fresh for a month and drying the remainder.

This reconstruction of an ancient activity carried within it clues for further questions. For instance, the diversity in the style of the projectile points found in this particular kill brings up matters of social or socioeconomic organization. Does such diversity indicate the coalescence of a special task force, made up of representatives from several Paleo-Indian groups?[58]

In another Paleo-Indian study, E. N. Wilmsen (1970) attempted a broader reconstruction of culture and society than that seen in the behavioral reconstruction of a single kill site activity locus. Wilmsen took as his sample a series of artifact collections from eight North American Paleo-Indian sites. Diagnostic fluted projectile points enabled him to make his initial selection of these sites and to assign them to period and cultural position, but Wilmsen was interested in going beyond this to intensive attribute analyses of all the artifacts (and debris) from the sites. He particularly emphasized such attributes as flake angles, edge angles, and artifact dimensions, which were susceptible to quantitative scale rankings. Quantitative treatment, he points out, allows for measurement of variation (and, in effect, measurement of cultural change). His artifact types were based on these descriptive quantitative-qualitative data, on functional inferences, and geographic-chronologic-associational information. The processes of artifact manufacture were analyzed with reference to raw materials, technological variation, and functional variation. Armed with this impressive analysis of his data, Wilmsen then turned to the question of site activities. Site variation, he states, is structured by interacting subsystems of the society and culture. It reflects different cultural responses to divergent ecological opportunities, the size and social composition of the groups involved, and the duration and periodicity of occupation (involving task activities, degree of mobility for these activities, and seasonability of resources). From this study of variation among his eight sites, he came up with an initial two-fold classification: "limited activity locations" and "multiple activity locations." Among the former were the Blackwater Draw, Horner, Williamson, and Shoop sites; and to these we could add the Olsen-Chubbuck location just discussed. Wilmsen's prime example of a multiple activity location is the Lindenmeier site in Colorado (see Roberts, 1933b, 1936).

Excavation data from Lindenmeier indicate that it was occupied seasonally over a very long period of years. Activity loci were determined from artifact and debris findings. A kill site was defined by the presence of the remains of nine young bison associated with only a few artifacts, mostly projectile points. Other spots were localized by concentrations of flint-chipping and bone-working debris, indicating manufactories. Many tools and weapons were made of locally obtained stone, others had been chipped out of exotic materials — but even most of these had been made at Lindenmeier. Wilmsen's interpretation of the Lindenmeier multiple activity location, derived from all these and other data, is that it was not only a multipurpose site but a multiband site as well. Occupied seasonally, it provided a place where various bands gathered together for hunting cooperation, exchange of diverse raw materials, technological information, and general socializing.

With this view of early Native American life as a much more complex structured one than that built around the single activity of big game hunting, Wilmsen then ventures to discuss the processes of site localization, the resolving choices involving living space and resources, segmentation into smaller specialized activity groups, the convergence of these into small family bands, and the convergence of these into multiband stations, as at Lindenmeier. He speculates about cultural change in these circumstances. A group enters a new environment. Here, it would apply its old techniculture, which would, in time, be modified in the new environment; and, a prolonged development would produce a technology distinctive from the parent culture. Technological, functional, social, and ecological processes were structurally related in the Paleo-Indian cultural system, as indeed they are in any cultural system. Wilmsen's view is a fully systemic one: technological procedures of the Paleo-Indians were directed toward a production of useful tools. Changes in resource patterns elicited changes in functional responses. Patterns of sociocultural interaction were adapted to ecological opportunities and task-performance requirements.

Do these studies by Wheat and Wilmsen reflect a new attitude, as we have claimed? For the Olsen-Chubbuck analysis, one might argue that inferences about the behavior of the bison herd and the hunters could all have been made within the common-sensical scope of traditional archaeology — and it is true that similar inferences have been made before. Nevertheless, Wheat has provided the necessary information for understanding larger patterns of Paleo-Indian behavior. Wilmsen, adopting a more comprehensive New Archaeological approach, attempts to expand this goal. Has he accomplished something different from what a traditionally oriented archaeologist might have achieved? We believe that he has, for the following reason: Wilmsen's emphasis on variability in the archaeological record allows his data to be related to ongoing ethnographical and ethnoarchaeological studies of hunting and gathering bands; because of this, he is in a better position than traditional archaeologists to coordinate archaeological and ethnoarchaeological data toward the testing of ideas about the adaptations of bands to their environments. The older typological emphasis simply would not allow such kinds of studies.

For further examples of attitudinal changes in American archaeology, let us go on to a later developmental stage, that of the beginnings of New World agriculture. As early as the 1950s, following MacNeish's (1950, 1958)[59] work in the Mexican Tamaulipas caves, it had become apparent to many American archaeologists that the origins of New World agriculture should be conceived of as "a process rather than an event." Stratigraphy in the dry preserving cave dusts had demonstrated that early cultivation of plants had proceeded only very gradually over the millennia—had been, indeed, a very "slow-footed revolution" (Willey and Phillips, 1958, p. 145). But this important new insight was only the beginning; the next question was how it all happened. As we have noted above, Kent Flannery (1968a) approached this question with a systems-theory model, drawing upon new data from MacNeish's (1967) further fieldwork in the Tehuacan Valley and his own studies in Oaxaca (Flannery, Marcus, and Kowalewski, 1981; Flannery, ed., 1986).

To review Flannery's model very briefly, plant cultivation began in the central and south Mexican highlands as early as 5000 B.C. or even earlier. This early selective planting was a part of a hunting-collecting subsistence system, which utilized a number of wild plants. A very primitive maize appears in the Tehuacan sequence at about 5000 B.C., possibly a true wild ancestor of *Zea mays* (Mangelsdorf, 1974) but, most likely, a very early mutant representing an evolutionary link between teosinte *(Zea mexicana)* and domesticated maize (Beadle, 1977). If the latter hypothesis is correct, it would imply that the wild teosinte seed-bearing grass, through harvesting and selection, had become a domesticate. For a long while, however, this had little effect on the system of food procurement; wild plant-collecting still dominated the scene. Then, at about 3000 B.C., there are indications in the archaeological record of population increases, changes in settlement location, and a more sedentary lifestyle, all of which suggest that maize and other associated early cultivars were beginning to have notable social and cultural effects on the inhabitants of these regions. These changes were accompanied by spectacular improvements in the maize itself, with the plant becoming

Maize cobs from the Tehuacan Valley, Mexico. This series illustrates an evolutionary sequence in the development of maize, from ca. 5000 B.C. to A.D. 1500 (right). (From R. S. MacNeish, Robert S. Peabody Foundation for Archaeology)

a more valuable food source. By 2000 to 1500 B.C., a significant threshold had been crossed: 200 to 250 kilograms of maize could be harvested per planted hectare, a ratio sufficient to sustain a sedentary community of the size found in the Tehuacan Valley. And, closing the circle of evidence, at this time the first permanent villages, situated on good farming soils, became the dominant settlement form in the valley.

When this hypothesis was promulgated, it seemed very satisfactory—and it still does, up to a point. It explains how things happened, in the sense of diagramming the articulations between humans and plants and the interrelated developmental courses of both. What is still lacking is an explanation of *why*. Why make the step from plant-collecting to plant-cultivation? It is now clear that this crucial step did not occur at that point in the sequence where hunters and gatherers selected the first wild seeds for desultory doorside planting, *ca.* 5000 B.C., but further along, (*ca.* 2000–1500 B.C.) where the decision was made to devote substantial labor to the clearing and planting of extensive fields. Such a decision would have been crucial, because, once such labor had been diverted from the more traditional economic pursuits of wild plant-gathering, with attendant rescheduling of seasonal work groups and behavior, it would have been difficult to turn back to old ways. This difficulty could have been realized in famines of a single year or two, if farming production had not come up to expectations; or, it could have made itself felt over a more extended time-period, if short-term success had led to population increases that then could not have been maintained as the result of agricultural reversals. It is quite possible that such difficulties and failures did occur in what must have been the tentative steps toward a basic dependence on the production of food rather than the collection of food. But what were the factors that lay behind the decision to "gamble" on farming—in this case, maize farming?

The question is not an easy one to answer, but by the 1970s American archaeologists had become increasingly suspicious of overly simple linear explanation. This is, perhaps, the main difference in the search for causal and processual understanding now as opposed to a few years ago. This change owes much to the New Archaeology, and its systemic approach is seen in various writings about the switch to effective agriculture.[60] Thus, working from a base of Peruvian data, M. N. Cohen (1977a) is quite critical of Flannery's (1968a) Mexican model, because it locates the prime focus of change in the maize plant mutation, transforming a primitive cultivar into a potentially major food source and thereby beginning the whole systemically linked series of processes that led to the agricultural revolution. To Cohen, this is the "old bias" for simple cause-and-effect relationships. Yet, Cohen, in his writings (1977a, 1977b, 1978) seems to place primary emphasis on population growth as the triggering factor in the rise of agriculture. This reverses the classic archaeological-anthropological position of some years ago, in which the invention and development of agriculture was seen to trigger population growth.[61] Cohen directs his attention primarily to the Peruvian data, and we will return to this later; but how does the idea of population growth as the trigger for farming fit the Mesoamerican data?

The answer is that it does not fit the data, at least not very well. Ancient upland Mexico was not densely populated at *ca.* 5000 to 3000 B.C., nor was any other part of Mesoamerica, although the question as to what constitutes population "pressure," even under conditions of seemingly high density, remains open. The need for subsistence increase over and above that of hunting-collecting procurement would not seem to have been indicated for this period. And, certainly, there are no signs of a rapid population increase in any region, such as the Tehuacan Valley, that would support the idea of an influx of peoples from some other region. This appears to dispose of Binford's (1968c) "tension zone" hypothesis, where agricultural origins are seen as the result of population overflow from an optimum wild resource region (such as a coastal shellfishing locale) into a marginal environmental zone (semiarid uplands) where plant cultivation becomes a forced or necessary alternative to maintain the population. So we are still left with the basic question as to which development precedes (and causes) the other. For the moment, one can only agree with Bray (1977a) that neither population increase nor effective agriculture can be given priority. So far, at least, we can only consider them as causally interrelated factors.

For Peru, the story is somewhat different from that for Mesoamerica, but, in its own way, the sequence is equally complex and resistant to easy causal explanations. In the Peruvian highlands, MacNeish (MacNeish 1969; MacNeish, Nelken-Turner, and Cook, 1970) has again led the way in the field investigations. He has shown that such cultivars as the lima bean and the common bean were domesticated in the Andean valleys prior to 5000 B.C. It seems almost certain that this domestication from wild species occurred quite separately from similar domestications in Mesoamerica. Further, it seems quite probable that these and other Andean domesticates were early tropical lowland cultivars that were introduced from the Amazon. Maize was the earliest Mesoamerican introduction into this Peruvian highland incipient cultivation context; it appears in MacNeish's sequences at 3000 to 2500 B.C. On the Peruvian coast, the lima bean, the common bean, and maize did not appear until the fourth to the second millennium B.C., and they are clearly imports from the highlands.

Cohen (1977a), as noted previously in connection with "population-growth determinism," seems drawn to this interpretation of the Peruvian story. He feels that models of human cultural systems that stress the maintenance of equilibrium should be replaced by those stressing change through expanding populations. Until Peruvian coastal populations that were dependent on *lomas* (fog-vegetation) hunting and plant-collecting grew to a sufficient size, they had no need for serious farming in the coastal valleys. Such an additional population buildup occurred on the coast with the exploitation of fishing resources, which began in an intensive way after 3000 B.C. As a result, by the end of the third millennium B.C., the Peruvian coastal peoples opted to make the switch to agriculture; they rapidly adopted and intensified their use of various cultivated plants that had been available, via their highland contacts, since 4000 B.C.[62]

Important advances have also been made in understanding the rise of agriculture in North America. For a long time, it was generally considered that Pre-Columbian farming in the southwestern and eastern United States was simply a matter of the diffusion of domesticated food plants northward from Mesoamerica, with maize (*Zea mays*) being the essential key crop. Now we know that the story was much more complicated than that. Mesoamerican diffusions, north through Mexico, were of course significant. Maize apparently spread into southern New Mexico perhaps early in the first millennium B.C. (Berry, 1985; Minnis, 1985), and this food plant eventually became the main domesticated staple of Southwestern cultures after about A.D. 500. In eastern North America, however, there was a gradual development of crop domestication based upon local North American plants. B. D. Smith (1989) has offered a succinct synthesis of what happened in the river valleys of these Eastern Woodlands. Between about 2000 and 1000 B.C., the Archaic foragers of the East brought four local North American plants under domestication. These were a subspecies of the cucurbit squash (*Cucurbita pepo* ssp. *ovifera*), the marshelder (*Iva annua*), the sunflower (*Helianthus annuus*), and the chenopod (*Chenopodium berlandieri*). For a good many centuries, these plants, although showing genetic changes as the result of cultivation, served as a part of a hunting-collecting diet; but by the Middle Woodland Period (250 B.C.–A.D. 200) this local agriculture had become the source of a significant part of the diet, and the cultural transformations and elaborations that characterize the Hopewellian climax of the Middle Woodland Period are almost certainly attributed to this local Eastern Woodland agriculture. It was also at this time that the first maize appeared in Hopewellian and related contexts. Presumably, this Mesoamerican cultigen had been introduced via the southwestern United States. Maize, however, seems to have been no more

A view of Russell Cave, an important Archaic Period site in Alabama with early domesticates. (From the United States National Museum, the Smithsonian Institution, and Bruce D. Smith)

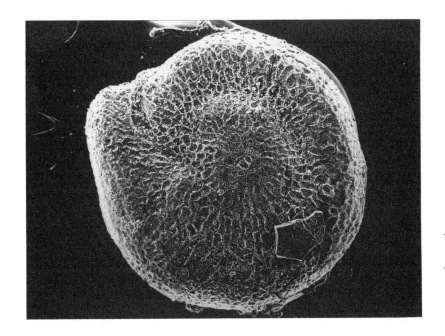

Photomicrograph of a prehistoric pericarp of genus Chenopodium, *from Archaic Period levels of Russell Cave, Alabama. Mean maximum fruit diameter: 1.3 mm. (From the United States National Museum, the Smithsonian Institution, and Bruce D. Smith)*

than a minor adjunct to the local Eastern Woodland farming patterns until after about A.D. 800 when agriculture became fully maize-centered and remained so throughout the prehistoric sequence. As Smith points out, this complex and fascinating archaeological history of agriculture in eastern North America has been made possible by a number of scientific aids and techniques of the recent decades, including scanning electron microscopy as a means of studying minute changes in plant remains and stable carbon isotope analysis of human bone as a means of determining the diets of the ancient populations.

In all of these areas, we see the beginnings of plant domestication in contexts that antedate fully developed agriculture and notable population upswings. Economically effective as opposed to incipient, farming seems to appear in all these sequences more or less simultaneously with the first large populations. Thus, it is difficult to come to firm conclusions about the causal factors behind agricultural origins at this stage of our knowledge and research. Population pressure may be a causal factor as much as a result; there are other obvious factors: natural habitat resources, soils, and climate in any given situation, as well as the condition of sedentary life which is related to farming but not inevitably tied to it. Certainly, a sedentary lifestyle is, in part, a cultural decision—a choice. At the same time, if ecological and demographical factors cannot be singled out as deterministic single causes, the New Archaeologist has been equally unwilling to accept only "cultural decision" or "cultural choice" as explanations, as they seem to be an obscurantist retreat from grappling with problems of explanation. That is, cultural decisions are deemed suitable for analytical investigation only insofar as they are susceptible to systemic analysis along with all the other factors that pertain to the human condition.

What are the factors and forces that led to the rise of cities and civilization? This question or set of questions has a fascination as great or greater than that concerning the origins of agriculture. It has engaged the attention of archaeologists in the Old World, and it is now a primary concern of many of those working in the Americas, especially in Mesoamerica.

We have referred to the studies of R. F. Millon (ed., 1973) at Teotihuacan, in the Valley of Mexico. The studies of this great Pre-Columbian metropolis have been continued (by Millon, the Mexican government, and many others; see, for example, Cabrera, Rodriguez, and Morales, 1982; Cowgill, Altschul, and Sload, 1984; McClung and Rattray, eds., 1987; Sugiyama, 1989; Storey, 1992), and data accruing from these studies and other explorations in Mexico, especially those of R. E. Blanton and his colleagues at the ancient Zapotec capital of Monte Alban, provide the focus of an ongoing New Archaeological debate on the urbanization process and related matters. The data that have been amassed and interpreted on such mammoth sites have also been complemented by those from the regions within which the cities lie. These data on settlement patterns and settlement systems are now coming in from many regions and locales, such as the Basin of Mexico surveys of W. T. Sanders (1965, 1976, 1981), J. R. Parsons (1968, 1971, 1976), and Blanton (1972a, 1972b, 1976a), which relate to Teotihuacan, and Oaxacan surveys by Flannery and his associates (see Flannery, 1976; Blanton, 1981; Blanton and Kowalewski, 1981, among others). In *The Early Mesoamerican Village*, Flannery has assembled the building blocks of settlement systems and the urbanization process by analyzing archaeological data on household, community, village, regional, and interregional levels. It is now apparent that urbanism, at least in its developmental dimensions, can only be viewed from this wider perspective.

Broadly speaking, two general points of view have emerged in the most recent debates about the urbanization process in Mesoamerica. One such view holds that subsistence technology and population pressure work in concert as the primary forces in the rise of the city and its political counterpart, the state. The other view would put less emphasis on these economic factors, maintaining instead that symbiotic interaction among communities, with political and ideological factors playing just as important roles as economic ones, are the key integrative forces leading to the urban phenomenon. Proponents of neither view, however, adhere exclusively to the monocausal factors, so that there is at least a consensus that the problem must be considered in a systemic context of interacting variables.

The spatial-temporal coordinates of the rise of Teotihuacan are well defined. Prior to 200 B.C., the largest population concentrations in the Basin of Mexico were in its southern portions, while to the northeast, in the zone of Teotihuacan, there were only small hamlet communities. Then, between 200 B.C. and A.D. 1 (Patlaclhique Phase), a large town of 10,000 persons sprang up at Teotihuacan. In the first century A.D. (Tzacualli Phase), this town enjoyed a phenomenal growth, burgeoning into a city of 50,000 to 60,000 inhabitants. Subsequently, in the succeeding centuries (the Miccaotli, Tlamimilolpa, and Xolalpan Phases), growth continued, so that by A.D. 600 the city of Teotihuacan had a population estimated at between 125,000 and 200,000 in a congested area of 20 square kilometers. After A.D. 600, there was a period of some decline (Metepec Phase), although Teotihuacan's status as a metropolis still continued; but, at about A.D. 700, it underwent a rapid decline and

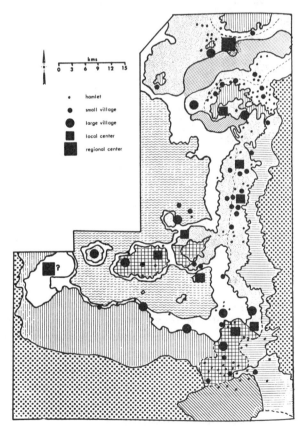

The settlement pattern of a portion of the Basin of Mexico ca. 200 B.C.–A.D. 100. Teotihuacan is the regional center, represented by the large black square at the top of the map. At this time, there were many other local centers and large villages. (From Parsons, 1976, copyright University of New Mexico Press and School of American Research.)

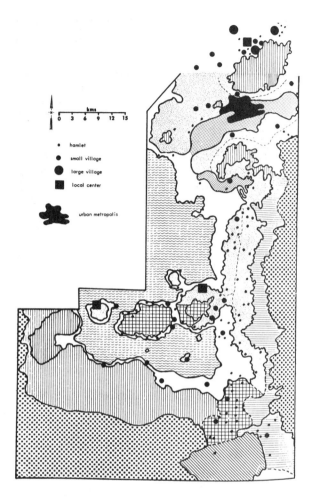

The settlement pattern of a portion of the Basin of Mexico during the height of Teotihuacan's power (ca. A.D. 400–700). The metropolis of Teotihuacan is the large irregular blob at the top of the map. Note the reduction or elimination of many former local centers and large villages. (From Parsons, 1976, copyright University of New Mexico Press and School of American Research)

ceased to function as a large city. Concomittant with the rise of the Teotihuacan urban zone was the semidepopulation of the remainder of the Teotihuacan Valley and, eventually, much of the Basin of Mexico. While some communities continued to exist separately from the growing city, these became much fewer in number, smaller in size, or both. What appeared to have been rival centers in earlier times disappeared or were greatly reduced. Some may have served as administrative subcenters in the Teotihuacan state system. Outlying hamlets and villages were, in many cases, specialized occupational communities, established for the extraction of salt or obsidian or as nodes on a trading network.

Within the great city itself, the population was housed in closely spaced apartment compounds. These varied in size, but all appear larger

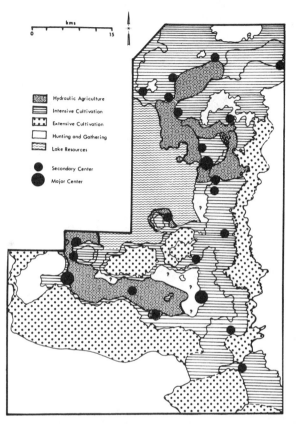

The settlement pattern of a portion of the Basin of Mexico after the decline and virtual abandonment of Teotihuacan. The period is that of the Aztec Horizon (ca. A.D. 1200–1520). Note the numerous major and secondary centers that have now sprung up. (From Parsons, 1976, copyright University of New Mexico Press and School of American Research)

than the dwellings of single or even extended families. Millon speculates that the 30 to 100 or more persons housed in each were probably linked in some way, by kinship or perhaps by a combination of kinship and craft or occupational allegiances. The Teotihuacan compound is a unique residential form for Mesoamerica, and Millon (1976) has made the suggestion that it may have served as an incorporative unit designed to assimilate incoming populations from the countryside as these were drawn in, voluntarily or involuntarily, to the metropolis. At the heart of the city were great public buildings—pyramids, temples, and palaces. The apartment compounds closer to the city center tended to be larger and more elaborate, so that something of a social spectrum—from upper to lower classes—is projected on a center-to-periphery axis; however, there are exceptions to this. Some compounds, or groups of compounds, have been identified as craft *barrios* for the working of obsidian or the manufacture of pottery or figurines. Millon estimates that one-quarter of the inhabitants of the city were engaged as artisans, traders, or bureaucrats. The remaining three-quarters are assumed to have been

engaged in agriculture. These, presumably, were at the bottom of the social scale, lived at the edges of the city, and often walked considerable distances to and from their fields.

The cosmopolitan and international flavor of the city of Teotihuacan is attested to by the evidences of its far-flung trade. Exotic goods are found within the city, and Teotihuacan or Teotihuacan-controlled and influenced products found throughout Mesoamerica. In the period of A.D. 200 to 600, it was clearly the greatest city of its time for the area, and there is no denying the appropriateness of the term *city*.

In attempting to answer questions about its nature and appearance, Sanders has long held to an interaction of forces involving agricultural production, population growth and expansion, competition among groups, and the emergence of a single dominant polity in the Basin of Mexico (and even farther away) as the primary determining factors in the rise of Teotihuacan as a great city (Sanders and Price, 1968; Sanders, Parsons, and Logan, 1976). Teotihuacan's rapid growth and success are attributed to irrigation agriculture, which was a necessity in the Teotihuacan Valley. Teotihuacan then set about eliminating its other rivals in the several sections or valleys of the Basin, such as Texcoco, Chalco, and others. In the Sanders-Parsons-Logan model, this growth of Teotihuacan's size, power, and prestige was further augmented and buttressed by its role as a trading center and the systemically related manufactories that developed there as well as by its growing political and religious importance; however, the driving force was essentially that of population pressure.

Critics of this position, such as Blanton (1976b), would see population growth as an epiphenomenon of sociocultural evolution rather than as the cause of sociocultural evolution. To follow this out, as societies become more complex and multipartite, there is an increased demand for labor power, with population growth a response to this demand. For Blanton (1976a) the causes behind increasing social complexity are to be found in symbiotic relationships between human groups. In this, he follows Flannery's (1972a) widened definition of the *ecosystem*, which involves not just people in relation to natural environment but humans in all their relationships, or, in Flannery's words, "everything which transmits information is within the province of ecology" (1972a, p. 400). Thus, exotic trade goods may be looked upon as banked wealth, not only because they are made of rare raw materials (such as jade) and represent time and skill in their manufacture but because they are sanctified with supernatural value or have an ideological ingredient. Community leaders, such as those participating in the "Olmec sphere," to use an example cited by Flannery (1968b), who were able to take advantage of this kind of ideology or information, were also able to control trade networks.

Teotihuacan architecture. Facing page top: Pyramid of the Sun with palace complex in foreground; bottom: "Palace of the Sun" complex. (From Millon, 1976, by permission of the author and the University of New Mexico Press)

Such control and political centralization, in Blanton's opinion, was a first step toward a state organization, which would have had a need for more people, for population growth (see also Charlton, 1978).

Leaving aside, for the moment, the causal question as to whether population growth or symbiosis through trade was the key mechanism in the rise of the urban center, we might ask another, more general question: Is the diachronic configuration of the Teotihuacan and Teotihuacan Valley development the normal or the inevitable one for urban development? Does it apply to all of Mesoamerica or to other parts of the world? The main outlines of this diachronic model would seem to be the following: A number of small communities in a region, such as the Basin of Mexico, are nucleated around individual political-religious centers of small autonomous towns. In the course of their existence, for whatever reasons, they amalgamate into a large center or metropolis, with the antecedent smaller centers being abandoned or notably depopulated.

Blanton (1978), in a recent large-scale study of Monte Alban, says that this model does not apply to the growth of that city. Monte Alban is located atop a series of hills at the juncture of three arms of the Valley of Oaxaca, a smaller basin than that of the Valley of Mexico but one nonetheless with a great agricultural potential. This city, according to recent interpretations (see Flannery, Marcus, and Kowalewski, 1981; Blanton, 1981; Marcus, ed., 1990) was founded around 500 B.C. by peoples from the preceding Rosario phase villages in the vicinity of Monte Alban.

A Rosario Phase (700–500 B.C.) building at San Jose Mogote in the Valley of Oaxaca with Kent Flannery and Joyce Marcus standing in the foreground. (From Robert D. Drennan)

It can be speculated that its ruling elite may have come from San Jose Mogote, a sizable Rosario Phase town in the northern arm of the Valley of Oaxaca. Blanton views the city as a political rather than an economic center, with its location due to political rather than economic factors. Thus, it is situated well away from the best alluvial lands and has no water sources on its hilltop site. In addition, it did not become a major center of economic production, according to Blanton, throughout its urban history. It reached its apogee at about the same time as Teotihuacan and was a distant rival of that city, although its population probably never exceeded 30,000 people.

Sanders and Santley (1978; see also Sanders and Nichols, 1988) vigorously reject this "disembedded capital" interpretation. In their opinion, there is adequate agricultural land in the immediate vicinity of Monte Alban to have sustained its natural growth as another of the several competing Oaxaca Basin towns—except, in this case, it seemed to be the most successful one and subjugated the others. They also reject Blanton's arguments that Monte Alban was less diversified and specialized in its craft manufactures than was Teotihuacan. In brief, to their way of thinking, Monte Alban paralleled the Teotihuacan configuration of urban development in the important essentials.

As is evident from this discussion, the search for the forces of change that lead to urban civilization is no easy task. Even at a fairly low level of interpretation, the basic field data of archaeology are susceptible to varying emphases and construals that may build toward quite different results. The problem must be approached in a systemic frame of reference, and yet, given the nature and limitations of archaeology, it is extremely difficult to isolate causal factors in the systemic matrix. Millon (1976), who is inclined to see ideology as deserving more consideration as a prime cause in the rise of Teotihuacan than some of his colleagues, has argued that we cannot resolve matters by combining ecology and population pressure, trade and information flow, and ideology into an ecosystem approach, as Flannery has advocated. To do so (Millon, 1976, p. 247) "entails either reductionism or the encompassing of so much that the 'explanations' offered are untestable."

And so the debate goes on. But it is, to our way of thinking, a better debate than it used to be. There are now boundaries, frames of reference, fixed points in the archaeological past, and arguments have to be referred to these. Some of this archaeological structure results from continued work in the traditional way—from formal definitions that have been sharpened, from distributional studies, and from more exact chronological controls—but some of it has grown from an awareness that, whether one seeks monocausal or multicausal explanations, the data must be reviewed in a systemic manner in regional rather than local

The floor of an Early Formative wattle-and-daub house at San Jose Mogote is sprayed with water in order to enhance soil color differences. A postmold is visible in front of the archaeologist with the sprayer. (From Joyce Marcus and Kent Flannery)

The Valley of Oaxaca, Mexico as seen from the ancient city of Monte Alban (from Jeremy A. Sabloff).

A "danzante" carved stone monument from the earliest phase of occupation at Monte Alban in the Valley of Oaxaca. The carving shows what most scholars consider to be a captive figure. (From Jeremy A. Sabloff)

contexts (see Fish and Kowalewski, eds., 1990), and conjectures and hypotheses must be submitted to close scrutiny and testing.

Ancient Maya civilization, perhaps because of its exotic lowland jungle setting and spectacular intellectual and artistic achievements, has always stood somewhat apart from other Mesoamerican and New World civilizational developments. The degree to which this separateness can be justified or understood has been undergoing examination in the Modern Period, and a number of revisions now characterize our thinking about the Maya. First, it has been established that the old Maya populations of the Mexican and Central American lowlands were much larger than was previously believed. Second, we now know that these populations—at least in some places and in some periods—were congregated into densities of urban or near-urban proportions (Culbert and Rice, eds., 1990). Third, it has been demonstrated that the Maya jungle farmers were not irrevocably committed to swidden or slash-and-burn agriculture but that they also practiced more intensive modes of cultivation. And fourth, it has also become apparent that ancient Maya social and political structure was much more complex than thought in earlier models.[63]

It would be an exaggeration to claim that these rather profound shifts in views have resulted solely from the innovations of a New Archaeology; they have come about in the context of substantial new data accrual. Nevertheless, we think it fair to say that new attitudes have played an important role in our changing perspectives on Maya archaeology.[64] Foremost among these has been a willingness to examine Maya prehistory from a systemic point of view. This does not necessarily mean formal systems theory; rather, it has been a commonsense understanding that culture and society can be seen profitably as a system with subsystemic parts; that, in the growth and functionings of these parts, an overall view is an advantage, and that changes in one part have repercussive effects on others. Operationally, this has meant that archaeologists have made their greatest progress by advancing along as many research fronts as possible and that new discoveries in the ecological interface and in the reading of hieroglyphic texts (to choose examples as disparate—new-fashioned and old-fashioned—as can immediately be called to mind) are important not only in themselves but in that each has reinforced the other.

A striking and basic example of systemic relationships within Maya culture (as well as in the interrelatedness of research) concerns the complex of population-subsistence relationships. For a long time, prevailing opinion held that swidden cultivation of maize—the system observed in the Maya Lowlands at the ethnohistorical period—placed a low ceiling on population size and community densities. This limited agricultural potential and sparse population were seen as the natural correlates of a settlement and social system of essentially "vacant" political-religious centers and scattered farming hamlets. The argument was set and circular.[65] The circle was broken with field information that began to be collected during the 1960s on settlement patterns (Bullard, 1960; Carr and Hazard, 1961; Willey and others, 1965; Haviland, 1966; Tourtellot, 1970). Small structures — "house mounds" — found surrounding, and between, major centers were simply too numerous to allow for the standard low population estimates. Moreover, the data from the vicinity of Tikal indicated a concentration of population in and around

Downslope face of agricultural terrace in the Rio Bec region. Note the rubble-filled drainage system immediately behind and below the terrace wall. (From Turner, 1974, Science, 185, Fig. 4, copyright 1974 by the American Association for the Advancement of Science, Washington, D.C.)

that ceremonial center that looked suspiciously urban (Haviland, 1969, 1970). All of this seemed systemically incompatible with an economic base of only swidden maize farming;[66] and archaeologists began to look for evidence of more intensive food production. This resulted in the discoveries of hydraulic agriculture. Extensive agricultural terraces were found in the Rio Bec region of southern Campeche. The labor that must have been expended to construct them is too great to allow for any other interpretation than that such terraces had made possible an annual, or very short-fallow, cropping. The other intensification technique, which may have been of even greater and more ancient importance that the terracing, is that of raised fields and canals. The problem was too much water, and the need was for drainage. This method of farming was practiced along seasonally flooded rivers or sluggish streams and in the *bajos* or swamps of the Maya Lowlands. Crops were grown on the raised fields or ridges, which were fed with constant moisture from the canals by capillary action. Surveys have disclosed raised field and canal patterns along rivers flowing into the Gulf of Mexico and the Caribbean, and vast tracts of *bajo* land are seen from the air as being gridded with what appear to be human-made canals. Such raised-field cultivation is known to be highly productive on an annual basis; if it was employed

View of ancient Maya raised fields on the margin of "Pulltrouser Swamp," between the New and Hondo Rivers in Northern Belize. (From Alfred H. Siemens)

by the ancient Maya to the extent suggested by these recent surveys, then higher Maya settlement densities are more easily explained.[67]

Investigations of the settlement-population-subsistence nexus have also led to questions of social and political organization. One such question is that of large-scale territorial organization. Lowland Maya settlement includes imposing centers of palace and temple-type buildings, similar but smaller centers, and clusters or hamlets of "house mounds." W. R. Bullard (1960) proposed a model of major-center-minor-center-hamlet organization, with the implication that such a settlement model also recapitulated a sociopolitical hierarchy. Later workers have followed this up in a more systemic way, attempting to plot formal central-place hexagons around centers (Flannery, 1972; Marcus, 1973; Hammond, 1974). Such efforts, although experimental, are of great interest. We do not yet know the reality of settlement and governmental hierarchies; for one thing, extensive settlement surveys are still too few in this jungle-covered terrain. Yet, it seems undeniable that a ranking of some kind existed.

This integration, this bringing together of multiple lines of Maya research, has carried over very nicely into the traditional and esoteric spheres of the Mayanists. In the 1970s Joyce Marcus (1976) plotted out the distributions of Maya "emblem glyphs" — or glyphic signs designating cities or ruling lineages — as a means of determining political hierarchies and allegiances among such cities. This pioneering effort has since been greatly expanded and refined by the numerous translations of Maya hieroglyphic texts that have occurred since that time (see Culbert, ed., 1991). We now have insights into the details of city-to-city wars, conquests, royal intermarriages, alliances, ideology, and gender that bring ancient Maya politics to life (Schele and Miller, 1986; Fash, 1988; Houston, 1989; Schele and Freidel, 1990; Joyce, 1991), and the interface

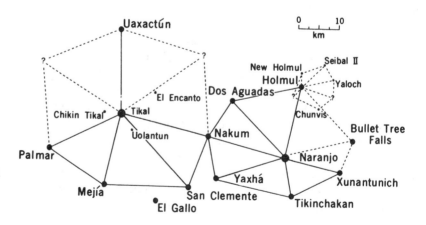

Hexagonal lattices or central-place plottings of major (Tikal, Naranjo) and lesser Maya centers of the Late Classic Period. (From Marcus, 1976, copyright Dumbarton Oaks, Washington, D.C.)

Maya emblem glyphs, identified as to site (or ruling lineage). Such glyphs were, in effect, insignia or coats-of-arms for major Maya Lowland sites. (From Marcus, 1976, copyright Dumbarton Oaks, Washington, D.C.)

between the "dirt" archaeology of settlement patterns and systems and the histories that the Maya themselves recorded promises to be the most exciting research focus in the field in the decades immediately ahead.

Equally fascinating have been the conjoined studies of urban activities, such as trade, hieroglyphic writing, art, and burial practices at Tikal, which attest to dynastic matters and throw light on Mesoamerican international politics. Thus, obsidian, identified as coming from central Mexican sources and widely known as a Teotihuacan export, is found at

Water lily motifs in Maya art from Palenque. (Redrawn from Rands, 1953)

Water lily motifs in Maya art. The Jaguar-lily association from Yucatan. (Redrawn from Rands, 1953)

Crocodile with water lilies attached to extremities and fish nibbling at those tied to the forelegs. (Redrawn from Maudslay, 1889–1902, Vol. 1)

Tikal at about the beginning of the fourth century A.D. A few decades afterward, dignitaries with Teotihuacan costuming and symbols are represented on Tikal monuments. Further hieroglyphic and iconographic study has identified these personages with the appearance of a probable Teotihuacan-derived ruler, one "Curl-Nose," who apparently married into the old resident Maya Tikal ruling lineage. This man and his descendant, "Stormy Sky," brought about significant calendrical and religious reforms that synthesized old Maya Lowlands ideologies with those of central Mexico. All of this is particularistic and historical—for the first time, actual individuals are identified from fourth and fifth century A.D. Maya history—yet, at the same time, it opens the way for processual study, for an understanding of how trade, politics, and religious innovation and change operated in this one situation. Perhaps in this case, the truly crucial results have come from the old approaches—hieroglyphic and iconographic study—but we think it unlikely that these results would have had the same meaning and interest without the broader New Archaeological perspective.[68]

If the majority of the credit in these Tikal studies goes to the side of humanism and history, we can offer a case in which the "dirt archaeologists," aided by natural and social scientists, have led the way in settlement-population-subsistence investigations that have aided our understanding of Maya art and iconography. D. E. Puleston (1977, p. 450), in commenting on the raised cultivation fields and their interspersed canals, notes that "they combine into a single fascinating system, one conducted to serve a civilization that understood and commemorated in its iconography the ecological relationships it was built on." He has given us a new view of Maya art, one emphasizing its preoccupation with aquatic fauna and flora—fish, water birds, turtles, crocodiles, and the water lily—all of which are tropical Central American species at home in sluggish riverine or still-water environments. Among these, the lily is a symbol for abundance, and it is frequently associated with maize symbols as well as with the major Maya deity, the crocodilian Itzam Na. The ambiance is that of the wet lowlands; the symbolism links subsistence and the powers of life. None of this is far-fetched; we see here a linkage of Maya subsystems. "Ideologies and the images of the mind are not random creations out of nothing. They articulate, through whatever screens of fantasy, with the real world" (Willey, 1985).

Research in Peruvian and Central Andean archaeology has been concerned, in very large part, with many of the same questions that have been asked in Mesoamerica. What is the relationship between agriculture and the rise of complex societies? And what are the courses and causes of the further evolution of civilization and the state? In answering these questions, one of the most innovative interpretations has been put

forward by M. E. Moseley. He begins his monograph *The Maritime Foundations of Andean Civilization* (1975a, p. 1) by saying: "This case study will demonstrate that the widely accepted maxim that only an agricultural economy can support the foundations of civilization is inoperative in the case of the coastal Andean cultural development." He goes on to emphasize the differences between Mesoamerican and Peruvian cultural growth. In so doing, he bridges both the Peruvian origins of agriculture and the rise of civilization. Moseley's data for this study are drawn from the Peruvian desert coast, with its oasis valleys, especially those valleys that constitute the region of the central coast. The early populations here had followed a subsistence pattern of land-hunting and *lomas* plant-gathering for many millennia. A few cultivated plants had been a part of this pattern, but these were of minor economic importance (see our previous discussion of the rise of Peruvian agriculture in this chapter). In the fourth millennium B.C., marine produce began to play a larger part in this coastal subsistence economy; and, after 3000 B.C., shellfish and fish became an important part of the economy.

The population increase from the land-hunting and *lomas*-collecting era, with its small scattered and seminomadic communities, to the maritime-dependent sedentary villages and towns is on the order of a thirty-fold increase. This was accompanied by a notable increase in craft

View of an artificial "corporate labor" construction mound at Aspero, on the central Peruvian coast. The mound is at the lower edge of the quebrada in which the site is located. Modern irrigated fields are in the distance, and the ocean lies just off to the right. (From G. R. Willey)

A cross-section showing the artificial construction of an Aspero preceramic period construction. Note the layering of adobe and stones. (From G. R. Willey)

development, especially in cotton textiles, and by the appearance of an art style, for the decoration of textiles, carved gourds, and small bone and stone objects, that signals an established iconographic system carrying esoteric knowledge. Mortuary practices became sufficiently differentiated to imply status differences among individuals; and, most significantly, corporate labor constructions were built at a number of these maritime sites. These were constructed of clay, stone, and adobe. Some were flat-topped platforms of considerable size, as at Aspero and Rio Seco; others were complexes of huge, masonry-walled rooms, such as those found at Paraiso, near the Chillon River delta. The archaeological evidence for this late preceramic, maritime-subsistence period is such that a complex social order must be posited for its people. There was centralized direction of the economy and of its political-religious functions. Moseley has made his point that these phenomena can occur in a context other than an agricultural one. He also goes on to argue that these developments in centralization of authority and corporate labor patterns "preadapted" the Peruvian coastal populations for irrigation agriculture and rapid state-formation (see also Moseley, 1974). These things appear with the Initial Period in Peruvian chronology, shortly after 1750 B.C.

Although there is still some room for discussion about the role of agriculture and its increasing economic importance in the last centuries of the 2500–1750 B.C. period, Moseley's interpretations have forced archaeologists to take a new look at the processes that led to civilization in the Peruvian coastal regions. These processes would appear to be significantly different from those operating in ancient Mesoamerica. At the same time, viewing the Andean area as a whole and incorporating both coast and highland zones, there are also some basic similarities. One of these similarities is that a maritime economy on the coast brought the resident populations an appreciable distance toward civilization but not all the way. Moseley's use of the term *foundations of civilization* is, in this sense, apt. Large sedentary populations and a nonegalitarian social order had been created from a maritime subsistence base, but this "chiefdom" stage was not a state. The state did not come into being in Peru until fully effective agriculture, with its extensive inventory of food crops, linked both coast and highlands in wider interaction spheres. In

The restored stone masonry construction of the site of Paraiso in the Chillon Valley, central Peruvian coast. This late preceramic period site is situated a short distance from the ocean. (From G. R. Willey)

this developmental sequence, there is a parallel with Mesoamerica, as well as with Old World areas of primary civilizational growth.

This concept of "interaction spheres" has enabled archaeologists to understand more fully the ecological and other systemic workings in the rise of civilization; R. S. MacNeish, T. C. Patterson, and D. L. Browman (1975) have applied this approach in very wide geographical perspective. They have compared the archaeological sequences of events in four Peruvian regions. One of these is the Ancon-Chilca region of the central coast, in effect the zone of Moseley's study. The others are upland regions: Huarochiri on the western approaches of the Andes, Huancayo-Junin in the Upper Mantaro Valley, and Ayacucho-Huanta in the Middle Mantaro and eastern slopes of the Andes. Although different subsistence strategies were employed in different regions and even in different parts of regions, there was a surprising amount of region-to-region movement and interchange in the early preagricultural periods. This last point is readily traced in domesticated animals and food plants, especially after about 400 B.C. In the period from 2500 to 1750 B.C., there is evidence for self-sufficient economic networks within each region, although coast-highland exchange had by no means ceased. During the Initial Period (1750–1050 B.C.), this formation of self-sufficient regional economies (and, probably, political entities) notably increased and the authors make the point that this process appears to have occurred first on the coast, spreading somewhat later to the highlands. One of its features is the establishment of political, religious, and economic centers, notable for their public architecture, that served as centralizing points for specialized communities exploiting various microniches within the region. Seen from this vantage point of what MacNeish and his colleagues call the "Central Peruvian Prehistoric Interaction Sphere," the Chavin style of the Early Horizon (1050–450 B.C.) can be interpreted as a religious or ideological system that, with centralizing economic forces, created a multiregional synthesis. Such an interpretation is not necessarily assigning primacy of causal forces to the economic realm, but it does enable the archaeologist to see economics (raw materials and other trade goods) and ideology (art and iconography) in a comparable perspective. Mac-Neish, Patterson, and Browman examine the remainder of the prehistoric sequence in this fashion, with periods of greater or lesser regional self-sufficiency being contrasted with those of strong stylistic horizon ties, such as the Huari-Tiahuanaco and the Inca.

The interaction sphere can also be examined in smaller geographical frames of reference, as W. H. Isbell (1977) has done in his analysis of a sector of the Huari (Wari) state in the Mantaro Basin. Here, Isbell identifies (from its setting and archaeological contents) a specialized agricultural site (Jargampata) that was a part of the old Huari system of

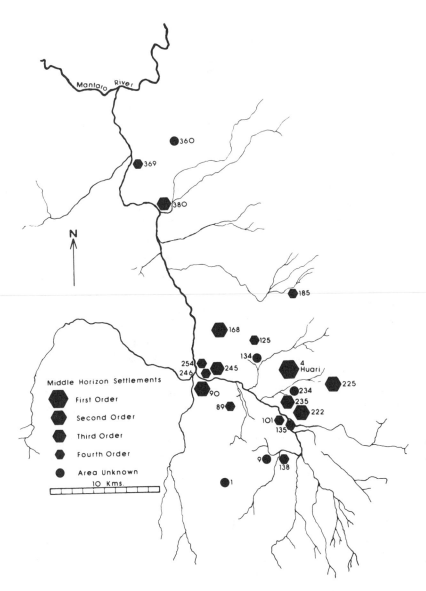

Middle Horizon sites of the
Ayacucho Valley, Peru, with the
capital of Huari and locations of
second, third, and fourth order sites.
(From Isbell and Schreiber, 1978,
reproduced by permission of the
Society for American Archaeology
from American Antiquity, 43:378,
1978)

rural-urban interchange. Encompassing a somewhat broader scope geographically, economically, and politically, Isbell and Katharina
Schreiber (1978) have also attempted to plot out the settlement hierarchy
that characterized the entire Huari system in an attempt to test the
hypothesis that his interaction sphere was indeed a state. Their results,
although not fully definitive, are highly suggestive that Huari-linked
sites so qualify (see also Isbell and McEwan, eds., 1991). In another paper,

D. L. Browman (1978) analyzed the contemporaneous "Tiahuanaco state" of the South Titicaca Basin from a related perspective.

Before leaving the Andean civilizations, we should pose the central question that has fascinated Americanists concerned with the Pre-Columbian high civilizations. Why were the end results of Mesoamerican and Andean civilizations so strikingly different? We refer here to the form and nature of such cities as Teotihuacan and Tenochtitlan, on the one hand, and Chan Chan and Cuzco, on the other. The Mesoamerican cities were bustling, crowded, mercantile metropoli, with resident populations well over 100,000. The Peruvian governmental centers were without large population aggregates and without the same kind of commercial functions. Perhaps we are exaggerating the differences, but we do not believe so. These cities seem to be the expressions of the two differing world views of the two cultural traditions.

The ultimate question as to causes of the differences perhaps will never be answered, but other Peruvian work offers data for comparison with Mesoamerica. These studies have been carried out at Chan Chan, the North Coast capital of the Chimu empire, which flourished between about A.D. 1200 and 1470. Michael E. Moseley, who has emphasized Peruvian-Mesoamerican differences on earlier chronological and developmental levels, Carol J. Mackey (Moseley and Mackey, eds., 1974; Moseley and Day, eds., 1982), and their colleagues have conducted these Chan Chan investigations. Again, although with quite different data, Moseley (1975b) argues for the uniqueness of the Peruvian achievement. He sees Chan Chan, which covers 20 square kilometers (about the same area as Teotihuacan), as urban only in a rather special sense. The central constructions are huge, high-walled adobe quadrangles. These were not primarily residential units but combined palaces-administrative-offices-warehouses-and-burial-places. There are nine of these, and Moseley interprets them as the seats and (later) burial places of the successive Chimu kings. Somewhat similar but much smaller compounds are found nearby these large ones. They are believed to have been the residences of high officials and nobility. In other precincts of the site are the remains of much poorer and flimsier dwellings. These are quite numerous, and in an among them are the debris of artisans. The whole city is estimated by Moseley to have numbered no more than 25,000 to 30,000 persons, with the bulk of the population made up of the lower class craftsmen. Agricultural workers are presumed to have lived in farmsteads and villages scattered through the valley.

Chan Chan's urban qualities seem to be features that were tolerated rather than features of comprehensive planning. Structures for administrative functions and royal and elite housing were the plan. This would have been in keeping with Inca state policy, and Moseley feels that Inca

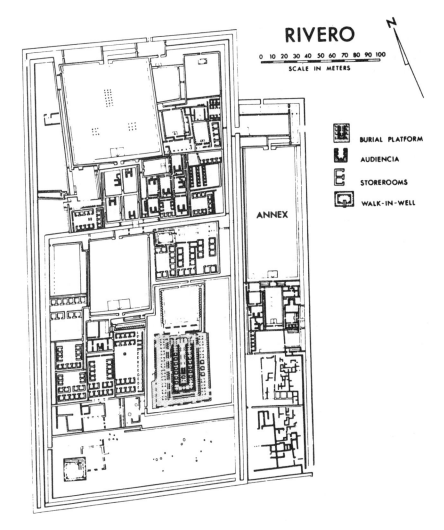

RIVERO

0 10 20 30 40 50 60 70 80 90 100
SCALE IN METERS

N

⊔ BURIAL PLATFORM

⊔ AUDIENCIA

E STOREROOMS

⊡ WALK-IN-WELL

ANNEX

The Rivero Compound at Chan Chan. It is divided into three sectors, with a fourth as an east side annex. The audiencia courts or chambers, with the U-shaped structures, are in the north sector, and numerous small storage rooms are also seen here and in the middle sector. The large shaded area, in the southeast corner of the middle sector, is a looted burial platform. (From Moseley, 1975b, Science, *Vol. 187, Fig. 2, copyright 1975 by the American Association for the Advancement of Science, Washington, D.C.)*

models can be applied to the Chimu data. Unlike Teotihuacan or Tenochtitlan, Chan Chan was not a market center but a key node on a vast redistributive system. Why the divergence from what may seem to us the more normal model—the Mesoamerican "true urban" model? One can partially answer this—or perhaps only defer an answer—by replying that Chan Chan and Cuzco are consistent with the Andean tradition of labor rather than commodities as the unit of value and of the lack of need for a market. This functional, systemic way of looking at things is part of the New Archaeological approach. It may not provide the ultimate causal answers, but it brings us closer to them than we have been before.

Our concentration of interest on Mesoamerica and Peru should not make us lose sight of the fact that much of the work influenced by the New Archaeology has been going on in other areas. For southwestern North America, there are numerous examples of new approaches. To choose one, Michael Glassow (1972) has done a rather formal systems analysis of the change from Early to Late Basketmaker cultures, utilizing such concepts as energy flow, energy storage, and conversion. The factor of population increase was linked to subsistence stress, which in turn was linked to the development of a more complex "facilities" system by the later Basketmaker. As in Flannery's Mesoamerican study of the rise of Mexican upland agriculture, this change was reflected in a decrease in wild foods and a corresponding increase in cultivated plants. Throughout the archaeological record of the Early to Late Periods, the evidence indicates a systemic shift in modes of cooking, storage, and housing, all of which pertain to the greater energy expansion necessitated by the larger population.

A second Southwestern study from the 1970s is reminiscent of the regional interaction analyses that we have described for Mesoamerica and Peru.[69] In fact, author J. H. Altschul (1978) refers to his analytical unit as the "Chacoan Interaction Sphere." Altschul begins with the observation that studies of Pueblo Bonito and other large Chaco Canyon

A view of the Chaco Canyon, New Mexico environment, looking east from the site of Hungo Pavi. (From Lynne Sebastian)

towns have focused attention too narrowly on what had happened at these loci. The story of their development from A.D. 750 to 1150 can only be properly understood by seeing these large towns as closely interrelated with the larger San Juan Basin-Chaco Canyon as a whole. While admitting that the big Chaco Canyon sites may have been the centers for a chiefdom-type political structure, Altschul says this is, as yet, far from certain. One problem is the difficulty in distinguishing in the archaeological record between a sociopolitical organization based on duality *(moieties)* and one based on a hierarchial organization *(sodalities)*. San Juan-Chaco settlement remains and architecture leave room for both interpretations. Population pressure and the need for centralized authority in connection with water control, land rights, other adjudications, and defense are all factors leading either to community fission or to political centralization. The mechanism of moieties and sodalities can serve for community integration up to a point in population aggregation, but, beyond this point, more authoritarian structures seem to be needed. The San Juan-Chacoan data reveal that, after A.D. 1050, towns of secondary size (smaller than Pueblo Bonito or Chettro Ketl but larger than previous outlying communities) did spring up outside Chaco Canyon. This looks suspiciously like hierarchial ordering by sites, with a capital (Pueblo Bonito) controlling an interaction network through subcapitals, and, as such, is strongly suggestive of chiefdoms (see also more recent writings including Vivian, 1990; Sebastian, 1992; and the publications of the Chaco Center, United States National Park Service).

Modern Period archaeological research in the eastern part of North America also reveals some interesting New Archaeological approaches. A very broad-scale study in the 1970s was *The Cache River Archaeological Project: An Experiment in Contract Archaeology* (Schiffer and House, 1975). It is based on a program of surveys carried out in northeastern Arkansas, and it has a special timeliness, in that it addresses the problem of how to reconcile research interests and problem-directed archaeology with the necessities of salvage. There is heavy reliance on mathematics and quantitative treatments. One problem—the nature of Paleo-Indian complex settlement and settlement function—is reminiscent of Wilmsen's study, to which we have already referred. Settlement models, involving "central-base" and specialized function camps, are constructed as hypotheses, and these hypotheses are tested against the lithic and ecological data. The difficulties and uncertainties in the analytical procedures are carefully laid out by Schiffer, Morse, and others.

Of greater substantive interest, at least to a wider audience, are the eastern North American studies using the evolution of sociopolitical organization as a central theme. Christopher S. Peebles and Susan M. Kus (1977) offer one of these, a theoretical critique of chiefdom-type

The great flat-topped, pyramidal earth mound at Moundville, Alabama. A replica of the presumed Precolumbian temple has been constructed on the summit, and there has also been a restoration of stairs on the original earth ramp leading to the mound summit. (From Alabama Museum of Natural History and Vernon James Knight)

societies and how these have been, or may be, appraised in the archaeological record. Peebles and Kus are especially concerned with the criteria of economic redistribution. They argue, quite correctly to our way of thinking, that redistribution is not necessarily a hallmark of chiefdom organization but can occur in egalitarian contexts. Conversely, as they show from the literature, ethnographically documented chiefdoms are sometimes without extensive redistributive systems. They see institutionalized offices of leadership and centralization of power as more definitive; from the archaeological perspective, they see hierarchy of settlement types and sizes, more elaborate burial treatment of some women and children than some males, and large-scale public works as the material manifestations of such institutionalization and concentration of power. With regard to settlement criteria, it is their belief that at least one hierarchial level above the ordinary residential community is the minimum for the ranked or chiefly society. They test this and other propositions with the Moundville data from northern Alabama. This was a sizable town, a palisaded zone of 300 acres, with an estimated resident population of 3,000 persons in the period of A.D. 1200 to 1500. As indicated by its big earth mound constructions and status burials, this was a regional capital. Contemporaneous mound sites of secondary size are found in the region that would appear to be representative of the middle-level settlement in the interaction network. In addition, such traits as evidences for craft specialization (within the Moundville perimeter), exotic trade goods and their concentrations at the capital and in secondary centers, and religious and military specialization all reinforce the case for the cultural complexity of Moundville and its related communities (see the recently published volume by Welch, 1991 for the latest thinking on the Moundville chiefdom; see also Powell, 1988).

Comparable studies have also been carried out for Cahokia, the largest prehistoric earth mound complex in the eastern United States. There has been considerable debate over the "urban" condition of this site (see O'Brien, 1972; M. L. Fowler, 1973, ed., 1974, 1975, 1978, 1989; Hall, 1974, 1991; Fowler and others, 1975; Milner, 1990) and over the nature of its immediate and supporting settlement pattern, its wider influences (see Emerson and Lewis, eds., 1991), and the sociopolitical inferences to be drawn therefrom. One difficulty is the paucity of reliable information, in spite of the century or more of archaeological digging in the area. Furthermore, the location is on the borders of the metropolitan area of St. Louis, and much of the site has been destroyed or otherwise obliterated. Because of this, accurate settlement data of the sort available for the Mesoamerican surveys at Teotihuacan or Monte Alban is not available. Nevertheless, what information is available does attest to the fact that Cahokia most nearly approached being a true city of any site in ancient North America. Population estimates for the period of its climax (*ca.* A.D. 1050–1250) most often are in the range of 10,000 to 20,000 people within a zone of 13 to 16 square kilometers. Such a size compares favorably with Teotihuacan in its earlier stages or with classic Monte Alban.

The development from egalitarian to nonegalitarian societies has also been documented through discoveries in Ecuador (Lathrap, Marcos, and Zeidler, 1977), Colombia, and Panama. The Real Alto site in Ecuador dates from 3400 to 1500 B.C. The site is located on farming land within a few kilometers of the sea. The culture represented is the Valdivia which, apparently, had an agricultural rather than a maritime economy. The ancient community covers an area of 400 by 300 meters. Permanent house dwellings were arranged in two opposite long rows. In the open space between these rows, the inhabitants had begun to construct artificial platform mounds as early as 3300 B.C. The houses, which were constructed with large wooden posts, were of a size adequate for extended families. The authors estimate a population of 1,500 persons by 3100 B.C. After that, although ceremonial construction and activity increased, focusing on a burial or charnel house mound and a platform fiesta mound in the plaza area, residential population decreased. This was the result of a process of fissioning into smaller outlying but permanent farming villages to feed the expanding population. Along with this population movement, centralized direction and political-religious ceremonialism rapidly developed in the original

A Mississippian pottery vessel with a skull-and-bones design, from Moundville, Alabama. (From Alabama Museum of Natural History and Vernon James Knight)

town center. The chiefly aspects of this ceremonialism are seen in human sacrifices and retainer burials of high status individuals in the burial mound.

Sociopolitical and economic evolution have not been the only concerns of 1970s research. Donald W. Lathrap (1973), basing himself in the archaeology and ethnography of the Amazonian tropical forest, authored a fascinating study that links religious art and its meaning to this evolutionary process and to the interareal relationships of Pre-Columbian American cultures. In this analysis, he is concerned with Peruvian Chavin art and its origins in tropical forest mythology and economy. His analysis is similar to that of Puleston's (1977) on Maya art, to which we have referred earlier.[70] It should be stressed that neither work is an aesthetic exercise in a vacuum; both are grounded in problems of agricultural technologies and their links to total cultural systems. Lathrap selects the Tello Obelisk, a well-known monument from the North Peruvian highland site of Chavin de Huantar, for his analysis. Following some of Tello's (1960) and Rowe's (1967) earlier suggestions as to the meanings of the representations on this carved stone monument, he gives us a convincing case for a dual presentation of the "Great Cayman" deity, a creature of the tropical forest who is conceived of as the bringer of important cultigens to the Andean area and in this sense is a founder of Peruvian civilization. Depictions of the bottle gourd, the chili pepper, and the root crops achira and manioc are shown as growing out of the two bodies of the deity. Throughout, Lathrap's interpretation is fortified by references to tropical-forest and Peruvian ethnography, which offer insights into native religion and myth that are consistent with the reconstruction.

Another example of a systemic analysis of art and iconography is the research of Olga Linares (1977), in which she links symbolism to both natural ecology and to political-religious values and organization. She analyzes the well-known Cocle and Macaracas polychrome art styles. Pottery of this tradition was made by the peoples of Central Panama's petty chiefdoms of late Pre-Columbian times for burial with the important dead (see Lothrop, 1937–42). The placing of this pottery, often partially destroyed or "killed," in the graves, along with rich offerings in gold and other ornaments, is interpreted as a validation of rank and prowess, a kind of public relations for the departed and his aristocratic lineage. In addition to human representations, the depictions on the handsomely painted ware are those of animals—but, as Linares emphasizes, of a certain class of animals. Animals useful as food are rarely or never portrayed; instead, all those shown are fighting creatures—crocodiles, rapacious birds, sharks, stingrays, and even stinging insects. These animals are, of course, familiar in the natural environment of the cul-

Stylized crocodile motif in Macaracas (Panama) pottery art. Note the prominent teeth and claws. (From Linares, 1977, copyright Dumbarton Oaks, Washington, D.C.)

tures, but their symbolic meaning is as warriors. Is the interpretation proven beyond a shadow of a doubt? No, but we see the attempt as one in the right direction for a broader and a processual understanding of ancient societies.

"Aggressive" animal motifs in Cocle (Panama) pottery art. (From Linares, 1977, copyright Dumbarton Oaks, Washington, D.C.)

One of the first advocates in the 1970s for the new approach was Stanley South. In his book *Method and Theory in Historical Archaeology* (1977a), South argues that historical archaeology can and should be an important contributor to the development of archaeological theory. As Schuyler (1970, p. 86) has previously noted, "Historic Sites Archaeology can correct documentary error, fill in lacunae in the record, certainly, but can it make a major contribution to our understanding of the past? The answer is patently becoming more and more a strong affirmative." Moreover, South points out, as have others (such as Deetz, 1977, in another influential work in historical archaeology in the 1970s), how the data base of historical archaeology can be used to test various archaeological techniques, methods, and assumptions.

Historical archaeologists frequently are able to control the dating of their materials with relatively high precision. With sources such as Ivor Noël Hume's *A Guide to the Artifacts of Colonial America* (1970) available to them, historical archaeologists in the eastern United States, can carefully date a wide variety of artifacts. Building on this base, for example, South (1972) has been able to create a very useful and accurate "mean

"Aggressive" shark and stingray motifs in Macaracas (Panama) pottery art. (From Linares, 1977, copyright Dumbarton Oaks, Washington, D.C.)

ceramic date formula" to provide fine-scale dates for sites on the basis of the pottery sherds discovered at these sites.

A major thrust of South's (1977a) book is to show how the nature of historic-site data, along with tight dating, allows the historical archaeologist to identify patterns more readily in the archaeological record. South discusses such patterns as the "Brunswick Pattern of Refuse Disposal," the "Carolina Artifact Pattern," and the "Frontier Artifact Pattern"; he shows how his ceramic formula can be used to identify other patterns, such as a Spanish Majolica "Horizon." As Lewis Binford (1977, p. xi) says in the Foreword to the book: "Stanley South is doing in this book what Francois Bordes did for European paleolithic studies, namely arguing the necessity for quantitative studies as the very basis for pattern recognition." South maintains that the identification and verification of statistically significant artifact patterns in the archaeological record is the first step toward explanation. In other words, he sees explanation of these patterns in terms of the cultural processes that caused them as the principal intellectual task of the anthropological archaeologist.[71]

We have already referred to the work of Deetz and Dethlesen on New England gravestones and to their use of historical data to test archaeological methods and assumptions. Although our discussion and the references cited in this chapter focus on British Colonial history, historical archaeologists in the Americas are concerned with a much wider range of data than that encompassed by our discussion. Deetz's (1962–63) innovative study of La Purisima Mission in California is an example of the range and potential of historic-sites research (see also Thomas, 1988). The excavations of this Spanish mission revealed the history and processes of Spanish acculturation of the Native Americans, including data on division of labor and the forced changes away from traditional activities. For example, males gave up flint chipping and were put to work at other tasks more in keeping with their new condition.

Closer to the present, J. S. Otto's (1977) excavations into a nineteenth-century Georgia plantation, exposing upper-class planter, middle-class overseer, and slave quarters, linked ceramic types and shapes to status positions in a statistically significant manner. Otto showed how ceramic forms related to the dietary habits of each class (also see Singleton, 1985; Crader, 1990).

Currently, historical archaeology has become a booming subfield within archaeology with a number of dynamic new directions (see, for example, Spencer-Wood, ed., 1987). As we shall see below, recent historical archaeology also has become a fertile ground for Postprocessual studies which provide alternatives to the New Archaeology in the Modern Period (see, for example, Leone 1984, and some of the essays in Leone and Potter, eds., 1988).

This brief review is, we think, sufficient to show the degree to which some of the major themes of New Archaeological thinking—a search for cause and process in culture change and problem-oriented research planning—has influenced the mainstream course of American archaeology from the 1960s through the 1980s. Most American archaeologists have not abandoned their interests in culture history, but they have attempted to turn this interest in new directions. Explanation as well as description has become a part of this "cultural history" they are seeking to recover. But the outlook for archaeology continues to change. Still newer voices of the last decade or so have challenged the New Archaeology, telling us that explanation and a comprehension of process are not enough, or at least not all of the story. They argue that understanding goes beyond or subsumes explanation and process and that the latter two cannot be properly achieved without the former. Such voices pose a critical challenge to the New Archaeology. How can we evaluate them in our overview of the Modern Period in American archaeology?

In the initial sections of this chapter we have outlined the concepts of the New Archaeology and have cited examples of its methodology. It is our thesis that these concepts and methods have been the principal defining ideas for what we are designating as the Modern Period in American archaeology. In making this case, we have attempted to show how these ideas of the New Archaeology have influenced—both directly and explicitly, as well as indirectly and implicitly—the mainstream of Americanist archaeological research. This can be seen in the clear emphasis on the problem-oriented investigations, in the attempts at a greater scientific rigor and quantification in the handling of data,

POSTPROCESSUAL
REACTIONS TO THE
NEW ARCHAEOLOGY

and in a strong concern with processual explanation in culture change. This has been accompanied, in varying degrees, by a pronounced ecological bias in interpretations and a basic neo-evolutionist-materialist philosophy.

In view of all this, can we say that these New Archaeological innovations are the only thing that has happened to American archaeology over the past three decades, and that they forecast its inevitable directions for the future? Certainly, some of the things just enumerated—a sense of problem, attention to the evaluation of inferences, and a concern with process—seem obvious goals in the future pursuit of archaeology. Nevertheless, and within the last fifteen years, serious dissenting voices have been raised against the positivistic and programmatic nature of the New Archaeology, and such voices have grown stronger, as well as increased in number during that time.

These criticisms of the New Archaeology have been grouped together under the rubric of *Postprocessual Archaeology* — in contradistinction to the Processualism of the New Archaeology, and while they are philosophically and conceptually varied, they share one common element: they are all antagonistic to the idea that the myriad human events of the archaeological past can be fully understood and appreciated by "scientific and objective" procedures alone. Indeed, these critics of the New Archaeology would hold that the archaeological past is not directly accessible in any truly objective way. Instead, in their view, the past is constructed by archaeologists who, by the very fact that they are living in the present, can have only a subjective view of that past. Broadly speaking, then, Postprocessualism is characterized by particularist and relativist views of the past, along with the conviction that the past is socially constructed (see, for example, Hodder, 1987; see also Salmon, 1992).

Postprocessual opinions in archaeology began to appear in Britain in the late 1970s. Bruce Trigger (1991a), citing Laudan (1990), characterizes them as a part of a broader intellectual movement of our times, one which reflects a growing sense of crisis in Western society and which first surfaced in the arts and literature before affecting the social sciences. Earlier roots of these relativistic attitudes of Postprocessual Archaeology also may be said to have antecedents in the historical scholarship of R. G. Collingwood (1945), and, going still farther back, they can be related to the anti-positivist philosophies of Hegel and Kant. British archaeologists whose Postprocessual writings contrast strongly with the American neo-evolutionist-positivist New Archaeological school are Ian Hodder (1978, 1984, 1985, 1991) and Michael Shanks and Christopher Tilley (1987a, 1987b, 1989); but this should not be presented too strictly as a division of opinion between British and American scholars as postprocessual relativism has also had an appeal to some American archaeologists. Many of these are individuals (Deetz, 1977; Fritz, 1978; Leone, 1982; Conkey, 1982) who have felt that the New Archaeological rejection of historical, psychological, and symbolic factors was too confining (see Redman, 1991). But let us turn to a more detailed consideration of Postprocessual Archaeological opinion.

Ian Hodder is a strong proponent of what might be called a "contextual" or "hermeneutic" brand of Postprocessualism (see also Patterson, 1989; Preucel, 1991). According to this way of thinking, archaeological remains are to be "read" and interpreted as "texts" and, as it might follow from this, the eloquence of the interpreter is important. Hodder has spoken out in unequivocal terms against the New Archaeological point of view. According to him, it is grounded in a "timeless past" which, in eschewing culture history, seeks a processual explanation of human behavior in the archaeological record through the concepts of utility, control, and adaptation In contrast, Hodder's brand of Postprocessualism relies heavily on historical context and particularity for, according to him, it is only in such historical contexts that past behavior can be understood (see especially Hodder, 1985). Hodder (1991) has referred to Christopher Hawkes' (1954) "ladder of inference," as it operates within an empiricist and positivist framework. We ascend the ladder with confidence on its lower rungs of the natural environmental interface, technology, and economy. Even as we go on up to social archaeology — via the study of settlement patterns and systems — it is not so bad; but when we attempt to climb higher, into ritual, symbolism, and ideology, there is nothing to hold onto. Hodder feels that then the best the Processual Archaeologist can do is to climb down and confine his or her efforts to the lower rungs of the ladder where the concerns are essentially those of humans as biological beings in natural environmental settings. Or the preferred alternative open to the Postprocessualist would be to continue the ascent of the ladder — but a ladder contained within a specific culture historical context. In brief, Hodder (1991) holds that the American New Archaeology, with its processualist agenda has remained intransigently ecological, evolutionist, and materialist; and, as such, it is out of step with a world anthropology which is now concerned with gender, power, ideology, text, structure, and — above all — history. In his opinion, it will be only through such a broadening of vision that archaeologists will be able to come to grips with process in culture change.[72]

Critical Archaeology is another category of Postprocessualism (Shanks and Tilley, 1987a, 1987b, 1989; *cf.* R. Watson, 1990). How can archaeology deal with ideology? Moreover, as M. P. Leone (1982) has asked, how can "mind" be recovered from archaeological contexts? The New Archaeologists held "mind" to be unreconstructable and "paleopsychology," a hopeless enterprise for the archaeologist (Binford 1965). Leone, in disagreement, cites the work of the French Paleolithic archaeologist, Leroi-Gorhan (1967, 1968), who has essayed an interpretation of the meanings behind Paleolithic cave paintings as revealed in their nature and spatial disposition on the cave wall, establishing a structural-symbolic dichotomy between "death-dealing" and "life-giving" figures. Deetz's (1977) recognition of a pattern of bilateral symmetry in colonial New England artifacts, house layouts, and gravestones is another such symbolic expression, as is the separation between certain themes in prehistoric Panamanian art which Olga Linares (1977) has recognized (also see above).

In further addressing such questions, Leone (1982) calls for a Neo-Marxist critical self-awareness on the part of the archaeologist (see also Patterson, 1989; Preucel, 1991). Critical Archaeology sees ideology as a powerful social force with more than the epiphenomenal role that neo-evolutionists would assign to it. Not only does it serve to mask socioeconomic and political divisions within society, but ideology can be creative in that it directs and determines culture change so that to ignore it is to fail to fully explain processes of change and, thereby, to achieve the processualist goals which the New Archaeology sets as its primary goals. Leone's principal research has been in North American historical archaeology where he has attempted to provide a self-consciousness and a self-understanding on the part of investigators as to the motivations behind what they are doing. Why are certain questions asked? What are the intellectual investments and the expectations on the part of the archaeologists and the sponsors of the investigations? As he says, " . . . we do not see the past as it appeared to those who lived in it. We see it somewhat polarized by present-day interests and insights" (Leone, 1983). In the excavations and related researches that he and his colleagues have carried out in Annapolis, Maryland, they drive home the point that there are "different pasts" (Leone, 1984; Leone and Patter, 1984, 1988; Leone, Potter, and Shackel, 1987). Thus, the citizens of Annapolis have structured for themselves a past that aids and legitimatizes its contemporary activities as a place of touristic interest. They focus upon a "golden age" (*ca.* 1760–84) before the city's economic eclipse by the rise of Baltimore. The establishment of the Naval Academy there is given little attention, and the institution of slavery which once flourished there is ignored. But, in spite of this awareness of "different pasts," Leone and his colleagues are not calling for untrammeled relativism nor a complete rejection of positivism and objectivity. Instead, they see the purpose of Critical Archaeology as a way to allow archaeologists to make interpretations that will be less contingent upon the dominant political, economic, and social thinking of their own time—and, ultimately, more objective. This approach, to our minds, eschews the more extreme relativism—some might say nihilism—that appears to have characterized British critical thinking to date (see, for example, Shanks and Tilley, 1987a, 1987b; cf. R. Watson, 1990).

Another aspect of Critical Archaeology is *Gender Archaeology* (see, for example, Conkey and Spector, 1984; Gero, 1985; Gero and Conkey, eds., 1991; Walde and Willows, eds., 1991; Claassen, ed., 1992). The critique here is against gender bias both in research and in the profession. In relation to the former, it takes as its starting point the idea that much, or most, of archaeology, at least up until very recent times, has been heavily skewed on the side of understanding or explaining male activities of the past—or at least those activities conceived of as male by the predominantly male cadres of archaeologists. As Alison Wylie (1991) points out, by ignoring women and generalizing about societies and cultures from such a male perspective alone, we are missing much of the record. What tools, what houses, what activities might be associated with women? A good example of what a wider perspective can offer is exemplified by some recent research of Christine A. Hastorf (1991). This research was in a Peruvian highland setting and concerned immediately Pre-Inca and Inca times. Isotope analyses of human skeletons showed that in the Pre-Inca Period the diet of men and women had been essentially the same. After the Inca takeover of the local state and its incorporation into the empire, this situation was radically changed in that male skeletons showed appreciable intakes of maize while female ones did not. The reasons behind this maize-deprivation of the women are not altogether clear. Perhaps it had something to do with "male dominance" ideas of the Inca Empire. Or, as Hastorf suggests, it may link to what early historic accounts tell us of the empire's organization of the state labor forces. According to this, such labor corvees were traditionally well supplied with chicha (or maize beer). In any event, insights and questions were opened here into facets of Pre-Columbian Peruvian behavior that would have been missed if gender information had not been gathered.[73] Certainly, a gendered archaeology raises the recognition of individual variability in the past.

Contextualism, the varieties of Critical Archaeology, Gender Archaeology—do these critical reactions destroy the New Archaeology and its Processualism? Are the lines between Processualism and Postprocessualism irrevocably drawn? Are the Processualists so firmly committed to a neo-evolutionist, materialist outlook in their search for "covering laws" in the explanation of human behavior that they cannot turn back from, or at least in some way moderate, their course? And are the Postprocessualists doomed to pursue a relativism to the point where it negates all efforts to explain and understand a meaningful past in any usefully comparative terms? While some of the polemics that have been generated in the Processualism versus Postprocessualism debate might suggest all this to be the case, we are unconvinced that intransigence has proceeded to such extremes on either side of the debate. We would point out that Processualists and Postprocessualists are interested in the same things—in understanding and explaining the past. Charles Redman (1991) sees a continuity between them—expressed in the fact that more than one Postprocessualist began in the Processualist camp. Certainly, the New Archaeological concern with methods and how interpretive conclusions were reached relates to postprocessual relativism, just as the New Archaeological emphasis on seeing objects, features, and sites within their meaningful contexts has a resonance with postprocessual contextualism. And a reading of the volume, *Processual and Postprocessual Archaeologies: Multiple Ways of Knowing the Past* (R. W. Preucel, ed., 1991), a collection of essays deriving from a seminar in which archaeologists from both sides of the debate participated, also reveals common ground. Whether or not a synthesis or an integration of Processualism and Postprocessualism is in the making is something else again. Redman (1991) would hope for it; A. C. Spaulding (1988) thought, rather, that a coexistence between two systems of knowing, rather than any fusion of the two, would be the more likely resolution, and one of us, in half-seriousness, has commented that, inasmuch as neither the processual or postprocessual approaches has succeeded all that well so far, a synthesis of the two might not do any better.[74] Still, and in a more serious vein, we would agree with Patty Jo Watson (1991) that a binary standoff between science versus history, explanation versus understanding, or objectivity versus subjectivity—or however we might want to phrase the issue—will only end up being unproductive.

To date, one of the most satisfactory statements we have read on the question of where archaeology—and American archaeology—may be going is Bruce Trigger's (1991b) "Constraint and Freedom: A New Synthesis for Archaeological Explanation." In spite of its title, it is not a synthesis in the sense of laying out any hard-and-fast methodological guidelines for "how to do" archaeology, but it is an extraordinarily well-thought-out consideration of just what the problems are that confront archaeologists in their difficult task of interpreting the past. Some statements of Trigger's concerning the debate between neo-evolutionism and historical particularism are especially worth repeating:

Bruce G. Trigger. (Photo by B. Welch)

"If anything has been made clear as a result of over 100 years of anthropological research, it is that human behavior is less orderly than neoevolutionists have have assumed but not as random as some historical particularists, including Ian Hodder in his more extreme formulations, want to suppose. . . . Neither the extremes of neoevolutionism nor those of historical particularism seem to correspond to what can be observed about human behavior." (Trigger, 1991b, p. 554)

In other words, the task confronting the archaeologist will not be an easy one, or one that is facilitated by readily applied doctrinal solutions.

Trigger refers to two types of "constraints" on social and cultural development and change of which the archaeologist must be aware: (1) *external constraints* deriving from ecological, technological, and economic factors and which tend to be universal in their applications; and (2) *internal constraints* pertaining to knowledge, beliefs, values, and culturally-conditioned habits and which tend to be specific to historically-related cultures. There is *strong* predictability about social and cultural behavior in the *external* category, and there is *some* predictability in the *internal* category. However, it is with interpretations within the latter category that the conflicts between the New Archaeologists and the Postprocessualists lie. The external constraints of natural environment, a productive subsistence economy, and large population concentrations provide strong conditioning factors for the development of an hierarchically organized social and political structure, but the internal constraints of particular ideological traditions will give significantly different forms to this hierarchically organized structure, forms that are not otherwise predictable. Or, as Trigger has put it, the external constraints of an ecological or systemic nature operate independently of human volition so that their evolutionary trajectory is to a large extent predictable. On the other hand, the internal constraints of a value-oriented or ideological kind are far more contingent upon the particularities of their contexts so that events are predictable only within a specific historical or cultural tradition.

Because of this latter circumstance, Trigger advocates a return to the direct-historical approach in which an historical or ethnographic present is utilized as a point of departure for understanding and explaining that particular archaeological past (see also Willey, 1953d, 1977, with reference to "specific historical analogy"). New Archaeology, from its beginnings (Binford, 1965, 1989), has eschewed the direct-historical approach on the grounds that it is "unscientific" and that the archaeologist cannot rely on past-to-present continuities in material culture and the meanings that pertain to it. Trigger is aware of these difficulties, and he is not advocating that archaeologists so limit themselves. He concedes the importance of the New Archaeological "middle-range theory" (Binford, 1977a), although he sees it as largely concerned with external constraints. What Trigger is asking for is an approach which will utilize both external and internal constraints to arrive at a more complete and meaningful understanding of the past (see also P. J. Watson, 1991).

In regard to the whole question of the uses of analogies in understanding the past, Alison Wylie has pointed out—in an important and insightful article on "The Reaction Against Analogy" (1985; see also 1989a,b)[75]—that Postprocessual Archaeologists have correctly argued that bridging or middle-range arguments based on actualistic or historic research do not eliminate the subjective biases also found in traditional analogies, since the actualistic research still reflects the biases of the researchers. Given such problems, some archaeologists have maintained that middle-range efforts have doubtful utility (see the discussion in Wylie 1989a; also see, for example, Hodder 1982, 1991a,b; Miller 1982). Others, most notably Richard Gould (1980; see also the Gould versus Patty Jo Watson debate, 1982; *cf.* Binford 1983b, 1989), in seeking ways to avoid the difficulties in analogical procedures, have argued that archaeologists should cease their heavy reliance on analogy. However, analogy-free archaeology does not appear to be feasible or, to our mind, desirable.[76] Rather, as Wylie and other scholars such as Diane Gifford-Gonzalez (1991) have emphasized, bridging research, stripped of earlier claims that it could circumvent traditional problems of subjectivity, can still provide important source-side support for the validity of analogies (without claiming "objectivity") and in this manner strengthen (but not "prove") the inferences of past behaviors that the analogies provide. That is to say, the stronger the links between activities and material patterning in the present or relatively recent history, the greater the potential utility of inferences from similar material patterning in the archaeological record to past behaviors. In this regard, middle-range or bridging studies can still play useful rules in helping to assign generally acceptable meanings to the archaeological record and understandings about past cultural processes.

We admit that there is no easy resolution to the dilemma of the Processualism versus Postprocessualism confrontation. We would add one comment, however, one which also has been offered by several of our colleagues. This is that "postprocessual" is a misnomer and, obviously, a term of the moment utilized for the want of a better designation. For processual explanation in archaeology is by no means behind us; instead, it remains a major goal in American archaeology—and in all archaeology. Rather than turning their backs on process, one of the Postprocessualist arguments is that the Processualists have not been going about processual explanation in the right way and that their goals, as they set about it, have been too limited. A better term for what has been lumped together as Postprocessual Archaeology might be *Contextual Archaeology*. Perhaps the word and its connotations are broad enough to subsume historically contextual, hermeneutic, and the various critical approaches.

In contemplating this Processualism versus Postprocessualism, or "scientific" versus "humanistic," dilemma in archaeology, one of us has stated elsewhere:

> . . . that much of the admirable edifice of archaeology as we know it—incorporating such things as the principles of typology, seriation, stratigraphy, and artifactual association, as well as the formalization of theories for bridging from archaeological data to human behavior—is largely a contribution of the "scientific" tradition. (Willey, 1991, p. 198)

And we adhere to this statement here. Archaeology will not progress in an intellectual atmosphere of undisciplined relativism. Some arguments are more soundly based on the evidences to be obtained in the real world than others:

> But at the same time, the "humanistic" tradition has kept alive the idea that cultural choice, human choice, has always been an important element in guiding our destiny, from remote times forward, and that there is no easy way to formulate covering laws that will predict what these choices will be. (Willey, 1991, p. 198)

We leave it there. We think that the ideas of New—or Processual—Archaeology have moved us forward a great distance from where we were before the beginning of what we are calling the Modern Period in American archaeology. But we also would agree with the postprocessual rejection of the doctrine that the contingent and the mental must be excluded from archaeology's confrontation of the past. While the philosophical positions of Processualism and Postprocessualism are probably not reconcilable, an expanded Processual Archaeology that incorporates facets of the postprocessual critique certainly is feasible, and, to our mind, advantageous.[77] An American archaeology that combines the many strengths of New Archaeological perspectives with concern for the elucidation of mental and ideological phenomena, as well as more material ones, will be more vital than either of the strict alternatives.

NOTES

1. See Sabloff (1992b) for a comment on Trigger (1989) in this regard.
2. See Harris (1968) for extended discussion and references.
3. See White (1949) for a collection of writings by him up to that date.
4. See South (1955) and Haag (1959) for criticism of Willey and Phillips (and others) on this count.
5. Willey (1960b); see also Willey's (1961) review of Sahlins and Service (eds., 1960), in which he questions the nature of causality in evolution as expressed by the writers of the essays.
6. Childe (1934, 1936, 1943) and especially his *Social Evolution* (1951). Childe is best known to American archaeologists as an evolutionist, although much of his writing was actually modified diffusionism (Trigger, 1980b; see also McNairn, 1980; Green, 1981; Manzanilla, ed., 1988).
7. See the exchange between Opler (1961) and Meggers (1961). Opler (1961, p. 13), for example, states: "Apparently the 'practical tool kit' Dr. Meggers urges upon 'the field anthropologist' is not quite so new as she represents, and its main contents seem to be a somewhat shopworn hammer and sickle."
8. Caldwell (1959); see Wissler (1917) for an earlier use of the term.
9. Binford (1962, 1963, 1964, 1965, 1967a, 1967b, 1968b, 1968c, 1968d).
10. Binford received graduate anthropological training at the University of Michigan and has taught subsequently at the Universities of Chicago, California at Santa Barbara, California at Los Angeles, and New Mexico and, currently, at Southern Methodist University.
11. Trigger (1989) recently has presented an argument on the rise of the New Archaeology and evolutionary thought that differs from the one we have just offered. Trigger (Ibid., p. 295) asserts that:

... during the decade following the publication of Taylor's *A Study of Archaeology* the concept of processual change within cultural systems had achieved a new level of importance in American archaeology. While this was encouraged by developments within archaeology, in particular the study of ecology and settlement patterns, it was also promoted by the growing popularity of neo-evolutionary anthropology, with its emphasis on cultural regularities.

He goes on to contend that Binford's polemics polarized the field and "made the New Archaeology appear to be a dramatic break with the past rather than a continuation and intensification of the functionalist and processual trends that had been developing in American and Western European archaeology since the 1930s." He concludes that "Binford's polemics disguised a considerable degree of consensus about the general direction in which American archaeology should evolve."

While clearly agreeing with Trigger that there were important continuities between the New Archaeology and the archaeology of the 1940s and 1950s, a position that we maintained in the first edition of this book in 1974, we believe that his reading of the intellectual situation in American anthropology and archaeology of the 1950s is off the mark. A careful examination of the literature of the 1940s and 1950s does not reveal a strong or widespread tide of evolutionary thought. William Haag's (1959) review article on "The Status of Evolutionary Theory in American Archaeology," for example, indicates only a limited number of evolutionary efforts in the field. If anything, Trigger's argument that evolutionary considerations stimulated processual thinking might well be reversed with growing processual emphases in the 1950s helping pave the way for the ascendancy of evolutionary thought in the 1960s.

12. Yarnell (1964); Cleland (1966); also McPherron (1967). The overall project was organized by James B. Griffin.

13. Flannery received graduate training at the University of Chicago and has taught for many years at the University of Michigan where he is the James B. Griffin Distinguished University Professor of Anthropology.

14. See especially Flannery (1968a); see also Flannery (1965, 1967a, 1967b, 1969), Coe and Flannery (1964, 1967), and Hole, Flannery, and Neely (1968).

15. See Flannery, Kirkby, Kirkby, and Williams (1967); Flannery (1968b); Flannery and Schoenwetter (1970); Flannery, ed. (1976, 1986); Flannery and Marcus, eds. (1983); Blanton et al. (1982); Kowalewski et al. (1989); Marcus, ed. (1990).

16. Odum (1953, 1971).

17. See Vayda and Rappaport (1968, pp. 493–494); also Trigger (1971) on the importance of open systems analysis; Rappaport's New Guinea study (1968) is a fine social-anthropological example to which archaeologists can look for analogies to their own work. See also Moran, ed. (1990).

18. Bertalanffy (1950); Wiener (1950, 1961); see also the articles in Buckley, ed. (1968) and Emery, ed. (1969); cf. M. Salmon (1978).

19. Flannery (1968a); see also Doran (1970) for an early introduction to systems theory and archaeology.

20. Clarke (1968); see also comments by Rouse (1970); Mayer-Oakes (1970); Moberg (1970); and Hymes (1970), along with the reply by Clarke (1970). Another development with British antecedents is the use of locational analysis (see Haggett, 1965).

21. For full discussion of advances in the use of statistics and the computer in archaeological research in the 1960s, the reader is referred to the excellent reviews of the subject by George Cowgill (1967a, 1967b, 1968) and Donald Tugby (1969). Also see Ascher and Ascher (1963); Kuzara, Mead, and Dixon (1966); Hole and Shaw (1967); Hodson (1969, 1970); Dunnell (1970); Gelfand (1971). In addition, see Freeman and Brown (1964); Deetz (1971); Hill (1966); and Longacre (1968), among others. Longacre (1970) contains a useful general discussion. However, see Cowgill (1977); Harpending (1977); Thomas (1978); and B. Hole (1980) for trenchant criticisms of archaeologists' use—and abuse—of statistical techniques.

22. Doran (1970); Hodder, ed. (1978); Sabloff, ed. (1981); also see Thomas (1972); Cordell (1975); Zubrow (1976); Hosler, Sabloff, and Runge (1977); Zimmerman (1977); Lowe (1985); Aldenderfer (1991).

23. See the cautionary article by Brothwell (1969).

24. Some examples from the recent literature on quantitative methods in archaeology are Doran and Hodson (1975); Thomas (1976); Christenson and Read (1977); Clark (1976); Drennan (1976); Orton (1980); Aldenderfer, ed. (1987).

25. See, among others, Mueller, ed. (1975); S. Plog (1978); Nance (1983).

26. Caldwell (1965); Struever and Houart (1972).

27. See Sabloff (1990) for a general overview.

28. See especially Binford (1968a, 1968d); Fritz and Plog (1970); Spaulding (1968).

29. See Hempel (1965); see also Preucel (1991).

30. See, among others, Fritz and Plog (1970); Watson, LeBlanc, and Redman (1971); Tuggle, Townsend, and Riley (1972); Morgan (1973); Sabloff, Beale, and Kurland (1973).

31. See, for example, Courbin (1989).

32. A follow-up volume appeared in the mid-1980s (Watson, LeBlanc, and Redman, 1984).

33. For more recent considerations of the study of mortuary practices, see, for example, Goldstein (1980); Chapman, Kinnes, and Randsborg, eds. (1981) and O'Shea (1984), among others.

34. Deetz's (1960) dissertation thus precedes Binford's (1962) article, and Deetz deserves credit as an independent pioneer of New Archaeology apart from the University of Chicago group led by Binford (see also Deetz 1965, 1968a).

35. Hill (1968, p. 120; see also 1966); Hill, Longacre, and Leone all worked in Southwestern archaeol-

ogy with Paul S. Martin, who, as we have noted, was one of the first to express dissatisfaction with traditional archaeology, and who gave further expressions to those dissatisfactions in collaboration with his younger Southwestern colleagues.

36. Whallon (1968); see Allen and Richardson (1971) for a critical review of the use of such concepts as "matrilocal residence" and "clans" by the New Archaeologists.

37. See, for example, Sanders (1968) or Sanders and Price (1968).

38. See, for example, M. D. Coe (1968a, 1968b) or Willey (1962, 1971); see also Flannery and Marcus (1976).

39. These ideas were developed in various ways with Olmec and Maya data by Flannery (1968b); Rathje (1971); and M. C. Webb (1964); see also Willey and Shimkin (1971).

40. A Society for Historical Archaeology, with a journal *Historical Archaeology,* was founded in the United States in 1967.

41. A number of good examples of the general trends in theoretical thinking in the earlier part of the 1970s can be found in three useful edited collections of papers: Mark Leone's *Contemporary Archaeology* (1972), Charles Redman's *Research and Theory in Current Archaeology* (1973), and Colin Renfrew's *Explanations of Culture Change* (1973). A review of these trends from a non-Americanist perspective can be found in Klejn (1977), while a general critique can be found in Gandara (1980–81). See also Lamberg-Karlovsky, ed. (1989, Part I) for examples of more recent perspectives.

42. Schiffer (1972, 1976, 1987); Schiffer and Rathje (1973); see also Sullivan (1978).

43. See Willey in Tax and others (1953b, p. 252) for these definitions. Ascher (1961) has referred to general comparative analogy as the new analogy and to specific historical analogy as the old analogy. Actually, general comparative analogy may be the older of the two—at least with reference to many nineteenth-century studies, with their strong evolutionary (and universalistic) orientations.

44. See his use of ethnographic analogy in the context of Mississippi Valley archaeology (Binford, 1967b).

45. See, for example, Chang (1958) and especially Chang (1967a), for this archaeologist's concern with process.

46. For an insightful discussion of differing views of the nature of the archaeological record, see Patrik (1985).

47. Binford (1977a, 1978a, 1978b, 1981b, 1983a, 1983b, 1989); Binford and Sabloff (1982); Sabloff (1982a, 1982b, 1989a); Wylie (1985, 1989a, b); Sabloff, Binford, and McAnany (1987); Pinsky and Wylie, eds. (1989), among many others; see Sabloff (1983, 1986, 1989b, 1990, 1992a) for applications in Mesoamerican archaeology; see also Raab and Goodyear (1984) for a variant definition of middle-range that follows Merton (1968), and Grayson (1986) for an historical discussion.

48. See Hayden and Nelson (1981); Hayden and Cannon (1982); Killion (1987); Smyth (1989); Arnold (1991) for some recent examples.

49. As this discussion indicates, Binford's middle-range theory and Schiffer's behavioral archaeology appear to be quite similar despite their arguments to the contrary (see, for example, Binford 1981a; Schiffer 1985a, 1985b, 1988), although Binford's efforts appear broader in that they seem more directly concerned with building general theories about long-term culture processes.

50. Nevertheless, the growing concern with methodology on the part of many processual archaeologists—although eminently justified in our opinion—was not without its detractors. Harkening back to the early theoretical promises of the New Archaeology in the 1960s, some archaeologists argued that the field should redirect its attention back to the building of general theory (Moore and Keene, 1983); also see Flannery (1982) for another critique.

51. As an example, Stanley South's (1977a; see also 1955, 1977b) book *Method and Theory in Historical Archaeology* is a strong exposition of the evolutionary perspective.

52. Other important works include, among others, Carneiro (1970); Webster (1975); Gall and Saxe (1977); Peebles and Kus (1977); Claessen and Skalnik, eds. (1978); Cohen and Service (1978); Hill, ed. (1977); Haas (1982); Sanders and Webster (1978); Sanders, Wright and Adams (1984); Wright (1986); and Spencer (1990).

53. See also Boserup (1965), P. Smith (1972), and Spooner (1972).

54. See Kirch (1980); Johnson and Earle (1987); Brumfiel and Earle, eds. (1987); Drennan and Uribe, eds. (1987); Sanderson (1990); Drennan (1991); Rambo (1991); Yengoyan (1991).

55. Blanton et al. (1982); Flannery and Marcus, eds. (1983); Sanders, Parsons, and Santley (1979); Herrera, Drennan, and Uribe, eds. (1989); Kowalewski et al. (1989); also see Fish and Kowalewski, eds. (1990). For the most up-to-date thinking from a New Archaeological perspective on regional studies in general, see Rossignol and Wandsnider, eds. (1992).

56. See McGuire (1992) for an excellent, in-depth analysis of Marxist thinking in archaeology and a helpful discussion of the relationship between materialism and Marxism, and see Gilman (1989) for an insightful discussion of the use of Marxist ideas in American archaeology; see also Harris (1979) and Trigger (1985); in addition, see Sanoja and Vargas (1974) and Gandara, Lopez, and Rodriquez (1988) for just two useful examples of the strong interest in Latin America in Marxist theory.

57. The traditional archaeological term *Paleo-Indian* is sometimes used in a more general way to refer to all Pleistocene inhabitants of the New World; but some authors, such as Wilmsen (1970), who will be cited in this section, would restrict it as defined here.

58. A later and more detailed study of an extinct bison kill site is that of G. C. Frison and his associates (Frison, 1974); this was the Casper site, identified with the Hell Gap lithic series, in Wyoming. In the several papers that make up this study, much attention was given to osteological remains in order to define the population structures of the bison herds, including age and seasonality. This study and other geological-ecological studies attempted to extract every bit of contextual information possible from the old activity locus.

59. For a review of discoveries pertaining to early American agriculture and the theoretical and methodological implications behind them, see MacNeish (1978).

60. For example, see C. A. Reed, ed. (1977); Rindos (1984); Wills (1988); B. D. Smith (1989); G. Fritz (1990).

61. Ester Boserup's (1965) influential book played a large part in this reversal of opinion.

62. For further details and ideas on this Peruvian coastal transition to agriculture, see M. E. Moseley (1975a); see also Pozorski and Pozorski (1990, 1991); Quilter et al. (1991); and Quilter (1991).

63. See Ashmore, ed. (1981); Becker (1979); Rice (1987); and Culbert, ed. (1991) for more detailed discussions. See also an article by Price (1978) on secondary state formation, in which she compares the relationships of the Maya Lowland socio-political order with those of Teotihuacan.

64. Sabloff (1990).

65. Willey and Shimkin (1973, pp. 473–484) summarize this.

66. As we have recounted elsewhere in this book, this change in attitude on the part of archaeologists was not without its precursors. O. G. Ricketson, Jr. (Ricketson and Ricketson, 1937) working some thirty years before, had been unhappy with the thin-population-swidden-cultivation reconstruction. At Uaxactun, he attempted the first Maya Lowland "house mound" survey in environs of that center, and, as the result of his research, he argued that population density was

too great to have been supported by long-fallow swidden farming. His argument was not generally accepted. Ironically, resurveys of the terrain examined by Ricketson show that his mound-counting erred on the short side, now suggesting populations even larger than those estimated by Ricketson (D. E. Puleston, personal communication, 1977).

67. A great many investigators have been involved in these studies of Maya subsistence practices. These will not be cited individually here, but *Prehispanic Maya Agriculture* (Harrison and Turner, eds., 1978) offers a useful survey of views on the subject and provides bibliographical coverage on the topics. See also Turner (1979).

68. A number of scholars have been involved in the Tikal research. The site was excavated in the 1956–66 period by the University of Pennsylvania under the field direction of Shook and, for most of the period, W. R. Coe (see Coe, 1965, for one summary). Hieroglyphic advances that helped make the Tikal readings and interpretations possible began with the work of Berlin (1958) and Proskouriakoff (1960, 1963–64); but Tikal studies directly referred to here are those of Coggins (1979) and Jones (1977). See also Miller (1986).

69. The interaction sphere concept was first developed in North American archaeology, in the eastern United States area (see Caldwell, 1965, and Chapter Five of this book).

70. Lathrap's article preceded Puleston's and is cited by Puleston.

71. The potential of the New Historical Archaeology as a contributor to the general goals of anthropological archaeology can be seen in a number of studies. A look at those reported or reprinted in edited volumes, such as *Research Strategies in Historical Archaeology* (South, ed., 1977) and *Historical Archaeology: A Guide to Substantive and Theoretical Contributions* (Schyuler, ed., 1978), can give the reader a feeling for the wide variety of productive research in the field. For an edited collection of historical archaeological studies from the 1980s, see *The Recovery of Meaning: Historical Archaeology in the Eastern United States* (Leone and Potter, eds., 1988). Excellent examples of book-length publications of recent research can be found in Deagan (1983), Rothschild (1990), and Ferguson (1992), among many others.

72. Processual Archaeology, with its techno-environmental, evolutionary concerns, also has been criticized for ignoring or discounting the significance of individual actions and motivations, that is what often is termed "free will" (see, for example, Hodder, 1991b). Such criticisms recall arguments directed against Leslie White's writings of the 1940s and 50s and effectively rebutted by White (see 1987, Part V; also see Barnes, 1960). Concern with processes is compatible with concern for individuals, and processual explanations do not necessarily deny the presence of human agencies.

73. There also is a growing interest in the role of female archaeologists in the development of the field (see, for example, Babcock and Parezo, 1988; Kehoe, 1992).

74. Summary comments at the Archaeology in the Year 2001 Conference organized by LuAnn Wandsnider at The Center for Archaeological Investigations, Southern Illinois University, Carbondale, May 1990; see also Sabloff (1992c).

75. Also see Salmon (1982); Kelley and Hanen (1988); and Gibbon (1989) for more general statements about archaeological inference and explanation; but *cf.* Dunnell (1989b).

76. It is interesting to note that more than forty years ago Walter Taylor also recognized problems with archaeology's inferential structure. He argued that while acknowledging the difficulties in evaluating inferences, archaeologists must persist in utilizing them. He states (1948, pp. 144–145):

The closeness with which his [the archaeologist's] groupings fit past actuality will be one prime measure of his service to anthropological and historiographic studies. . . . The empirical data with which the archaeologist has to work consist of the material objectifications of culture traits and their empirical attributes. . . . His work is entirely a pyramiding of inferences based on these foundations, and there is no remedy for this situation. It is in the nature of archaeological materials, and the student might as well face it! The only recourse for him is to make his multi-tude of required inferences congenial to the empirical facts and as acceptable as possible to his own reasoned opinion and that of his colleagues.

77. See Renfrew and Bahn (1991, pp. 431–434) for a discussion of Cognitive-Processual Archaeology; also see Flannery and Marcus (1976) and Hastorf and Johannessen (1991), among others.

Epilogue

In this history, we have recounted how American archaeology had its beginnings in an era of speculation about the New World and its inhabitants, how there was always a hard element of fact-searching within this ambience of speculation, and how this element provided the basis for what we have called the Classificatory-Descriptive Period of the archaeological discipline. Indeed, a formal discipline only emerged at this time, toward the middle of the nineteenth century; this emergence of an American archaeology was, of course, vitally influenced by prior European developments. These European developments are best seen in Denmark, in France, and in England: Thomsen's Three-Age System of archaeological classification, Boucher de Perthes' demonstration of Pleistocene Paleolithic cultures, archaeological researches in England, and finally the revolution in all scientific thought produced by Darwin's theory of evolution.

American archaeology then followed a course of its own, one in which the prehistory of the New World continents was seen to be an aspect of a larger subject, which also subsumed the ethnography, ethnology, and ethnohistory of the Native American population. Proper chronological perspective on American archaeological cultures did not become a major concern until after World War I. For various reasons, stratigraphy—the prime method of archaeological chronology—lagged in Americanist studies. It was not effectively employed until about 1914, the point in our history when what we have called the Classificatory-Descriptive Period, one concerned essentially with description and classification of remains, gave way to what we have designated as the Classificatory-Historical Period, when chronology became the prime order of the day. Great advances were made in chronological and chronological-geographical-distributional ordering in the early part of the Classificatory-Historical Period, from 1914 until 1940, and in some American areas local site and regional chronologies were linked together to effect area syntheses, the ultimate goal of the American archaeology of that time.

But this ultimate goal came to be seen as too limited and restrictive, and American archaeologists, under the stimulus of some social-anthropological colleagues, grew restive under these restrictions. They began to ask questions about cultural context and function and even to speculate, although perhaps without focus, about the processes of culture change. These trends characterized the latter half of our Classificatory-Historical Period, from about 1940 until 1960, although in this time they were expressed by a relative minority of the American archaeological profession. The mainstream of archaeological research remained in chronological-distributional ordering, and notable advances continued in this mainstream.

Out of these concerns with context and function, still other trends emerged in American archaeology. These came rapidly to the forefront, insofar as archaeological theory and methodology are concerned, after 1960, and we have seen this date as marking a division between our Classificatory-Historical Period and a new period, which we are calling the Modern Period. The innovations of the Modern Period have been dubbed by some as the New Archaeology. The watchword of the New Archaeology is process—the explanation of culture change, or, as its proponents would say, the explanation of the variability that is observed in the archaeological record through time and space.

In a sense, archaeology has come full circle, or, to follow an evolutionary conceit, a full spiral has been completed in the progressive development of American archaeology. The protoarchaeologists of the Speculative Period were concerned with explanation (in their definition of that term) of the wondrous phenomena of the New World and its peoples, but they were doomed to do no more than speculate. Then, in the wake of the rising tide of nineteenth-century science, an orderly archaeology emerged. It eventually mastered the dimension of chronology, and from there it went on to contextual reconstruction of past cultures and functional description. More recently, there has been a theoretical and methodological synthesis in American archaeology, in which the once discredited theory of cultural evolution has been made viable and applicable through models of general systems. This systemic outlook has brought archaeological research into the mainstream of the social sciences and of the other sciences in general. For, as a practitioner of another social science, David Easton (1965, p. xiii), has observed, "The perspectives of a systems analysis serve to link all of the sciences, natural and social, help to make communication among them possible and rewarding, and generate common kinds of problems that interdisciplinary discussion can help to resolve."

It is our belief that despite some recent criticisms of this new theoretical-methodological synthesis, American archaeology stands poised for a great stride forward. For the first time, archaeologists can now not only speculate but can also verify their speculations (or hypotheses) on the nature and causes of culture change. Nor do we mean to limit this observation to American archaeology alone (see, for example, Paddayya, 1990). Archaeology in the Americas remains American only in its particularities of subject matter. Inquiries into the whys and wherefores of the development of cultural complexity and the methodological approaches devised to serve these inquiries are clearly of worldwide scope.

One of the biggest challenges facing American archaeology in the Modern Period has been the reconciliation of the demands of new laws and governmental policies concerning the management of archaeological resources with the needs of the archaeological discipline as it attempts to put into practice its processual goals of explaining culture change. The challenge emerged in the late 1960s and early 1970s in the United States, as a result of the passage of such laws as the National Historic Preservation Act of 1966, the National Environmental Policy Act of 1969, and the Archaeological and Historic Preservation Act of 1974 (Moss-Bennett Bill), as well as Executive Order 11593 of 1971 (see McGimsey and Davis, 1977, pp. 9–15 for details); but this concern is also seen in other New World countries, such as Mexico, where cultural resource management is rapidly growing in importance.[1] The tension between archaeological goals and public policy has a lengthy history throughout the Americas, but the events of the past three decades have increased this tension to crisis proportions. The ways in which the demands of public policies are met in the long run by the archaeological profession will have a crucial impact on the future development of American archaeology.

From the start, the profession has had to cope with the mundane problems of setting standards for the fulfilling of contracts and for the elimination of shoddy fieldwork and reporting. As difficult as these practical problems may be, the intellectual ones have been just as imposing. The nature of the demands made on archaeologists by contractors — be they governmental or private agencies — makes the task of the archaeologist who wishes to both fulfill the contract and make a contribution to the growth of the science of archaeology a difficult one indeed. In many cases, the desires of the contracting agents understandably are narrow, and the time limitations are severe. With competitive bidding, private firms or government agencies are under pressure to award contracts to those willing to do an adequate job in the quickest time and with the least expenditure of funds. No matter how good the intentions of the contractors or contractees, the intellectual goals of the discipline and the time (and money) necessary to reach them are often regarded as frills.

Fortunately, in response to the demands of public archaeology (see McGimsey, 1971), cultural resource management in the United States— on both the federal and local levels—appears to have come of age. Productive use of data from contract-supported projects for broader processual goals has become commonplace in recent years (see Bareis and Porter, eds., 1984, for one excellent example). There are a number of successful federal programs that have promoted conservation, protection, and public education (see Smith and Ehrenhard, 1991). Moreover, there has been much progress in both archaeological protection and salvage on a wide American scale in Latin America, as well as North America, often related to the development of tourism and the broadening of access to archaeological sites and related museums.

This is not to say, however, that no problems remain. For instance, looting continues throughout the Americas, although there are growing curbs on the activities of the looters of the cultural heritage of North, Central, and South America. Certainly, increased efforts by archaeologists to cooperate with national and local governments in the promulgation and enforcement of laws governing antiquities are needed. In addition, the "gray literature" of unpublished—or worse, unknown or unaccessible—reports is an ongoing area of critical concern, as is the likelihood of reduced funding for archaeological research in the face of broad public needs. Moreover, archaeologists, particularly those practicing cultural resource management, regularly confront a host of ethical issues that are unlikely to disappear (see Green, ed., 1984, for a fuller discussion).

Archaeological research is increasingly undertaken in the public arena and crucial questions relating to issues such as economic development, environmental conservation, and fiscal priorities are certain to impinge on the advance of archaeological research with growing frequency and urgency. In addition, as archaeologists are now beginning to realize, they cannot ignore the impact of archaeology on the feelings and beliefs of various native peoples about issues such as the excavation, display, and repatriation of Native American burials. Archaeologists throughout the Americas clearly need to be aware of the modern social, political, economic, and ideological contexts of their fieldwork and analyses, and they will certainly have to engage the various publics with which they interact to a greater extent than they have in the past (see Leone and Preucel, 1992). Yet, if such "engagements" are undertaken with the same energy and insight that scholars apply to their research, there is every reason to believe that public interest and support of archaeology will continue, particularly as archaeological work is made increasingly relevant to the modern world.

Finally, we should emphasize that the rate of change in American archaeology and in worldwide archaeology has accelerated so rapidly in the last few years that it is difficult to predict what the discipline will be like in another few decades. Here in the New World, it is certain that substantive descriptive-chronological knowledge will continue to grow, as will material analyses, as developments in other sciences are brought to bear on archaeology.

To return to the theoretical and methodological levels, which have been the central concern of this history, we repeat that the outlook is bright. There are some clear difficulties and challenges but we optimistically predict they will be surmounted, particularly if the processual agenda is expanded to encompass ideological questions. One hazard American archaeology appears to be overcoming is an overemphasis on polemical rhetoric at the expense of substantive contribution. To return to our analogy of the talking dog, we think that the creature has demonstrated its power of speech; we must now look more to the content of its message.

Additionally, we are increasingly hopeful that American archaeology will avoid rigidity in theoretical and methodological thinking and that it will not fall into the trap of confusing the scientific and humanistic aims of the discipline. These goals are complementary. As has often been noted, good science is good humanism. In forging better theoretical and methodological tools to study the past, archaeologists hopefully will offer the world a richer perspective with which to view the events of today. We would also add that flexibility should be maintained with regard to assumptions about cultural processes and the primacy of one cultural subsystem over others in culture change. As yet we know so very little. Most of us feel that culture evolves, but we still do not know just how and in what circumstances. These, indeed, are the great questions of archaeology and of cultural history in general. They are extraordinarily difficult and complex questions, but questions that American archaeologists can and should attempt to answer.

In conclusion, the development of American archaeology over the past 150 years has witnessed a tremendous growth of research and knowledge about the prehistoric and historic past of the New World. Archaeologists have significantly greater understandings of the past than they had even a decade ago, let alone the century since the beginnings of academic archaeology. If our view in this book is both progressive and presentist, as some critics have charged, then so be it. The growth of archaeological knowledge has been cumulative to date, and it is impossible to avoid judging the achievements of past scholars in light of current biases and modern professional values (*cf.* Trigger, 1985b, 1989; Gruber, 1991; Hill, 1991).

While some view the intellectual pluralism in the archaeology of the 1990s with trepidation or even despair, we find the archaeological scene in the last decade of the twentieth century both exciting and encouraging. Processual Archaeology is alive and well, we believe, and if it becomes enriched by a positive response to postprocessual criticisms of its previously restricted research agenda, as we optimistically expect it will, then American archaeology will continue to prosper and increase our insights into how and why past cultures developed the way they did.

NOTES

1 . The literature abounds with new names for activities that were traditionally labeled "salvage archaeology" prior to the spate of new laws and changes in archaeological perspectives. As Goodyear, Raab, and Klinger (1978, p. 159) point out, "The impact of contract research is already reflected in the proliferation of labels and a new literature, which attempt to identify and systematize efforts by the profession to cope with the new research conditions. These include contract archaeology (Schiffer and House, eds., 1975), public archaeology (McGimsey, 1972), conservation archaeology (Lipe, 1974; Schiffer and Gumerman, 1977), and cultural resource management (CRM) (Lipe and Lindsay, 1974; McGimsey and Davis, 1977)."

BIBLIOGRAPHY

ABBOTT, CHARLES C. On the Discovery of Supposed Paleolithic Implements from the Glacial Drift in the Valley of the Delaware River, near Trenton, New Jersey. *Tenth Annual Report of the Peabody Museum*, vol. 2, 30–43. Cambridge, Mass., 1977.

ADAIR, JAMES. *The History of the American Indian, particularly those nations adjoining to the Mississippi, east and west Florida, Georgia, South and North Carolina, and Virginia; containing an account of their origins, language, manners . . . and other particulars sufficient to render it a complete Indian system . . . also an appendix . . . with a new map of the country referred to in the history.* Dilly, London, 1775.

ADAMS, RICHARD E. W. Manuel Gamio and Stratigraphic Excavation. *American Antiquity*, vol. 26, no. 1, 99, 1960.

ADAMS, ROBERT M. Some Hypotheses on the Development of Early Civilizations. *American Antiquity*, vol. 21, no. 3, 227–32, 1956.

———. The Evolutionary Process in Early Civilizations. In *Evolution After Darwin*, Sol Tax, ed., vol. 2, 153–68. University of Chicago Press, Chicago, 1960.

———. *The Evolution of Urban Society. Early Mesopotamia and Prehispanic Mexico.* Aldine, Chicago, 1966.

———. Illicit International Traffic in Antiquities. *American Antiquity*, vol. 36, no. 1, ii–iii, 1971.

ADOVASIO, J. M., J. DONAHUE, K. CUSHMAN, R. C. CARLISLE, R. STUCKENRATH, J. D. GUNN and W. C. JOHNSON. Evidence from Meadowcroft Rockshelter. In *Early Man in the New World*, R. Shutler, Jr., ed., 163–190. Sage Publications, Beverly Hills, California, 1983.

AITKEN, MARTIN J. Magnetic Location. In *Science in Archaeology*, revised edition, D. Brothwell and E. Higgs, eds., 681–994. Basic Books, New York, 1969.

ALCINA, FRANCH. J. *Manual de arqueologia Americana.* Aguilar, Madrid, 1965.

ALDENDERFER, M. S. The Analytical Engine: Computer Simulation and Archaeological Research. In *Archaeological Method and Theory*, M. B. Schiffer, ed., 195–249. University of Arizona Press, Tucson, 1991.

ALDENDERFER, M. S., ed. *Quantitative Research in Archaeology Progress and Prospects.* Sage Publications, Newbury Park, California, 1987.

ALLEN, WILLIAM L. and JAMES B. RICHARDSON III. The Reconstruction of Kinship from Archaeological Data: The Concepts, Methods, and the Feasibility. *American Antiquity*, vol. 36, no. 1, 41–53, 1971.

ALLIBONE, T. E. *The Impact of the Natural Sciences on Archaeology.* Joint Symposium of the Royal Society and British Academy, London, 1970.

ALTSCHUL, J. H. Development of the Chacoan Interaction Sphere. *Journal of Anthropological Research*, vol. 34, no. 1, 109–147, 1978.

ALTSCHULER, MILTON. On the Environmental Limitations of Mayan Cultural Development. *Southwestern Journal of Anthropology*, vol. 14, no. 2, 189–198, 1958.

AMBROSETTI, JUAN B. La Antigua Ciudad de Quilmes (Valle Calchaqui). *Boletin Instituto Geografia Argentino*, vol. 17, 33–70, 1897.

———. El Sepulero de 'La Paya' ultimamente descubierto en los Valles Callchaquies (Provincia de Salta). *Arqueologia Argentina*, vol. 1, ser. 3, 119–148, 1902.

———. Exploraciones arqueológicas en la Pampa Grande (Prov. de Salta). *Revista de la Universidad de Buenos Aires*, vol. 6, no. 1, 1906.

———. Exploraciones arqueológicas en la ciudad prehistorica de 'La Paya' (Valle Calchaqui, Provincia de Salta). *Revista de la Universidad de Buenos Aires*, vol. 8, no. 3, 1908.

AMEGHINO, FLORENTINO. Une nouvelle industrie lithique. *Anales del Museo Nacional de Buenos Aires*, vol. 12, ser. 3, 189–204, 1911.

———. *La Antigüedad del Hombre en El Plata*. Cultura Argentina, Buenos Aires, 1918.

ANDERSON, DOUGLAS D. A Stone Age Campsite at the Gateway to America. *Scientific American*, vol. 218, no. 6, 24–33, 1968.

———. Akmak: An Early Archaeological Assemblage from Onion Portage, Northwest Alaska. *Acta Arctica*, vol. 16, 1970.

ANDERSON, KEITH M. Ethnographic Analogy and Archaeological Interpretation. *Science*, vol. 163, no. 3863, 133–138, 1969.

APARICIO, FRANCISCO DE. The Archaeology of the Paraná River. In *Handbook of South American Indians*, Julien H. Steward, ed., vol. 3, 57–67. Bureau of American Ethnology, Bulletin 143. Washington, D. C., 1948.

ARMILLAS, PEDRO. A Sequence of Cultural Development in Meso-America. In *A Reappraisal of Peruvian Archaeology*, W. C. Bennett, ed.. Society for American Archaeology, Memoir 4, 105–112, 1948.

———. Tecnologia, formaciones socio-económicas y religión en Mesoamérica. In *The Civilizations of Ancient America*, Sol Tax, ed., vol. 1, 19–30. University of Chicago Press, Chicago, 1951.

———. Cronologia y periodificación de la historia de la America precolumbina. *Journal of World History*, vol. 3, no. 2, 463–503, 1956.

ARMILLAS, PEDRO, ANGEL PALERM, and ERIC R. WOLF. A Small Irrigation System in the Valley of Teotihuacan. *American Antiquity*, vol. 21, no. 4, 396–399, 1956.

ARNOLD, P. J. III. *Domestic Ceramic Production and Spatial Organization: A Mexican Case Study in Ethnoarchaeology*. Cambridge University Press, Cambridge, 1991.

ASCHER, MARCIA and ROBERT ASCHER. Chronological Ordering by Computer. *American Anthropologist*, vol. 65, no. 5, 1045–1052, 1963.

ASCHER, ROBERT. Analogy in Archaeological Interpretation. *Southwestern Journal of Anthropology*, vol. 17, no. 4, 317–325, 1962.

ASHMORE, WENDY, ed. *Lowland Maya Settlement Patterns*. University of New Mexico, Albuquerque, 1981.

ASHMORE, WENDY and G. R. WILLEY. An Historical Introduction to the Study of Lowland Maya Settlement Patterns. In *Lowland Maya Settlement Patterns*, W. Ashmore, ed., pp. 1–16. University of New Mexico Press, Albuquerque, 1981.

ATWATER, CALEB. Description of the Antiquities Discovered in the State of Ohio and Other Western States. *Transactions and Collections of the American Antiquarian Society*, vol. 1, 105–267. Worcester, 1820.

d'AZEVEDO, WARREN and others, eds. *The Current Status of Anthropological Research in the Great Basin: 1964*. Desert Research Institute, Social Sciences and Humanities Publications, no. 1. Reno, 1966.

BABCOCK, B. A. and N. J. PAREZO. *Daughters of the Desert; Women Anthropologists and the Native American Southwest, 1880–1980: An Illustrated Catalogue*. University of New Mexico Press, Albuquerque, 1988.

BANCROFT, HUBERT H. *The Native Races*. Bancroft, San Francisco, 1882.

BANDELIER, ADOLF F. On the Art of War and Mode of Warfare of the Ancient Mexicans. *Tenth Annual Report of the Peabody Museum*, vol. 2, 95–161. Cambridge, Mass., 1877.

———. On the Tenure and Distribution of Lands, and the Customs with Respect to Inheritance, among the Ancient Mexicans. *Eleventh Annual Report of the Peabody Museum*, 385–448. Cambridge, Mass., 1878.

———. On the Social Organization and Mode of Government of the Ancient Mexicans. *Twelfth Annual Report of the Peabody Museum*, vol. 2, 557–669. Cambridge, Mass., 1879.

———. Report on the Ruins of the Pueblo of Peos. *Papers of the Archaeological Institute of America*, America Series, vol. 1, 37–133. London, 1881.

———. Final Report of Investigations Among the Indians of the Southwestern United States. *Papers of the Archaeological Institute of America*, vol. 4, 1–591. Cambridge, Mass., 1892.

———. *The Islands of Titicaca and Koati*. Hispanic Society of America, New York, 1910.

BANDI, HANS-GEORG. *Eskimo Prehistory*, translated by Ann E. Keep, Studies in Northern Peoples No. 2. University of Alaska Press, College, 1969.

BANNISTER, BRYANT. Dendrochronology. In *Science in Archaeology*, D. Brothwell and E. Higgs, eds., 161–176. Basic Books, New York, 1963.

———. Dendrochronology. In *Science in Archaeology*, revised edition, D. Brothwell and E. Higgs, eds., 191–205. Basic Books, New York, 1969.

BAREIS, C. F. and J. W. PORTER, eds. *American Bottom Archaeology.* University of Illinois Press, Urbana, 1984.

BARNES, H. E. Foreword. In *Essays in the Science of Culture in Honor of Leslie A. White,* G. E. Dole and R. L. Carneiro, eds., xi–xlvi. Thomas Y. Crowell, New York, 1960.

BARTH, FREDRIK. Cultural Development in Southern South America: Yahgan and Alakaluf vs. Ona and Tehuelche. *Acta Americana,* vol. 6, 192–99, 1948.

————. Ecologic Adaptation and Cultural Change in Archaeology. *American Antiquity,* vol. 15, no. 4, 338–39, 1950.

BARTON, BENJAMIN S. *Observations on Some Parts of Natural History.* C. Dilly, London, 1787.

————. *New Views of the Origin of the Tribes and Nations of America.* John Bioren, Philadelphia, 1797.

————. *Fragments of the Natural History of Pennsylvania,* pt. I. John Bioren, Philadelphia, 1799.

BARTRAM, WILLIAM. *Travels Through North and South Carolina, Georgia, East and West Florida, the Cherokee Country, the Extensive Territories of the Muscogulges or Creek Confederacy and the Country of the Chactaws.* James and Johnson, Philadelphia, 1791.

BASTIAN, ADOLPH. Die Monumente in Santa Lucia Cotzumalhuapa. *Zeitschrift für Ethnologie,* vol. 8, 322–326, 403–404, 1876.

BATES, MARSTON. Human Ecology. In *Anthropology Today,* prepared under the chairmanship of A. L. Kroeber, 700–713. University of Chicago Press, Chicago, 1953.

BATRES, LEOPOLDO. *Teotihuacán ó la Ciudad Sagrada de los Tolteca.* Mexico, D. F., 1906.

BAUDEZ, CLAUDE F. Cultural Development in Lower Central America. In *Aboriginal Cultural Development in Latin America: An Interpretative Review,* B. J. Meggers and C. Evans, eds., 45–54. Anthropological Society of Washington, Washington, D. C., 1963.

————. Central America. *Archaeologia Mundi.* Nagel, Geneva and London, 1970.

BAYARD, DONN T. Science, Theory, and Reality in the "New Archaeology." *American Antiquity,* vol. 34, no. 4, 376–384, 1969.

BEADLE, GEORGE W. The Origins of Zea Mays. In *Origins of Agriculture,* Charles A. Reed, ed., 615–637. Aldine, Chicago, 1977.

BEALS, RALPH L. Father Acosta on the First Peopling of the New World. *American Antiquity,* vol. 23, no. 2, 182–183, 1957.

BECKER M. J. Priests, Peasants, and Ceremonial Centers: The Intellectual History of a Model. In *Maya Archaeology and Ethnohistory,* N. Hammond and G. R. Willey, eds., 3–20. University of Texas Press, Austin, 1979.

BELL, ROBERT E. and DAVID A. BAERREIS. A Survey of Oklahoma Archaeology. *Bulletin of the Texas Archaeological and Paleontological Society,* vol. 22, 7–100. Lubbock, 1951.

BELMONT, JOHN S. and STEPHEN WILLIAMS. *The Foundations of American Archaeology,* mimeographed. Peabody Museum, Cambridge, Mass., 1965.

BENNETT, JOHN W. Recent Developments in the Functional Interpretation of Archaeological Data. *American Antiquity,* vol. 9, no. 2, 208–219, 1943.

————. Middle American Influences on Cultures of the Southeastern United States. *Acta Americana,* vol. 2, 25–50, 1944a.

————. The Interaction of Culture and Environment in the Smaller Societies. *American Anthropologist,* vol. 46, no. 4, 461–478, 1944b.

————. Empiricist and Experimental Trends in Eastern Archaeology. *American Antiquity,* vol. 11, no. 3, 198–200, 1946.

BENNETT, WENDELL C. Excavations at Tiahuanaco. *Anthropological Papers of the American Museum of Natural History,* vol. 34, pt. 3, 359–494. New York, 1934.

————. Excavations in Bolivia. *Anthropological Papers of the American Museum of Natural History,* vol. 34, pt. 4, 329–507. New York, 1936.

————. Archaeology of the North Coast of Peru. *Anthropological Papers of the American Museum of Natural History,* vol. 37, pt. 1, 1–153. New York, 1939.

————. Interpretations of Andean Archaeology. *Transactions of the New York Academy of Sciences,* series 2, vol. 7, 95–99. New York, 1945.

————. The Peruvian Co-Tradition. In *A Reappraisal of Peruvian Archaeology,* W. C. Bennett, ed., 1–7. Society for American Archaeology, Memoir 4. Menasha, Wisc., 1948.

————. *The Gallinazo Group, Virú Valley, Peru.* Yale University Publications in Anthropology, no. 43. New Haven, 1950.

BENNETT, WENDELL C. and JUNIUS B. BIRD. *Andean*

Culture History. American Museum of Natural History Handbook Series, no. 15. New York, 1949.

BENNETT, WENDELL C., EVERETT F. BLEILER, and FRANK H. SOMMER. *Northwest Argentine Archaeology.* Yale University Publications in Anthropology, no. 38. New Haven, 1948.

BERLIN, HEINRICH. El glifo "emblema" en las inscripciones Mayas. *Journal de la Société des Américanistes,* vol. 47, 111–119, 1958.

BERNAL, IGNACIO. Evolución y alcance de las culturas Mesoamericanas. In *Esplendor del México antiguo,* C. Cook de Leonard, ed., vol. 1, 97–126. Centro de Investigaciones Anthropologicas de Mexico, Mexico, D.F., 1959.

———. *The Olmec World,* translated by Doris Heyden and Fernando Horcasitas. University of California Press, Berkeley, 1969.

———. Maya Antiquaries. In *Social Process in Maya Prehistory,* N. Hammond, ed., 19–44. Academic Press, London, 1977.

———. *A History of Mexican Archaeology.* Thames and Hudson, London, 1980.

BERRY, M. S. The Age of Maize in the Greater Southwest: A Critical Review. In *Prehistoric Food Production in North America,* R. I. Ford, ed., pp. 279–307. University of Michigan Museum of Anthropology, Anthropological Papers, no. 75. Ann Arbor, 1985.

BERTALANFFY, LUDWIG VON. The Theory of Open Systems in Physics and Biology. *Science,* vol. 111, 23–29, 1950.

BIBBY, GEOFFREY. *The Testimony of the Space.* Knopf, New York, 1956.

BIEDER, R. E. *Science Encounters the Indian, 1820–1880: The Early Years of American Ethnology.* University of Oklahoma, Norman, 1986.

BINFORD, LEWIS R. Archaeology as Anthropology. *American Antiquity,* vol. 28, no. 2, 217–225, 1962.

———. "Red Ochre" Caches from the Michigan Area: A Possible Case of Cultural Drift. *Southwestern Journal of Anthropology,* vol. 19, no. 1, 89–108, 1963.

———. A Consideration of Archaeological Research Design. *American Antiquity,* vol. 29, no. 4, 425–451, 1964.

———. Archaeological Systematics and the Study of Cultural Process. *American Antiquity,* vol. 31, no. 2, 203–210, 1965.

———. Comment on K. C. Chang's 'Major Aspects of the Interrelationship of Archaeology and Ethnology.' *Current Anthropology,* vol. 8, no. 3, 234–235, 1967a.

———. Smudge Pits and Hide Smoking: The Use of Analogy in Archaeological Reasoning. *American Antiquity,* vol. 32, no. 1, 1–12, 1967b.

———. Archaeological Perspectives. In *New Perspectives in Archaeology,* S. R. Binford and L. R. Binford, eds., 5–33. Aldine, Chicago, 1968a.

———. Methodological Considerations of the Archaeological Use of Ethnographic Data. In *Man the Hunter,* R. B. Lee and I. Devore, eds., 268–273. University of Chicago Press, Chicago, 1968b.

———. Post-Pleistocene Adaptations. In *New Perspectives in Archaeology,* S. R. Binford and L. R. Binford, eds., 313–341. University of Chicago Press, Chicago, 1968c.

———. Some Comments on Historical Versus Processual Archaeology. *Southwestern Journal of Anthropology,* vol. 24, no. 3, 267–275, 1968d.

———. Mortuary Practices: Their Study and Potential. In *Approaches to the Social Dimensions and Mortuary Practices,* J. A. Brown, ed. Society for American Archaeology, Memoir 25, 58–67. Washington, D. C., 1971.

———. Comments on Evolution. In *An Archaeological Perspective,* L. R. Binford, ed., 105–113. Aldine, Chicago, 1972.

———. Forty-seven Trips. In *Contributions to Anthropology: The Interior Peoples of Northern Alaska,* E. Hall, Jr., ed., 299–381. Archaeological Survey of Canada, paper no. 49. National Museum, Ottawa, 1976a.

———. Review of *Cherokee Archaeology: A Study of The Appalachian Summit* by B. C. Keel and *Cherokee Prehistory: The Pisgah Phase in The Appalachian Summit Region* by R. Dickens, Jr., *Journal of Anthropological Research,* vol. 32, 295–296, 1976b.

———. General Introduction. In *For Theory Building in Archaeology: Essays on Faunal Remains, Aquatic Resources, Spatial Analysis and Systematic Modeling,* L. R. Binford, ed., 1–10. Academic Press, New York, 1977a.

———. Foreword to *Method and Theory in Historical Archaeology* by Stanley South. Academic Press, New York, 1977b.

———. Dimensional Analysis of Behavior and Site Structure: Learning from an Eskimo Hunting Stand. *American Antiquity*, vol. 43, 330–361, 1978a.

———. *Nunamiut Ethnoarchaeology*. Academic Press, New York, 1978b.

———. Behavioral Archaeology and the "Pompeii Promise." *Journal of Anthropological Research*, vol. 37, 195–208, 1981a.

———. *Bones: Ancient Men and Modern Myths*. Academic Press, New York, 1981b.

———. *In Pursuit of the Past*. Thames and Hudson, London, 1983a.

———. *Working at Archaeology*. Academic Press, New York, 1983b.

———. *Debating Archaeology*. Academic Press, New York, 1989.

BINFORD, L. R., ed. *For Theory Building in Archaeology: Essays on Faunal Remains, Aquatic Resources, Spatial Analysis, and Systematic Modeling*. Academic Press, New York, 1977.

BINFORD, L. R. and W. J. CHASKO, JR. Nunamiut Demographic History: A Provocative Case. In *Demographic Anthropology*, Ezra B. W. Zubrow, ed., 63–143. School of American Research Advanced Seminar Series. University of New Mexico Press, Albuquerque, 1976.

BINFORD, L. R. and JACK B. BERTRAM. Bone Frequencies—and Attritional Processes. In *For Theory Building in Archaeology*, L. R. Binford, ed., 77–156. Academic Press, New York, 1977.

BINFORD, L. R. and J. A. SABLOFF. Paradigms, Systematics and Archaeology. *The Journal of Anthropological Research*, vol. 38, 137–153, 1982.

BINFORD, SALLY R. and LEWIS R. BINFORD., eds. *New Perspectives in Archaeology*. Aldine, Chicago, 1968.

BIRD, JUNIUS B. Antiquity and Migrations of the Early Inhabitants of Patagonia. *The Geographical Review*, vol. 28, no. 2, 250–275, 1938.

———. Excavations in Northern Chile. *Anthropological Papers of the American Museum of Natural History*, vol. 38, pt. 4a, 171–318. New York, 1943.

———. The Cultural Sequence of the North Chilean Coast. In *Handbook of South American Indians*, Julian H. Steward, ed., vol. 2, 587–94. Bureau of American Ethnology, Bulletin 143. Washington, D. C., 1946a.

———. The Archaeology of Patagonia. In *Handbook of South American Indians*, Julian H. Steward, ed., vol. 1, 17–24, Bureau of American Ethnology, Bulletin 143. Washington, D. C., 1946b.

———. Preceramic Cultures in Chicama and Virú. In *A Reappraisal of Peruvian Archaeology*, W. C. Bennett, ed., 21–28. Society for American Archaeology, Memoir 4, Menasha, Wisc., 1948.

BIRKERT-SMITH, KAJ. *The Eskimos*. Methuen, London, 1936 [revised ed., 1959].

BISHOP, RONALD L. and FREDERICK W. LANGE, eds. *The Ceramic Legacy of Anna O. Sheppard*. University Press of Colorado, Boulder, 1991.

BLANTON, R. E. Prehispanic Adaptation in the Ixtapalapa Region, Mexico. *Science*, vol. 175, no. 4028, 1317–1326, 1972a.

———. *Prehispanic Settlement Patterns of the Ixtapalapa Peninsula Region, Mexico*. Occasional Papers in Anthropology, no. 6. Pennsylvania State University Press, University Park, 1972b.

———. The Role of Symbiosis in Adaptation and Sociocultural Change in the Valley of Mexico. In *The Valley of Mexico*, Eric R. Wolf, ed., 181–203. School of American Research, Advanced Seminar Series. University of New Mexico Press, Albuquerque, 1976a.

———. Appendix: Comment on Sanders, Parsons, and Logan. In *The Valley of Mexico*, Eric R. Wolf, ed., 179–181. School of American Research, Advanced Seminar Series. University of New Mexico Press, Albuquerque, 1976b.

———. *Monte Alban, Settlement Patterns at the Ancient Zapotec Capital*. Academic Press, New York, 1978.

———. The Rise of Cities. *Supplement to the Handbook of Middle American Indians, Vol 1: Archaeology*. V. R. Bricker and J. A. Sabloff, eds., 392–402. University of Texas Pres, Austin, 1981.

BLANTON, R. E. and S. A. KOWALEWSKI. Monte Alban and After in the Valley of Oaxaca. *Supplement to the Handbook of Middle American Indians, Vol. 1: Archaeology*. R. Bricker and J. A. Sabloff, eds., 94–116. University of Texas Press, Austin, 1981.

BLANTON, R. E., S. A. KOWALEWSKI, G. M. FEINMAN, and JILL APPEL. *Monte Alban's Hinterland, Part 1: Prehispanic Settlement Patterns of the Central and Southern Parts of the Valley of Oaxaca, Mexico*. Prehistory and Human Ecology of the Valley of Oaxaca, vol. 7, K. V.

Flannery and R. E. Blanton, eds. Memoir 15. Museum of Anthropology, University of Michigan, Ann Arbor, 1982.

BLOM, FRANS F. *The Maya Ball-Game pok-ta-pok.* Middle American Research Institute, Publication 4, no. 13, 485–530. Tulane University, New Orleans, 1932.

BOAS, FRANZ. Archaeological Investigations in the Valley of Mexio by the International School, 1911–12. In *Eighteenth International Congress of Americanists,* pt. 1, 176–179. London, 1913.

———. *Race, Language, and Culture.* Macmillan, New York, 1940.

BOLLAERT, WILLIAM. *Antiquarian, Ethnological, and Other Researches in New Granada, Equador, Peru, and Chile.* D. Lane, London, 1860.

BOMAN, ERIC. *Antiquitiés de la région Andine de la république Argentine et du désert d'Atacama.* Le Soudier, Paris, 1908.

BONAVIA, DUCCIO and A. GROBMAN. Sistema de depositos y almacentamiento durante et periodo preceramic en la Costa del Peru. *Journal de la Société des Américanistes,* vol. 66, 21–42, 1979.

BORDEN, CHARLES E. Fraser River Archaeological Project, Progress Report, April 20, 1961. *Anthropology Papers of the National Museum of Canada,* no. 1–6. Ottawa, 1961.

BÓRMIDA, MARCELO. Arqueologia de las altas cotas de La Costa Norpatagónica. *Thirty-seventh International Congress of Americanists,* vol. 3, 345–374. Buenos Aires, 1968.

BOSCH-GIMPERA, PEDRO. *L'America precolumbiana. Nuova storia universale dei popoli e delle civilta,* vol. 7. Torino, 1971.

BOSERUP, ESTHER. *The Conditions of Agricultural Growth: The Economics of Agrarian Change Under Population Pressure.* Aldine, Chicago, 1965.

BOUGHEY, A. S. *Man and Environment; an Introduction to Human Ecology and Evolution.* Macmillan, New York, 1971.

BRACKENRIDGE, HENRY M. *On the Population and Tumuli of the Aborigines of North America.* In a letter from H. M. Brackenridge, Esq., to Thomas Jefferson, read October 1. Baton Rouge, 1813.

BRAIDWOOD, ROBERT J. *Prehistoric Man.* Chicago Natural History Museum Popular Series in Anthropology, no. 37. Chicago, 1948.

———. *The Near East and the Foundations for Civilization.* Condon Lectures. Oregon State System for Higher Education, Eugene, 1952.

———. Archaeology and the Evolutionary Theory. In *Evolution and Anthropology: A Centennial Appraisal,* 76–89. Anthropological Society of Washington, Washington, D. C., 1959.

BRAIDWOOD, ROBERT J. and GORDON R. WILLEY, eds. *Courses Toward Urban Life,* Viking Fund Publications in Anthropology, no. 32. Chicago, 1962.

BRAINERD, GEORGE W. The Place of Chronological Ordering in Archaeological Analysis. *American Antiquity,* vol 16, no. 4, 301–313, 1951.

BRAY, WARWICK. From Predation to Production: The Nature of Agricultural Evolution in Mexico and Peru. In *Problems in Economic and Social Archaeology,* 74–95. Westview Press, Boulder, Col., 1977a.

———. From Foraging to Farming in Early Mexico. In *Hunters, Gatheres and First Farmers Beyond Europe,* J. V. S. Megaw, ed., 225–250. Leicester University Press, Leicester, 1977b.

BREW, JOHN O. Mexican Influence upon the Indian Cultures of the Southwestern United States in the Sixteenth and Seventeenth Centuries. In *The Maya and Their Neighbors,* C. I. Hay and others, eds., 341–348. Appleton-Century, New York, 1940.

———. The Uses and Abuses of Taxonomy. *Archaeology of Alkali Ridge, Southeastern Utah,* Papers of the Peabody Museum, vol. 21, 44–66. Cambridge, Mass., 1946.

BREW, JOHN O., ed. *One Hundred Years of Anthropology.* Harvard University Press, Cambridge, Mass., 1968.

BRICKER, VICTORIA R. and JEREMY A. SABLOFF, eds. *Supplement to the Handbook of Middle American Indians, Vol. 1: Archaeology.* University of Texas Press, Austin, 1981.

BRILL, ROBERT H., ed. *Science and Archaeology.* M.I.T. Press, Cambridge, Mass., 1971.

BRINTON, DANIEL G. *The Maya Chronicles.* Brinton's Library of Aboriginal American Literature, no. 1. Philadelphia, 1882.

———. *The Annals of the Cakchiquels.* Brinton's Library of Aboriginal American Literature, no. 6. Philadelphia, 1885.

BROTHWELL, DON R. Stones, Pots and People. In *Science in Archaeology,* revised edition, D. Brothwell and E. Higgs, eds., 669–680. Basic Books, New York, 1969.

BROTHWELL, DON R. and E. HIGGS, eds. *Science in Archaeology*, revised edition. Basic Books, New York, 1969.

BROWMAN, D. L. Towards the Development of the Tiahuanaco (Tiwanaku) State. In *Advances in Andean Archaeology*, D. L. Browman, ed., 327–350. Mouton, The Hague, 1978.

BROWN, JAMES A. The Dimensions of Status in Burials at Spiro. In *Approaches to the Social Dimensions of Mortuary Practices*, J. A. Brown, ed., 92–112. Society for American Archaeology, Memoir 25. Washington, D. C., 1971.

BROWN, JAMES A., ed. *Approaches to the Social Dimensions of Mortuary Practices*. Society for American Archaeology, Memoir 25. Washington, D. C., 1971.

BRUMFIEL, ELIZABETH and TIMOTHY K. EARLE, eds. *Specialization, Exchange, and Complex Society*. Cambridge University Press, Cambridge, 1987.

BRYAN, A. L. Paleoenvironments and Cultural Diversity in Late Pleistocene South America. *Quartenary Research*, vol. 3, 237–256, 1973.

———. An Overview of Paleo-American Prehistory from a Circum-Pacific Perspective. In *Early Man in America*, A. L Bryan, ed. University of Alberta, Department of Anthropology, Occasional Papers, no. 1. Edmonton, 1978.

BRYAN, KIRK and LOUIS R. RAY. *Geologic Antiquity of the Lindenmeier Site in Colorado*. Smithsonian Institution Miscellaneous Collection, vol. 99, no. 2. Washington, D. C., 1940.

BUCKLEY, WALTER, ed. *Modern Systems Research for the Behavioral Scientist: A Sourcebook*. Aldine, Chicago, 1968.

BULLARD, W. R., JR. The Maya Settlement Pattern in Northeastern Peten, Guatemala. *American Antiquity*, vol 25, 355–372, 1960.

BULLEN, RIPLEY P. S. T. Walker, an Early Florida Archaeologist. *Florida Anthropologist*, vol. 4, 46–49, Gainesville, 1951.

BUSHNELL, GEOFFREY H. *Peru*, second edition, Ancient Peoples and Places Series, G. Daniel, ed. Praeger, New York, 1963.

BUSHNELL, GEOFFREY H. and C. B. M. MCBURNEY. New World Origins Seen from the Old World. *Antiquity*, vol. 33, 93–101, 1959.

BUTLER, B. ROBERT. *The Old Cordilleran Culture in the Pacific Northwest*. Occasional Papers of the Idaho State University Museum, no. 5. Pocatello, 1961.

BYERS, D. S. and R. S. MACNEISH, eds. *The Prehistory of the Tehuacan Valley*, 5 vols. University of Texas Press, Austin, 1967–1976.

CABRERA, RUBEN, IGNACIO RODRIGUEZ, and NOEL MORALES. *Teotihuacan 80–82, Primeros Resultados*. Instituto Nacional de Antropologia, Mexico, D. F., 1982.

CALDWELL, JOSEPH R. *Trend and Tradition in the Prehistory of the Eastern United States*. Illinois State Museum Scientific Papers, vol. 10, and the American Anthropological Association, Memoir 88. Springfield and Menasha, 1958.

———. The New American Archaeology. *Science*, vol. 129, no. 3345, 303–307, 1959.

———. Interaction Spheres in Prehistory. In *Hopewellian Studies*, J. R. Caldwell and R. L. Hall, eds. Springfield, Illinois State Museum Scientific Papers, vol. 12, 133–143, 1965.

CANALS FRAU, SALVADOR. *Prehistoria de América*. Editorial Sudamericana, Buenos Aires, 1950.

———. *Las Civilizaciones Prehispanicas de América*. Buenos Aires, 1955.

CARNEIRO, R. L. A Theory of the Origin of the State. *Science*, vol. 169, 733–738, 1970.

CARR, CHRISTOPHER, ed. *For Concordance in Archaeological Analysis: Bridging Data Structure, Quantitative Technique, and Theory*. Westport Publishers, Kansas City, 1985.

CARR, ROBERT F. and JAMES E. HAZARD. *Map of the Ruins of Tikal, El Peten, Guatemala*. University of Pennsylvania Museum Monographs, Tikal Report no. 11, 1961.

CARVER, JONATHAN. *Travels Through the Interior Parts of North America in the Years 1766, 1767, and 1768*. S. Price and R. Cross, Dublin, 1779.

CASANOVA, EDUARDO, The Cultures of the Puna and the Quebrada of Humuhuaca. In *Handbook of South American Indians*, Julian H. Steward, ed., vol. 2, 619–632. Bureau of American Ethnology, Bulletin 143. Washington, D. C., 1946.

CASAS, BARTOLOMÉDE LAS. *Apologética Historia de las Indias*, M. Serrano y Sanz, ed. Bailliere, Madrid, 1909.

————. *Historia de las Indias.* Gonzalo de Paparaz, ed., 3 vols. M. Aguilar, Madrid, 1927.

————. *Apologética Historia Sumaria,* edition prepared by Edmundo O'Gorman. Madrid, 1967.

CASO, ALFONSO. *Exploraciones en Oaxaca, Quinta y Sexta Temporadas, 1936–1937.* Pan American Institute of Geography and History, Publication 34. Tacubaya, Mexico, 1938.

————. Calendario y Escritura de las antiguas culturas de Monte Alban. In *Obras Completas de Miguel Othón de Mendizábal.* Talleres Gráficos de la Nación, D. F., Mexico, 1946.

CASTELNAU, FRANCIS DE. *Expédition dans les parties centrales de l'Amérique du Sud, troisieme partie: Antiquités des Incas et autres peuples anciens.* Bertrand, Paris, 1854.

CATHERWOOD, FREDERICK. *View of Ancient Monuments in Central America, Chiapas, and Yucatan.* Vizetally, London, 1844.

CHANG, KWANG-CHIH. Study of the Neolithic Social Grouping: Examples from the New World. *American Anthropologist,* vol. 60, no. 2, 298–334, 1958.

————. *Rethinking Archaeology.* Random House, New York, 1967a.

————. Major Aspects of the Interrelationship of Archaeology and Ethnology. *Current Anthropology,* vol. 18, no. 3, 227–243, 1967b.

————. Toward a Science of Prehistoric Society. In *Settlement Archaeology,* K. C. Chang, ed., 1–9. National Press Books, Palo Alto, 1968.

CHANG, KWANG-CHIH, ed. *Settlement Archaeology.* National Press Books, Palo Alto, 1968.

CHAPMAN, ROBERT, IAN KINNAS, and KLAUS RANDSBERG, eds. *The Archaeology of Death,* New Directions in Archaeology. Cambridge University Press, Cambridge, 1981.

CHARD, CHESTER S. The Old World Roots: Review and Speculations. *University of Alaska Anthropological Papers,* vol. 10, no. 2, 115–121. College, 1963.

CHARLTON, T. H. Teotihuacan, Tepeapulco, and Obsidian Exploitation. *Science,* vol. 200, no. 4247, 1227–1236, 1978.

CHARNAY, DÉSIRÉ. *The Ancient Cities of the New World.* Harper, New York, 1887.

CHILDE, V. GORDON. *The Most Ancient East.* Paul Kegan, London, 1934.

————. *Man Makes Himself.* Watts, London, 1936.

————. *What Happened in History.* Pelican Books, London and New York, 1943.

————. *Social Evolution.* Watts, London, 1951.

CHRISTENSON, A. and D. W. READ. Numerical Taxonomy, R-mode Factor Analysis, and Archaeological Classification. *American Antiquity,* vol. 42, 163–179, 1977.

CIGLIANO, E. M. *El Ampajanguense,* Instituto de Antropologia, Rosario, Universidad Nacional de Litoral, 1962.

CLAASSEN, CHERYL, ed. *Exploring Gender Through Archaeology.* Monographs in World Archaeology, No. 11. Prehistory Press, Madison, 1992.

CLAESSEN, H. J. M. and P. SKALNIK, eds. *The Early State.* Mouton, The Hague, 1978.

CLARK, G. A. More on Contingency Table Analysis, Decision Making Criteria and the Use of Log Linear Models. *American Antiquity,* vol. 41, 259–273, 1976.

CLARK, J. GRAHAME D. *The Mesolithic Settlement of Northern Europe.* Cambridge University Press, Cambridge, 1936.

————. *Archaeology and Society.* Methuen, London, 1939.

————. *Prehistoric England.* S. Batsford, London, 1940.

————. *Prehistoric Europe: The Economic Basis.* Methuen, London, 1952 (reprinted 1972).

————. The Economic Approach to Prehistory. *Proceedings of the British Academy,* vol. 39, 215–238, 1953.

————. *Excavations at Starr Carr.* Cambridge University Press, Cambridge, 1954.

CLARKE, DAVID L. *Analytical Archaeology.* Methuen, London, 1968.

————. Reply to the Comments on *Analytical Archaeology. Norwegian Archaeological Review,* vol. 34, nos. 3–4, 25–34. 1970.

CLARKE, DAVID L., ed. *Models in Archaeology.* Methuen, London, 1972.

————. *Spatial Archaeology.* Academic Press, London, 1977.

CLAVIJERO, FRANCISCO J. *The History of Mexico,* translated by Charles Cullen. Thomas Dobson, Philadelphia, 1817.

CLELAND, CHARLES E. *The Prehistoric Animal Ecology and Ethnology of the Upper Great Lakes Region.* University of Michigan Museum Anthropological Papers, no. 29. Ann Arbor, 1966.

CLEWLOW, C. WILLIAM and ALEŠ HRDLIČKA Some Thoughts on the Background of Early Man. *Kroeber Anthropological Society Papers*, vol. 42, 26–46, 1970.

CLINTON, DE WITT. *A Memoir on the Antiquities of the Western Parts of the State of New York*. E. and E. Hosford, Albany, 1820.

COE, JOFFRE L. *The Formative Cultures of the Carolina Piedmont*. Transactions, American Philosophical Society, vol. 54, pt. 5. Philadelphia, 1964.

COE, MICHAEL D. *Mexico*. Thames and Hudson, London and New York, 1962.

———. *The Maya*. Thames and Hudson, London and New York, 1966.

———. San Lorenzo and the Olmec Civilization. *Proceedings, Dumbarton Oaks Conference on the Olmec*, 41–78. Washington, D. C., 1968a.

———. *America's First Civilization*. American Heritage, New York, 1968b.

COE, MICHAEL D. and CLAUDE F. BAUDEZ. The Zoned Bichrome Period in Northwestern Costa Rica. *American Antiquity*, vol. 26, no. 4, 505–515, 1961.

COE, MICHAEL D. and KENT V. FLANNERY. Microenvironments and Mesoamerican Prehistory. *Science*, vol. 143, no. 3607, 650–654, 1964.

———. *Early Cultures and Human Ecology in South Coastal Guatemala*, Smithsonian Contributions to Anthropology, vol. 3. Washington, D. C., 1967.

COE, WILLIAM R. Environmental Limitation on Maya Culture: A Reexamination. *American Anthropologist*, vol 59, 328–335, 1957.

———. Tikal: Ten Years of Study of a Maya Ruin in the Lowlands of Guatemala. *Expedition*, vol. 8, no. 1, 50–56, 1965.

COGGINS, CLEMENCY. A New Order and the Role of the Calendar: Some Characteristics of the Middle Classic Period at Tikal. In *Maya Archaeology and Ethnohistory*, N. Hammond and G. R. Willey, eds., 38–50. University of Texas Press, Austin, 1979.

COHEN, M. N. Population Presence and the Origins of Agriculture: An Archaeological Example from the Coast of Peru. In *Origins of Agriculture*, C. A. Reed, ed., 135–177. Mouton, The Hague, 1977a.

———. *The Food Crisis in Prehistory*. Yale University Press, New Haven, 1977b.

———. Archaeological Plant Remains from the Central Coast of Peru. *Ñawpa Pacha*, vol. 16, 23–51, 1978.

COHEN, RONALD and ELMAN R. SERVICE, eds. *Origins of the State, the Anthropology of Political Evolution*. Institute for the Study of Human Issues, Philadelphia, 1978.

COLE, FAY-COOPER and THORNE DEUEL. *Rediscovering Illinois*. University of Chicago Publications in Anthropology. University of Chicago Press, Chicago, 1937.

COLLIER, DONALD. *Cultural Chronology and Change as Reflected in the Ceramics of the Virú Valley, Peru*. Chicago Natural History Museum, Fieldiana: Anthropology, vol. 43. Chicago, 1955.

COLLINGWOOD, R. G. *The Idea of History*. Oxford University Press, Oxford, 1946.

COLLINS, HENRY B., JR. Potsherds from Choctaw Village Sites in Mississippi. *Journal of the Washington Academy of Sciences*, vol. 17, no. 10, 259–263, 1927.

———. *Archaeology of St. Lawrence Island, Alaska*. Smithsonian Miscellaneous Collections, vol. 96, no. 1. Washington, D. C., 1937.

———. Outline of Eskimo Prehistory. *Essays in Historical Anthropology*. Smithsonian Miscellaneous Collections, vol. 100, 533–592. Washington, D. C., 1940.

COLTON, HAROLD S. and LYNDON L. HARGRAVE. *Handbook of Northern Arizona Pottery Wares*. Museum of Northern Arizona Bulletin, no. 11. Flagstaff, 1937.

CONKEY, MARGARET W. Boundaries in Art and Society. In *Symbolic and Structural Archaeology*, I. Hodder, ed., 15–128. Cambridge University Press, Cambridge, 1982.

CONKEY, MARGARET W. and JOAN M. GERO. Tensions, Pluralities, and Engendering Archaeology: An Introduction to Women and Prehistory. In *Engendering Archaeology: Women and Prehistory*, J. M. Gero and M. W. Conkey, eds., 3–30. Basil Blackwell, London, 1991.

CONKEY, MARGARET W. and JANET SPECTOR. Archaeology and the Study of Gender. In *Advances in Archaeological Method and Theory*, vol. 7, M. B. Schiffer, ed., 1–38. Academic Press, New York, 1984.

COOK DE LEONARD, CARMEN, ed. *Esplendor del México antiguo*, 2 vols. Centro de Investigaciiones Anthropologicos de Mexico, Mexico, D.F., 1959.

COOK, ROBERT M. Archaeomagnetism. In *Science in Ar-*

chaeology, revised edition, D. Brothwell and E. Higgs, eds., 76–87. Basic Books, New York, 1969.

COOK, SHERBURNE F. A Reconsideration of Shell-mounds with Respect to Population and Nutrition. *American Antiquity*, vol. 12, no. 1, 50–53, 1946.

———. Physical Analysis as a Method for Investigating Prehistoric Habitation Sites. *University of California Archaeological Survey Reports*, no. 7, 2–5. Berkeley, 1950.

———. Dating Prehistoric Bone by Chemical Analysis. In *Viking Fund Publications in Anthropology*, no. 28, 223–245. New York, 1960.

COOK, SHERBURNE F. and H. C. EZRA-COHN. An Evaluation of the Fluorine Dating Method. *Southwestern Journal of Anthropology*, vol. 15, no. 3, 276–290, 1959.

COOK, SHERBURNE F. and ROBERT F. HEIZER. Archaeological Dating by Chemical Analysis of Bone. *Southwestern Journal of Anthropology*, vol. 9, no. 2, 231–238, 1953.

CORDELL, LINDA S. Predicting Site Abandonment at Wetherill Mesa. *The Kiva*, vol. 40, no. 3, 189–202, 1975.

———. *Prehistory of the Southwest*. Academic Press, New York, 1984.

COURBIN, P. *What is Archaeology?* University of Chicago Press, Chicago, 1989.

COVARRUBIAS, MIGUEL. *Indian Art of Mexico and Central America*. Knopf, New York, 1957.

COWGILL, GEORGE L. Computer Applications in Archaeology. *American Federation of Information Processing Societies Conference Proceedings*, vol. 31, 331–337. Washington, D. C., 1967a.

———. Computers and Prehistoric Archaeology. In *Computers in Humanist Research*, E. A. Bowles, ed., 47–56. Prentice-Hall, Englewood Cliffs, N. J., 1967b.

———. Archaeological Applications of Factor, Cluster, and Proximity Analyses. *American Antiquity*, vol. 33, no. 3, 367–375, 1968.

———. Albert Spaulding and Archaeological Method and Theory. *American Antiquity*, vol. 42, no. 3, 325–330, 1977a.

———. The Trouble with Significance Tests and What We Can Do About It. *American Antiquity*, vol. 42, no. 3, 350–368, 1977b.

COWGILL, GEORGE L., JEFFREY H. ALTSCHUL, and REBECCA S. SLOAD. Spatial Analysis of Teotihuacan: A Mexican Metropolis. In *Intrasite Spatial Analysis in Archaeology*, H. J. Hietala, ed., 154–195. Cambridge University Press, Cambridge, 1984.

CRADER, DANA C. Slave Diet at Monticello. *American Antiquity*, vol. 55, 690–717, 1990.

CRAWFORD O. G. S. The Distribution of Early Bronze Age Settlements in Britain. *Geographical Journal*, vol. 40, no. 3, 183–217. London, 1912.

———. *Man and His Past*. Oxford University Press, London, 1921.

CRESSMAN, LUTHER S. Man in the World. In *Man, Culture, and Society*, H. L. Shapiro, ed., 139–167. Oxford University Press, New York, 1956.

CRESSMAN, LUTHER S. and others. *Cultural Sequences at the Dalles, Oregon*. Transactions, American Philosophical Society, vol. 50, pt. 10. Philadelphia, 1960.

CRONE, GERALD. R. *The Discovery of America*. New York, 1969.

CRUMLEY, CAROLE L. A Dialectical Critique of Hierarchy. In *Power Relations and State Formation*. T. C. Patterson and C. W. Gailey, eds., 155–169. Archaeology Section, American Anthropological Association, Washington, D.C., 1987.

CULBERT, T. P., ed. *Classic Maya Political History*. Cambridge University Press, Cambridge, 1991.

CULBERT, T. P. and D. S. RICE, eds. *Precolumbian Maya Population History*. University of New Mexico Press, Albuquerque, 1990.

CUMMINGS BYRON. The Ancient Inhabitants of the San Juan Valley. *Bulletin of the University of Utah*, vol. 3, no. 3, pt. 2. Salt Lake City, 1910.

CUSHING, FRANK H. A Study of Pueblo Pottery as Illustrative of Zuñi Culture Growth. *Bureau of American Ethnology, Fourth Annual Report*, 467–521. Washington, D. C., 1886.

———. Preliminary Notes on the Origin, Working Hypothesis and Primary Researches of the Hemenway . . . Expedition. *Seventh International Congress of Americanists*, 151–194. Berlin, 1890.

DALL, WILLIAM H. On Succession in the Shell-Heaps of the Aleutian Islands. In *Contributions to North American Ethnology*, vol. 1, 41–91. U. S. Department of the Interior, Washington, D. C., 1877.

DANIEL, GLYN E. *A Hundred Years of Archaeology*. Duckworth, London, 1950.

———. *The Idea of Prehistory*. Penquin Books, Harmondsworth, England, 1964.

———. *The Origins and Growth of Archaeology*. Penguin Books, Harmondsworth, England, 1967.

———. One Hundred Years of Old World Prehistory. In *One Hundred Years of Anthropology*, J. O. Brew, ed., 57–96. Harvard University Press, Cambridge, Mass., 1968.

DARRAH, WILLIAM C. *Powell of the Colorado*. Princeton University Press, Princeton, 1951.

DAWSON, J. W. *Fossil Men and Their Modern Representatives*. Dawson Brothers, Montreal, 1880.

DEAGAN, KATHLEEN. *Spanish St. Augustine: The Archaeology of a Colonial Creole Community*. Academic Press, New York, 1983.

DEBENEDETTI, SALVADOR. Exploración arqueológica en los cementerios prehistoricos de la Isla de Tilcara. *Revista de la Universidad de Buenos Aires*, vol. 6, 1910.

———. Influencias de la cultura de Tiahuanaco en la region del noroeste Argentino. *Revista de la Universidad de Buenos Aires*, vol. 17, 326–352, 1912.

DEETZ, JAMES J. F. *An Archaeological Approach to Kinship Change in Eighteenth Century Arikara Culture*. Ph. D. dissertation, Harvard University, Cambridge, Mass., 1960.

———. Archaeological Investigations at La Purisima Mission. *Annual Reports of the University of California Archaeological Survey*, vol. 5, 161–244. Los Angeles, 1962–63.

———. *The Dynamics of Stylistic Change in Arikara Ceramics*. University of Illinois Series in Anthropology, no. 4. Urbana, 1965.

———. The Inference of Residence and Descent Rules from Archaeological Data. In *New Perspectives in Archaeology*, S. R. Binford and L. R. Binford, eds., 41–49. Aldine, Chicago, 1968a.

———. Late Man in North America: Archaeology of European Americans. In *Anthropological Archaeology in the Americas*, B. J. Meggers, ed., 121–130. Washington, D. C., 1968b.

———. *In Small Things Forgotten: The Archaeology of Early American Life*. Anchor Press, Garden City, 1977.

DEETZ, JAMES J. F. and EDWIN DETHLEFSEN. The Doppler Effect and Archaeology: A Consideration of the Spatial Aspects of Seiation. *Southwestern Journal of Anthropology*, vol. 21, 196–206, 1965.

———. Some Social Aspects of New England Colonial Mortuary Art. In *Approaches to the Social Dimensionsllll of Mortuary Practices*, J. A. Brown, ed. Society for American Archaeology, Memoir 25, 30–38. Washington, D.C., 1971.

DEGARMO, G. D. Identification of Prehistoric Intrasettlement Exchange. In *Exchange Systems in Prehistory*, T. K. Earle and J. E. Ericson, eds., 153–170. Academic Press, New York, 1977.

DEJARNETTE, D. L. and S. B. WIMBERLY. *The Bessemer Site*. Geological Survey of Alabama, Museum Paper 17. University of Alabama, Tuscaloosa, 1941.

DELORIA, VINE, JR. *Custer Died for Your Sins: An Indian Manifesto*. Macmillan, London, 1969.

DEL RIO, ANTONIO and PAUL F. CABRERA. *Description of the Ruins of an Ancient City, Discovered near Palenque, in the Kingdom of Guatemala, in Spanish America;* followed by *Teatro Critico Americano*. London, 1822.

DERBY, ORVILLE A. Artificial Mounds of the Island of Marajó, Brazil. *American Naturalist*, vol. 13, no. 4, 224ff, 1879.

DETHLEFSEN, EDWIN and JAMES J. F. DEETZ. Death's Heads, Cherubs, and Willow Trees: Experimental Archaeology in Colonial Cemeteries. *American Antiquity*, vol. 31, no. 4, 502–511, 1966.

DEUEL, THORNE. Basic Cultures of the Mississippi Valley. *American Anthropologist*, vol. 37, no. 3, 429–445, 1935.

DEXTER, RALPH W. Contributions of Frederic Ward Putnam to Ohio Archaeology. *Ohio Journal of Science*, vol. 65, no. 3, 110–117, 1965.

———. Frederick Ward Putnam and the Development of Museums of Natural History and Anthropology in the United States. *Curator*, vol. 9, no. 2, 151–155, 1966a.

———. Putnam's Problems Popularizing Anthropology. *American Scientist*, vol. 54, no. 3, 315–332, 1966b.

DILLEHEY, THOMAS D. *Paleoenvironment and Site Context. Monte Verde: A Late Pleistocene Settlement in Chile*, vol. 1. Smithsonian Institution Press, Washington, D. C., 1989.

DILLEHEY, THOMAS D. and DAVID J. MELTZER, eds. *The First Americans: Search and Research*. CRC Press, Boca Raton, Florida, 1991.

DINCAUZE, DENA. An Archaeo-logical Evaluation of

the Case for Pre-Clovis Occupations. In *Advances in World Archaeology*, Vol. 3, Fred Wendorf and Angela Close, eds., 275–323. Academic Press, New York, 1984.

DI PESO, CHARLES C. Cultural Development in Northern Mexico. In *Aboriginal Cultural Development in Latin America: An Interpretative Review*, B. J. Meggers and C. Evans, eds. Smithsonian Miscellaneous Collection, vol. 146, no. 1, 1–16. Washington, D. C., 1963.

DI PESO, CHARLES C. and others. *The Upper Pima of San Cayetano del Tumacacori: An Archaeological Reconstruction of the Ootam of Pimeria Alta*. Amerind Foundation, Publication 7. Dragoon, Ariz., 1956.

DISSELHOFF, HANS-DIETRICH. *Geschichte der Altamerikanischen Kulturen*, revised and enlarged edition. Oldenbourg, Munich, 1967.

DORAN, JAMES E. Systems Theory, Computer Simulations, and Archaeology. *World Archaeology*, vol. 1, no. 3, 829–898, 1970.

DORAN, JAMES E. and F. R. HODSON. *Mathematics and Computers in Archaeology*. Edinburgh University Press, Edinburgh, 1975.

DORSEY, G. A. Archaeological Investigations on the Island of La Plata, Ecuador. *Field Columbian Museum Archaeological Series*, vol. 22, no. 5, 245–280. Chicago, 1901.

DRAY, WILLIAM H. *Laws and Explanation in History*. Oxford University Press, Oxford, 1957.

———. *Philosophical Analysis and History*, W. H. Dray, ed. Harper & Row, New York, 1966.

———. *Philosophy of History*. Prentice-Hall, Englewood Cliffs, N. J., 1967.

DRENNAN, R. D. A Refinement of Chronological Seriation Using Nonmetric Multidimensional Scaling. *American Antiquity*, vol. 41, no. 3, 290–302, 1976.

———. Cultural Evolution, Human Ecology, and Empirical Research. In *Profiles in Cultural Evolution*. A. T. Rambo and K. Gillogly, eds., 113–136. Anthropological Papers, Museum of Anthropology, University of Michigan, Ann Arbor, 1991.

DRENNAN, R. D. and C. A. URIBE, eds. *Chiefdoms in the Americas*. University Press of America, Lanham, 1987.

DRUCKER, PHILLIP. *La Venta, Tabasco: A Study of Olmec Ceramics and Art*. Bureau of American Ethnology, Bulletin 153. Washington, D. C., 1952.

DRUCKER, PHILLIP, ROBERT F. HEIZER, and ROBERT J. SQUIER. *Excavations at La Venta, Tabasco, 1955*. Bureau of American Ethnology, Bulletin 170. Washington, D. C., 1959.

DUNNELL, ROBERT C. Seriation Method and Its Evaluation. *American Antiquity*, vol. 35, no. 3, 305–319, 1970.

———. Sabloff and Smith's "The Importance of Both Analytic and Taxonomic Classification in the Type-Variety System." *American Antiquity*, vol. 36, no. 1, 115–118, 1971.

———. Style and Function: A Fundamental Dichotomy. *American Antiquity*, vol. 43, no. 2, 192–202, 1978.

———. Evolutionary Theory and Archaeology. In *Advances in Archaeological Method and Theory*, vol. 3, M. B. Schiffer, ed., 62–74. Academic Press, New York, 1980.

———. Science, Social Science, and Common Sense: The Agonizing Dilemma of Modern Archaeology. *Journal of Anthropological Research*, vol. 38, 1–25, 1982.

———. The Concept of Progress in Cultural Evolution. In *Evolutionary Progress*, M. H. Nitecki, ed., 169–194. University of Chicago Press, Chicago, 1988.

———. Aspects of the Application of Evolutionary Theory in Archaeology. In *Archaeological Thought in America*, C. C. Lamberg-Karlovsky, ed., 35–49. Cambridge University Press, Cambridge, 1989a.

———. Philosophy of Science and Archaeology. In *Critical Traditions in Contemporary Archaeology: Essays in the Philosophy, History, and Socio-Politics of Archaeology*, V. Pinsky and A. Wylie, eds., 5–9. Cambridge University Press, Cambridge, 1989b.

———. Methodological Impacts of Catastrophic Depopulation on American Archaeology and Ethnology. In *Columbian Consequences*, vol. 3, D. H. Thomas, ed., 561–580. Smithsonian Institution Press, Washington, D. C., 1991.

DUPAIX, GUILLAUME. *Antiquités Mexicaines; relation des trois expéditions du Capitaine Dupaix, ordonnées en 1805, 1806, et 1807 . . . par MM. Baradère de St. Priest*. Paris, 1834.

DURÁN, FRAY DIEGO. *The Aztecs: The History of the Indies of New Spain*, translated by Doris Heyden and Fernando Hocasitas. Orion Press, New York, 1964.

EARLE, TIMOTHY K. Chiefdoms in Archaeological and Ethnohistorical Perspective. *Annual Review of Anthropology*, vol. 16, 279–308, 1987.

EARLE, TIMOTHY K., ed. *Chiefdoms: Power, Economy, and Ideology.* Cambridge University Press, Cambridge, 1991.

EARLE, TIMOTHY K. and J. E. ERICKSON, eds. *Exchange Systems in Prehistory.* Academic Press, New York, 1977.

EASTON, DAVID. *Framework for Political Analysis.* Prentice-Hall, Englewood Cliffs, N. J., 1965.

EKHOLM, GORDON F. Transpacific Contacts. In *Prehistoric Man in the New World,* J. D. Jennings and E. Norbeck, eds., 489–510. University of Chicago Press, Chicago, 1964.

ELVAS, GENTLEMAN OF. The Narrative of the Expedition of Hernando de Soto. In *Spanish Explorers in the Southern United States,* Theodore H. Lewis, ed., 127–272. Scribner's, New York, 1907.

EMERSON, THOMAS E. and R. BARRY LEWIS, eds. *Cahokia and the Hinterlands: Middle Mississippian Cultures of the Midwest.* University of Illinois Press, Urbana, 1991.

EMERY, F. E., ed. *Systems Thinking.* Penguin Books, New York, 1969.

EMORY, WILLIAM H. Notes of a Military Reconnaissance from Fort Leavenworth, in Missouri, to San Diego, in California, Including Parts of the Arkansas, Del Norte, and Gila Rivers. *30th Congress, 1st session, Senate Executive Docket 7.* Washington, D. C., 1848.

EMPERAIRE, JOSE M., ANNETTE LAMING-EMPERIRE, and HENRI REICHLEN. La grotte Feli et autres sites de la región volcanique de la Patagonie chilienne. *Journal de la Société des Américanistes*, vol. 52, 169–254, 1964.

ENGEL, FRÉDÉRIC. Le complexe préceramique d'El Paraiso (Pérou). *Journal de la Société des Américanistes*, vol. 55, no. 1, 43–96, 1967.

ESTRADA, EMILIO. *Ensayo preliminar sobre la arqueologia del Milagro, Guayaquil.* Publicaciones del Museo Victor Emilio Estrada. Guayaquil Ecuador, 1954.

———. *Prehistoria de Manabí.* Publicaciones del Museo Victor Emilio Estrada, no. 4. Guayaquil, 1957.

EULER, R. C. and G. J. GUMERMAN, eds. *Investigations of the Southwestern Anthropological Research Group: An Experiment in Archaeological Cooperation.* Museum of Northern Arizona, Flagstaff, 1978.

EVANS, CLIFFORD and B. J. MEGGERS. Formative Period Cultures in the Guayas Basin, Coastal Ecuador. *American Antiquity*, vol. 22, no. 3, 235–246, 1957.

———. *Archaeological Investigations in British Guiana,* Bureau of American Ethnology, Bulletin 177. Washington, D. C., 1960.

EVANS, FRANCIS C. Ecosystem as the Basic Unit in Ecology. *Science*, vol. 123, 1127–1128, 1956.

FAGAN, B. M. *Elusive Treasure: The Story of Early Archaeologists in the Americas,* Scribner's, New York, 1977.

FARABEE, WILLIAM C. Exploration at the Mouth of the Amazon, *Museum Journal of the University Museum,* vol. 12, no. 13, 142–161. Philadelphia, 1921.

FASH, W. L., JR. A New Look at Maya Statecraft from Copan, Honduras. *Antiquity*, vol. 62, 157–169, 1988.

FERDON, EDWIN N., JR. Agricultural Potential and the Development of Cultures. *Southwestern Journal of Anthropology*, vol. 15, 1–19, 1959.

FERGUSON, LELAND. *Uncommon Ground: Archaeology and Early African America, 1650–1800.* Smithsonian Institution Press, Washington, D. C., 1992.

FERNANDEZ, J. *Historia de la arqueologia Argentina.* Anales de Aqueologia y Etnologia, Universidad Nacional de Cuyo, vols. 34–35, Mendoza, 1982.

FEWKES, JESSE W. Anthropology. In *The Smithsonian Institution, 1846–1896,* G. B. Goode, ed., 745–72. Washington, D. C., 1897.

———. The Aborigines of Porto Rico and Neighboring Islands. *Bureau of American Ethnology, Twenth-fifth Annual Report.* Washington, D. C., 1907.

———. Casa Grande, Arizona. *Bureau of American Ethnology, Twenth-eighth Annual Report,* 35–179. Washington, D. C., 1912.

———. A Prehistoric Island Culture Area of America. *Bureau of American Ethnology, Thirty-fourth Annual Report,* 35–281. Washington, D. C., 1922.

FIEDEL, S. J. *Prehistory of the Americas.* Cambridge University Press, New York, 1987.

FIGGINS, JESSE D. The Antiquity of Man in America. *Natural History*, vol. 27, no. 3, 229–239, 1927.

FISH, S. K. and S. A. KOWALEWSKI, eds. *The Archaeology of Regions: A Case for Full Coverage Survey.* Smithsonian Institution Press, Washington, D. C., 1990.

FISK, H. N. *Summary of the Geology of the Lower Alluvial*

Valley of the Mississippi River. Mississippi River Commission, War Department, Corps of Engineers, Washington, D. C., 1944.

FITTING, JAMES E. Environmental Potential and the Post-Glacial Readaptation in Eastern North America. *American Antiquity,* vol. 33, no. 4, 441–445, 1968.

———. *The Archaeology of Michigan; A Guide to the Prehistory of the Great Lakes Region.* Garden City Press, Garden City, 1970.

FITTING, J. E., ed. *The Development of North American Archaeology.* Anchor Press-Doubleday, Garden City, N. Y., 1973.

FLANNERY, KENT V. The Ecology of Eary Food Production in Mesopotamia. *Science,* vol. 147, no. 3663, 1247–1256., 1965.

———. Culture History vs. Cultural Process: A Debate in American Archaeology. *Scientific American,* vol. 217, 119–122, 1967a.

———. Vertebrate Fauna and Hunting Patterns. in *The Prehistory of the Tehuacan Valley,* vol. 1, *Environment and Subsistence,* D. S. Byers, ed., 132–177. R. S. Peabody Foundation, Andover, Mass.; University of Texas Press, Austin, 1967b.

———. Archaeological Systems Theory and Early Mesoamerica. In *Anthropological Archaeology in the Americas,* B. J. Meggers, ed., 67–87. Washington, D. C., 1968a.

———. The Olmec and the Valley of Oaxaca: A Model for Inter-Regional Interaction in Formative Times. In *Dumbarton Oaks Conference on the Olmec,* E. P. Benson, ed., 79–110. Washington, D. C., 1968b.

———. Origins and Ecological Effects of Early Domestication in Iran and the Near East. In *The Domestication and Exploitation of Plants and Animals,* G. W. Dimbleby and P. J. Ucko, eds., 73–100. Aldine, Chicago, 1969.

———. The Cultural Evolution of Civilizations. *Annual Review of Ecology and Systematics,* vol. 3, 399–426. Palo Alto, 1972a.

———. Summary Comments: Evolutionary Trends in Social Exchange and Interaction. In *Social Exchange and Interaction,* E. N. Wilmsen, ed., 129–136. University of Michigan, Museum of Anthropology, Anthropological Papers, no. 46. Ann Arbor, 1972b.

———. The Origins of Agriculture. *Annual Review of Anthropology,* vol. 2, 271–310. Palo Alto, 1973.

———. The Golden Marshalltown: A Parable for the Archaeology of the 1980s. *American Anthropologist,* Vol. 84, 265–278, 1982.

FLANNERY, KENT V., ed. *The Early Mesoamerican Village.* Academic Press, New York, 1976.

———. *Guila Naquitz: Archaic Foraging and Early Agriculture in Oaxaca, Mexico.* Academic Press, Orlando, 1986.

FLANNERY, KENT V. and others. Farming Systems and Political Growth in Ancient Oaxaca. *Science,* vol. 158, no. 3800, 445–454, 1967.

FLANNERY, KENT V. and JOYCE MARCUS. Formative Oaxaca and the Zapotec Cosmos. *American Scientist,* vol. 64, no. 4, 374–383, 1976.

FLANNERY, K. V. and JOYCE MARCUS, eds. *The Cloud People: Divergent Evolution of the Zapotec and Mixtec Civilizations.* Academic Press, Orlando. 1983.

FLANNERY, K. V., JOYCE MARCUS, and S. A. KOWALEWSKI. The Preceramic and Formative of the Valley of Oaxaca. In *Supplement to the Handbook of Middle American Indians, Vol. 1: Archaeology,* V. R. Bricker and J. A. Sabloff, eds., pp. 48–93. University of Texas Press, Austin, 1981.

FLANNERY, KENT V. and JAMES SCHOENWETTER. Climate and Man in Formative Oaxaca. *Archaeology,* vol. 23, no. 2, 144–152, 1970.

FLEMING, S. *Dating in Archaeology: A Guide to Scientific Techniques.* St. Martin's Press, New York, 1976.

FORD, JAMES A. *Ceramic Decoration Sequence at an Old Indian Village Site, Near Sicily Island, Louisiana.* Anthropological Study no. 1, Department of Conservation, Louisiana State Geological Survey. New Orleans, 1935.

———. *Analysis of Indian Village Site Collections from Louisiana and Mississippi.* Anthropological Study no. 2, Department of Conservation, Louisiana State Geological Survey. New Orleans, 1936.

———. A Chronological Method Applicable to the Southeast. *American Antiquity,* vol. 3, no. 3, 260–264, 1938.

———. *Report of the Conference on Southeastern Pottery Typology,* mimeographed. Ceramic Repository, Museum of Anthropology, University of Michigan, Ann Arbor, 1938.

———. Cultural Dating of Prehistoric Sites in the Virú Valley, Peru. *Anthropological Papers of the*

American Museum of Natural History, vol. 43, pt. 1. New York, 1949.

———. Measurements of Some Prehistoric Design Developments in the Southeastern States. *Anthropological Papers of the American Museum of Natural History*, vol. 44, pt. 3. New York, 1952.

———. Letter, Spaulding's Review of Ford. *American Anthropologist*, vol. 56, 109–112, 1954a.

———. Comment on A. C. Spaulding, "Statistical Techniques for the Discovery of Artifact Types." *American Antiquity*, vol. 19, no. 4, 390–391, 1954b.

———. On the Concept of Types. *American Anthropologist*, vol. 56, 42–53, 1954c.

———. *A Quantitative Method for Deriving Cultural Chronology*, Pan American Union Technical Manual, no. 1. Washington, D. C., 1962.

———. *A Comparison of Formative Cultures in the Americas: Diffusion or the Psychic Unity of Man?*. Smithsonian Institution Contributions to Anthropology, vol. II. Washington, D. C., 1969.

FORD, JAMES A., PHILIP PHILLIPS, and WILLIAM G. HAAG. The Jaketown Site in West-Central Mississippi. *Anthropological Papers of the American Museum of Natural History*, vol. 45, pt. 1. New York, 1955.

FORD, JAMES A. and GORDON R. WILLEY. An Interpretation of the Prehistory of the Eastern United States. *American Anthropologist*, vol. 43, no. 3, 325–363, 1941.

———. The Virú Valley: Background and Problems. *Anthropological Papers of the American Museum of Natural History*, vol. 43, pt. 1. New York, 1949.

FÖRSTEMANN, ERNST W. Commentary on the Maya Manuscripts in the Royal Public Library of Dresden. *Papers of the Peabody Museum*, vol. 4, no. 2, 49–266. Cambridge, Mass., 1906.

FOSTER, JOHN W. *Prehistoric Races of the United States*. S. C. Griggs, Chicago, 1873.

FOWKE, GERARD. Stone Art. *Bureau of American Ethnology, Thirteenth Annual Report*, 47–184. Washington, D. C., 1896.

FOWLER, M. L. Cahokia: Ancient Capital of the Midwest. Addison-Wesley Module in Anthropology, no. 48, 3–38. Reading, Mass., 1974.

———. A Pre-Columbian Urban Center on the Mississippi. *Scientific American*, vol. 233, no. 2, 93–101, 1975.

———. Cahokia and the American Bottom: Settlement Archaeology. In *Mississippian Settlement Patterns*, B. D. Smith, ed., 455–478. Academic Press, New York, 1978.

———. *The Cahokia Atlas: A Historical Atlas of Cahokia Archaeology*. Studies in Illinois Archaeology, no. 6, Illinois Historic Preservation Agency, Springfield, 1989.

FOWLER, M. L., ed. *Explorations into Cahokia Archaeology*, Illinois Archaeological Survey, Bulletin no. 7. University of Illinois, Urbana, 1973.

FOWLER, M. L. and others. *Perspectives in Cahokia Archaeology*, Illinois Archaeological Survey, Bulletin no. 10. University of Illinois, Urbana, 1975.

FOX, CYRIL. *The Archaeology of the Cambridge Region*. Cambridge University Press, Cambridge, 1932.

———. The Personality of Britain. *Man*, vol. 32, 202ff., 1932.

FREEMAN, JOHN F. University Anthropology: Early Departments in the United States. *Papers of the Kroeber Anthropological Society*, vol. 32, 78–90. Berkeley, 1965.

FREEMAN, L. G., JR., and J. A. BROWN. Statistical Analysis of Carter Ranch Pottery. In *Chapters in the Prehistory of Eastern Arizona, II*, P. S. Martin and others, eds., 126–154. Chicago Museum of Natural History, Fieldiana: Anthropology, vol. 55. Chicago, 1964.

FRIED, M. H. *The Evolution of Political Society*. Random House, New York, 1967.

FRIEDMAN, I., R. L. SMITH, and D. CLARK. Obsidian Dating. In *Science in Archaeology*, revised edition, D. Brothwell and E. Higgs, eds., 62–75. Basic Books, New York, 1969.

FRISON, G. C., ed. *The Casper Site, a Hell Gap Bison Kill on the High Plains*. Seminar Press, New York, 1974.

FRITZ, GAYLE J. Multiple Pathways to Farming in Precontact Eastern North America. *Journal of World Prehistory*, vol. 4, 387–436, 1990.

FRITZ, JOHN M. Paleopsychology Today: Ideational Systems and Human Adaptation in Prehistory. In *Social Anthropology: Beyond Subsistence and Dating*, C. L. Redman et al, eds., 37–59. Academic Press, New York, 1978.

FRITZ, JOHN M. and FRED T. PLOG. The Nature of Archaeological Explanation. *American Antiquity*, vol. 35, no. 4, 405–412, 1970.

GALL, PATRICIA and A. A. SAXE. The Ecological Evolution of Culture: The State as Predator in Succession Theory. In *Exchange Systems and Prehistory*, T. Earle and J. Ericson, eds., 255–268. Academic Press, New York, 1977.

GALLATIN, ALBERT. A Synopsis of the Indian Tribes Within the United States East of the Rocky Mountains, in the British and Russian Possessions in North America. *Archaeologia Americana*, vol. 2, 1–422, 1836.

———. Notes on the Semi-Civilized Nations of Mexico, Yucatan, and Central America. *Transactions of the American Ethnological Society*, vol. 1. New York, 1845.

GAMIO, MANUEL. Arqueologia de Atzcapotzalco, D. F., Mexico. *Proceedings, Eighteenth International Congress of Americanists*, 180–187. London, 1913.

———. *La Poblacion del Valle de Teotihuacan*, 3 vols. Secretaria de Fomento, Mexico, 1922.

GANDARA, MANUEL. La vieja "nueva arqueologia." *Boletin de Antropología Americana*, vols. 2–3, 7–45 and 7–70, 1980–81.

GANDARA, MANUEL, FERNANDO LOPEZ, and IGNACIO RODRIQUEZ. Arqueología y Marxismo en Mexico. *Boletin de Antropología Americana*, vol. 11, 5–17, 1985.

GANN, THOMAS W. F. Mounds in Northern Honduras. *Bureau of American Ethnology, Nineteenth Annual Report*, pt. 2, 655–692. Washington, D. C., 1900.

GARCÍA DE PALACIO, DIEGO. Description de la province de Guatemala, Envoyée au Roi d'Espagne en 1576, par le licencié Palacios. In *Recueil de Documents et Mémoires Originaux sur l'Historie des Possesiones Espagnoles*, H. Ternaux-Compana, ed. Paris, 1840.

GARCILASO DE LA VEGA. *The Florida of the Inca: A History of the Adelantado, Hernando de Soto, Governor and Captain General of the Kingdom of Florida, and Other Heroic Spanish and Indian Cavaliers*, translated by John Grier Varner and Jeannette Johnson Varner. University of Texas Press, Austin, 1951.

———. *Royal Commentaries of the Incas*, 2 vols., translated with an Introduction by Harold V. Livermore. University of Texas Press, Austin, 1966.

GARDINER, PATRICK, ed. *Theories of History*. Free Press, Glencoe, Ill., 1959.

GAYTON, ANNA H. The Uhle Collections from Nieveria. *University of California Publications in American Archaeology and Ethnology*, vol. 21, no. 8, 305–329. Berkeley, 1927.

GAYTON, ANNA H. and ALFRED L. KROEBER. The Uhle Pottery Collections from Nazca. *University of California Publications in American Archaeology and Ethnology*, vol. 24, no. 1, 1–21. Berkeley, 1927.

GELFAND, ALAN E. Seriation Methods for Archaeological Materials. *American Antiquity*, vol. 36, no. 3, 263–274, 1971.

GERO, JOAN M. Socio-Politics and the Woman-at-Home Ideology. *American Antiquity*, vol. 50, no. 2, 342–350, 1985.

GERO, JOAN M. and MARGARET W. CONKEY, eds. *Engendering Archaeology: Women and Prehistory*. Basil Blackwell, London, 1991.

GIBBON, GUY. *Explanation in Archaeology*. Basil Blackwell, Oxford, 1989.

GIBBS, GEORGE. Instructions for Archaeological Investigations in the United States. *Smithsonian Institution Annual Report for 1861*, 392–396. Washington, D. C., 1862.

GIDDINGS, JAMES L. The Archaeology of Bering Strait. *Current Anthropology*, vol. 1, no. 2, 121–138. Chicago, 1960.

———. *The Archaeology of Cape Denbigh*. Brown University Press, Providence, 1964.

GIFFORD, EDWARD W. Composition of California Shellmounds. *University of California Publications in American Archaeology and Ethnology*, vol. 12, no. 1, 1–29. Berkeley, 1916.

GIFFORD, JAMES C. The Type-Variety Method of Ceramic Classification as an Indicator of Cultural Phenomena. *American Antiquity*, vol. 25, no. 31, 341–347, 1960.

GIFFORD-GONZALEZ, DIANE. Bones Are Not Enough: Analogues, Knowledge, and Interpretive Strategies in Zooarchaeology. *Journal of Anthropological Archaeology*, vol. 10, 215–254, 1991.

GILMAN, A. Marxism in American Archaeology. In *Archaeological Thought in America*, C. C. Lamberg-Karlovsky, ed., 63–73. Cambridge University Press, Cambridge, 1989.

GIVENS, DOUGLAS R. *Alfred Vincent Kidder and the Development of American Archaeology*. University of New Mexico Press, Albuquerque, 1992.

GLADWIN, HAROLD S. *Excavations at Casa Grande, Ari-*

zona. Papers of the Southwest Museum, no. 2. Los Angeles, 1928.

———. *Excavations at Snaketown,* vol. 2: Comparisons and Theories. Medallion Papers, no. 26. Globe, Ariz., 1937.

GLADWIN, HAROLD S. and others. *Excavations at Snaketown: Material Culture.* Medallion Papers, no. 25, vol. 1. Globe, Ariz., 1937.

GLADWIN, WINIFRED and HAROLD S. GLADWIN. *A Method for the Designation of Ruins in the Southwest.* Medallion Papers, no. 1. Pasadena, 1928a.

———. *The Use of Potsherds in an Archaeological Survey of the Southwest.* Medallion Papers, no. 2. Pasadena, 1928b.

———. *The Red-on-Buff Culture of the Gila Basin.* Medallion Papers, no. 31. Globe, 1929.

———. *A Method for the Designation of Southwestern Pottery Types.* Medallion Papers, no. 7. Globe, 1930.

———. *Some Southwestern Pottery Types. Series II.* Medallion Papers, no. 10, Globe, 1931.

———. *A Method for the Designation of Cultures and Their Variations.* Medallion Papers, no. 15. Globe, 1934.

———. *The Eastern Range of the Red-on-Buff Culture.* Medallion Papers, no. 16. Globe, 1935.

GLASSOW, M. A. Changes in the Adaptations of Southwestern Basketmakers: A Systems Perspective. In *Contemporary Archaeology, A Guide to Theory and Contributions,* M. P. Leone, ed., 289–303. Southern Illinois University Press, Carbondale, 1972.

GOELDI, EMILIO A. *Excavações archaeológicas en 1895, pt. 1. Memories do Museu Goeldi, Belém do Pará, Brazil, 1900.*

GOETZMANN, WILLIAM H. *Army Exploration in the American West, 1803–1863.* Yale University Press, New Haven, 1959.

———. *Exploration and Empire.* Knopf, New York, 1967.

GOGGIN, JOHN M. Cultural Traditions in Florida Prehistory. In *The Florida Indian and His Neighbors,* J. W. Griffin, ed., 13–44. Rollins College, Winter Park, 1949.

GOLDSCHMIDT, WALTER R. *Man's Way: A Preface to the Understanding of Human Society.* World, Cleveland, 1959.

GOLDSTEIN, LYNNE GAIL. *Mississippian Mortuary Practices: A Case Study of Two Cemeteries in the Lower Illinois Valley.* Northwestern University Archaeology Program, Evanston, 1980.

GONZALEZ, ALBERTO R. La Estratigrafia de la Gruta de Intihuasi (Prov. de San Luis, R. A.) y sus relaciones con otros sitios precerámicos de Sudamérica. *Revista del Instituto de Antropología,* vol. 1, 5–302. Córdoba, 1960.

———. The La Aguada Culture of Northwestern Argentina. In *Essays in Precolumbian Art and Archaeology,* S. K. Lothrop and others, eds., 389–420. Harvard University Press, Cambridge, 1961.

———. Cultural Development in Northwestern Argentina. In *Aboriginal Cultural Development in Latin America: An Interpretative Review,* B. J. Meggers and C. Evans, eds. Smithsonian Miscellaneous Collection, vol. 1240, no. 1, 103–118. Washington, D. C., 1963.

GONZÁLEZ SUÁREZ, FEDÉRICO. *Estudio histórico sobre los Cañaris, antiguos habitantes de la provincia del Azuay, en la Republica del Ecuador.* Imprenta del Clero, Quito, 1878.

———. *Los aborigenes de Imbabura y del Carchi.* Tipografia Salesiana, Quito, 1910.

GOODMAN, JOSEPH T. The Archaic Maya Inscriptions. In *Biologia Centrali Americana,* A. P. Maudslay, ed., pt. 8, Appendix to vol. 1. Porter and Dulau, London, 1897.

———. Maya Dates. *American Anthropologist,* vol. 7, 642–647, 1905.

GOODYEAR, A. C., L. M. RAAB, T. C. KLINGER. The Status of Archaeological Research Design in Cultural Resource Management. *American Antiquity,* vol. 43, no. 2, 159–173, 1978.

GORDON, GEORGE B. *Prehistoric Ruins of Copan, Honduras.* Memoirs of the Peabody Museum, Harvard University, vol. 10. Cambridge, Mass., 1896.

———. *The Hieroglyphic Stairway; Ruins of Copan.* Memoirs of the Peabody Museum, Harvard University, vol. 1, no. 6. Cambridge, Mass., 1902.

GORENSTEIN, SHIRLEY. History of American Archaeology. In *Perspectives on Anthropology.* American Anthropologiccal Association Special Publication, no. 10. Washington, D.C., 1976.

GOULD, R. A. *Living Archaeology.* Cambridge University Press, Cambridge, 1980.

GOULD, R. A. and P. J. WATSON. A Dialogue on the Meaning and Use of Analogy in Ethnoarchaeological Reasoning. *Journal of Anthropological Archaeology,* vol. 1, 355–381, 1982.

GRAEBNER, FRITZ. *Methode der Ethnologie.* Winter's Universitätsbuchhandlung, Heidelberg, 1911.

GRAHAM, IAN. Juan Galindo, Enthusiast. *Estudios de Cultura Maya,* vol. 3, 11–36. Mexico, D.F., 1963.

———. Introduction and Catalogue. In *The Art of Maya Hieroglyphic Writing.* Peabody Museum, Cambridge, Mass., 1971.

———. Lord Kingsborough, Sir Thomas Phillips, and Obadiah Rich: Some Biographical Notes. In *Social Process in Maya Prehistory,* N. Hammond, ed., 45–57. Academic Press, London, 1977.

GRAHAM, JOHN A. George C. Engerrand in Mexico, 1907–1917. *Bulletin of Texas Archaeological Society,* vol. 32, 19–31. 1962.

GRAYSON, D. K. Eoliths, Archaeological Ambiguity, and the Generation of "Middle-Range" Research. In *American Archaeology Past and Future,* D. J. Meltzer, D. D. Fowler, and J. A. Sabloff, eds., 135–162. Smithsonian Institution Press, Washington, D.C., 1986.

GREEN, ERNESTINE L., ed. *Ethics and Values in Archaeology.* Free Press, New York, 1984.

GREEN, SALLY. *Prehistorian: A Biography of V. Gordon Childe.* Moonraker Press, Bradford-on-Avon, England, 1981.

GRIFFIN, JAMES. B. *The Fort Ancient Aspect: Its Cultural and Chronological Position in Mississippi Valley Archaeology.* University of Michigan Press, Ann Arbor, 1943.

———. Culture Change and Continuity in Eastern United States. In *Man in Northeastern North America,* F. Johnson, ed., 37–95. R. S. Peabody Foundation, Andover, Mass., 1946.

———. The Study of Early Cultures. In *Man, Culture, and Society,* H. L. Shapiro, ed., 22–48. Oxford University Press, New York, 1956.

———. The Pursuit of Archaeology in the United States. *American Archaeologist,* vol. 61, 379–88, 1959.

———. Some Prehistoric Connections Between Siberia and America. *Science,* vol. 131, no. 3403, 801–812, 1960.

———. Eastern North American Archaeology: A Summary. *Science,* vol. 156, no. 3772, 175–191, 1967.

GRIFFIN, JAMES B., ed. *Essays on Archaeological Methods.* Anthropological Papers of Anthropology, no. 8. Ann Arbor, 1951.

———. *Archaeology of Eastern United States.* University of Chicago Press, Chicago, 1952.

GROOD, HUGO DE. *Desertatio de Origini Gentium Americanarum.* Amsterdam and Paris, 1643.

GRUBER, J. W. Review of *A History of Archaeological Thought* by B. D. Trigger. *Science,* vol. 251, 1116–1117, 1991.

GUAMAN POMA DE AYALA, FELIPE. *Nueva corónica y buen gobierno,* 1613 [original manuscript in the Kongelige Bibliothek, Copenhagen; also published in *Travaux et Memoires,* vol. 23, Institut d'Ethnologie, Paris, 1936].

GUIDON, N. Las unidades culturales de São Raimundo Nonato—sudeste del Estado Piaui, Brasil. In *New Evidence for the Pleistocene Peopling of the Americas,* A. L. Bryan, ed., 157–171. Center for the Study of the First Americans, University of Maine, Orono, 1986.

GUMERMAN, G. J. The Reconciliation of Theory and Method in Archaeology. In *Conservation Archaeology: A Guide for Cultural Resource Management Studies,* M. Schiffer and G. Gumerman, eds., 97–106. Academic Press, New York, 1977.

GUMERMAN, G. J. and D. A. PHILLIPS, JR. Archaeology Beyond Anthropology. *American Antiquity,* vol. 43, no. 2, 184–192, 1978.

HAAG, WILLIAM G. Recent Work by British Archaeologists. *Annals of the Association oof American Geographers,* vol. 43, 298–303, 1957.

———. The Status of Evolutionary Theory in American Archaeology. In *Evolution and Anthropology: A Centennial Appraisal,* 90–105. Anthropological Society of Washington, Washington, D.C., 1959.

———. Twenty-five Years of Eastern Archaeology. *American Antiquity,* vol. 27, no. 1, 16–23, 1961.

———. Federal Aid to Archaeology in the Southeast, 1933–1942. *American Antiquity,* vol. 50, 272–280, 1985.

HAAS, JONATHAN. *The Evolution of the Prehistoric State.* Columbia University Press, New York, 1982.

HABERLAND, WOLFGANG. *Archaeologische Untersuchungen in Südost-Costa Rica.* Acta Humboldtiana, Series Geographia et Ethnographica, no. 1. Wiesbaden, 1959.

———. Die Kulturen Meso-und Zentral-Amerikas. In *Handbuch der Kulturgeschichte*, 3–192. Frankfurt, 1969.

HAGEN, VICTOR VON. *Maya Explorer: John Lloyd Stephens and the Lost Cities of Central America and Yuctán.* University of Oklahoma Press, Norman, 1947.

HAGGETT, PETER. *Locational Analysis in Human Geography.* St. Martin's Press, London, 1965.

HALL, E. T. Dating Pottery by Thermoluminescence. In *Science in Archaeology*, revised edition, D. Brothwell and E. Higgs, eds., 106–108. Basic Books, New York, 1969.

HALL, R. L. *Some Problems of Identity and Process in Cahokia Archaeology.* Paper presented at a Symposium on Mississippian Cultural Development, 1974.

———. Cahokia Identity and Interaction Models of Cahokia Missippian. In *Cahokia and the Hinterlands: Middle Mississippian Cultures of the Midwest*, T. E. Emerson and R. B. Lewis, eds., 3–34. University of Illinois Press, Urbana, 1991.

HALLOWELL, A. I. The Beginnings of Anthropology in America. In *Selected Papers from the American Anthropologist, 1888–1920*, Frederica de Laguna, ed., 1–90. American Anthropological Association, Evanston, 1960.

HAMMOND, NORMAN. The Distribution of Late Classic Maya Major Ceremonial Centres in the Central Area. In *Mesoamerican Archaeology – New Approaches*, Norman Hammond, ed., 313–335. Duckworth, London, 1974.

HANKE, LEWIS. *The Spanish Struggle for Justice in the Conquest of America.* University of Pennsylvania Press, Philadelphia, 1949.

———. *Bartolomé de las Casas: An Interpretation of His Life and Writings.* M. Nijhoff, The Hague, 1951.

HARDESTY, DONALD L. The Ecosystem Model, Human Energetics and the Analysis of Environmental Relations. *The Western Canadian Journal of Archaeology*, vol. 2, no. 2, 1–17. Edmonton, 1971.

HARGRAVE, LYNDON L. *Guide to Forty Pottery Types from Hopi Country and the San Francisco Mountains, Arizona.* Museum of Northern Arizona, Bulletin 1. Flagstaff, 1932.

HARPENDING, H. C. Review of *Mathematics and Computers in Archaeology* by J. E. Doran and F. R. Hodson. *Journal of Anthropological Research*, vol. 33, 352–353, 1977.

HARRIS, D. R. The Prehistory of Tropical Agriculture: An Ethnoecological Model. In *The Explanation of Culture Change: Models in Prehistory*, A. C. Renfrew, ed., 391–418. Duckworth, London, 1973.

HARRIS, MARVIN. *The Rise of Anthropological Theory.* Crowell, New York, 1968.

———. *Cultural Materialism: The Struggle for a Science of Culture.* Random House, New York, 1979.

HARRIS, THADDEUS M. *The Journal of a Tour into the Territory Northwest of the Alleghany Mountains; Made in the Spring of the Year 1805.* Manning and Loring, Boston, 1805.

HARRISON, P. D. and B. L. TURNER II, eds. *Pre-Hispanic Maya Agriculture.* University of New Mexico Press, Albuquerque, 1978.

HARRISON, WILLIAM H. A Discourse on the Aborigines of the Ohio Valley. In *Transactions of the Historical and Philosophical Society of Ohio*, vol. 1, pt. 2. Cincinnati, 1839.

HARTMAN, CARL V. *Archaeological Researches in Costa Rica.* Royal Ethnological Museum, Stockholm, 1901.

———. *Archaeological Researches on the Pacific Coast of Costa Rica.* Memoirs of the Carnegie Museum, vol. 3, no. 1. Pittsburgh, 1907.

HARTT, CHARLES F. The Ancient Indian Pottery of Marajó, Brazil. *American Naturalist*, vol. 5, 259–271, 1871.

HARVEY, DAVID. *The Condition of Postmodernity: An Enquiry into the Origin of Culture Change.* Basil Blackwell, Oxford, 1989.

HASTORF, CHRISTINE A. Gender, Space, and Food in Prehistory. In *Engendering Archaeology: Women and Prehistory*, J. M. Gero and M. W. Conkey, eds., 132–159. Basil Blackwell, London, 1991.

HASTORF, CHRISTINE A. and S. JOHANNESSEN. Understanding Changing People/Plant Relationships in the Prehispanic Andes. In *Processual and Postprocessual Archaeologies: Multiple Ways of Knowing the Past*, R. Preucel, ed., 140–155. Center for Archaeological Investigations, Southern Illinois University, Occasional Paper no. 10. Carbondale, 1991.

HAURY, EMIL W. *Roosevelt: 9 : 6, a Hohokam Site of the Colonial Period.* Medallion Papers, no. 11. Globe, 1932.

———. *The Canyon Creek Ruin . . . of the Sierra Ancha.* Medallion Papers, no. 14. Globe, 1934.

———. *The Mogollon Culture of Southwestern New Mexico.* Medallion Papers, no. 20. Globe, 1936a.

———. Some Southwestern Pottery Types, Series IV. Medallion Papers, no. 19. Globe, 1936b.

———. *Excavation in the Forestdale Valley, East-Central Arizona.* University of Arizona Social Science Bulletin, no. 12. Tucson, 1940.

HAURY, EMIL W. and others. *The Stratigraphy and Archaeology of Ventana Cave.* University of Arizona Press, Albuquerque and Tucson, 1950.

HAVEN, SAMUEL F. *Archaeology of the United States.* Smithsonian Contributions to Knowledge, vol. 8, art. 2. Washington, D.C., 1856.

HAVILAND, W. A. *Maya Settlement Patterns: A Critical Review.* Middle American Research Institute, Publication 26. Tulane University, New Orleans, 1966.

———. A New Population Estimate for Tikal, Guatemala. *American Antiquity,* vol. 34, no. 4, 429–433, 1969.

———. Tikal, Guatemala and Mesoamerican Urbanism. *World Archaeology,* vol. 2, no. 2, 186–199, 1970.

HAWKES, C. F. C. Archaeological Theory and Method: Some Suggestions from the Old World. *American Anthropologist,* vol. 56, no. 1, 155–168, 1954.

HAY, CLARENCE L. and others. *The Maya and Their Neighbors.* Appleton-Century, New York, 1940.

HAYDEN, BRIAN and A. CANNON. Where the Garbage Goes: Refusal Disposal in the Maya Highlands. *Journal of Anthropological Archaeology,* vol. 2, 117–163, 1983.

HAYDEN, BRIAN and MARGARET NELSON. The Use of Chipped Lithic Material in the Contemporary Maya Highlands. *American Antiquity,* vol. 46, 885–898, 1981.

HAYNES, C. VANCE, JR. Fluted Projectile Points: Their Age and Dispersion. *Science,* vol. 145, no. 3639, 1408–1413, 1964.

———. Carbon-14 Dates and Early Man in the New World. In *Pleistocene Extinctions; the Search for a Cause,* P. S. Martin and H. E. Wright, Jr., eds., 267–268. Proceedings of the Seventh Congress of the International Association for Quartenary Research, vol. 6. Yale University Press, New Haven, 1967.

HAYNES, HENRY W. The Prehistoric Archaeology of North America. In *Narrative and Critical History of America,* Justin Winsor, ed. Houghton Mifflin, Boston, 1889.

———. Progress of American Archaeology During the Past Ten Years. *Journal of the Archaeological Institute of America,* ser. 2, vol. 4, 17–39, 1900.

HAYWOOD, JOHN. *The Natural and Aboriginal History of Tennessee, Up to the First Settlements Therein by the White People, in the Year 1768.* Nashville, 1823.

HEART, JONATHAN. Account of Some Remains of Ancient Work on the Muskingun, with a Plan of these Works. *Columbian Magazine,* vol. 1, 425–427, 1787.

———. Observations on the Ancient Mounds. In *Topographical Description of the Western Territory,* Gilbert Imlay, ed. Debrett, London, 1792.

HEINE-GELDERN, ROBERT VON. Die Asiatische Herkunft, der Südamerikanischen Metalltechnik. *Paideuma,* vol. 5, 347–423, 1954.

———. Representations of the Asiatic Tiger in the Art of the Chavin Culture: A Proof of Early Contacts Between China and Peru. *Actas del 33rd Congreso Internacional de Americanistas,* 321–326. San José, 1959a.

———. Chinese Influence in Mexico and Central America: The Tajin Style of Mexico and the Marble Vases from Honduras. *Actas del 33rd Congreso Internacional de Americanistas,* 207–210. San Jose, 1959b.

———. The Problem of Transpacific Influences in Mesoamerica. In *Handbook of Middle America Indians,* R. Wauchope and others, eds., vol. 4, 277–297. University of Texas Press, Austin, 1966.

HEIZER, ROBERT F. The Direct-Historical Approach in California Archaeology. *American Antiquity,* vol. 7, no. 2, 98–122ff., 1941.

———. Preliminary Report on the Leonard Rockshelter Site, Pershing County, Nevada. *American Antiquity,* vol. 17, no. 2, 89–98, 1951.

———. Long-Range Dating in Archaeology. In *Anthropology Today,* edited under the chairmanship of A. L. Kroeber, 3–42. University of Chicago Press, Chicago, 1953.

———. Primitive Man as an Ecologic Factor. *Papers of the Kroeber Anthropological Society,* no. 13, 1–31. Berkeley, 1955.

———. Physical Analysis of Habitation Residues. In

Viking Fund Publications in Anthropology, no. 28, 93–142. New York, 1960.

———. The Western Coast of North America. In *Prehistoric Man in the New World,* J. D. Jennings and E. Norbeck, eds., 117–148. University of Chicago Press, Chicago, 1964.

HEIZER, ROBERT F., ed. *The Archaeologist at Work.* Harper & Row, New York, 1959.

HEIZER, ROBERT F. and FRANKLIN FENENGA. Archaeological Horizons in Central California. *American Anthropologist,* vol. 41, 378–399, 1939.

HELM, JUNE. The Ecological Approach to Anthropology. *American Journal of Anthropology,* vol. 67, no. 6, 630–639, 1962.

HEMPEL, C. G. *Aspects of Scientific Exploration and Other Essays in the Philosophy of Science.* Free Press, New York, 1965.

———. *Philosophy of Natural History.* Prentice-Hall, Englewood Cliffs, N.J., 1966.

HENRY, JOSEPH. Editorial Comment. *Annual Report of the Smithsonian Institution for 1874,* 335. Washington, D.C., 1875.

HENSHAW, HENRY W. Animal Carvings from the Mounds of the Mississippi Valley. *U.S. Bureau of American Ethnology, Second Annual Report 1880/1881,* 4–35. Washington, D.C., 1883.

HERRERA, L. F., R. D. DRENNAN, and C. A. URIBE, eds. *Prehispanic Chiefdoms in the Valle de La Plata.* University of Pittsburgh Memoirs in Latin American Archaeology, no. 2. Pittsburgh, 1989.

HESTER, JAMES J. A Comparative Typology of New World Cultures. *American Anthropologist,* vol. 64, no. 5, 1001–1015, 1962.

HEWETT, EDGAR L. *Antiquities of the Jemez Plateau, New Mexico.* U.S. Bureau of American Ethnology, Bulletin 32. Washington, D.C., 1906.

HILBERT, PETER F. *Archäologische Untersuchungen am Mittleren Amazonias.* Dietrich Riemer Verlag, Berlin, 1968.

HILL, JAMES N. A Prehistoric Community in Eastern Arizona. *Southwestern Journal of Anthropology,* vol. 22, no. 1, 9–30, 1966.

———. Broken K Pueblo: Patterns of Form and Function. In *New Perspectives in Archaeology,* S. R. Binford and L. R. Binford, eds., 103–143. Aldine, Chicago, 1968.

———. Archaeology and the Accumulation of Knowledge. In *Processual and Postprocessual Archaeologies: Multiple Ways of Knowing,* R. W. Preucel, ed., 42–53. Center for Archaeological Investigations, Southern Illinois University, Occasional Paper No. 10. Carbondale, 1991.

HILL, JAMES N., ed. *Explanation of Prehistoric Change.* School of American Research, Advanced Seminar Series. University of New Mexico Press, Albuquerque, 1977.

HINSLEY, C. M. *Savages and Scientists: The Smithsonian Institution and the Development of American Anthropology, 1846–1910.* Smithsonian Institution Press, Washington, D.C., 1981.

———. From Shell-heaps to Stelae. In *Objects and Others: Essays on Museums and Material Culture.* Edited by G. P. Stocking, Jr., 49–74. History of Anthropology, vol. 3. University of Wisconsin Press, Madison, 1985.

HIRSCHBERG, RICHARD and JOAN F. HIRSCHBERG. Meggers' Law of Environmental Limitation on Culture. *American Anthropologist,* vol. 59, 890–892, 1957.

HODDER, IAN, Theoretical Archaeology: A Reactionary View, In *Symbolic and Structural Archaeology,* I. Hodder, ed., 1–16. Cambridge University Press, Cambridge, 1982.

———. Archaeology in 1984. *Antiquity,* vol. 58, 25–32, 1984.

———. Postprocessual Archaeology. In *Advances in Archaeological Method and Theory,* M. Schiffer, ed., vol. 8, 1–26. Academic Press, New York, 1985.

———. The Contribution of the Long Term. In *Archaeology as Long-term History,* I. Hodder, ed., 1–8. Cambridge University Press, Cambridge, 1987.

———. Postprocessual Archaeology and the Current Debate. In *Processual and Postprocessual Archaeologies: Multiple Ways of Knowing the Past,* R. W. Preucel, ed., 30–41. Center for Archaeological Investigations, Southern Illinois University, Occasional Paper no. 10. Carbondale, 1991a.

———. *Reading the Past: Current Approaches to Interpretation in Archaeology,* second edition. Cambridge University Press, Cambridge, 1991b.

HODDER, IAN, ed. *Simulation Studies in Archaeology.* New Directions in Archaeology. Cambridge University Press, Cambridge, 1978.

HODGE, FREDERICK W., ed. *Handbook of American Indians North of Mexico*, 2 pts. Bureau of American Ethnology, Bulletin 30. Washington, D.C., 1907–10.

HODSON, FRANK R. Classification by Computer. In *Science in Archaeology*, revised edition, D. Brothwell and E. Higgs, eds., 649–660. Basic Books, New York, 1969.

———. Cluster Analysis and Archaeology: Some New Developments and Applications. *World Archaeology*, vol. 1, no. 3, 299–320, 1970.

HOLE, BONNIE. Sampling in Archaeology: A Critique. *Annual Review of Anthropology*, vol. 9, 217–234, 1980.

HOLE, FRANK. Questions of Theory in the Explanation of Culture Change in Prehistory. In *Explanation of Culture Change: Models in Prehistory*, C. Renfrew, ed., 19–34. Duckworth, London, 1973.

———. Editorial. *American Antiquity*, vol. 43, no. 2, 151–152, 1978.

HOLE, FRANK, KENT V. FLANNERY and JAMES NEELY. *Prehistoric and Human Ecology of the Deh Luran Plain*. Memoirs of the University of Michigan, Museum of Anthropology, no. 1. Ann Arbor, 1968.

HOLE, FRANK and ROBERT F. HEIZER. *An Introduction to Prehistoric Archaeology*. Holt, Rinehart and Winston, New York, 1966 (second edition, 1969; third edition, 1973).

HOLE, FRANK and MARY SHAW. *Computer Analysis of Chronological Seriation*. Rice University Studies, vol. 53, no. 3. Houston, 1967.

HOLMBERG, ALLEN R. Virú: Remnant of an Exalted People. *Patterns for Modern Living*, 367–416. The Delphian Society, Chicago, 1950.

HOLMES, WILLIAM H. Evidences of the Antiquity of Man on the Site of the City of Mexio. *Transactions of the Anthropological Society of Washington*, vol. 3, 68–81. Washington, D.C., 1885.

———. Ancient Art of the Province of Chiriqui. *Bureau of American Ethnology, Sixth Annual Report 1884/85*, 3–187. Washington, D.C., 1888.

———. Modern Quarry Refuse and the Paleolithic Theory. *Science* vol. 20, 295–297, 1892.

———. *Archaeological Studies Among the Ancient Cities of Mexico*. Field Columbian Museum Anthropological Series, vol. 1, no. 1. Chicago, 1895-7.

———. Aboriginal Pottery of the Eastern United States. *Bureau of American Ethnology, Twentieth Annual Report*. Washington, D.C., 1903.

———. Areas of American Culture Characterization Tentatively Outlined as an Aid in the Study of the Antiquities. *American Anthropologist*, vol. 16, no. 3, 413–446, 1914.

HOLSER, DOROTHY, J. A. SABLOFF, and DALE RUNGE. Simulation Model Development: A Case Study of the Classic Maya Collapse. In *Social Process in Maya Prehistory*, N. Hammond, ed., 553–590. Academic Press, London, 1977.

HORN, GEORGE. *De Originibus Americanis*. Leyden, 1652.

HOUGH, WALTER. Archaeological Field Work in Northeastern Arizona. *U.S. National Museum Annual Report for 1901*, 279–358. Washington, D.C., 1903.

———. Experimental Work in American Archaeology and Ethnology. In *Holmes Anniversary Volume*, 194–197. J. W. Bryan Press, Washington, D.C., 1916.

———. William Henry Holmes. *American Anthropologist*, vol. 35, 752–764, 1933.

HOUSTON, S. D. Archaeology and Maya Writing. *Journal of World Prehistory*, vol. 3, 1–32, 1989.

HOWARD, E. B. Evidence of Early Man in America. *The Museum Journal*, vol. 24, 53–171. Philadelphia, 1935.

HRDLIČKA, ALEŠ and OTHERS. *Early Man in South America*. Bureau of American Ethnology, Bulletin 52. Washington, D.C., 1912.

———. The Origin and Antiquity of the American Indian. *Annual Report of the Smithsonian Institute for 1923*, 481–494. Washington, D.C., 1925.

HUDDLESTON, LEE E. *Origins of the American Indians: European Concepts, 1492-1729*. University of Texas Press, Austin, 1967.

HUMBOLDT, ALEXANDER VON. *Political Essay on the Kingdom of New Spain*. Longmans, London, 1811.

———. *Researches Concerning the Institutions and Monuments of the Ancient Inhabitants of America*, translated by H. M. Williams. Longmans, London, 1814.

HUNTER-ANDERSON, ROSALIND L. A Theoretical Approach to the Study of House Form. In *For Theory Building in Archaeology: Essays on Fauunal Remains, Aquatic Resources, Spatial Analysis, and Systematic Modeling*, L. Binford, ed., 287–315. Academic Press, New York, 1977.

HYER, N. F. Ruins of the Ancient City of Aztlan. *Milwaukee Advertiser*, February 25, 1837.

HYMES, DELL H. Comments on *Analytical Archaeology*. *Norwegian Archaeological Review*, vol. 34, nos. 3–4, 16–21, 1970.

IHERING, HERMANN VON. A civilisacão prehistoria do Brazil meridional. *Revista do Museu Paulista*. vol. 1, 34–159, 1895.

IMBELLONI, JOSÉ.Culturas y geografía, cultural y raza. *Acta Venezolana*, 1, 129–140, 1945.

IRWIN-WILLIAMS, CYNTHIA. Archaic Culture History in the Southwestern United States. In *Early Man in Western North America*, Eastern New Mexico Contributions to Anthropology, vol. 1, no. 4, 48–54. Portales, 1968.

ISBELL, W. H. *The Rural Foundation for Urbanism: Economic and Stylistic Interaction Between Rural and Urban Communities in Eighth-Century Peru.* Illinois Studies in Anthropology, no. 10. University of Illinois Press, Urbana, 1977.

ISBELL, W. H. and G. F. MCEWAN, eds. *Huari Administrative Structure: Prehistoric Monumental Architecture and State Government.* Dumbarton Oaks, Washington, D.C., 1991.

ISBELL, W. H. and K. J. SCHREIBER. Was Huari a State? *American Antiquity*, vol. 43, no. 3, 372–390, 1978.

IVES, RONALD L. An Early Speculation Concerning the Asiatic Origin of the American Indian. *American Antiquity*, vol. 21, no. 4, 420–21, 1956.

IZUMI, SEIICHI. A Viewpoint Based on Material from the Kotosh Site. *Dumbarton Oaks Conference on Chavin*, E. P. Benson, ed., 49–72. Washington, D.C., 1971.

IZUMI, SEIICHI and TOSHIHIKO SONO. *Andes 2: Excavations at Kotosh, Peru, 1960.* Kadokawa, Tokyo, 1963.

JEFFERSON, THOMAS. *The Life and Selected Writings of Thomas Jefferson*, Adrienne Koch and William Reden, eds. Modern Library, New York, 1944.

JENNESS, DIAMOND. Archaeological Investigations in Bering Strait. *Annual Report of the National Museum of Canada for 1926.* Ottawa, 1928.

———. The Problem of the Eskimo. In *The American Aborigines. Their Origin and Antiquity*, D. Jenness, ed., 373–396. University of Toronto Press, Toronto, 1933.

JENNINGS, JESSE D. *Danger Cave.* Society for American Archaeology, Memoir 14. Washington, D.C., 1957.

———. Administration of Contract Emergency Archaeological Programs. *American Antiquity*, vol. 28, no. 3, 282–285, 1963.

———. The Desert West. In *Prehistoric Man in the New World*, J. D. Jennings and E. Norbeck, eds., 149–174. University of Chicago Press, Chicago, 1964.

———. *Prehistory of North America.* McGraw-Hill, New York, 1968.

———. *Prehistory of North America*, second edition. McGraw-Hill, New York, 1974.

———. *Prehistory of North America*, third edition. Mayfield, Mountain View, California, 1989.

JENNINGS, JESSE D. and EDWARD NORBECK. Great Basin Prehistory: A Review. *American Antiquity*, vol. 21, no. 1, 1–11, 1955.

JENNINGS. JESSE D. and EDWARD NORBECK, eds. *Prehistoric Man in the New World.* University of Chicago Press, Chicago, 1964.

JETER, M. D. *Edward Palmer's "Arkansaw Mounds."* University of Arkansas Press, Fayetteville, 1991.

JIJÓN Y CAAMAÑO, JACINTO. *Contribución al conocimiento de los aborigines de la provincia de Imbabura en la República del Ecuador*, Estudio de Prehistoria Americana, II. Blass, Madrid, 1914.

———. Nueva contribución al conocimiento de los aborigenes de la provincia de Imbabura. *Boletin de la Sociedad Equatoriana de Estudios Historicos Americanos*, vol. 4, 1–120, 183–244, 1920.

———. *Puruhá. Contribución al concimiento de los aborigenes de la provincia de Chimborazo, de la República del Ecuador*, 2 vols. Academia Nacional de Historia de Ecuador, Quito, 1927.

JIMÉNEZ MORENO, WIGBERTO. Sintesis de la historia pretolteca de Mesoamerica. In *Esplendor del México Antiquo*, vol. 2, 1019–1108. Centro de Investigaciones Antropologicas de México, Mexico, D.F., 1959.

JOHNSON, A. W. and T. K. EARLE. *The Evolution of Human Societies: From Foraging Group to Agrarian State.* Stanford University Press, Stanford, 1987.

JOHNSON, FREDERICK. A Quarter Century of Growth in American Archaeology. *American Antiquity*, vol. 27, no. 1, 1–16, 1961.

———. Archaeology in an Emergency. *Science*, vol. 152, no. 3729, 1966.

JOHNSON, FREDERICK, ed. *The Boylston Street Fishweir.* Papers of the Robert S. Peabody Foundation for Archaeology, vol. 2. Andover, Mass., 1942.

JOHNSON, FREDERICK, and OTHERS. *Prehistoric America and the River Valleys*, prepared by the Committee for the Recovery of Archaeological Remains. R. S. Peabody Foundation, Andover, Mass., 1945.

JOHNSON, H. G. Revolution and Counter-Revolution in Economics. *Encounter*, vol. 36, no. 4, 23–33, 1971.

JONES, CHRISTOPHER. Inauguration Dates of Three Late Classic Rulers of Tikal, Guatemala. *American Antiquity*, vol. 42, no. 1, 28–60, 1977.

JONES, J. M. Recent Discoveries of Kjokkenmodings. *Anthropological Review and Journal of the Anthropological Society of London*, vol. 2, 223–226. London, 1864.

JONES, V. H. James Bennett Griffin, Archaeologist. In *Cultural Change and Continuity*, C. E. Cleland, ed., xxxxix–lxvii. Academic Press, New York, 1976.

JOSEPHY, ALVIN M., JR. Indians in History. *Atlantic*, vol 225, no. 6, 67–72, 1970.

JOYCE, ROSEMARY. *Cerro Palenque: Power and Ideology on the Maya Periphery*. University of Texas Press, Austin, 1991.

JOYCE, THOMAS A. *South American Archaeology*. Putnam, London, 1912.

———. *Mexican Archaeology*. Putnam, London, 1914.

———. *Central American and West Indian Archaeology*. Putnam, London, 1916.

JUDD, NEIL M. Arizona's Prehistoric Canals, from the Air. *Explorations and Fieldwork of the Smithsonian Institution in 1930*, 157–166. Washington, D.C., 1931.

———. *The Bureau of American Ethnology*. University of Oklahoma Press, Norman, 1967.

———. *Men Met Along the Trail*. University of Oklahoma Press, Norman, 1968.

KALM, PETER. *Travels into North America*, second edition. London, 1772.

KEHOE, ALICE B. Contextualizing Archaeology. In *Tracing Archaeology's Past: The Historiography of Archaeology*, A. L. Christenson, ed., 97–106. Southern Illinois University Press, Carbondale, 1989.

———. The Muted Class: Unshackling Tradition. In *Exploring Gender Through Archaeology*, Cheryl Claassen, ed., 23–32. Monographs in World Archaeology, no. 11. Prehistory Press, Madison, 1992.

KELLEY, DAVID H. Glyphic Evidence for a Dynastic Sequence at Quirigua, Guatemala. *American Antiquity*, vol. 27, no. 3, 323–335, 1962.

KELLEY, DAVID H. and DUCCIO BONAVIA. New Evidence for Pre-Ceramic Maize on the Coast of Peru. *Ñawpa Pacha*. no. 1, 39–42. Institute of Andean Studies, Berkeley, 1963.

KELLEY, JANE H. and MARSHA P. HANEN. *Archaeology and the Methodology of Science*. University of New Mexico Press, Albuquerque, 1988.

KEUR, DOROTHY L. *Big Bead Mesa*. Society for American Archaeology, Memoir 1. Menasha, Wisconsin, 1941.

KIDDER, ALFRED V. Pottery of the Pajarito Plateau and Some Adjacent Regions in New Mexico. *Memoirs of the American Anthropological Association*, vol. 2, pt. 6, 407–462. Lancaster, Pa., 1915.

———. *An Introduction to the Study of Southwestern Archaeology, with a Preliminary Account of the Excavations at Pecos*. Papers of the Southwestern Expedition, Phillips Academy, no. 1. Yale University Press, New Haven, 1924.

———. Southwestern Archaeological Conference. *Science*, vol. 66, 486–491, 1927.

———. *The Pottery of Pecos*, vol. 1. Papers of the Southwestern Expedition, Phillips Academy. Yale University Press, New Haven, 1931.

———. Speculations on New World Prehistory. In *Essays in Anthropology*, 143–152. Berkeley, 1936.

———. Archaeological Problems of the Highland Maya. In *The Maya and Their Neighbors*, C. L. Hay and others, eds., 117–25. Appleton-Century, New York, 1940.

KIDDER, ALFRED II. South American Penetrations in Middle America. In *The Maya and Their Neighbors*, C. L. Hay and others, eds., 441–459. Appleton-Century, New York, 1940.

KILLION, T. W. *Agricultural and Residential Site Structure Among Campesions in Southern Veracruz, Mexico: Building a Foundation for Archaeological Inference*. Ph.D. dissertation, Department of Anthropology, University of New Mexico, Albuquerque, 1987.

KING, THOMAS F. A Conflict of Values in American Archaeology. *American Antiquity*, vol. 36, no. 3, 253–262, 1971.

———. Resolving a Conflict of Values in American Archaeology. In *Conservation Archaeology: A Guide for Cultural Resource Management Studies*, M. Schiffer and G. Gumerman, eds., 87–96. Academic Press, New York, 1977.

KINGSBOROUGH, EDWARD. *Antiquities of Mexico.* Privately printed, London, 1831–48.

KIRBUS, F. B. *Historia de la arqueologia Argentina.* Editorial La Barca Grafica, Buenos Aires, 1976.

KIRCH, P. V. The Archaeological Study of Adaptation: Theoretical and Methodological Views. In *Advances in Archaeological Method and Theory,* M. B. Schiffer, ed., 101–156. Academic Press, New York 1980.

KIRCHOFF, PAUL. Mesoamerica. *Acta Americana,* vol. 1, 92–107, 1943.

KLEJN, L. S. A Panorama of Theoretical Archaeology. *Current Anthropology,* vol. 18, no. 1, 1–43, 1977.

KLUCKHOHN, CLYDE. Some Reflections on the Method and Theory of the Kulturkreislehre. *American Anthropologist,* vol. 38, no. 2, 157–196, 1936.

————. The Place of Theory in Anthropological Studies. *Philosophy of Science,* vol. 6, no. 3, 328–344, 1939.

————. The Conceptual Structure in Middle American Studies. In *The Maya and Their Neighbors,* C. L. Hay and others, eds., 41–51. Appleton-Century, New York, 1940.

KLUCKHOHN, CLYDE and PAUL REITER, eds. *Preliminary Report on the 1937 Excavations, Bc 50–51, Chaco Canyon, New Mexico.* University of New Mexico Anthropological Series, vol. 3, no. 2. Albuquerque, 1939.

KNOROZOV, Y. V. *Selected Chapters from the Writing of the Maya Indians,* translated by Sophie Coe, Russian Translation Series of the Peabody Museum, vol. 4. Cambridge, Mass., 1967.

KOWALEWSKI, S. A., G. M. FEINMAN, LAURA FINSTEN, R. E. BLANTON, and L. M. NICHOLAS. *Monte Alban's Hinterland, Part II. Prehistoric Settlement Patterns in Tlacolula, Etla, and Ocotlán, the Valley of Oaxaca, Mexico.* Museum of Anthropology, Memoirs 23. University of Michigan, Ann Arbor, 1989.

KRICKEBERG, WALTER. *Altmexikanische Kulturen.* Safari Verlag, Berlin, 1956.

————. Early Man in the New World. In *Prehistoric Man in the New World,* J. D. Jennings, and E. Norbeck, eds., 23–84. University of Chicago Press, Chicago, 1964.

KROEBER, ALFRED L. The Archaeology of California. In *Putnam Anniversary Volume,* 1–42. G. E. Stechert, New York, 1909.

————. Zuñi Potsherds. *Anthropological Papers of the American Museum of Natural History,* vol. 18, pt. 1, 7–37. New York, 1916.

————. On the Principle of Order in Civilizations as Exemplified by Changes of Fashion. *American Anthropologist,* vol. 21, no. 3, 2335–2363, 1919.

————. The Uhle Pottery Collections from Supe. *University of California Publications in American Archaeology and Ethnology,* vol. 21, 235–264. Berkeley, 1925a.

————. The Uhle Pottery Collections from Moche. *University of California Publications in American Archaeology and Ethnology,* vol. 21, 191–234. Berkeley, 1925b.

————. Archaic Culture Horizons in the Valley of Mexico. *University of California Publications in American Archaeology and Ethnology,* vol. 17, 373–408. Berkeley, 1925c.

————. The Uhle Pottery Collections from Chancay. *University of California Publications in American Archaeology and Ethnology,* vol. 21, no. 7, 265–304. Berkeley, 1926.

————. Coast and Highland in Prehistoric Peru. *American Anthropologist,* vol. 29, 625–653, 1927.

————. Cultural Relations Between North and South America. In *Proceedings of the Twenty-third International Congress of Americanists,* 5–22. New York, 1930.

————. Cultural and Natural Areas of Native North America. *University of California Publications in American Archaeology and Ethnology,* vol. 38, 1–242. Berkeley, 1939.

————. Conclusions. In *The Maya and Their Neighbors,* C. L. Hay and others, eds., 406–490. Appleton-Century, New York, 1940.

————. *Peruvian Archaeology in 1942.* Viking Fund Publications in Anthropology, no. 4. New York, 1944.

————. *Anthropology.* Harcourt, Brace and World, New York, 1948.

KROEBER, ALFRED L. and WILLIAM D. STRONG. The Uhle Pottery Collections from Ica. *University of California Publications in American Archaeology and Ethnology,* vol. 21, no. 3, 95–133. Berkeley, 1924a.

————. The Uhle Collections from Chincha. *University of California Publications in American Archaeology and Ethnology,* vol. 223, no. 1, 1–54. Berkeley, 1924b.

KUBLER, GEORGE. *The Art and Architecture of Ancient America. The Mexican, Maya, and Andean Peoples.* Pelican Books, Baltimore, 1962.

KUHN, THOMAS S. *The Structure of Scientific Revolutions.* University of Chicago Press, Chicago, 1962.

KUSHNER, GILBERT. A Consideration of Some Processual Designs for Archaeology as Anthropology. *American Antiquity,* vol. 35, no. 2, 125–132, 1970.

KUZARA, RICHARD S., GEORGE R. MEAD, and KEITH A. DIXON. Seriation of Anthropological Data: A Computer Program for Matrix-Ordering. *American Anthropologist,* vol. 68, no. 6, 1442–1455, 1966.

LAET, JOHANNES DE. *Notae ad Dissertationem Hugonis Grotti de Origine Gention Americanarium: Et Observationes Aliquot ad Meliorem Indaginem Difficillimae Illius Quaestionis.* Paris, 1643.

———. *Responsis ad Dissertationem Secundum Hugonis Grotti.* Amsterdam, 1644.

LAGUNA, FREDERICA DE. *The Archaeology of Cook Inlet, Alaska.* University of Pennsylvania, Philadelphia, 1934.

———. *The Archaeology of Prince William Sound, Alaska.* University of Washington Publications in Anthropology, no. 13. Seattle, 1956.

LAMBERG-KARLOVSKY, C. C. Operations Problems in Archaeology. *Bulletin of the American Anthropological Association,* vol. 3, no. 3, pt. 2, 111–114. Washington, D.C., 1970.

LAMBERG-KARLOVSKY, C. C., ed. *Archaeological Thought in America.* Cambridge University Press, Cambridge, 1989.

LANDA, DIEGO DE. *Relation de choses de Yucatan de Diego de Landa,* translated by Charles E. Brasseur de Bourbour. Paris, 1864.

———. *Relación de las cosas de Yucatán, a Translation,* Alfred M. Tozzer, ed. Papers of the Peabody Museum, vol. 18. Cambridge, Mass., 1941.

LANNING, E. P. *Peru Before the Incas.* Prentice-Hall, Englewood Cliffs, N.J., 1967.

LAPHAM, INCREASE A. *The Antiquities of Wisconsin,* Smithsonian Contributions to Knowledge, vol. 7, art. 4. Washington, D.C., 1855.

LARCO, HOYLE, RAFAEL. *Los Mochicas,* 2 vols. Casa Editora "La Cronica," Lima, 1938–40.

———. *Los Cupisniques.* Casa Editora "La Cronica," Lima, 1941.

———. *Cronologia arqueólogica del notre del Peru.* Hacienda Chiclin, Trujillo, 1948.

LARKIN, FREDERICK. *Ancient Man in America.* New York, 1880.

LARSEN, HELGE. Archaeology in the Arctic, 1935–60. *American Antiquity,* vol. 27, no. 1, 7–15, 1961.

LARSEN, HELGE and F. G. RAINEY. *Ipiutak and the Arctic Whale Hunting Culture.* Anthropological Papers of the American Museum of Natural History, vol. 42. New York, 1948.

LARSON, LEWIS H., JR. Archaeological Implications of Social Stratification at the Etowah Site, Georgia. In *Approaches to the Social Dimensions of Mortuary Practices,* J. A. Brown, ed., 58–67. Society for American Archaeology, Memoir 25. Washington, D.C., 1972.

LATCHAM, R. E. *La Alfareria indigena Chilena.* La Comision Oficial Organizadora de la Concurrencia de Chile a la Exposición Ibero-Americana de Sevilla, Santiago, 1928a.

———. *La Prehistoria Chilena.* La Comisión Oficial Organizadora de la Concurrencia de Chile a la Exposición Ibero-Americana de Seville, Santiago, 1928b.

LATHRAP, DONALD W. The Culture Sequence at Yarinacocha, Eastern Peru. *American Antiquity,* vol. 23, no. 4, 379–388, 1958.

———. *Yarinacocha: Stratigraphic Excavations in the Peruvian Montana,* Ph.D. dissertation. Harvard University, Cambridge, Mass., 1962.

———. *The Upper Amazon.* Praeger, New York, 1970.

———. The Tropical Forest and the Cultural Context of Chavin. *Dumbarton Oaks Conference on Chavín,* E. P. Benson, ed., 73–100. Washington, D.C., 1973.

———. Gifts of the Cayman: Some Thoughts on the Subsistence Basis of Chavin. In *Variation in Anthropology,* D. W. Lathrap and Jody Douglas, eds., 91–107. Illinois Archaeological Survey, Urbana, 1973.

LATHRAP, DONALD W., ed. An Archaeological Classification of Culture Contact Situations. In *Seminars in Archaeology: 1955,* R. Wauchope, ed., 1–30. Society for American Archaeology, Memoir 22. Washington, D.C., 1956.

LATHRAP, D. W., J. G. MARCOS, and JAMES ZEIDLER. Real Alto: An Ancient Ceremonial Center. *Archaeology,* vol. 30, no. 1, 2–14, 1977.

LAUDAN, L. *Science and Relativism: Some Key Controver-*

sies in the Philosophy of Science. University of Chicago Press, Chicago, 1990.

LEHMANN-HARTLEBEN, KARL. Thomas Jefferson, Archaeologist. American Journal of Archaeology, vol. 47, 161–163, 1943.

LEHMER, DONALD J. Introduction to Middle Missouri Archaeology. Anthropological Papers of the National Park Service, no. 2. Washington, D.C., 1971.

LE MOYNE, JACQUES. Brevis Narratio. de Bry, Frankfort, 1591.

LEON PORTILLA, MIGUEL. Pre–Columbian Literatures of Mexico. University of Oklahoma Press, Norman, 1969.

LEONARD, ROBERT D., and GEORGE T. JONES. Elements of an Inclusive Evolutionary Model for Archaeology. Journal of Anthropological Archaeology, vol. 6, 199–219, 1987.

LEONE, MARK P. Neolithic Economic Autonomy and Social Distance. Science, vol. 162, no. 3858, 1150–1151, 1968.

———. Some Opinions About Recovering Mind. American Antiquity, vol. 47, 742–760, 1982.

———. Method as Message: Interpreting the Past with the Public. Museum News, vol. 62, 34–41, 1983.

———. Interpreting Ideology in Historical Archaeology: Using the Rules of Perspective in the William Paca Garden in Annapolis, Maryland. In Ideology, Power, and Prehistory, D. Miller and C. Tilley, eds., 25–35. Cambridge University Press, Cambridge, 1984.

LEONE, MARK P., ed. Contemporary Archaeology. Southern Illinois University Press, Carbondale, 1972.

LEONE, M. P. and P. B. POTTER, JR. Archaeological Annapolis. University of Maryland, College Park, 1984.

———. Introduction: Issues in Historical Archaeology. In The Recovery of Meaning: Historical Archaeology in the Eastern United States, M. P. Leone and P. B. Parker, Jr., eds., 1–22. Smithsonian Institution Press, Washington, D.C., 1988.

LEONE, MARK P. and P. B. POTTER, JR., eds. The Recovery of Meaning: Historical Archaeology in the Eastern United States. Smithsonian Institution Press, Washington, D.C., 1988.

LEONE, MARK P., P. B. POTTER, JR., and P. A. SHACKEL. Toward a Critical Archaeology. Current Anthropology, vol. 28, 283–302, 1987.

LEONE, MARK P., and ROBERT W. PREUCEL. Archaeology

in a Democratic Society: A Critical Theory Perspective. In Quandaries and Quests: Visions of Archaeology's Future, LuAnn Wandsnider, ed., 115–135, Center for Archaeological Investigations, Occasional Paper No. 20. Southern Illinois University, Carbondale, 1992.

LE PAGE DU PRATZ, ANTOINE S. Histoire de la Louisiane, 3 vols. De Bure, Paris, 1758.

LEROI-GOURHAN, A. Treasures of Prehistoric Art. Abrams, New York, 1967.

LEVIN, MICHAEL E. On Explanation in Archaeology: A Rebuttal to Fritz and Plog. American Antiquity, vol. 38, 387–395, 1973.

LEWIS, THOMAS M. N. and MADELINE KNEBERG. The Prehistory of Chickamuga Basin in Tennessee. Tennessee Anthropological Papers, no. 1. Knoxville, 1941.

———. Hiwassee Island: An Archaeological Account of Four Tennessee Indian Peoples. University of Tennessee Press, Knoxville, 1946.

LIBBY, WILLARD F. Radiocarbon Dating, second edition. University of Chicago Press, Chicago, 1955.

LINARES, OLGA. Ecology and the Arts in Ancient Panama. Studies in Pre-Columbian Art and Archaeology, No. 37. Dumbarton Oaks, Washington, D.C., 1977.

LINNÉ, SIGVALD. Danien in the Past. Göteborgs Kungl. Vetenskaps-Och, Vittenkets-Samhalles Handlingar, Femte Foljden, Ser. A, Bd. 1, No. 3. Göteborg, Sweden, 1929.

LINTON, RALPH. The Study of Man. Appleton-Century, New York, 1936.

———. North American Cooking Pots. American Antiquity, vol. 9, no. 4, 1944.

LIPE, W. D. A Conservation Model for American Archaeology. Kiva, vol. 39, 213–245, 1974.

LIPE, W. D., and A. J. LINDSAY, eds. Proceedings of the 1974 Cultural Resource Management Conference, Denver, Colorado. Museum of Northern Arizona, Technical Series, 14. Flagstaff, 1974.

LONGACRE, WILLIAM A. Archaeology as Anthropology: A Case Study. Science, vol. 144, no. 3625, 1454–1455, 1964.

———. Changing Pattern of Social Integration: A Prehistoric Example from the American Southwest. American Anthropologist, vol. 68, no. 1, 94–102, 1966.

———. Some Aspects of Prehistoric Society in East-Central Arizona. In New Perspectives in Archaeology,

S. R. Binford and L. R. Binford, eds., 89–102. Aldine, Chicago, 1968.

———. Current Thinking in American Archaeology. *Bulletin of the American Anthropological Association*, vol. 3, no. 3, pt. 2, 126–138. Washington, D.C., 1970.

LOTHROP, SAMUEL K. *Pottery of Costa Rica and Nicaragua*, 2 vols. Contributions from the Museum of the American Indian, Heye Foundation, vol. 8. New York, 1926.

———. South America as Seen from Middle America. In *The Maya and Their Neighbors*, C. L. Hay and others, eds., 417–429. Appleton-Century, New York, 1940.

———. *Cocle, An Archaeological Study of Central Panama, Parts I and II*. Peabody Museum Memoirs, vols. 7 and 8. Harvard University, Cambridge, Mass., 1937–42.

———. The Diaguita of Chile. In *Handbook of South American Indians*, Julian H. Steward, ed., vol. 2, 633–636. Bureau of American Ethnology, Bulletin 143. Washington, D.C., 1946.

LOUNSBURY, FLOYD. On the Derivation and Reading of the "Ben-Ich" Prefix. In *Mesoamerican Writing Systems*, E. Benson, ed., 99–143. Dumbarton Oaks, Washington, D.C., 1973.

LOWE, J. W. G. *The Dynamics of Apocalypse: A Systems Simulation of the Classic Maya Collapse*. University of New Mexico Press, Albuquerque, 1985.

LOWIE, ROBERT H. Reminiscences of Anthropological Currents in America Half a Century Ago. *American Anthropologist*, vol. 58, no. 6, 995–1016, 1956.

LUBBOCK, JOHN. *Prehistoric Times*. London, 1865.

LUMBRERAS, LUIS G. Towards a Re-evaluation of Chavin. *Dumbarton Oaks Conference on Chavin*, E. P. Benson, ed., 1–28. Dumbarton Oaks, Washington, D.C., 1971.

LUND, P. W. Blik poa Brasiliens Dyreverden, etc. *Det Kongelige Danske Videnskabernes Selskabs Naturvidenskabelige og Mathematiske Afhandlinger, Niende Dul*, 195–196. Copenhagen, 1842.

LYNCH, BARBARA D. and THOMAS F. LYNCH. The Beginnings of a Scientific Approach to Prehistoric Arhaeology in Seventeenth and Eighteenth-Century Britain. *Southwestern Journal of Anthropology*, vol. 24, no. 1, 33–65, 1968.

LYON, PATRICIA J. Anthropological Activity in the United States, 1865–1879. *Kroeber Anthropological Society Papers*, no. 40, 8–37. Berkeley, 1969.

MCCLUNG DE TAPIA, EMILY and EVELYN RATTRAY, eds. *Teotihuacan: nuevos datos, nuevas síntesis, nuevos problemas*. Universidad Nacional Autónoma de México, Mexico, D. F. 1987.

MCCULLOH, JAMES H., JR. *Researches Philosophical and Antiquarian Concerning the Aboriginal History of America*. Fielding Lucas, Baltimore, 1829.

MACCURDY, GEORGE G. *A Study of Chiriquian Antiquities*. Memoirs of the Connecticut Academy of Sciences, vol. 3. New Haven, 1911.

MACNEISH, R. S. A Synopsis of the Archaeological Sequence in the Sierra de Tamaulipas. *Revista Mexicana de Estudios Antropologicos*, tomo 11, 79–96, 1950.

———. *Preliminary Archaeological Investigations in the Sierra de Tamaulipas, Mexico*. Transactions, American Philosophical Society, vol. 48, pt. 6. Philadelphia, 1958.

———. Ancient Mesoamerican Civilization. *Science*, vol. 143, no. 3606, 531–537, 1964a.

———. *Investigations in the Southwest Yukon: Part II, Archaeological Excavation, Comparisons and Speculations*. Papers of the R. S. Peabody Foundation for Archaeology, vol. 6, no. 1. Andover, Mass., 1964b

———. A Summary of the Subsistence. In *Prehistory of the Tehuacan Valley*, vol. 1, D. S. Byers, ed., 290–309. University of Texas Press, Austin, 1967.

———. *First Annual Report of the Ayacucho Archaeological-Botanical Project*. Andover, R. S. Peabody Foundation, 1969.

———. Early Man in the Andes. *Scientific American*, vol. 224, no. 4, 36–46, 1971.

———. Review of *A History of American Archaeology* by G. R. Willey and J. A. Sabloff. *American Anthropologist*, vol. 77, no. 2, 447–448, 1975.

———. *The Science of Archaeology?* Duxbury Press, North Scituate, Mass., 1975.

———. A History of North American Archaeology. Manuscript, 1981.

MACNEISH, R. S., ANTOINETTE NELKEN-TURNER, and ANGEL GARCIA COOK. *Second Annual Report of the Ayacucho Archaeological-Botanical Project*. R. S. Peabody Foundation, Andover, Mass., 1970.

MACNEISH, R. S., T. C. PATTERSON, and D. L. BROWMAN. *The Central Peruvian Prehistoric Interaction Sphere*. Papers of the R. S. Peabody Foundation for Archaeology. Andover, Mass., 1975.

MCGIMSEY, CHARLES R. III. Archaeology and the Law. *American Antiquity*, vol. 36, no. 2, 125–126, 1971.

———. *Public Archaeology*. Seminar Press, New York, 1972.

MCGIMSEY, CHARLES R. III and H. A. DAVIS, eds. *The Management of Archaeological Resources; The Airlie House Report*. Special Publication of the Society for American Archaeology, Washington, D.C., 1977.

MCGREGOR, JOHN C. *Southwestern Archaeology*. Wiley, New York, 1941.

———. *Southwestern Archaeology*, second edition. University of Illinois Press, Urbana, 1965.

MCGUIRE, R. H. *A Marxist Archaeology*. Academic Press, Orlando, 1992.

MCKERN, WILLIAM C. The Midwestern Taxomonic Method as an Aid to Archaeological Study. *American Antiquity*, vol. 4, 301–313, 1939.

———. On Willey and Phillips' Method and Theory in American Archaeology. *American Anthropologist*, vol. 58, 360–361, 1956.

MCKUSICK, MARSHALL. *The Davenport Conspiracy*. Office of the State Archaeologist, Report no. 1. Iowa City, 1979.

———. *The Davenport Conspiracy Revisited*. Iowa State University Press, Ames, 1991.

MCNAIRN, BARBARA. *Method and Theory of V. Gordon Childe*. Edinburgh University Press, Edinburgh, 1980.

MCPHERRON, ALAN. *The Juntenen Site and the Late Woodland Prehistory of the Upper Great Lakes Area*. Anthropological Papers of the University of Michigan Museum of Anthropology, no. 30. Ann Arbor, 1967.

MADISON, JAMES. A Letter on the Supposed Fortification of the Western Country from Bishop Madison of Virginia to Dr. Barton. *Transactions of the American Philosophical Society*, vol. 6. Philadelphia, 1803.

MALER, TEOBERT. *Researches in the Central Portion of the Usumatsintla Valley*. Memoirs of the Peabody Museum, vol. 2, no. 1. Cambridge, Mass., 1901.

———. *Researches in the Central Portion of the Usumatsintla Valley*. Memoirs of the Peabody Museum, vol. 2, no. 2. Cambridge, Mass., 1903.

———. *Explorations of the Upper Usumatsintla and Adjacent Region: Altar de Sacrificios, Seibal, Itsimte-Sacluk,*

Cankuen. Memoirs of the Peabody Museum, vol. 4, no. 1. Cambridge, Mass., 1908.

MANGELSDORF, PAUL C. *Corn, its Origin, Evolution, and Improvement*. Harvard University Press, Cambridge, 1974.

MANGELSDORF, PAUL C. and EARLE C. SMITH. New Archaeological Evidence on Evolution in Maize. *Botanical Museum Leaflets*, Harvard University, vol. 13, no. 8, 213–247. Cambridge, Mass., 1949.

MANNERS, ROBERT A., ed. *Process and Pattern in Culture: Essays in Honor of Julian H. Steward*. Aldine, Chicago, 1964.

MANZANILLA, LINDA, ed. *Colloquio V. Gordon Childe: estudios sobre las revoluciones neolítica y urbana*. Instituto de Investigaciones Antropologicas, Arqueología, Serie Monografías, vol. 2. Universidad Nacional Autónoma de México, Mexico, D. F., 1988.

MARCANO, G. Ethnographie précolombienne du Venezuela, Vallées d'Aragua et de Caracas. *Mémoires d'Anthropologie*, ser. 2, vol. 4, 1–86, 1889.

MARCUS, JOYCE. Territorial Organization of the Lowland Classic Maya. *Science*, vol. 180, no. 4089, 911–916, 1973.

———. *Emblem and State in the Classic Maya Lowlands*. Dumbarton Oaks, Washington, D.C., 1976.

MARCUS, JOYCE, ed. *Debating Oaxaca Archaeology*. Anthropological Papers, no. 84. Museum of Anthropology, University of Michigan, Ann Arbor, 1990.

MARKHAM, SIR CLEMENTS R. *Cuzco: A Journey to the Ancient Capital of Peru*. Chapman and Hall, London, 1856.

———. On the Geographical Positions of the Tribes Which Formed the Empire of the Yucas. *Journal of the Royal Geographical Society*, vol. 41, 281–338, 1871.

———. *A History of Peru*. Charles H. Siegel, Chicago, 1892.

– – –. *The Incas of Peru*. E. P. Dutton, New York, 1910.

MÁQUEZ MIRANDA, FERNANDO. The Diaguita of Argentina. In *Handbook of South American Indians*, Julian H. Steward, ed., vol. 2, 637–654. Bureau of American Ethnology, Bulletin 143. Washington, D.C., 1946a.

———. The Chaco-Santiagueño Culture. In *Handbook of South American Indians*, Julian H. Steward, ed., vol. 2, 655–660. Bureau of American Ethnology, Bulletin 143. Washington, D.C., 1946b.

MARTIN, PAUL S. Early Development in Mogollon Research. In *Archaeological Researches in Retrospect*, G. R. Willey, ed., 3–33. Winthrop, Cambridge, 1974.

MARTIN, PAUL S., CARL LLOYD, and ALEXANDER SPOEHR. Archaeological Works in the Ackman-Lowry Area, Southwestern Colorado, 1937. *Field Museum of Natural History Anthropological Series*, vol. 23, no. 2, 217–304. Chicago, 1938.

MARTIN, PAUL S., GEORGE L. QUIMBY, and DONALD COLLIER. *Indians Before Columbus*. University of Chicago Press, Chicago, 1947.

MARTIN, PAUL S. and JOHN RINALDO. Modified Basket Maker Sites, Ackman-Lowry Area, Southwestern Colorado, 1938. *Field Museum of Natural History Anthropological Series*, vol. 23, no. 3, 305–499. Chicago, 1939.

———. The Southwestern Co-Tradition. *Southwestern Journal of Anthropology*, vol. 7, 215–229, 1951.

MARTIN, PAUL S., JOHN RINALDO, and MARJORIE KELLY. The SU Site, Excavations at a Mogollon Village, Western New Mexico, 1939. *Field Museum of Natural History Anthropological Series*, vol. 32, no. 1. Chicago, 1940.

MARTIN, PAUL S., LAWRENCE ROYS, and GERHARDT VON BONIN. Lowry Ruin in Southwestern Colorado. *Field Museum of Natural History Anthropological Series*, vol. 23, no. 1. Chicago, 1936.

MARUYAMA, MOGOROH. The Second Cybernetics: Deviation-Amplifying Mutual Causal Processes. *American Scientist*, vol. 51, no. 2, 164–179, 1963.

MASON, J. ALDEN. *The Ancient Civilizations of Peru*. Pelican Books, Baltimore, 1957.

MASON, OTIS T. Influence of Environment upon Human Industries or Arts. *Annual Report of the Smithsonian Institution for 1895*, 639–665. Washington, D.C., 1895.

———. Environment. In *Handbook of American Indians*, F. W. Hodge, ed., 427–430. Bureau of American Ethnology, Bulletin 30. Washington, D.C., 1905.

MATHIASSEN, THERKEL. *Archaeology of the Central Eskimos*. Report of the Fifth Thule Expedition, 1921–24, vol. 4. Copenhagen, 1927.

———. The Eskimo Archaeology of Greenland. *Annual Report of the Smithsonian Institution for 1936*, 397–404. Washington, D.C., 1937.

MATTOS, ANIBAL. Lagoa Santa Man. In *Handbook of South American Indians*, Julian H. Steward, ed., vol. 1, 399–400. Bureau of American Ethnology, Bulletin 143. Washington, D.C., 1946.

MAUDSLAY, ALFRED P. Archaeology. In *Biologia Centrali Americana*, 4 vols. Porter and Dulau, London, 1889–1902.

MAYER-OAKES, WILLIAM J. *Prehistory of the Upper Ohio Valley: An Introductory Study*. Carnegie Museum Anthropological Series, no. 2. Pittsburgh, 1955.

———. A Developmental Concept of Pre-Spanish Urbanization in the Valley of Mexico. *Middle American Research Records*, vol. 2, no. 8, 167–175. Tulane University, New Orleans, 1961.

———. Comments on *Analytical Archaeology*. *Norwegian Archaeological Review*, vol. 34, nos. 3–4, 12–16, 1970.

MEANS, PHILIP A. A Survey of Ancient Peruvian Art. *Transactions of the Connecticut Academy of Arts and Sciences*, vol. 21, 315–324, 1917.

———. *Ancient Civilizations of the Andes*. Scribner's, New York, 1931.

MEEHAN, EUGENE J. *Explanation in Social Science, a System Paradigm*. Dorsey, Homewood, Ill. 1968.

MEGGERS, BETTY J. Environmental Limitation on the Development of Culture. *American Anthropologist*, vol. 56, no. 5, 801–824, 1954.

———. The Coming of Age of American Archaeology. In *New Interpretations of Aboriginal American Culture History*, 116–129. Washington, D.C., 1955.

———. Functional and Evolutionary Implications of Community Patterning. In *Seminars in Archaeology: 1955*, R. Wauchope, ed., 129–157. Society for American Archaeology, Memoir 11. Washington, D.C., 1956.

———. Environment and Culture in the Amazon Basin: An Appraisal of the Theory of Environmental Determinism. In *Studies in Human Ecology*, Angel Palerm and others, ed., 71–90. Pan American Union Social Sciences Monograph, no. 3. Washington, D.C., 1957.

———. Field Testing of Cultural Law: A Reply to Morris Opler. *Southwestern Journal of Anthropology*, vol. 17, no. 14, 352–354, 1961.

———. *Ecuador*. Praeger, New York, 1966.

MEGGERS, BETTY J. and CLIFFORD EVANS. *Archaeological Investigations at the Mouth of the Amazon*. Bureau of

American Ethnology, Bulletin 167. Washington, D.C., 1957.

———. Review of *Method and Theory in American Archaeology* by G. Willey and P. Phillips. *American Antiquity*, vol. 24, no. 2, 195–196, 1958.

———. An Experimental Formulation of Horizon Styles in the Tropical Forest Area of South America. In *Essays in Pre-Columbian Art and Archaeology*, S. K. Lothrop and others, eds., 372–388. Harvard University Press, Cambridge, Mass., 1961.

———. *Aboriginal Cultural Development in Latin America: An Interpretative Review.* Smithsonian Miscellaneous Collection, vol. 146, no. 146, no. 1. Washington, D.C., 1963.

MEGGERS, BETTY J., CLIFFORD EVANS, and EMILIO ESTRADA. *Early Formative Period of Coastal Ecuador.* Smithsonian Contributions to Anthropology, vol. 1. Washington, D.C., 1965.

MEIGHAN, CLEMENT W. Excavations in Sixteenth Century Shellmounds at Drake's Bay, Marin County. *Reports of the California Archaeological Survey*, no. 9, 27–322. Berkeley, 1950.

———. The Little Harbor Site, Catalina Island: An Example of Ecological Interpretation in Archaeology. *American Antiquity*, vol. 24, no. 4, 383–405, 1959.

———. The Growth of Archaeology in the West Coast and the Great Basin, 1935–60. *American Antiquity*, vol. 27, no. 1, 33–38, 1961.

———. Pacific Coast Archaeology. In *The Quaternary of the United States*, H. E. Wright, Jr. and D. G. Frey, eds., 709–722. Seventh Congress of the International Association for Quarternary Research. Princeton, 1965.

MEIGHAN, CLEMENT W. and others. Ecological Interpretation in Archaeology. *American Antiquity*, vol. 24, no. 1, 1–23 and no. 2, 131–150, 1958.

MELDGAARD, JORGEN A. On the Formative Period of the Dorset Culture. In *Prehistoric Cultural Relations Between the Arctic and Temperate Zones of North America*, J. M. Campbell, ed., 92–95. Arctic Institute of North America Technical Paper no. 11. Montreal, 1962.

MELTZER, D. J. The Antiquity of Man and the Development of American Archaeology. In *Advances in Archaeological Method and Theory*, vol. 6, M. B. Schiffer, ed., 1–51. Academic Press, New York, 1983.

———. North American Archaeology and Archaeologists, 1879–1934. *American Antiquity*, vol. 50, 249–260, 1985.

———. Late Pleistocene Human Adaptations in Eastern North America. *Journal of World Prehistory*, vol. 2, 1–52, 1988.

———. Why Don't We Know When the First People Came to North America? *American Antiquity*, vol. 54, 471–490, 1989.

MENGHIN, OSWALD F. A. *Weltgeschichte der Steinzeit.* Anton Schroll, Vienna, 1931.

———. Das Protolithikum in Amerika. *Acta Praehistorica*, no. 1, 1957.

MENZEL, DOROTHY. Style and Time in the Middle Horizon. *Ñawpa Pacha*, no. 2, 1–106, 1964.

MENZEL, DOROTHY, JOHN ROWE, and LAWRENCE E. DAWSON. *The Paracas Pottery of Ica, a Study in Style and Time.* University of California Publications in American Archaeology and Ethnology, vol. 50. Berkeley, 1964.

MERRIAM, C. HART. William Healy Dall. *Science*, vol. 65, no. 1684, 345–347, 1927.

MERTON, R. K. *Social Theory and Social Structure.* Free Press, New York, 1968.

MERWIN, RAYMOND E. and GEORGE C. VAILLANT. *The Ruins of Holmul, Guatemala.* Memoirs of the Peabody Museum, vol. 3, no. 2. Cambridge, Mass., 1932.

MIDDENDORF, E. W. *Peru*, 3 vols. Robert Oppenheim, Berlin, 1893–5.

MILLER, A. G. *Maya Rulers of Time.* University Museum, Philadelphia, 1986.

MILLER, DANIEL. Explanation and Social Theory in Archaeological Practice. In *Theory and Explanation in Archaeology*, C. Renfrew, M. Rowlands, and B. Seagraves, eds., 83–95. Academic Press, New York, 1982.

MILLER, TOM. Evolutionism and History in American Archaeology. *Tebiwa*, vol. 2, no. 2, 55–56, 1959.

MILLON, RENÉ F. Teotihuacán. *Scientific American*, vol. 216, no. 6, 38–48, 1967.

———. Teotihuacán: Completion of Maps of Giant Ancient City in the Valley of Mexico. *Science*, vol. 170, 1077–1082, 1970.

———. Social Relations in Ancient Teotihuacan. In *The Valley of Mexico*, E. R. Wolf, ed., 205–249. School of American Research, Advanced Seminar Series. University of New Mexico Press, Albuquerque, 1976.

MILLON, RENÉ F., ed. *Urbanization of Teotihuacan, Mexico*, vol. 1: The Teotihuacan Map (Parts One and Two, Text and Maps). University of Texas Press, Austin, 1973.

MILLS, WILLIAM C. Baum Prehistoric Village. *Ohio State Archaeological and Historical Quarterly*, vol. 16, no. 2, 113–193. Columbus, 1906.

———. Explorations of the Edwin Harness Mound. *Ohio State Archaeological and Historical Quarterly*, vol. 25, no. 3, 262–398, 1907.

MILNER, G. R. The Late Prehistoric Cahokia Cultural System of the Mississippi River Valley: Foundations, Florescence, and Fragmentation. *Journal of World Prehistory*, vol. 4, 1–44, 1990.

MINNIS, P. E. Domesticating People and Plants in the Greater Southwest. In *Prehistoric Food Production in North America*, R. I. Ford, ed., 309–339. University of Michigan Museum of Anthropology, Anthropological Papers, no. 75. Ann Arbor, 1985.

MINNIS, P. E., and C. L. REDMAN, eds. *Perspectives on Southwestern Prehistory*. Westview Press, Boulder, Col., 1990.

MIRAMBELL SILVA, LORENA. Excavaciones en un sitio pleistocénico de Tlapacoya, Mexico. *Boletín del Instituto Nacional de Antropología e Historia*, no. 29, 37–41. Mexico, D.F., 1967.

MITRA, PANCHANAN. *A History of American Anthropology*. University of Calcutta Press, Calcutta, 1933.

MOBERG, CARL-AXEL. Comments on *Analytical Archaeology. Norwegian Archaeological Review*, vol. 34, nos. 3–4, 21–24, 1970.

MONTAGU, M. F. ASHLEY. Earliest Acounts of the Association of Human Artifacts with Fossil Mammals in North America. *Science*, vol. 95, 380–381, 1942.

MOORE, CLARENCE B. Certain Sand Mounds of the St. John's River, Florida. *Journal of the Academy of Natural Sciences of Philadelphia*, vol. 10, 1894.

———. Certain River Mounds of Duval County, Florida. *Journal of the Academy of Natural Sciences of Philadelphia*, vol. 10, 1896.

———. Certain Aboriginal Remains of the Northwest Florida Coast, pt. 2. *Journal of the Academy of Natural Sciences of Philadelphia*, vol. 12, 1902.

———. Antiquities of the St. Francis, White and Black Rivers, Arkansas. *Journal of the Academy of Natural Sciences of Philadelphia*, vol. 14, 1910.

MOORE, J. A. and A. S. KEENE, eds. *Archaeological Hammers and Theories*. Academic Press, New York, 1983.

MOORHEAD, WARREN K. *Primitive Man in Ohio*. Putnam, New York, 1892.

———. *The Stone Age in North America*, 2 vols. Houghton Mifflin, Boston, 1910.

———. *A Report on the Archaeology of Maine*. Publications of the Department of Archaeology, Philadelphia Academy, Publication 5. Andover, Mass., 1922.

———. *The Cahokia Mounds*. University of Illinois Bulletin, vol. 26, no. 4. Urbana, 1928.

MORAN, EMILIO F., ed. *The Ecosystem Approach in Anthropology: From Concept to Practice*. University of Michigan Press, Ann Arbor, 1990.

MORGAN, C. G. Archaeology and Explanation. *World Archaeology*, vol. 4, 259–276, 1973.

MORGAN, LEWIS H. Montezuma's Dinner. *North American Review*, vol. 122, 265–308, 1876.

———. *Ancient Society*. Henry Holt, New York, 1877.

MORGAN, RICHARD G. and JAMES H. RODABAUGH. *Bibliography of Ohio Archaeology*. Ohio State Archaeological and Historical Society, Columbus, 1947.

MORLEY, SYLVANUS G. Excavations at Quirigua, Guatemala. *National Geographic Magazine*, vol. 24, 339–361, 1913.

———. *The Ancient Maya*. Stanford University Press, Stanford, 1946.

MORLEY, SYLVANUS G. and G. W. BRAINERD. *The Ancient Maya*, third edition. Stanford University Press, Stanford, 1956.

MORLOT, A. VON. General Views on Archaeology. *Annual Report of the Smithsonian Institution for 1860*, 284–343. Washington, D.C., 1861.

MOSELEY, MICHAEL E. Organizational Preadaptation to Irrigation: The Evolution of Early Water-Management Systems in Coastal Peru. In *Irrigation's Impact on Society*, T. E. Downing and McGuire Gibson, eds. Anthropological Papers of the University of Arizona, no. 25. Tucson, 1974.

———. *The Maritime Foundations of Andean Civilization*. Cummings, Menlo Park, Calif., 1975a.

———. Chan Chan: Andean Alternative of the Preindustrial City. *Science*, vol. 187, 219–225, 1975b.

MOSELEY, MICHAEL E. and KENT C. DAY, eds. *Chan Chan: Andean Desert City*. A School of American Research Book. University of New Mexico Press, Albuquerque, 1982.

MOSELEY, MICHAEL E. and CAROL J. MACKEY, eds. *Twenty-four Architectural Plans of Chan Chan, Peru*. Peabody Museum Press, Cambridge, Mass., 1974.

MOSELEY, MICHAEL E. and GORDON R. WILLEY. Aspero, Peru: A Reexamination of the Site and Its Implications. *American Antiquity*, vol. 38, no. 4, 452–468, 1973.

MUELLER, J. W., ed. *Sampling in Archaeology*. University of Arizona Press, Tucson, 1975.

MÜLLER-BECK, HANSJÜRGEN. Paleohunters in America: Origins and Diffusions. *Science*, vol. 152, no. 3726, 1191–1210, 1966.

NADAILLAC, JEAN FRANCOIS, MARQUIS DE. *Prehistoric America*, translated by N. d'Anvers, W. H. Dall, ed. G. P. Putnam's Sons, New York and London, 1884.

NANCE, J. D. Regional Sampling in Archaeological Survey: The Statistical Perspective. In *Advances in Archaeological Method and Theory*, vol. 6, M. B. Schiffer, ed., 289–356. Academic Press, New York, 1983.

NAROLL, RAOUL S. Floor Area and Settlement Population. *American Antiquity*, vol. 27, no. 4, 587–589, 1962.

NELSON, NELS C. Shellmounds of the San Francisco Bay Region. *University of California Publications in American Archaeology and Ethnology*, vol. 7, no. 4, 319–348. Berkeley, 1909.

———. The Ellis Landing Shellmound. *University of California Publications in American Archaeology and Ethnology*, vol. 7, no. 5, 357–426. Berkeley, 1910.

———. Pueblo Ruins of the Galisteo Basin. *Anthropological Papers of the American Museum of Natural History*, vol. 14, pt. 1. New York, 1914.

———. Chronology of the Tano Ruins, New Mexico. *American Anthropologist*, vol. 18, no. 2, 150–80, 1916.

———. Notes on Pueblo Bonito. In *Pueblo Bonito*, G. H. Pepper, ed., Anthropological Papers of the American Muiseum of Natural History, vol. 27. New York, 1920.

———. The Antiquity of Man in America in the Light of Archaeology. In *The American Aborigines, Their Origin and Antiquity*, D. Jenness, ed., 85–130. University of Toronto Press, Toronto, 1933.

NETTO, LADISLÁU. Investigacoes sobre a archeologia Brazileira. *Archivos do Museo Nacional*, vol. 6, 257–555, 1885.

NEWELL, H. PERRY, and ALEX D. KRIEGER. *The George C. Davis Site, Cherokee County, Texas*, Society for American Archaeology, Memoir 5. Menasha, 1949.

NICHOLS, FRANCES S., compiler. *Index to Schoolcraft's "Indian Tribes of the United States,"* Bureau of American Ethnology, Bulletin 152. Washington, D.C., 1954.

NICHOLSON, HENRY B. Settlement Pattern Analysis in Contemporary American Archaeology. *American Anthropologist*, vol. 60, no. 6, 1189–1192, 1958.

NOËL HUME, IVOR. *Historical Archaeology*. Knopf, New York, 1969.

———. *A Guide to the Artifacts of Colonial America*. Knopf, New York, 1970.

NORDENSKIÖLD, ERLAND VON. Urnengräber und Mounds im Bolivianischen Flachlande. *Braessler Arhives*, vol. 3, 205–255, 1913.

———. *Comparative Ethnographical Studies IV: The Copper and Bronze Ages in South America*. Elanders Boktryckeri Aktiebolag, Göteberg, 1921.

———. *Origin of the Indian Civilizations in South America*. Comparative Ethnographical Studies, no. 9. Elanders Boktryckeri Aktiebolag, Göteborg, 1931.

NÖRDENSKIÖLD, GUSTAF VON. *The Cliff Dwellers of the Mesa Verde, Southwestern Colorado; Their Pottery and Implements*, translated by D. L. Morglan. Norstedt, Stockholm, 1893.

NUTTALL, ZELIA. The Island of Sacrificios. *American Anthropologist*, vol. 12, 257–295, 1910.

OAKLEY, KENNETH P. Analytical Methods of Dating Bones. In *Science in Archaeology*, revised edition, D. Brothwell and E. Higgs, eds., 35–45. Basic Books, New York, 1969.

O'BRIEN, P. J. Urbanism, Cahokia, and Middle Mississippian. *Archaeology*, vol. 25, no. 3, 188–197, 1972.

ODUM, EUGENE P. *Fundamentals of Ecology*. Saunders, Philadelphia, 1953.

———. *Ecology*. Holt, Rinehart and Winston, New York, 1963.

———. *Fundamentals of Ecology*, third edition. Saunders, Philadelphia, 1971.

OPLER, MORRIS E. Cultural Evolution, Southern Athapaskans, and Chronology in Theory. *Southwestern Journal of Anthropology*, vol. 17, no. 1, 1–20, 1961.

ORTON, C. *Mathematics in Archaeology*. Collins, London, 1980.

OSGOOD, CORNELIUS. *Ingalik Material Culture*. Yale University Publications in Anthropology, no. 2. New Haven, 1940.

———. *The Ciboney Culture of Cayo Redondo, Cuba*. Yale University Publications in Anthropology, no. 25. New Haven, 1942.

O'SHEA, J. *Mortuary Variability: An Archaeological Investigation*. Academic Press, New York, 1984.

OTTO, J. S. Artifacts and Status Differences — A Comparison of Ceramics from Planter, Overseer, and Slave Sites on an Antebellum Plantation. In *Research Strategies in Historical Archaeology*, Stanley South, ed., 91–118. Academic Press, New York, 1977.

OUTES, FELIX F. La Edad de la piedra en Patagonia. *Anales del Museo Nacional de Buenos Aires*, vol. 12, 203–575, 1905.

———. Arqueología de San Blas, provincia de Buenos Aires. *Anales del Museo Nacional de Buenos Aires*, vol. 14, 249–275, 1907.

———. *Los Querandies*. Impreuta Martin Biedma, Buenos Aires, 1897.

PADDAYYA, K. *The New Archaeology and Aftermath: A View from Outside the Anglo-American World*. Ravish, Pune, India, 1990.

PALERM, ANGEL. The Agricultural Basis of Urban Civilization in Mesoamerica. In *Irrigation Civilizations: A Comparative Study*. Pan American Union Social Sciences Monograph, no. 1, 28–42. Washington, D.C., 1955.

PALERM, ANGEL and E. R. WOLF. Ecological Potential and Cultural Development in Mesoamerica. In *Studies in Human Ecology*, Pan American Union Social Sciences Monograph, no. 3. 1–37. Washington, D.C., 1957.

PARKER, ARTHUR C. *Excavations in an Erie Indian Village and Burial Site at Ripley, Chataqua County, New York*. New York State Museum, Bulletin 117. Albany, 1907.

———. *Archaeological History of New York*, New York State Museum, Bulletins 235–238. Albany, 1922.

PARSONS, J. R. Teotihuacan, Mexico, and its Impact on Regional Demography. *Science*, vol. 162, 872–877, 1968.

———. *Prehistoric Settlement Patterns in the Texcoco Region, Mexico*. Memoirs of the Museum of Anthropology, University of Michigan, no. 3. Ann Arbor, 1971.

———. Settlement and Population History of the Basin of Mexico. In *The Valley of Mexico*, E. R. Wolf, ed., 69–101. School of American Research, Advanced Seminar Series. University of New Mexico Press, Albuquerque, 1976.

PARSONS, LEE A. The Nature of Horizon Markers in Middle American Archaeology. *Anthropology Tomorrow*, vol. 5, no. 2, 98–121, 1957.

PARSONS, SAMUEL H. *Discoveries Made in the Western Country*. Memoirs of the American Academy of Arts and Sciences, vol. 2. Boston, 1793.

PATRIK, LINDA E. Is There an Archaeological Record? In *Advances in Archaeological Method and Theory*, vol. 8, M. B. Schiffer, ed., 27–62. Academic Press, Orlando, 1985.

PATTERSON, CLAIR C. Native Copper, Silver, and Gold Accessible to Early Metallurgists. *American Antiquity*, vol. 36, no. 3, 286–321, 1971.

PATTERSON, THOMAS C. Chavin: An Interpretation of Its Spread and Influence. *Dumbarton Oaks Conference on Chavín*, E. P. Benson, ed., 29–48. Washington, D.C., 1971.

———. The Last Sixty Years: Toward a Social History of Americanist Archaeology in the United States. *American Anthropologist*, vol. 88, 7–26, 1986.

———. History and the Post-Processual Archaeologies. *Man*, vol. 24, 555–566, 1989.

———. Some Theoretical Tensions Within and Between Processual and Postprocessual Archaeologists. *Journal of Anthropological Archaeology*, vol. 9, 189–200, 1990.

PATTERSON, THOMAS C. and CHRISTINE W. GAILEY, eds. *Power Relations and State Formation*. Archaeology Section, American Anthropological Association, Washington, D.C., 1987.

PATTERSON, THOMAS C. and EDWARD P. LANNING. Changing Settlement Patterns on the Central Peruvian Coast. *Ñawpa Pacha*, vol. 2, 113–123, 1964.

PEEBLES, CHRISTOPHER S. Moundville and Surrounding Sites: Some Structural Consideration of Mortuary Practices II. In *Approaches to the Social Dimensions of Mortuary Practices*, J. A. Brown, ed. Society for American Archaeology, Memoir 25, 68–91. Washington, D.C., 1971.

PEEBLES, CHRISTOPHER S. and SUSAN M. KUS. Some Archaeological Correlates of Ranked Societies. *American Antiquity*, vol. 42, no. 3, 421–448, 1977.

PEET, STEPHEN D. *Prehistoric America*, 5 vols. American Antiquarian, Chicago, 1892–1905.

PETERSON, FREDERICK A. *Ancient Mexico*. Putnam, New York, 1959.

PETRIE, W. M. FLINDERS. Sequences in Pre-historic Remains. *Journal of the Royal Anthropological Institute of Great Britain and Ireland*, vol. 29, 295–301, 1899.

———. *Methods and Aims in Archaeology*. Macmillan, London, 1904.

PHILLIPS, PHILIP. Middle American Influences on the Archaeology of the Southwestern United States. In *The Maya and Their Neighbors*, C. L. Hay and others, eds., 349–367. Appleton-Century, New York, 1940.

———. Alfred Marston Tozzer, 1877–1954. *American Antiquity*, vol. 21, no. 1, 72–80, 1955.

———. The Role of Transpacific Contacts in the Development of New World Pre-Columbian Civilizations. In *Handbook of Middle American Indians*, R. Wauchope and others, eds., vol. 4, 296–319. University of Texas Press, Austin, 1966.

PHILLIPS, PHILIP, JAMES A. FORD, and JAMES B. GRIFFIN. *Archaeological Survey in the Lower Mississippi Alluvial Valley, 1940–47*. Papers of the Peabody Museum, vol. 25. Cambridge, Mass., 1951.

PHILLIPS, PHILIP and GORDON R. WILLEY. Method and Theory in American Archaeology: An Operational Basis for Culture-Historical Integration. *American Anthropologist*, vol. 55, 615–633, 1953.

PIDGEON, WILLIAM. *Traditions of De-coo-dah, and Antiquarian Researches*. Horace Thayer, New York, 1858.

PIGGOTT, STUART. Prehistory and Evolutionary Theory. In *Evolution After Darwin*, Sol Tax, ed., vol. 2, 85–98. University of Chicago Press, Chicago, 1960.

PIÑA CHAN, ROMAN. *Una visión del Mexico prehispánico*. Instituto de Investigaciones Historicas, Universidad Nacional Autonoma de México, Serie de Culturas Mesoamericanos, no. 1. Mexico, 1967.

PINSKY, VALERIE and ALISON WYLIE, eds. *Critical Traditions in Contemporary Archaeology*. New Directions in Archaeology. Cambridge University Press, Cambridge, 1989.

PLOG, FRED T. *The Study of Prehistoric Change*. Academic Press, New York, 1974.

———. Systems Theory in Archaeological Research. *Annual Review of Anthropology*, vol. 4, 207–224. Palo Alto, 1975.

PLOG, STEPHEN. Sampling in Archaeological Surveys: A Critique. *American Antiquity*, vol. 43, 280–285, 1978.

POLLOCK, HARRY E. D. Sources and Methods in the Study of Maya Architecture. In *The Maya and Their Neighbors*, C. L. Hay and others, eds., 179–201. Appleton-Century, New York, 1940.

POPPER, KARL R. *The Poverty of Historicism*, second edition. Rutledge and Kegan Paul, London, 1961.

POWELL, JOHN W. Introduction. In *Annual Report of the Bureau of Ethnology to the Secretary of the Smithsonian Institution*, vol. 1. Washington, D.C., 1879–80.

POWELL, MARY LUCAS. *Status and Health in Prehistory: A Case Study of the Moundville Chiefdom*. Smithsonian Institution Press, Washington, D.C., 1988.

POZORSKI, SHEILA and THOMAS POZORSKI. Reexamining the Critical Preceramic/Ceramic Period Transition: New Data from Coastal Peru. *American Anthropologist*, vol. 92, 481–491, 1990.

———. The Impact of Radiocarbon Dates on the Maritime Hypothesis: Response to Quilter. *American Anthropologist*, vol. 93, 454–455, 1991.

PRESCOTT, WILLIAM H. *History of the Conquest of Mexico*. Harper, New York, 1843.

PREUCEL, R. W. The Philosophy of Archaeology. In *Processual and Postprocessual Archaeologies: Multiple Ways of Knowing the Past*, R. W. Preucel, ed., 17–29. Center for Archaeological Investigations, Occasional Paper no. 10. Southern Illinois University, Carbondale, 1991.

PREUCEL, R. W., ed. *Processual and Postprocessual Archaeologists: Multiple Ways of Knowing the Past*. Center for Archaeological Investigations, Occasional Paper no. 10. Southern Illinois University, Carbondale, 1991.

PRICE, BARBARA J. Secondary State Formation: An Explanatory Model. In *Origins of the State, The Anthropology of Political Evolution*, Ronald Cohen and E. R. Service, eds., 161–186. Institute for the Study of Human Issues, Philadelphia, 1978.

PROGRAMA NACIONAL DE PESQUISAS ARQUEOLÓGICAS.

Resultados Preliminaries de Primerio, Segundo, e Terceiro Anos, Publicacâos Avulsas, nos. 6, 10, and 13. Belem, 1967–69.

PROSKOURIAKOFF, TATIANA. Historical Implications of a Pattern of Dates at Piedras Negras, Guatemala. *American Antiquity*, vol. 25, no. 4, 454–475, 1960.

———. Historical Data in the Inscriptions of Yaxchilan, Part I. *Estudios de Cultura Maya*, vol. 3, 149–167. Universidad Nacional Autónoma de México, Mexico, D.F., 1963.

———. Historical Data in the Inscription of Yaxchilan, Part II. *Estudios de Cultura Maya*, vol. 4, 177–201. Universidad Nacional Autónoma de México, Mexico, D.F., 1964.

PRUDDEN, THEOPHIL M. An Elder Brother to the Cliff-Dwellers. *Harper's New Monthly Magazine*, vol. 95, June, 56–63, 1897.

PULESTON, D. E. The Art and Archaeology of Hydraulic Agriculture in the Maya Lowlands. In *Social Process in Maya Prehistory: Studies in Memory of Sir Eric Thompson*, Norman Hammond, ed., 63–71. Academic Press, London, 1977.

PUTNAM, FREDERIC W. The First Notice of the Pine Grove or Forest River Shellheap. *Bulletin of the Essex Institute*, vol. 15, 86–92, 1883.

———. On Methods of Archaeological Research in America. *Johns Hopkins University Circular*, vol. 5, no. 49, 89. Baltimore, 1886.

———. A Problem in American Anthropology. *Proceedings of the American Association for the Advancement of Science*, vol. 48, 1–17, 1899.

———. The Serpent Mound of Ohio. *Century Illustrated Magazine*, vol. 39. April, 871–888, 1890.

QUILTER, JEFFREY. Problems with the Late Preceramic of Peru. *American Anthropologist*, vol. 93, 450–454, 1991.

QUILTER, JEFFREY, BERNARDINO E. OJEDA, D. M. PEARSALL, D. H. SANDWEISS, J. G. JONES, and E. S. WING. Subsistence Economy of El Paraiso, an Early Peruvian Site. *Science*, vol 251, 277–283, 1991.

QUIMBY, GEORGE I. Cultural and Natural Areas Before Kroeber. *American Antiquity*, vol. 19, 317–331, 1954.

———. Habitat, Culture, and Archaeology. In *Essays in the Science of Culture*, G. E. Dole and R. L. Carneiro, eds., 380–389. Crowell, New York, 1960a.

———. *Indian Life in the Upper Great Lakes, 11,000 B.C.*

to A.D. 1800. University of Chicago Press, Chicago, 1960b.

———. A Brief History of WPA Archaeology. In *The Uses of Anthropology*, W. Goldschmidt, ed., 110–123. Special Publication of the American Anthropological Association, Washington, D.C., 1979.

RAAB, L. M. and A. C. GOODYEAR. Middle Range Theory in Archaeology: A Critical Review of Origins and Applications. *American Antiquity*, vol. 49, 255–268, 1984.

RAFINESQUE, CONSTANTINE S. *Ancient History or Annals of Kentucky*. Frankfort, 1824.

RAINEY, FROELICH G. and ELIZABETH K. RALPH. Archaeology and Its New Technology. *Science*, vol. 153, no. 3743, 1481–1491, 1966.

RAMBO, A. T. The Study of Cultural Evolution. In *Profiles in Cultural Evolution*, A. T. Rambo and K. Gillogly, eds., 23–109. Anthropological Papers, Museum of Anthropology, University of Michigan, no. 85. Ann Arbor, 1991.

RANDS, R. L. *The Water Lily in Maya Art: A Complex of Alleged Asiatic Origin*. Bureau of American Ethnology, Smithsonian Institution, Anthropological Papers, no. 34, Bulletin 151. Washington, D.C., 1953.

RAPPAPORT, ROY A. *Pigs for the Ancestors: Ritual in the Ecology of a New Guinea People*. Yale University Press, New Haven, 1968.

RATHJE, WILLIAM L. Socio-Political Implications of Lowland Maya Burials: Methodology and Tentative Hypotheses. *World Archaeology*, vol. 1, no. 3, 359–374, 1970.

———. The Origin and Development of Lowland Classic Maya Civilization. *American Antiquity*, vol. 36, no. 3, 275–285, 1971.

———. Classic Maya Development and Denouement: A Research Design. In *The Classic Maya Collapse*, T. P. Culbert, ed., 405–454. School of American Research, Advanced Seminar Series. University of New Mexico Press, Albuquerque, 1973.

———. The Garbage Project: A New Way of Looking at the Problems of Archaeology. *Archaeology*, vol. 27, no. 4, 236–241, 1974.

———. Archaeological Ethnography . . . Because Sometimes It Is Better to Give Than to Receive. In *Explorations in Ethnoarchaeology*, R. Gould, ed., 49–75. School of American Research, Advanced Seminar Series. University of New Mexico Press, Albuquerque, 1978.

RATHJE, WILLIAM L. and GAIL C. HARRISON. Monitoring Trends in Food Utilization: Application of an Archaeological Method. In *Anthropology and the Assessment of Nutritional Status*, Federation Proceedings, vol. 37, no. 1, 9–14, 1978.

RATHJE, WILLIAM L. and MICHAEL MCCARTHY. Regularity and Variability in Contemporary Garbage. In *Research Strategies in Historical Archaeology*, Stanley South, ed., 261–286. Academic Press, New York, 1977.

RAU, CHARLES. *The Archaeological Collection of the United States National Museum, in Charge of the Smithsonian Institution.* Smithsonian Contributions of Knowledge, vol. 22, no. 4. Washington, D.C., 1876.

———. *The Palenque Tablet in the United States National Museum, Washington, D.C.*. Smithsonian Contributions to Knowledge, vol. 22, art. 5. Washington, D.C., 1879.

REDMAN, C. L. Research and Theory in Current Archaeology: An Introduction. In *Research and Theory in Current Archaeology*, C. L. Redman, ed., 5–26. Wiley, New York, 1973.

———. Distinguished Lecture in Archaeology. In Defense of the Seventies — The Adolescence of New Archaeology. *American Anthropologist*, vol. 93, 295–307, 1991.

REDMAN, C. L., ed. *Research and Theory in Current Archaeology.* Wiley, New York, 1973.

REED, C. A., ed. *Origins of Agriculture.* Mouton, The Hague, 1977.

REICHEL-DOLMATOFF, GERARDO. *Colombia.* Praeger, New York, 1965a.

———. *Excavaciones Arqueológicas en Puerto Hormiga (Departamento de Bolívar).* Publicaciones de la Universidad de Los Andes, Antropologia 2. Bogotá, 1965b.

REID, J. J. and D. E. DOYEL, eds. *Emil Haury's Prehistory of the American Southwest.* University of Arizona Press, Tucson, 1986.

REID, J. J., W. L. RATHJE, and M. B. SCHIFFER. Expanding Archaeology. *American Antiquity*, vol. 39, 126–129, 1974.

REISS, WILHELM, and ALTHONS STÜBEL. *The Necropolis of Ancón in Peru*, 3 vols. Berlin, 1880–87.

RENFREW, COLIN. *The Emergence of Civilization: The Cyclades and the Aegean in the Aegean in the Third Millennium* B.C. Methuen, London, 1972.

RENFREW, COLIN, ed. *The Explanation of Culture Change: Models in Prehistory.* Duckworth, London, 1973.

RENFREW, COLIN and PAUL BAHN. *Archaeology: Theories, Methods, and Practices.* Thames and Hudson, London, 1991.

RESTREPO, VINCENTE. *Los Chibchas antes de la Conquista Española.* Imprenta de La Luz, Bogotá, 1895.

REYMAN, JONATHAN E., ed. *Rediscovering Our Past: Essays on the History of American Archaeology.* Worldwide Archaeological Series 2, Avebury, Aldershot, Great Britain, 1992.

RHOADES, ROBERT E. Archaeological Use and Abuse of Ecological Concepts and Studies: The Ecotone Example. *American Antiquity*, vol. 43, 608–614, 1978.

RICE, PRUDENCE M. Economic Change in the Lowland Maya Late Classic Period. In *Specialization, Exchange, and Complex Societies*, Elizabeth M. Brumfiel and Timothy K. Earle, eds., 76–85. Cambridge University Press, Cambridge, 1987.

RICHARDS, HORACE G. Reconsideration of the Dating of the Abbott Farm Site at Trenton, New Jersey. *American Journal of Science*, vol 237, no. 5, 345–354, 1939.

RICKETSON, OLIVER G., JR., and EDITH B. RICKETSON. *Uaxactun, Guatemala, Group E: 1926–1931.* Carnegie Institution of Washington, Publication 477. Washington, D.C., 1937.

RILEY, CARROLL L. and others, eds. *Man Across the Sea: Problems of Pre-Colombian Contacts.* University of Texas Press, Austin, 1971.

RINDOS, DAVID. *The Origins of Agriculture.* Academic Press, Orlando, 1984.

———. Undirected Variation and the Darwinian Explanation of Cultural Change. *Archaeological Method and Theory*, vol. 1, M. B. Schiffer, ed., 1–46. University of Arizona Press, Tucson, 1989.

RITCHIE, WILLIAM A. The Algonkin Sequence in New York. *American Anthropologist*, vol. 34, 406–414, 1932.

———. A Perspective of Northeastern Archaeology. *American Antiquity*, vol. 4, no. 2, 94–112, 1938.

———. *The Archaeology of New York State.* Garden City Press, Garden City, 1965.

ROBERTS, FRANK H. H., JR. *Shabik'eshchee Village, a Late Basketmaker Site in the Chaco Canyon, New Mexico.* Bureau of American Ethnology, Bulletin 992. Washington, D.C., 1929

———. *The Ruins of Kiatuthlanna, Eastern Arizona.* Bureau of American Ethnology, Bulletin 100. Washington, D.C., 1931.

———. *The Village of the Great Kivas on the Zuñi Reservation, New Mexico.* Bureau of American Ethnology, Bulletin 111. Washington, D.C., 1932.

———. A Survey of Southwestern Archaeology. *American Anthropologist,* vol. 37, no. 1, 1–33, 1935a.

———. *A Folsom Complex: Preliminary Report on Investigations at the Lindenmeier Site in Northern Colorado.* Smithsonian Miscellaneous Collections, vol. 94, no. 4. Washington, D.C., 1935b.

———. *Additional Information on the Folsom Complex.* Smithsonian Miscellaneous Collections, vol. 95, no. 10. Washington, D.C., 1936.

———. Archaeology in the Southwest. *American Antiquity,* vol. 3, no. 1, 3–33, 1937.

———. *Archaeological Remains of the Whitewater District, Eastern Arizona.* Bureau of American Ethnology, Bulletin 121. Washington, D.C., 1939.

———. Developments in the Problem of the North American Paleo-Indian. In *Essays in Historical Alnthropology in North America.* Smithsonian Miscellaneous Collections, vol. 100, 51–116. Washington, D.C., 1940.

ROBERTSON, WILLIAM. *The History of America,* 2 vols. Strahan, London, 1777.

ROBINSON, W. S. A Method for Chronologically Ordering Archaeological Deposits. *American Antiquity,* vol. 16, no. 4, 293–300, 1951.

ROOSEVELT, ANNA C. *Moundbuilders of the Amazon: Geophysical Archaeology on Marajo Island, Brazil.* Academic Press, San Diego, 1991.

ROSEN, ERIC VON. *Archaeological Researches on the Frontier of Argentina and Bolivia in 1901–1902.* Stockholm, 1904.

———. *Popular Account of Archaeological Research During the Swedish Chaco-Cordillera Expedition, 1901–1902.* C. E. Fritze, Stockholm, 1924.

ROSSIGNOL, JACQUELINE and LUANN WANDSNIDER, eds. *Space, Time, and Archaeological Landscapes.* Plenum, New York, 1992.

ROTHSCHILD, NAN A. *New York City Neighborhoods: The 18th Century.* Academic Press, San Diego, 1990.

ROUSE, IRVING. *Prehistory in Haiti, A Study in Method.* Yale University Publications in Anthropology, no. 21. New Haven, 1939.

———. *Culture of the Ft. Liberté Region, Haiti.* Yale University Publications in Anthropology, no. 24. New Haven, 1941.

———. The Strategy of Culture History. In *Anthropology Today,* A. L. Kroeber and others, eds., 57–76. University of Chicago Press, Chicago, 1953a.

———. The Circum-Caribbean Theory, an Archaeological Test. *American Anthropologist,* vol. 55, 188–200, 1953b.

———. On the Use of the Concept of Area Co-Tradition. *American Antiquity,* vol. 19, no. 3, 221–225, 1954.

———. On the Correlation of Phases of Culture. *American Anthropologist,* vol. 57, no. 4, 713–722, 1955.

———. Settlement Patterns in the Caribbean Area. In *Prehistoric Settlement Patterns in the New World,* G. R. Willey, ed. Viking Fund Publications in Anthropology, no. 23, 165–172. New York, 1956.

———. Culture Area and Co-Tradition. *Southwestern Journal of Anthropology,* vol. 13, 123–133, 1957.

———. The Classification of Artifacts in Archaeology. *American Antiquity,* vol. 25, no. 3, 313–323, 1960.

———. The Caribbean Area. In *Prehistoric Man in the New World,* J. Jennings and E. Norbeck, eds., 389–417. University of Chicago Press, Chicago, 1964a.

———. Prehistory in the West Indies. *Science,* vol. 144, no. 3618, 499–514, 1964b.

———. Archaeological Approaches to Cultural Evolution. In *Explorations in Cultural Anthropology,* Ward H. Goodenough, ed., 455–468. Mcgraw-Hill, New York, 1964c.

———. Seriation in Archaeology. In *American Historical Anthropology, Essays in Honor of Leslie Spier,* C. L. Riley and W. W. Taylor, eds., 153–195. Southern Illinois University Press, Carbondale, 1967.

———. Prehistory, Typology, and the Study of Society. In *Settlement Archaeology,* K. C. Chang, ed., 10–30. National Press Books, Palo Alto, 1968.

———. Comments on *Analytical Archaeology. Norwegian Archaeological Review,* vol. 34, nos. 3–4, 4–12. Oslo, 1970.

ROWE, JOHN H. Technical Aids in Anthropology: A Historical Survey. In *Anthropology Today*, A. L. Kroeber and others, eds., 895–940. University of Chicago Press, Chicago, 1953.

———. *Max Uhle, 1856–1944: A Memoir of the Father of Peruvian Archaeology*, University of California Publications in American Archaeology and Ethnology, vol. 46, no. 1. Berkeley, 1954.

———. Archaeological Dating and Cultural Process. *Southwestern Journal of Anthropology*, vol. 15, no. 4, 317–324, 1959b.

———. Carl Hartman and his Place in the History of Archaeology. *Thirty-third International Congress of Americanists*, vol. 2, 268–279. San José, 1959b.

———. Cultural Unity and Diversification in Peruvian Archaeology. In *Men and Cultures*, A. F. Wallace, ed. Selected Papers of the Fifth International Congress of Anthropological and Ethnological Sciences, 627–631. University of Pennsylvania Press, Philadelphia, 1960.

———. Stratigraphy and Seriation. *American Antiquity*, vol. 26, no. 3, 324–330, 1961.

———. Alfred Louis Kroeber, 1876–1960. *American Antiquity*, vol. 27, no. 3, 395–415, 1962a.

———. Worsaae's Law and the Use of Grave Lots for Archaeological Dating. *American Antiquity*, vol. 28, no. 2, 129–137, 1962b.

———. *Chavín Art*. Museum of Primitive Art, New York, 1962c.

———. Stages and Periods in Archaeological Interpretation. *Southwestern Journal of Anthropology*, vol. 18, no. 1, 40–54, 1962d.

———. Urban Settlements in Ancient Peru. *Nawpa Pacha*, vol. 1, no. 1, 1–27, 1963.

———. The Renaissance Foundations of Anthropology. *American Anthropologist*, vol. 67, no. 1, 1–20, 1965.

———. Diffusionism and Archaeology. *American Antiquity*, vol. 31, no. 3, 334–338, 1966.

———. Form and Meaning in Chavin Art. In *Peruvian Archaeology, Selected Readings*, J. H. Rowe and Dorothy Menzel, eds., 72–103. Peek Publications, Palo Alto, California, 1967.

———. Review of *A History of American Archaeology* by G. R. Willey and J. A. Sabloff. *Antiquity*, vol. 49, no. 194, 156–158, 1975.

ROWSE, A. L. *The Elizabethans and America*. Harper, New York, 1959.

RUBENKO, SERGEI I. The Ust'-Kanskaia Paleolithic Cave Site, Siberia. *American Antiquity*, vol. 27, no. 2, 203–215, 1961.

SABLOFF, JEREMY A. Major Themes in the Past Hypotheses of the Collapse. In *The Classic Maya Collapse*, T. P. Culbert, ed., 35–40. School of American Research, Advanced Seminar Series. University of New Mexico Press, Albuquerque, 1973.

———. Review of *The Origins of Maya Civilizations*, R. E. W. Adams, ed. *Journal for Anthropological Research*, vol. 34, 154–155, 1978.

———. Background. In *Simulations in Archaeology*, J. A. Sabloff, ed., 3–10. School of Advanced Research, Advanced Seminar Series. University of New Mexico Press, Albuquerque, 1981.

———. Recent Trends in the Development of American Archaeology. In *Crisis in Anthropology: View from Spring Hill, 1980*, E. A. Hoebel, R. Currier, and S. Kaiser, eds., 293–299. Garland Publishing, New York, 1982a.

———. When the Rhetoric Fades: A Brief Appraisal of Intellectual Trends in American Archaeology During the Past Two Decades. *Bulletin of the Schools of Oriental Research*, vol. 242, 1–6, 1982b.

———. Classic Maya Setlement Pattern Studies: Past Problems, Future Prospects. In *Prehistoric Settlement Patterns, Essays in Honor of Gordon R. Willey*, E. Z. Vogt and R. M. Leventhal, eds., 413–422. Peabody Musum, Harvard University and University of New Mexico Press, Cambridge, Mass., and Albuquerque, 1983.

———. Interaction Among Classic Maya Polities: A Preliminary Examination. In *Peer Polity Interaction and Socio-Political Change*, C. Renfrew and J. F. Cherry, eds., 109–116. Cambridge University Press, Cambridge, 1986.

———. Analyzing Recent Trends in American Archaeology from a Historic Perspective. In *Explaining Archaeology's Past: Method and Theory in the History of Archaeology*, A. Christensen, ed., 34–40. Southern Illinois University Press, Carbondale, 1989a.

———. *The Cities of Ancient Mexico*. Thames and Hudson, New York, 1989b.

———. *The New Archaeology and the Ancient Maya.* Scientific American Library. W. H. Freeman, New 1990.

———. Interpreting the Collapse of Classic Maya Civilization: A Case Study of Changing Archaeological Perspectives. In *Meta-Archaeology*, L. Embree, ed. Boston Studies in the Philosophy of Science, Kluwer Academic Press. Boston, 1992a (in press).

———. Review of *A History of Archaeological Thought* by B. G. Trigger. *Philosophy of Science*, 1992b (in press).

———. Visions of Archaeology's Future: Some Comments. In *Quandaries and Quests: Visions of Archaeology's Future*, LuAnn Wandsnider, ed., 266–272. Center for Archaeological Investigation, Southern Illinois University, Carbondale, Occasional Paper 20, 1992c.

SABLOFF, JEREMY A., ed. *Simulations in Archaeology.* School of American Research, Advanced Seminar Series. University of New Mexico Press, Albuquerque, 1981.

SABLOFF, JEREMY A., A. T. BEALE, and A. KURLAND. Recent Developments in Archaeology. *The Annals of the American Academy of Political and Social Science*, vol. 408, 103–118, 1973.

SABLOFF, JEREMY A., LEWIS R. BINFORD, and PATRICIA A. MCANANY. Understanding the Archaeological Record. *Antiquity*, vol. 61, 203–209, 1987.

SABLOFF, JEREMY and C. C. LAMBERG-KARLOVSKY, eds. *Ancient Civilization and Trade.* School of American Research, Advanced Seminar Series. University of New Mexico Press, Albuquerque, 1975.

SABLOFF, JEREMY A. and ROBERT E. SMITH. The Importance of Both Analytic and Taxonomic Classification in the Type-Variety System. *American Antiquity*, vol. 34, no. 3, 278–285, 1969.

SABLOFF, JEREMY A. and GORDON R. WILLEY. The Collapse of Maya Civilization in the Southern Lowlands: A Consideration of History and Process. *Southwestern Journal of Anthropology*, vol. 23, no. 4, 311–336, 1967.

SAITTA, D. J. Dialectics, Critical Inquiry, and Archaeology. In *Critical Traditions in Contemporary Archaeology*, V. Pinsky and A. Wylie, eds., 38–43. Cambridge University Press, Cambridge, 1989.

SAHAGÚN. FRAY BERNARDINO DE. *Florentine Codex; General History of the Things of New Spain,* translated by Charles E. Dibble and Arthur J. O. Anderson. Monographs of the School of American Research and the Museum of New Mexico, no. 14, pts. 2 and 6, 8–13. Santa Fé, 1950–53.

SAHLINS, M. D. and ELMAN R. SERVICE, eds. *Evolution and Culture.* University of Michigan Press, Ann Arbor, 1960.

SALMON, MERRILEE H. "Deductive" Versus "Inductive" Archaeology. *American Antiquity,* vol. 41, 376–381, 1976.

———. What Can Systems Theory Do for Archaeology? *American Antiquity,* vol. 43, no. 2, 174–183, 1978.

———. *Philosophy and Archaeology.* Academic Press, New York, 1982.

———. On the Possibility of Lawful Explanation in Archaeology. *Critica, Revista Hispanoamericana de Filosofía,* vol. 22, 87–114, 1990.

———. Postprocessual Explanation in Archaeology. In *Meta-Archaeology*, L. Embree, ed. Boston Studies in the Philosophy of Science. Kluwer Academic Press, Boston, 1992 (in press).

SALMON, MERRILEE H. and WESLEY C. SALMON. Alternative Models of Scientific Explanation. *American Anthropologist,* vol. 81, 61–74, 1979.

SANDERS, WILLIAM T. *The "Urban Revolution" in Central Mexico.* Undergraduate honors thesis, Harvard University, Cambridge, 1949.

———. *Tierra y Agua.* Ph.D. dissertation, Harvard University, Cambridge, 1956.

———. *Teotihuacan Valley Project, 1960–61, Mexico.* Pennsylvania State University, mimeographed. Pennsylvania State University, University Park, 1962.

———. *The Cultural Ecology of the Teotihuacan Valley.* Pennsylvania State University, University Park, 1965.

———. Hydraulic Agricultures, Economic Symbiosis and the Evolution of States in Central Mexico. In *Anthropological Archaeology in the Americas*, B. J. Meggers, ed., 88–107. Anthropological Society of Washington, Washington, D.C., 1968.

———. The Agricultural History of the Basin of Mexico. In *The Valley of Mexico*, E. R. Wolf, ed., 101–161. School of American Research, Advanced Seminar

Series, University of New Mexico Press, Albuquerque, 1976.

———. Ecological Adaptation in the Basin of Mexico: 23,000 B.C. to the Present. *Supplement to the Handbook of Middle American Indians, Vol. 1: Archaeology,* V. R. Bricker and J. A. Sabloff, eds., 147–197. University of Texas Press, Austin, 1981.

SANDERS, W. T. and JOSEPH MERINO. *New World Prehistory; Archaeology of the American Indian.* Foundations of Modern Anthropology Series. Prentice-Hall, Englewood Cliffs, N.J., 1970.

SANDERS, W. T. and DEBORAH L. NICHOLS. Ecological Theory and Cultural Evolution in the Valley of Oaxaca. *Current Anthropology,* vol. 29, 33–80, 1988.

SANDERS, W. T. and BARBARA J. PRICE. *Mesoamerica, the Evolution of a Civilization.* Random House, New York, 1968.

SANDERS, W. T. and others. *The Natural Environment, Contemporary Occupation and Sixteenth-Century Population of the Valley.* The Teotihuacan Valley Project, Final Report, vol. 1, Pennsylvania State University, Department of Anthropology Occasional Papers, no. 3. University Park, 1970.

SANDERS, W. T., J. R. PARSONS, and M. H. LOGAN. Summary and Conclusions. In *The Valley of Mexico,* E. R. Wolf, ed., 161–179. School of American Research, Advanced Serminar Series. University of New Mexico Press, Albuquerque, 1976.

SANDERS, W. T., J. R. PARSONS, and R. S. SANTLEY. *The Basin of Mexico: Ecological Processes in the Evolution of a Civilization.* Academic Press, New York, 1979.

SANDERS, W. T. and ROBERT S. SANTLEY. Review of *Monte Alban, Settlement Patterns at the Ancient Zapotec Capital* by R. E. Blanton. *Science,* vol. 202, 303–304, 1978.

SANDERS, W. T. and DAVID WEBSTER. Unilinealism, Multilinealism, and the Evolution of Complex Societies. In *Social Archaeology: Beyond Subsistence and Dating,* C. L. Redman et al., eds., 249–302. Academic Press, New York, 1978.

SANDERS, W. T., HENRY WRIGHT, and R. M. ADAMS. *On the Evolution of Complex Societies: Essays in Honor of Harry Hoijer, 1982.* Other Realities, vol. 6. Undena, Malibu, California, 1984.

SANDERSON, S. K. *Social Evolutionism: A Critical History.* Basil Blackwell, Oxford, 1990.

SANGER, DAVID. Prehistory of the Pacific Northwest Plateau as Seen from the Interior of British Columbia. *American Antiquity,* vol. 32, no. 2, 186–98, 1967.

SANOJA, MARIO, and IRAIDA VARGAS. *Antiques formaciones y modes de produccion Venezolanos: notas para el estudio de los processos de integración de la sociedad Venezuela (12,000 A.C.–1900D.C.).* Monte Avila, Caracas, 1974.

SAPIR, EDWARD. *Time Perspective in Aboriginal American Culture, A Study in Method.* Canada, Dept. of Mines, Geological Survey, Memoir 90, no. 13, Anthropological Series. Ottawa, 1916.

SAPPER, KARL. Altindianische Ansiedlungen in Guatemala und Chiapas. *Publications of the Königlichen Museum für Völkerunde,* vol. 4, 13–20. Berlin, 1895.

SARGENT, WINTHROP. A Letter from Colonel Winthrop Sargent to Dr. Benjamin Smith Barton Accompanying Drawings and Some Accounts of Certain Articles, Which Were Taken out of an Ancient Tumulus, or Grave in the Western Country. *Transactions of the American Philosophical Society,* vol. 4, 173–176. Philadelphia, 1799.

SAUER, CARL O. *Agricultural Origins and Dispersals.* American Geographical Society, New York, 1952.

SAVILLE, MARSHALL H. Explorations on the Main Structure of Copan, Honduras. *Proceedings of the American Association for the Advancement of Science,* no. 41, 271–275. Salem, 1892.

———. *The Antiquities of Manabí, Ecuador,* 2 vols. Contributions to South American Archaeology, Museum of the American Indian, Heye Foundation. New York, 1907–10.

SAYLES, EDWIN B. *Some Southwestern Pottery Types, Series V.* Medallion Papers, Gila Pueblo, no. 21. Globe, 1936.

SAYLES, EDWIN B. and ERNST ANTEVS. *The Cochise Culture.* Medallion Papers, Gila Pueblo, no. 29. Globe, 1941.

SCHÁVELZON, DANIEL WILLIAM. *Holmes y el origen de la estratigrafia cientifica en Mexico (1884).* Paper presented at a conference on the history of archaeology in Mesoamerica, Mexico City, 1984.

SCHELE, LINDA and DAVID A. FREIDEL. *A Forest of Kings.* William Morrow, New York, 1990.

SCHELE, LINDA and MARY E. MILLER. *The Blood of Kings.* Kimbell Art Museum, Fort Worth, 1986.

SCHIFFER, M. B. Archaeological Context and Systematic Context. *American Antiquity*, vol. 37, 372–375, 1972.

———. *Behavioral Archaeology*. Academic Press, New York, 1976.

———. Is There a "Pompeii Premise" in Archaeology? *Journal of Anthropological Research*, vol. 41, 18–41, 1985a.

———. Review of *Working at Archaeology* by L. R. Binford. *American Antiquity*, vol. 50, 191–193, 1985b.

———. *Formation Processes of the Archaeological Record*. University of New Mexico Press, Albuquerque, 1987.

———. The Structure of Archaeological Theory. *American Antiquity*, vol. 53, 461–485, 1988.

SCHIFFER, M. B. and G. J. GUMERMAN, eds. *Conservation Archaeology: A Guide for Cultural Resource Management Studies*. Academic Press, New York, 1977.

SCHIFFER, M. B. and J. H. HOUSE, eds. *The Cache River Archaeological Project: An Experiment in Contract Archaeology*. Arkansas Archaeological Survey, Research Series. University of Arkansas, S. Fayetteville, 1975.

SCHIFFER, M. B. and W. L. RATHJE. Efficient Exploitation of the Archaeological Record: Penetrating Problems. In *Research and Theory in Current Archaeology*, C. Redman, ed., 169–179. Wiley, New York, 1973.

SCHMIDT, ERICH F. *Time-Relations of Prehistoric Pottery Types in Southern Arizona*. Anthropological Papers of the American Museum of Natural History, vol. 30, pt. 5. New York, 1928.

SCHOBINGER, JUAN. *Prehistoria de Suramérica*. Nueva Colección Labor, no. 95. Editorial Labor, S. A., Barcelona, 1969.

SCHOOLCRAFT, HENRY R. *Historical and Statistical Information Respecting the History, Condition, and Prospects of the Indian Tribes of the United States, Part IV*. Philadelphia, 1854.

SCHROEDER, ALBERT H. The Hakataya Cultural Tradition. *American Antiquity*, vol. 23, no. 2, 176–178, 1957.

———. Unregulated Diffusion from Mexico into the Southwest Prior to A.D. 700. *American Antiquity*, vol. 30, no. 3, 297–309, 1965.

SCHULTZ, ADOLPH H. Biological Memoir of Aleš Hrdlička. *Biological Memoirs of the National Academy of Sciences*, vol. 23. Memoir 12, 305–338. Washington, D.C., 1945.

SCHUMACHER, PAUL. Remarks on the Kjokkenmoddings on the Northwest Coast of America. *Annual Report of the Smithsonian Institution for 1873*, 354–362. Washington, D.C., 1874.

SCHUYLER, ROBERT L. Historical and Historic Sites Archaeology as Anthropology: Basic Definitions and Relationships. *Historical Archaeology*, vol. 4, 83–89, 1970.

SCHUYLER, ROBERT L., ed. *Historical Archaeology: A Guide to Substantive and Theoretical Contributions*. Baywood, Farmingdale, N.Y., 1978.

SCHWARTZ, DOUGLAS W. *Conceptions of Kentucky Prehistory*. University of Kentucky Press, Lexington, 1967.

———. North American Archaeology in Historical Perspective. *Actes du XIe Congrès International d'Histoire de Sciences*, vol. 2, 311–315. Warsaw and Cracow, 1968.

———. An Overview and Initial Analysis of a Conceptual Inventory of American Archaeology. In *Eighth Congress of Anthropological and Ethnological Sciences, Part C, Prehistory and Archaeology*, 172–174, 1970.

SEARS, WILLIAM H. The Study of Social and Religious Systems in North American Archaeology. *Current Anthropology*, vol. 2, no. 3, 223–231, 1961.

SEBASTIAN, LYNNE. *The Chaco Anasazi: Sociopolitical Evolution in the Prehistoric Southwest*. Cambridge University Press, Cambridge, 1992.

SERRANO, ANTONIO. The Sambaquís of the Brazilian Coast. In *Handbook of South American Indians*, Julian H. Steward, ed., vol. 1, 401–407. Bureau of American Ethnology, Bulletin 143. Washington, D.C., 1946.

SERVICE, E. R. *Primitive Social Organization*. Random House, New York, 1962.

———. *Origins of the State and Civilization*. Norton, New York, 1975.

SETZLER, FRANK M. Archaeological Perspectives in the Northern Mississippi Valley. *Essays in Historical Anthropology*, Smithsonian Miscellaneous Collections, col. 100, 253–290. Washington, D.C., 1940.

SHANKS, MICHAEL and CHRISTOPHER TILLEY. *Re-constructing Archaeology*. Cambridge University Press, Cambridge, 1987a.

———. *Social Theory and Archaeology*. Polity Press, Cambridge, 1987b.

———. Archaeology into the 1990s. *Norwegian Archaeological Review*, vol. 22, 1–12, 1989.

SHENNAN, STEPHEN. Towards a Critical Archaeology. *Proceedings of the Prehistoric Society*, vol. 52, 327–356, 1986.

———. *Quantifying Archaeology*. Edinburgh University Press, Edinburgh, 1988.

SHEPPARD, ANNA O. *Ceramics for the Archaeologist*. Carnegie Institution of Washington Publication, no. 609. Washington, D.C., 1956.

SHETRONE, HENRY C. The Culture Problem in Ohio Archaeology. *American Anthropologist*, vol. 22, no. 2, 144–172, 1920.

———. *The Mound-Builders*. Appleton, New York, 1939.

SHIPPEE, ROBERT. The "Great Valley of Peru" and Other Aerial Photographic Studies by the Shippee-Johnson Peruvian Expedition. *The Geographical Review*, vol. 22, no. 1, 1–29. New York, 1932.

SHIPTON, CLIFFORD K. The American Antiquarian Society. *The William and Mary Quarterly*, 3rd series, vol. 2, April, 164–172, 1945.

———. The Museum of the American Antiquarian Society. In *A Cabinet of Curiosities*, W. M. Whitehall, ed., 35–48. University of Virginia Press, Charlottesville, 1967.

SILVERBERG, ROBERT. *Mound Builders of Ancient America: The Archaeology of a Myth*. New York Graphic Society, Greenwich, Conn., 1968.

SINGLETON, THERESA. *The Archaeology of Slavery and Plantation Life*. Academic Press, Orlando, 1985.

SMITH, B. D. The Origins of Agriculture in Eastern North America. *Science*, vol. 246, 1566–1571, 1989.

SMITH, G. S. and J. E. Ehrenhard, eds. *Protecting the Past*. CRC Press, Boca Raton, 1991.

SMITH, H. I. *The Prehistoric Ethnology of a Kentucky Site*. Anthropological Papers, American Museum of Natural History, no. 6, pt. 2. New York, 1910.

SMITH, P. E. L. *The Consequences of Food Production*. Addison-Wesley Module in Anthropology, 31. Reading, Mass., 1972.

SMITH, ROBERT E. *Preliminary Shape Analysis of Uaxactun Pottery*. Special Publications of the Carnegie Institution. Washington, D.C., 1936a.

———. *Ceramics of Uaxactun: A Preliminary Analysis of Decorative Techniques and Designs*. Special Publications of the Carnegie Institution. Washington, D.C., 1936b.

———. *Ceramic Sequence at Uaxactun, Guatemala*, 2 vols., Middle American Research Series, Publication 20. New Orleans, 1955.

SMYTH, M. P. Domestic Storage Behavior in Mesoamerica: An Ethnoarchaeological Approach. In *Archaeological Method and Theory*, vol. 1, M. B. Schiffer, ed., 89–136. University of Arizona Press, Tucson, 1989.

SOUTH, STANLEY A. Evolutionary Theory in Archaeology. *Southern Indian Studies*, vol. 7, 10–32, 1955.

———. Evolution and Horizon as Revealed in Ceramic Analysis in Historical Archaeology. In *The Conference on Historic Site Archaeology Papers, 1971*, vol. 6, no. 2, 71–106, 1972.

———. *Method and Theory in Historical Archaeology*. Academic Press, New York, 1977a.

———. Research Strategies in Historical Archaeology: The Scientific Paradigm. In *Research Strategies in Historical Archaeology*, Stanley South, ed., 1–12. Academic Press, New York, 1977b.

SOUTH, STANLEY A., ed. *Research Strategies in Historical Archaeology*. Academic Press, New York, 1977.

Southwestern Archaeological Conference Newsletters, vol. 1, nos. 1–5. Lexington, Kentucky, 1939.

SPAULDING, ALBERT C. Review of *Measurements of Some Prehistoric Design Developments in the Southeastern States* by J. A. Ford. *American Anthropologist*, vol. 55, 588–591, 1953a.

———. Statistical Techniques for the Discovery of Artifact Types. *American Antiquity*, vol. 18, no. 4, 305–313, 1953b.

———. Reply (to Ford). *American Antiquity*, vol. 19, no. 4, 391–393, 1954a.

———. Reply (to Ford). *American Anthropologist*, vol. 56, 112–114, 1954b.

———. Review of "Method and Theory in American Archaeology" by G. R. Willey and P. Phillips. *American Antiquity*, vol. 23, no. 1, 85–87, 1957.

———. The Dimensions of Archaeology. In *Essays in the Science of Culture*, G. E. Dole and R. L. Carneiro, eds., 437–456. Crowell, New York, 1960.

———. Explanation in Archaeology. In *New Perspec-*

tive in Archaeology, S. R. Binford and L. R. Binford, eds., 33–41. Aldine, Chicago, 1968.

———. Distinguished Lecture: Archaeology and Anthropology. *American Anthropologist*, vol. 90, 263–271, 1988.

SPENCER, CHARLES. On Tempo and Mode of State Formation: Neoevolutionism Reconsidered. *Journal of Anthropological Archaeology*, vol. 9, 1–30, 1990.

SPENCER, ROBERT F. and others, eds. *The Native Americans*. Harper & Row, New York, 1965.

SPENCER-WOOD, SUZANNE M., ed. *Consumer Choice in Historical Archaeology*. Plenum, New York, 1987.

SPIER, LESLIE. *An Outline for a Chronology of Zuñi Ruins*, Anthropological Papers of the American Museum of Natural History, vol. 18, pt. 3. New York, 1917.

———. N. C. Nelson's Stratigraphic Technique in the Reconstruction of Prehistoric Sequence in Southwestern America. In *Methods in Social Science*, S. A. Rice, ed., 275–283. University of Chicago Press, Chicago, 1931.

SPINDEN, HERBERT J. *A Study of Maya Art*. Memoirs of the Peabody Museum, vol. 6. Cambridge, Mass., 1913.

———. The Origin and Distribution of Agriculture in America. *Proceedings, Nineteenth International Congress of Americanists*, 269–276. Washington, D.C., 1917.

———. *Ancient Civilizations of Mexico and Central Mexico*. American Museum of Natural History Handbook Series, no. 3. New York, 1928.

———. Origin of Civilizations in Central America and Mexico. In *The American Aborigines, Their Origin and Antiquity*, D. Jenness, ed., 217–246. University of Toronto Press, Toronto, 1933.

SPOONER, BRIAN, ed. *Population Growth: Anthropological Implications*. M.I.T. Press, Cambridge, Mass., 1972.

SPORES, RONALD M. *The Mixtec Kings and Their People*. University of Oklahoma Press, Norman, 1967.

SPRIGGS, MATTHEW, ed. *Marxist Perspectives in Archaeology*. Cambridge University Press, Cambridge, 1984.

SQUIER, EPHRAIM G. Observations on the Aboriginal Monuments of the Mississippi Valley. *Transactions of the American Ethnological Society*, vol. 2, 131–207. New York, 1948.

———. *Aboriginal Monuments of New York* (later revised as *Antiquities of the State of New York*). Smithsonian Contributions to Knowledge, vol. 2. Washington, D.C., 1849.

———. *Nicaragua: Its People, Scenery, Monuments . . .*, 2 vols. Harper, New York, 1852.

———. Observations on the Archaeology and Ethnology of Nicaragua. *Transactions of the American Ethnological Society*, vol. 3, 83–158, 1853.

———. *Peru: Incidents of Travel and Exploration in the Land of the Incas*. Harper, New York, 1877.

SQUIER, EPHRAIM G. and E. H. DAVIS. *Ancient Monuments of the Mississippi Valley*. Smithsonian Contributions to Knowledge, vol. 1. Washington, D.C., 1848.

STEERE, J. B. *The Archaeology of the Amazon*, University of Michigan Official Publications, vol. 29, no. 9. Report of the Associate Director of the Museum of Anthropology. University of Michigan, Ann Arbor, 1927.

STEINEN, KARL VON DEN. Ausgrabungen am Valenciasee. *Globus*, vol. 86, no. 77, 101–8, 1904.

STEPHENS, JOHN L. *Incidents of Travel in Egypt, Arabia Petraea and the Holy Land*, 2 vols. Harper, New York, 1837.

———. *Incidents of Travel in Greece, Turkey, Russia and Poland*, 2 vols. Harper, New York, 1838.

———. *Incidents of Travel in Central America, Chiapas and Yucatan*, 2 vols. Harper, New York, 1841.

———. *Incidents of Travel in Yucatan*, 2 vols. Harper, New York, 1843.

STEPHENSON, ROBERT L. Administrative Problems of the River Basin Surveys. *American Antiquity*, vol. 28, no. 3, 277–81, 1963.

———. A Strategy for Getting the Job Done. In *Research Strategies in Historical Archaeology*, Stanley South, ed., 307–322. Academic Press, New York, 1977.

STERNS, FREDERICK H. A Stratification of Cultures in Eastern Nebraska. *American Anthropologist*, vol. 17, no. 1, 121–127, 1915.

STEWARD, JULIAN H. *Ancient Caves of the Great Salt Lake Region*. Bureau of American Ethnology, Bulletin 116. Washington, D.C., 1937a.

———. Ecological Aspects of Southwestern Society. *Anthropos*, vol. 32, 87–104, 1937b.

———. *Basin-Plateau Aboriginal Sociopolitical Groups.* Bureau of American Anthropology, Bulletin 120, 1–3ff. Washington, D.C., 1938.

———. The Direct Historical Approach to Archaeology. *American Antiquity*, vol. 7, no. 4, 337–433, 1942.

———. American Culture History in the Light of South America. *Southwestern Journal of Anthropology*, vol. 3, 85–107, 1947.

———. Culture Areas of the Tropical Forest. In *Handbook of South American Indians*, Julian H. Steward., ed., vol. 3, 883–899. Bureau of American Ethnology, Bulletin 143. Washington, D.C., 1948a.

———. A Functional-Developmental Classification of American High Cultures. In *A Reappraisal of Peruvian Archaeology*, W. C. Bennett, ed., Society for American Archaeology, Memoir 4, 103–104. Menasha, Wis., 1948b.

———. Cultural Causality and Law: A Trial Formulation of the Development of Early Civilizations. *American Anthropologist*, vol. 51, 1–27, 1949a.

———. South American Cultures: An Interpretative Summary. In *Handbook of South American Indians*, Julian H. Steward, ed., vol. 5, 669–772. Bureau of American Ethnology, Bulletin 143. Washington, D.C., 1949b.

———. *Irrigation Civilizations: A Comparative Study*, Julian H. Steward, ed. Pan American Union Social Science Monographs, no. 2. Washington, D.C., 1955a.

———. *Theory of Culture Change.* University of Illinois Press, Urbana, 1955b.

———. Toward Understanding Cultural Evolution. *Science*, vol. 153, 729–730, 1966.

STEWARD, JULIAN H., ed. *The Handbook of South American Indians*, 6 vols. Bureau of American Ethnology, Bulletin 143. Washington, D.C., 1946–50.

STEWARD, JULIAN H. and L. C. FARON. *Native Peoples of South America.* McGraw-Hill, New York, 1959.

STEWARD, JULIAN H. and FRANK M. SETZLER. Function and Configuration in Archaeology. *American Antiquity*, vol. 4, no. 1, 4–10, 1938.

STIRLING, MATTHEW W. The Historic Method as Applied to Southeastern Archaeology. In *Essays in Historical Anthropology of North America*, Smithsonian Miscellaneous Collections, vol. 100, 117–124. Washington, D.C., 1946.

———. *Stone Monuments of Southern Mexico.* Bureau of American Ethnology, Bulletin 138. Washington, D.C., 1943.

STODDARD, AMOS. *Sketches, Historical and Descriptive, of Louisiana.* Matthew Carey, Philadelphia, 1812.

STONE, DORIS Z. *Introduction to the Archaeology of Costa Rica.* Museo Nacional, San José, 1958.

STOREY, REBECCA. *Life and Death in the Ancient City of Teotihuacan: A Modern Paleodemographic Synthesis.* University of Alabama Press, Tuscaloosa, 1992.

STRONG, WILLIAM D. The Uhle Pottery Collections from Ancón. *University of California Publications in American Archaeology and Ethnology*, vol. 21, 135–190. Berkeley, 1925.

———. An Analysis of Southwestern Society. *American Anthropologist*, vol. 29, 1–61, 1927.

———. The Plains Culture Area in the Light of Archaeology. *American Anthropologist*, vol. 35, no. 2, 271–287, 1933.

———. *An Introduction to Nebraska Archaeology.* Smithsonian Miscellaneous Collections, vol. 93, no. 10. Washington, D.C., 1935.

———. Anthropological Theory and Archaeological Fact. In *Essays in Anthropology*, R. H. Lowie, ed., 359–368. University of California Press, Berkeley, 1936.

———. From History to Prehistory in the Northern Great Plains. In *Essays in Historical Anthropology of North America.* Smithsonian Miscellaneous Collections, vol. 100, 353–394. Washington, D.C., 1940.

———. Cultural Epochs and Refuse Stratigraphy in Peruvian Archaeology. In *A Reappraisal of Peruvian Archaeology*, W. C. Bennett, ed., 93–102. Society for American Archaeology, Memoir 4. Menasha, Wis., 1948.

———. The Value of Archaeology in the Training of Professional Anthropologists. *American Anthropologist*, vol. 54, 318–321, 1952.

STRONG, WILLIAM D. and CLIFFORD EVANS, JR. *Cultural Stratigraphy in the Virú Valley, Northern Peru: The Formative and Florescent Epoclhs.* Columbian Studdies in Archaeology and Ethnology, vol. 4. Columbia University Press, New York, 1952.

STRUEVER, STUART. Woodland Subsistence Settlement Systems in the Lower Illinois Valley. In *New Perspectives in Archaeology*, S. R. Binford and L. R. Binford, eds., 285–312. Aldine, Chicago, 1968a.

———. Problems, Methods and Organization: A Disparity in the Growth of Archaeology. In *Anthropological Archaeology in the Americas*, 131–151. Anthropological Society of Washington, Washington, D.C., 1968b.

STRUEVER, STUART and GAIL HOUART. An Analysis of the Hopewell Interaction Sphere. In *Social Exchange and Interaction*, E. Wilmsen, ed., 47–80. Museum of Anthropology, University of Michigan, Ann Arbor, 1972.

STÜBEL, ALPHONS and MAX UHLE. *Die Ruinenstaette von Tiahuanaco in Hochlande des alten Peru.* Karl W. Hiersemann, Leipzig, 1892.

STURTEVANT, WILLIAM C. *The Significance of Ethnological Similarities Between Southeastern North America and the Antilles.* Yale University Publications in Anthropology, no. 64. New Haven, 1960.

SUGIYAMA, S. Burials Dedicated to the Old Temple of Quetzalcoatl at Teotihuacan, Mexico. *American Antiquity*, vol. 54, 85–106.

SULLIVAN, A. P. Inference and Evidence in Archaeology: A Discussion of the Conceptual Problems. In *Advances in Archaeological Method and Theory*, vol. 1, M. B. Schiffer, ed., 183–222. Academic Press, New York, 1978.

SWANSON, EARL H., JR. Theory and History in American Archaeology. *Southwestern Journal of Anthropology*, vol. 15, 120–124, 1959.

SWARTZ, B. K., JR. A Logical Sequence of Archaeological Objectives. *American Antiquity*, vol. 32, no. 4, 487–498, 1967.

TANSLEY, A. G. The Use and Abuse of Vegetational Concepts and Terms. *Ecology*, vol. 16, 284–307, 1935.

TAX, SOL and OTHERS, eds. *An Appraisal of Anthropology Today, Supplement to Anthropology Today*, A. L. Kroeber, ed. University of Chicago Press, Chicago, 1953.

TAX, T. G. E. George Squier and the Mounds, 1845–1850. In *Toward a Science of Man: Essays in the History of Anthropology*, T. H. H. Thoresen, ed., 99–124. Mouton, The Hague, 1975.

TAYLOR, RICHARD C. Notes Respecting Certain Indian Mounds and Earthworks in the Form of Animal Effigies, Chiefly in the Wisconsin Territory, U.S. *American Journal of Science and Art*, vol. 34, 88–104, 1838.

TAYLOR, R. E. Science in Contemporary Archaeology. In *Advances in Obsidian Glass Studies*, R. E. Taylor, ed., 1–21. Noyes Press, Park Ridge, N.J., 1976.

———. Dating Methods in New World Archaeology. In *Chronologies in New World Archaeology*, R. E. Taylor and C. W. Meighan, eds., 1–27. Academic Press, New York, 1978.

TAYLOR, R. E., ED. *Advances in Obsidian Glass Studies.* Noyes Press, Park Ridge, N.J., 1976.

TAYLOR, WALTER W., JR. *A Study of Archaeology.* Memoir Series of the American Anthropologist Association, no. 69. Menasha, Wis., 1948.

———. Review of *New Perspectives in Archaeology*, S. R. Binford and L. R. Binford, eds. *Science*, vol. 165, 382–384, 1969.

TELLO, JULIO C. Vira-Kocha. *Inca*, vol. 1, 93–320 and 583–606. Museo Nacional, Lima, 1923.

———. *Antiguo Peru; primera epoca.* Editado por la Comisión Organizadora del Segundo Congreso Sudamericano de Turismo. Lima, 1929.

———. Origin y desarrollo de las civilizaciones prehistóricas Andinas. In *Actas y Trabajos Científicos, Twenty-seventh International Congress of Americanists*, vol. 1, 589–720. Lima, 1942.

———. Discovery of the Chavin Culture in Peru. *American Antiquity*, vol. 9, 135–160, 1943.

———. *Chavin: cultura matriz de la civilizacion Andina*, pt. 1, K. Mejia Xesspe, ed. Universidad de San Marcos, Lima, 1960.

THOMAS, CYRUS. Who Were the Moundbuilders? *American Antiquarian and Oriental Journal*, no. 2, 65–74, 1885.

———. *Report of the Mound Explorations of the Bureau of Ethnology.* Washington, D.C., 1894.

———. *Introduction to the Study of North American Archaeology.* Robert Clarke, Cincinnati, 1898.

———. Maudslay's Archaeological Work in Central

America. *American Anthropologist,* vol. 1, no. 3, 552–61, 1899.

THOMAS, DAVID H. A Computer Simulation Model of Great Basin Shoshonean Subsistence and Settlement Systems. In *Models in Archaeology,* D. Clarke, ed., 671–704. Methuen, London, 1972.

———. *Figuring Anthropology: First Principles of Probability and Statistics.* Holt, Rinehart and Winston, New York, 1976.

———. The Awful Truth about Statistics in Archaeology. *American Antiquity,* vol. 43, 231–244, 1978.

———. *Refiguring Anthropology: First Principles of Probability and Statistics.* Waveland Press, Prospect Heights, Ill., 1986.

———. Saints and Soldiers at Santa Catalina: Hispanic Designs for Colonial America. In *The Recovery of Meaning: Historical Archaeology in the Eastern United States,* M. P. Leone and P. B. Potter, Jr., eds., 73–140. Smithsonian Institution Press, Washington, D.C., 1988.

THOMPSON, DONALD E. Formative Period Architecture in the Casma Valley, Peru. In *Actas y Memorias, Thirty-fifth International Congress of Americanists,* vol. 1, 205–212. Mexico, D.F., 1964a.

———. Postclassic Innovations in Architecture and Settlement Patterns in the Casma Valley, Peru. *Southwestern Journal of Anthropology,* vol. 20, no. 1, 91–105, 1964b.

THOMPSON, EDWARD H. *The Chultunes of Labna, Yucatan.* Memoirs of the Peabody Museum, vol. 1, no. 3. Cambridge, Mass., 1897.

———. Ruins of Xkichmook, Yucatan. *Field Columbian Museum Anthropological Series,* vol. 2, no. 3, 209–29. Chicago, 1898.

———. *Archaeological Researches in Yucatan.* Memoirs of the Peabody Museum, vol. 31, no. 1. Cambridge, Mass., 1904.

THOMPSON, J. E. S. Maya Chronology: The Correlation Question. *Publications of the Carnegie Institution of Washington,* no. 456, 51–104. Washington, D.C., 1937.

———. *Excavations at San José, British Honduras.* Publications of the Carnegie Institution of Washington, no. 506. Washington, D.C., 1939.

———. *Late Ceramic Horizons at Benque Viejo, British*

Honduras. Publications of the Carnegie Institution of Washington, no. 528. Washington, D.C., 1940.

———. *Maya Hieroglyphic Writing: An Introduction.* Publications of the Carnegie Institution of Washington, no. 589. Washington, D.C., 1950.

———. *The Rise and Fall of Maya Civilization.* University of Oklahoma Press, Norman, 1954.

———. *Thomas Gage's Travels in the New World,* J. E. S. Thompson, ed. University of Oklahoma Press, Norman, 1958a.

———. Research in Maya Hieroglyphic Writing. In *Middle American Anthropology,* G. R. Willey, ed., 43–60. Pan American Union, Washington, D.C., 1958b.

THOMPSON, RAYMOND H. Review of *Archaeology from the Earth* by R. E. M. Wheeler. *American Antiquity,* vol. 21, no. 2, 188–189, 1955.

———. An Anthropological Approach to the Study of Cultural Stability, R. H. Thompson, ed. In *Seminars in Archaeology: 1955,* R. Wauchope, ed., 31–58. Society for American Archaeology, Memoir 11. Washington, D.C., 1956.

———. *Modern Yucatan Maya Pottery Making.* Society for American Archaeology, Memoir 15. Washington, D.C., 1958.

THURSTON, GATES P. *The Antiquities of Tennessee.* Robert Clarke, Cincinnati, 1890.

TITE, M. S. *Methods of Physical Examination in Archaeology.* Seminar Press, New York, 1972.

TORRES, LUIS M. Arqueologia de la Cuenca del Rio Paraná. *Revista del Musco de La Plata,* vol. 14, 53–122, 1907.

———. *Los Primitivas habitantes del Delta del Paraná.* Universidad Nacioinal de La Plata Biblioteca Centenaria, vol. 4. Buenos Aires, 1911.

TOURTELLOT, GAIR III. The Peripheries of Seibal: An Interim Report. In *Monographs and Papers in Maya Archaeology,* W. R. Bullard, ed., 405–421. Papers of the Peabody Museum, vol. 61. Cambridge, Mass., 1970.

TOZZER, ALFRED M. *A Preliminary Study of the Prehistoric Ruins of Tikal, Guatemala.* Memoirs of the Peabody Museum, vol. 5, no. 3, 93–135. Cambridge, 1913.

———. Report of the Director of the International School of Archaeology and Ethnology in Mexico for 1913–1914. *American Anthropologist*, vol. 17, no. 2, 391–395, 1915.

———. Chronological Aspects of American Archaeology. *Proceedings of the Massachusetts Historical Society*, vol. 59, 283–292. Boston, 1926.

———. Time and American Archaeology. *Natural History*, vol. 27, no. 3, 210–221, 1927.

———. Frederic Ward Putnam. *National Academy of Sciences Biographical Memoirs*, vol. 16, no. 4. Washington, D.C., 1935.

TREUTLEIN, T. E., trans. *Pfefferkorn's Description of the Province of Sonora.* Coronado's Quarto Centennial Publications, 1540–1940. Albuquerque, 1949.

TRIGGER, BRUCE G. Settlement as an Aspect of Iroquoian Adaptation at the Time of Contact. *American Anthropologist*, vol. 65, no. 1, 86–101, 1963.

———. Settlement Archaeology—its Goals and Promise. *American Antiquity*, vol. 32, no. 1, 149–161, 1967.

———. The Determinants of Settlement Patterns. In *Settlement Archaeology*, K. C., Chang, ed., 53–78. National Press Books, Palo Alto, 1968a.

———. Major Concepts of Archaeology in Historical Perspective. *Man*, vol. 3, no. 4, 527–541, 1968b.

———. Aims in Prehistoric Archaeology. *Antiquity*, vol. 44, no. 173, 26–37, 1970.

———. Archaeology and Ecology. *World Archaeology*, vol. 2, no. 3, 321–336, 1971.

———. Review of *A History of American Archaeology* by G. R. Willey and J. A. Sabloff. *Man*, vol. 9, no. 4, 632–633, 1974.

———. *Time and Traditions: Essays in Archaeological Interpretation.* Columbia University Press, New York, 1978.

———. Archaeology and the Image of the American Indian. *American Antiquity*, vol. 45, 662–676, 1980a.

———. *Gordon Childe: Revolutions in Archaeology.* Thames and Hudson, London, 1980b.

———. Marxism in Archaeology: Real or Spurious? *Reviews in Anthropology*, vol. 12, 114–123, 1985a.

———. Writing the History of Archaeology: A Survey of Trends. In *History of Anthropology*, vol. 3, G. W. Stocking, Jr., ed., 218–235. University of Wisconsin Press, Madison, 1985b.

———. *A History of Archaeological Thought.* Cambridge University Press, Cambridge, 1989.

———. Post-Processual Developments in Anglo-American Archaeology. Paper to be published in the *Norwegian Archaeological Review*, 1991a.

———. Constraint and Freedom: A New Synthesis for Archaeological Explanation. *American Anthropologist*, vol. 93, 551–569, 1991b.

TSHUDI, JOHANN. *Reisen Durch Súd-Amerika*, 5 vols. Leipzig, 1869.

TUGBY, DONALD J. Archaeology and Statistics. In *Science in Archaeology*, revised edition, D. Brothwell and Higgs, eds., 633–648. Basic Books, New York, 1969.

TUGGLE, H. DAVID, ALEX H. TOWNSEND, and THOMAS J. RILEY. Laws, Systems, and Research Design. *American Antiquity*, vol. 37, no.1, 3–12, 1972.

TURNER, B. L. II. Prehispanic Terracing in the Central Maya Lowlands: Problems of Agricultural Intensification. In *Maya Archaeology and Ethnohistory*, N. Hammond and G. R. Willey, eds., 103–115. University of Texas Press, Austin, 1979.

TURNER, B. L. II and P. D. HARRISON. Implications from Agriculture for Maya Prehistory. In *Prehispanic Maya Agriculture*, P. D. Harrison and B. L. Turner II, eds., 337–374. University of New Mexico Press, Albuquerque, 1978.

UHLE, MAX. *Pachacamac.* University of Pennsylvania Press, Philadelphia, 1903.

———. *The Emeryville Shellmound.* University of California Publications in American Archaeology and Ethnology, vol. 7, no. 1. Berkeley, 1907.

———. Über die Frühkulturen in der Umgebung von Lima. *Sixteenth International Congress of Americanists*, 347–370. Vienna, 1910.

———. Die Muschelhügel von Ancón, Peru. *Eighteenth International Congress of Americanists*, 22–45. London, 1913a.

———. Die Ruinen von Moche. *Journal de la Société des Americanistes de Paris*, vol. 10, 95–117, 1913b.

———. Sobre la Estación Paleolíon de Taltal. *Publicaciones del Museo de Ethnolgía*, vol. 31–50. Santiago, 1916.

———. La Arqueología de Arica y Tacna. *Boletin de la Sociedad Ecuatoriana de Estudios Historicos Americanos*, vol. 3, nos. 7 and 8, 1–48, 1919.

———. *Fundamentos etnicos y arqueologia de Arica y*

Tacna, second edition. Imprenta de la Universidad Central, Quito, 1922a.

———. Influencias Mayas en el Alto Ecuador. *Boletin de la Academia Nacional de Historia*, vol. 4, nos. 10 and 11, 205–246, 1922b.

———. Civilizaciones Mayoides de la Costa Pacifica de Sudamérica. *Boletin Academia Nacional de Historia*, vol. 6, 87–92, 1923.

UPHAM, STEADMAN. Adaptive Diversity and Southwestern Abandonment. *Journal of Anthropological Research*, vol. 4, 235–256, 1984.

VAILLANT, GEORGE C. *The Chronological Significance of Maya Ceramics*. Ph.D. dissertation, Harvard University, Cambridge, 1927.

———. *Excavations at Zacatenco*. Anthropological Papers of the American Museum of Natural History, vol. 32, pt. 1. New York, 1930.

———. *Excavations at Ticoman*. Anthropological Papers of the American Museum of Natural History, vol. 32, pt. 2. New York, 1931.

———. *Some Resemblances in the Ceramics of Central and North America*. Medallion Papers, no. 12. Globe, Ariz. 19322.

———. The Archaeological Setting of the Playa de Los Muertos Culture. *Maya Research*, vol. 1, no. 2, 87–100. Middle American Research Institute, Tulane University, New Orleans, 1934.

———. Chronology and Stratigraphy in the Maya Area. *Maya Research*, vol. 2, no. 2, 119–143. Middle American Research Institute, Tulane University, New Orleans, 1935.

———. History and Stratigraphy in the Valley of Mexico. *Scientific Monthly*, vol. 44, 307–324, 1937.

———. Patterns in Middle American Archaeology. In *The Maya and Their Neighbors*, C. L. Hay and others, eds., 295–305. Appleton-Century, New York, 1940.

———. *Aztecs of Mexico*. Garden City Press, Garden City, 1941.

VAILLANT, SUZANNAH B. and GEORGE C. VAILLANT. *Excavations at Gualupita*. Anthropological Papers of the American Museum of Natural History, vol. 35, no. 6. New York, 1934.

VAYDA, ANDREW P. and ROY A. RAPPAPORT. Ecology, Cultural and Noncultural. In *Introduction to Cultural Anthropology*, J. A. Clifton, ed., 477–497. Houghton Mifflin, Boston, 1968.

VERNEAU, RENE, and PAUL RIVET. *Ethnographie ancienne de L'Equateur*, 2 vols. Gauthier Villars, Paris, 1912–22.

VIVIAN, R. G. *The Chacoan Prehistory of the San Juan Basin*. Academic Press, San Diego, 1990.

WALCKENAËR, DE LARENAUDIÈRE, and JOMARD. Rapport sur le concours relatif à la Géographie et aux antiquités de l'Amérique Centrale. *Bulletin de la Sociéte de Géographie*, second series, vol. 5, 253–291, 1836.

WALDE, DALE and NOREEN WILLOWS, eds. *The Archaeology of Gender*. Archaeological Association of the University of Calgary, Calgary, 1991.

WALDECK, JEAN FRÉDÉRIC MAXIMILIAN, COUNTE DE. *Voyage pittoresque et archéologique dans la province d'Yucatan (Amérique Centrale), pendant les années 1834 et 1836*. Paris, 1838.

WALKER, S. T. Mounds, Shellheaps, Ancient Canal, etc., Florida. *Annual Report of the Smithsonian Institution for 1881*, 685. Washington, D.C., 1883.

WARING, ANTONIO J., JR., and PRESTON HOLDER. A Prehistoric Ceremonial Complex in the Southeastern United States. *American Anthropologist*, vol. 47, no. 1, 1–34, 1945.

WARREN, CLAUDE N. The San Dieguito Complex: A Review and Hypothesis. *American Antiquity*, vol. 32, no. 2, 168–186, 1967.

———. *The View from Wenas: A Study in Plateau Prehistory*. Occasional Papers of the Idaho State University Museum, no. 24. Pocatello, 1968.

WASHBURN, DOROTHY K. *A Symmetry Analysis of Upper Gila Area Ceramic Design*. Papers of the Peabody Museum, vol. 68. Cambridge, Mass., 1977.

WASHBURN, WILCOMB E. Joseph Henry's Conception of the Purpose of the Smithsonian Institution. In *A Cabinet of Curiosities*, W. N. Whitehall, ed., 106–166. University of Virginia Press, Charlottesville, 1967.

WATSON, PATTY JO. A Parochial Primer: The New Dissonance as Seen from the Midcontinental U.S.A. In *Processual and Postprocessual Archaeologies: Multiple Ways of Knowing the Past*, R. W. Preucel, et., 265–274. Center for Archaeological Investigations, Occasional Paper no. 10. Southern Illinois University, Carbondale, 1991.

WATSON, PATTY JO. and MICHAEL FOTIADIS. The Razor's Edge: Symbolic-Structuralist Archaeology and the Expansion of Archaeological Inference. *American Anthropologist,* vol. 92, 613–629, 1990.

WATSON, PATTY JO, S. A. LEBLANC, and CHARLES L. REDMAN. *Explanation in Archaeology, an Explicitly Scientific Approach.* Columbia University Press, New York, 1971.

———. *Archaeological Explanation: The Scientific Method in Archaeology.* Columbia University Press, New York, 1984.

WATSON, RICHARD A. Ozymandias, King of Kings: Postprocessual Radical Archaeology as Critique. *American Antiquity,* vol. 55, 673–689, 1990.

———. What the New Archaeology Has Accomplished. *Current Anthropology,* vol. 32, 275–291, 1991.

WAUCHOPE, ROBERT. Implications of Radiocarbon Dates from Middle and South America. *Middle American Research Records,* vol. 2, no. 2, 19–39. Tulane University, New Orleans, 1954.

———. *Lost Tribes and Sunken Continents.* University of Chicago Press, Chicago, 1962.

———. *Archaeological Survey of Northern Georgia.* Memoirs of the Society for American Archaeology, Memoir 21. Washington, D.C., 1966.

WAUCHOPE, ROBERT, ed. *Handbook of Middle American Indians,* vols. 1–16. University of Texas Press, Austin, 1964–76.

WEBB, MALCOM C. *The Post-Classic Decline of the Peten Maya: An Interpretation in the Light of a General Theory of State Society,* Ph.D. dissertation. University of Michigan, Ann Arbor, 1964.

WEBB, WILLIAM S. and DAVID L. DEJARNETTE. *An Archaeological Survey of Pickwick Basin in the Adjacent Portions of the States of Alabama, Mississippi, and Tennessee.* Bureau of American Ethnology, Bulletin 129. Washington, D.C., 1942.

WEBB, WILLIAM S. and C. E. SNOW. *The Adena People.* University of Kentucky Report in Anthropology and Archaeology, vol. 6. Lexington, 1945.

WEBSTER, DAVID. Warfare and the Evolution of the State: A Reconsideration. *American Antiquity,* vol. 40, 464–470, 1975.

WEDEL, WALDO R. *An Introduction to Pawnee Archaeology.* Bureau of American Ethnology, Bulletin 112. Washington, D.C., 1936.

———. *The Direct-Historical Approach in Pawnee Archaeology.* Smithsonian Miscellaneous Collections, vol. 97, no. 7. Washington, D.C., 1938.

———. Culture Sequence in the Central Great Plains. In *Essays in Historical Anthropology of North America.* Smithsonian Miscellaneous Collections, vol. 100, 291–352. Washington, D.C., 1940.

———. *Environment and Native Subsistence Economies in the Central Great Plains.* Smithsonian Miscellaneous Collections, vol. 100, no. 3. Washington, D.C., 1941.

———. Some Aspects of Human Ecology in the Central Plains. *American Anthropologist,* vol. 55, 499–514, 1953.

———. *Prehistoric Man on the Great Plains.* University of Oklahoma Press, Norman, 1961.

WELCH, PAUL D. *Moundville's Economy.* University of Alabama Press, Tuscaloosa, 1991.

WHALLON, ROBERT, JR. Investigations of Late Prehistoric Social Organization in New York State. In *New Perspectives in Archaeology,* S. R. Binford and L. R. Binford, eds., 223–244. Aldine, Chicago, 1968.

WHEAT, JOE BEN A Paleo-Indian Bison Kill. *Scientific American,* vol. 216, no. 1, 43–52, 1967.

WHEAT, JOE BEN, JAMES C. GIFFORD, and WILLIAM WASLEY. Ceramic Variety, Type Cluster, and Ceramic System in Southwestern Pottery Analysis. *American Antiquity,* vol. 24, no. 1, 34–47, 1958.

WHEELER, MORTIMER. *Archaeology from the Earth.* Oxford University Press, Oxford, 1954.

WHITE, LESLIE A. *The Science of Culture: A Study of Man and Civilization.* Farrar, Straus, New York, 1949.

———. *The Evolution of Culture.* McGraw-Hill, New York, 1959.

———. *Ethnological Essays,* B. Dillingham and R. L. Carneiro, eds. University of New Mexico Press, Albuquerque, 1987.

WHITNEY, JOSIAH D. *Cave in Calaveras County, California.* Annual Report of the Smithsonian Institution for 1867. Washington, D.C., 1872.

WIENER, CHARLES. *Pérou et Bolíví.* Librairie Hachette, Paris, 1880.

WIENER, NORBERT. *The Human Use of Human Beings: Cybernetics and Society.* Houghton Mifflin, New York, 1950.

———. *Cybernetics,* second edition. M.I.T. Press, Cambridge, Mass., 1961.

WILLEY, GORDON R. Ceramic Stratigraphy in a Georgia Village Site. *American Antiquity,* vol. 5, no. 2, 140–47, 1939.

———. A Supplement to the Pottery Sequence at Ancón. In *Archaeological Studies in Peru,* W. D. Strong, G. R. Willey, and J. M. Corbett, eds., 119–211. Columbia University Studies in Archaeology and Ethnology, vol. 1, no. 4. Columbia University Press, New York, 1943.

———. Horizon Styles and Pottery Traditions in Peruvian Archaeology. *American Antiquity,* vol. 11, 49–56, 1945.

———. The Archaeology of the Greater Pampa. In *Handbook of South American Indians,* Julian H. Steward, ed., 25–46. Bureau of American Ethnology, Bulletin 143, vol. 1. Washington, D.C., 1946a.

———. The Virú Valley Program in Northern Peru. *Acta Americana,* vol. 4, no. 4, 224–238, 1946b.

———. A Functional Analysis of "Horizon Styles" in Peruvian Archaeology. In *A Reappraisal of Peruvian Archaeology,* W. C. Bennett, ed., 8–15. Society for American Archaeology, Memoir 4. Menasha, 1948.

———. *Archaeology of the Florida Gulf Coast.* Smithsonian Miscellaneous Collections, vol. 113. Washington, D.C., 1949.

———. Growth Trends in New World Cultures. In *For the Dean: Anniversary Volume for Byron Cummings,* 223–247. National Park Service, Santa Fé, 1950.

———. Archaeological Theories and Interpretation: New World. In *Anthropology Today,* A. L. Kroeber and others, eds., 361–385. University of Chicago Press, Chicago, 1953a.

———. Comments on Cultural and Social Anthropology. In *An Appraisal of Anthropology Today,* S. Tax and others, ed., 229–230. University of Chicago Press, Chicago, 1953b.

———. *Prehistoric Settlement Patterns in the Virú Valley, Peru.* Bureau of American Ethnology, Bulletin 155. Washington, D.C., 1953c.

———. A Pattern of Diffusion-Acculturation. *Southwestern Journal of Anthropology,* vol. 9, 369–384, 1953d.

———. The Interrelated Rise of the Native Cultures of Middle and South America. In *New Interpretations of Aboriginal American Culture History.* Seventy-fifth Anniversary Volume, Anthropological Society of Washington, 28–45. Washington, D.C., 1955a.

———. The Prehistoric Civilizations of Nuclear America. *American Anthropologist,* vol. 57, no. 3, 571–593, 1955b.

———. Estimated Correlations and Dating of South and Central American Culture Sequences. *American Antiquity,* vol. 23, no. 4, 353–378, 1958.

———. New World Prehistory. *Science,* vol. 131, no. 3393, 73–83, 1960a.

———. Historical Patterns and Evolution in Native New World Cultures. In *Evolution After Darwin,* Sol Tax, ed., vol. 2, 111–141. University of Chicago Press, Chicago, 1960b.

———. Review of *Evolution and Culture,* M. D. Sahlins and E. R. Service, eds. *American Antiquity,* vol. 26, no. 3, 441–443, 1961.

———. The Early Great Styles and the Rise of the Pre-Colombian Civilizations. *American Anthropologist,* vol. 64, no. 1, 1–14, 1962.

———. *An Introduction to American Archaeology,* 2 vols. Prentice-Hall, Englewood Cliffs, N.J., 1966–71.

———. One Hundred Years of American Archaeology. In *One Hundred Years of Anthropology,* J. O. Brew, ed., 29–56. Harvard University Press, Cambridge, 1968a.

———. Settlement Archaeology: An Appraisal. In *Settlement Archaeology,* K. C. Chang, ed., 208–226. National Press Book, Palo Alto, 1968b.

———. Commentary on: The Emergence of Civilizations in the Maya Lowlands. In *Observations on the Emergence of Civilization in Mesoamerica,* R. F. Heizer and J. A. Graham, eds., 97–112. Contributions of the University of California Archaeological Research Facility, no. 11. Berkeley, 1971.

———. The Virú Valley Settlement Pattern Study. In *Archaeological Researches in Retrospect,* G. R. Willey, ed., 149–179. Winthrop, Cambridge, 1974.

———. Mesoamerican Civilization and the Idea of Transcendence. *Antiquity,* vol. 50, no. 199–200, 200–215, 1976.

———. A Consideration of Archaeology. *Daedalus,* vol. 106, no. 3, 81–96, 1977.

———. The Convergence of Humanistic and Scientific Approaches in Maya Archaeology. In *Gedenkschrift Gerdt Kutscher, Indiana 10*, Teil 2, 215–226. Gebr. Mann Verlag, Berlin, 1985.

———. *Portraits in American Archaeology*. University of New Mexico Press, Albuquerque, 1988.

———. Horizontal Integration and Regional Diversity: An Alternating Process in the Rise of Civilizations. *American Antiquity*, vol. 56, 197–215, 1991.

WILLEY, GORDON R., ed. *Prehistoric Settlement Patterns in the New World*. Viking Fund Publications in Anthropology, no. 23. New York, 1956.

WILLEY, GORDON R., and others. *Prehistoric Maya Settlements in the Belize Valley*. Papers of the Peabody Museum, vol. 54. Cambridge, Mass., 1965.

WILLEY, GORDON R. and CHARLES R. MCGIMSEY. *The Monagrillo Culture of Panama*. Papers of the Peabody Museum, vol. 49, no. 2. Cambridge, Mass., 1954.

WILLEY, GORDON R. and PHILIP PHILLIPS. Method and Theory in American Archaeology, II: Historical-Developmental Interpretations. *American Anthropologist*, vol. 57, 723–819, 1955.

———. *Method and Theory in American Archaeology*. University of Chicago Press, Chicago, 1958.

WILLEY, GORDON R. and D. B. SHIMKIN. The Collapse of Classic Maya Civilization in the Southern Lowlands: A Symposium Summary Statement. *Southwestern Journal of Anthropology*, vol. 27, no. 1, 1–18, 1971.

———. The Maya Collapse: A Summary View. In *The Classic Maya Collapse*, T. P. Culbert, ed., 457–503. School of American Research, Advanced Seminar eries. University of New Mexico Press, Albuquerque, 1973.

WILLIAMS, HOWEL. Petrographic Notes on Tempers of Pottery from Chupicuaro, Cerro de Tepelcate and Ticoman, Mexico. *Transactions of the American Philosophical Society*, vol. 45, no. 5, 576–80, 1956.

WILLIAMS, HOWEL and ROBERT F. HEIZER. Sources of Rocks Used in Olmec Monuments. *Contributions of the University of California Archaeological Research Facility*, no. 1, 1–40. Berkeley, 1965.

WILLIAMS, STEPHEN. *Anthropology 239: Archaeology of Eastern North America*. Class Syllabus, Harvard University, Department of Anthropology, 1964.

———. *Fantastic Archaeology: The Wild Side of North American Prehistory*. University of Pennsylvania Press, Philadelphia, 1991.

WILLIS, ERIC H. Radiocarbon Dating. In *Science in Archaeology*, revised edition, D. Brothwell and E. Higgs, eds., 46–47. Basic Books, New York, 1969.

WILLS, W. H. Early Agriculture and Sedentism in the American Southwest: Evidence and Interpretations. *Journal of World Prehistory*, vol. 2, 445–488, 1988.

WILLOUGHBY, CHARLES CLARK. Pottery of the New England Indians. *Putnam Anniversary Volume*, 83–101. G. E. Stelchert, New York, 1909.

WILMSEN, EDWIN N. An Outline of Early Man Studies in the United States. *American Antiquity*, vol. 31, no. 2, 1972–192, 1965.

———. *Lithic Analysis and Cultural Inference: A Paleo-Indian Case*. Archaeological Papers of the University of Arizona, no. 16. University of Arizona Press, Tucson, 1970.

WILSON, DANIEL. *Prehistoric Man: Researches into the Origin of Civilization in the Old and New World*, 2 vols. Macmillan, London, 1862.

WILSON, DAVID. *Prehispanic Settlement Patterns in the Lower Santa Valley, Peru*. Smithsonian Institution Press, Washington, D.C., 1988.

WILSON, THOMAS. Chipped Stone Classifications. *Report of the U. S. National Museum for 1897*, 887–944. Washington, D.C., 1899.

WINSOR, JUSTIN, ed. The Progress of Opinion Respecting the Origin and Antiquity of Man in America. In *Narrative and Critical History of America*, vol. 1, 369–412. Boston, 1889.

WINTEMBERG, W. J. *Uren Prehistoric Village Site, Oxford County, Ontario*. National Museum of Canada, Bulletin no. 51. Ottawa, 1928.

———. *Roebuck Prehistoric Village Site, Grenville County, Ontario*. National Museum of Canada, Bulletin no. 83. Ottawa, 1936.

———. *Lawson Prehistoric Village Site, Middlesex County, Ontario*. National Museum of Canada, Bulletin no. 94. Ottawa, 1939.

WINTERS, H. D. *The Riverton Culture: A Second Millenium Occupation in the Central Wabash Valley*. Illinois State Museum, Reports of Investigations, no. 13, and the Illinois Archaeological Survey, Monograph no. 1. Springfield, 1969.

WISSLER, CLARK. Material Cultures of the North American Indians. *American Anthropologist*, vol. 16, no. 3, 447–505, 1914.

———. The New Archaeology. *The American Museum Journal*, vol. 17, 100–101, 1917.

———. Dating Our Prehistoric Ruins. *Natural History*, vol. 21, 13–26, 1921.

———. *The American Indian*, third edition. Oxford University Press, New York, 1938.

———. The American Indian and the American Philosophical Society. *Proceedings of the American Philosophical Society*, vol. 86, 189–204. Philadelphia, 1942.

WITTFOGEL, KARL A. *Oriental Despotism.* Yale University Press, New Haven, 1957.

WITTRY, WARREN L. and ROBERT E. RITZENTHALER. The Old Copper Complex: An Archaic Manifestation in Wisconsin. *American Antiquity*, vol. 21, no. 3, 244–254, 1956.

WOLF, ERIC R., ed. *The Valley of Mexico.* School of American Research, Advanced Seminar Series. University of New Mexico Press, Albuquerque, 1976.

WOLF, ERIC R. and ANGEL PALERM. Investigation in the Old Acolhua Domain, Mexico. *Southwestern Journal of Anthropology*, vol. 11, no. 3, 265–281, 1955.

WOODBURY, RICHARD B. Review of *A Study of Archaeology* by W. W. Taylor. *American Antiquity*, vol. 19, no. 3, 292–296, 1954.

———. Nels C. Nelson and Chronological Archaeology. *American Antiquity*, vol. 25, no. 3, 400–401, 1960a.

———. Nelson's Stratigraphy. *American Antiquity*, vol. 26, no. 1, 98–99, 1960b.

———. *Alfred V. Kidder.* Columbia University Press, New York, 1973.

WORMINGTON, H. MARIE. *Ancient Man in North America,* fourth edition. Denver Museum of Natuiral History Popular Series, no. 4. Denver, 1957.

———. *Prehistoric Indians of the Southwest,* fifth edition. Denver Museum of Natural History Popular Series, no. 7. Denver, 1961.

WORSAAE, JENS J. A. *Danmarks Oldtid Oplyst ved Oldsager og Gravhøie.* Copenhagen, 1843.

WRIGHT, H. T. The Evolution of Civilizations. In *American Archaeology Past and Future.* D. J. Meltzer, D. D.

Fowler, and J. A. Sabloff, eds., 323–365. Smithsonian Institution Press, Washington, D.C., 1986.

WRIGHT, H. T. and G. A. JOHNSON. Population Exchange, and Early State Formation in Southwestern Iran. *American Anthropologist*, vol. 79, 267–289, 1975.

WRIGHT, JAMES V. Type and Attribute Analysis: Their Application to Iroquois Culture History. *Proceedings of the 1965 Conference on Iroquois Research*, 99–100. Alblany, 1967.

WRIGHT, JOHN H., and others. Report of the Committee on Archaeological Nomenclature. *American Anthropologist*, vol. 11, 114–119, 1909.

WYLIE, ALISON. The Reaction Against Analogy. In *Advances in Archaeological Method and Theory*, M. Schiffer, ed., vol. 8, 63–111. Academic Press, New York, 1985.

———. The Interpretive Dilemma. In *Critical Traditions in Contemporary Archaeology*, V. Pinsky and A. Wylie, eds., 18–277. Cambridge University Press, Cambridge, 1989a.

———. Matters of Fact and Matters of Interest. In *Archaeological Approaches to Cultural Identity*, S. Shennan ed., 94–109. Unwin Hyman, London, 1989b.

———. Gender Theory and the Archaeological Record. In *Engendering Archaeology, Women and Prehistory*, J. M. Gero and M. W. Conkey, eds., 31–56. Basil Blackwell, London, 1991.

———. On "Heavily Decomposing Red Herrings": Scientific Method in Archaeology and the Ladening of Evidence with Theory. In *Meta-Archaeology*, L. Embree, ed. Boston Studies in the Philosophy of Science, Kuwer Academic Press, Boston, 1992 (in press).

WYMAN, JEFFRIES. An Account of the Fresh-Water Shell-Heaps of the St. Johns River, Florida. *American Naturalist*, vol. 2, nos. 8 and 9, 393–403 and 449–63, 1863a.

———. An Account of Some Kjoekken, Moeddings, or Shell-Heaps, in Maine and Massachusetts. *American Naturalist*, vol. 1, 561–84, 1868b.

———. Fresh-Water Shell Mounds of the St. John's River, Florida. *Memoirs of the Peabody Academy of Science*, no. 4, 3–94, 1875.

YARNELL, RICHARD A. *Aboriginal Relationships Between*

Culture and Plant Life in the Upper Great Lakes Basin. Anthropological Papers of the Museum of Anthropology of the University of Michigan, no. 23. Ann Arbor, 1964.

YENGOYAN, A. A. Evolutionary Theory in Ethnological Perspectives. In *Profiles in Cultural Evolution,* A. T. Rambo and K. Gillogly, eds., 3–22. Anthropological Papers, Museum of Anthropology, University of Michigan, no. 85. Ann Arbor, 1991.

ZEISBERGER, DAVID. History of the Northern American Indians, A. B. Hulbert and W. N. Schwarze, eds.

Ohio Archaeological and Historical Quarterly, vol. 19, 1–189, 1910.

ZIMMERMAN, L. J. *Prehistoric Locational Behavior: A Computer Simulation.* Office of the State Archaeologist, University of Iowa, Report 10. Iowa City, 1977.

ZUBROW, EZRA B. W. Carrying Capacity and Dynamic Equilibrium in the Prehistoric Southwest. *American Antiquity,* vol. 36, 127–138, 1971.

———. Models and Complexity in Archaeological Simulations. *Newsletter of Computer Archaeology,* vol. 12, no. 2, 1–16, 1976.

Name Index

*Page numbers in italics indicate illustrations. The letter "n"
following page numbers indicates references to notes sections
at the end of chapters.*

Abbott, Charles C., 52
Acosta, Fray José de, 18
Adair, James, 16
Adams, Robert M., 218, 219, 309n
Adovasio, James M., 258
Aitken, Martin J., 186
Alcina Franch, José, 200, 212n
Aldenderfer, Mark S., 307n
Aldiss, Brian, 214
Allen, William L., 308n
Allibone, T. E., 185
Altschul, J. H., 268, 290–291
Altschuler, Milton, 179
Ambrosetti, Juan B., 83–84
Ameghino, Florentino, 84
Amsden, Charles A., 149n
Anderson, Douglas D., 198, 212n
Anderson, Keith M., 247–248
Antevs, Ernst, 150n
Aparicio, Francisco de, 151
Armillas, Pedro, 179, 195, 207,
  210n–211n
Arnold, Philip J., III, 308n
Ascher, Marcia, 307n
Ascher, Robert, 307n, 308n
Ashmore, Wendy, 309n
Atwater, Caleb, 6, 13, 14, 33, 34
Aubrey, John, 2
Azevedo, Warren L. d', 212n

Babcock, Barbara A., 310n
Baerreis, David A., 212n
Bahn, Paul, 311n
Baldwin, C. C., 45
Bancroft, Hubert H., 45
Bandelier, Adolf, 57, 73–74, 76, 101

Bandi, Hans-Georg, 212n
Bannister, Bryant, 131, 185
Bareis, Charles F., 315
Barnes, Harry Elmer, 310n
Barth, Frederik, 182, 211n
Barton, Benjamin Smith, 24, 25
Bartram, John, 24
Bartram, William, 21, 24–25
Bastian, Adolph, 65–66
Bates, Marston, 226
Batres, Leopoldo, 66
Baudez, Claude F., 149n, 212n
Beadle, George W., 262
Beale, A. T., 307n
Beals, Ralph L, 18
Becker, Marshall, 309n
Bell, Robert E., 212n
Belmont, John S., 25, 36n, 92n
Belzoni, Giovanni, 2
Bennett, John W., 158–160, 162, 208n,
  209n, 211n
Bennett, Wendell C., 106, 107, 120,
  130, 160, 205, 210n, 212n
Benton, Thomas Hart, 33
Berlin, Henrich, 193, 310n
Bernal, Ignacio, 29, 37n, 92, 94n, 193,
  195, 201
Berry, Michael S., 266
Bertalanffy, Ludwig von, 226, 307n
Bertram, Jack B., 250
Bibby, Geoffrey, 1
Bieder, R. E., 92n
Binford, Lewis R., 210n, 221–225,
  227, 228, 232–233, 240, 245,
  247–253, *255*, 264, 296, 300, 303,
  304, 306n, 307n, 308n

Binford, Sally R., 221–222
Bird, Junius B., 137, 151n, 192, 210n,
  211n
Birket-Smith, Kaj, 136
Bishop, Ronald L., 186
Blanton, Richard E., 268, 273–275,
  307n, 309n
Bleiler, Everett F., 212n
Boas, Franz, 11n, 91, 92, 94n, 95n, 98,
  102, 109–110, 148n
Bodin, Jean, 21
Bollaert, William, 84
Boman, Eric, 84
Bonin, Gerhardt von, 106
Borden, Charles E., 212n
Bordes, Francois, 296
Bórmida, Marcelo, 192
Bosch-Gimpera, Pedro, 213n
Boserup, Esther, 309n
Boucher de Perthes, Jacques, 3, 15,
  52, 312
Boughey, Arthur S., 226
Bowditch, Charles P., 73
Brackenridge, Henry M., 24, 25
Braidwood, Robert J., 218
Brainerd, George W., 186, 209n, 212n
Brasseur de Bourbourg, C. E., 73
Bray, Warwick, 265
Breuil, Henri Édouard Prosper, 99
Brew, John O., 93n, 137, 210n
Bricker, Victoria R., 212n
Brill, Robert H., 186, 229
Brinton, Daniel G., 73, 90
Brothwell, Don R., 210n, 211n, 307n
Brown, James A., 233, 234, 307n
Browman, David L., 286, 288

Subject Index

*Page numbers in italics indicate illustrations. The letter "n"
following page numbers indicates references to notes sections
at the end of chapters.*